Librarianship—Quo Vadis?

Librarianship—Quo Vadis?

Opportunities and Dangers As We Face the New Millennium

Herbert S. White

2000
LIBRARIES UNLIMITED, INC.
Englewood, Colorado

Libraries Unlimited, Inc.
P.O. Box 6633
Englewood, CO 80155-6633
1-800-237-6124
www.lu.com

Library of Congress Cataloging-in-Publication Data

White, Herbert S.
    Librarianship--quo vadis? : opportunities and dangers as we face the new millennium /
Herbert S. White.
        p. cm.
    Includes bibliographical references and index.
    ISBN 1-56308-807-X
    1. Library science--Forecasting. 2. Library science--United States--Forecasting. 3.
Information science--Forecasting. 4. Information science--United States--Forecasting. I.
Title.

Z665 .W59 2000
020--dc21   00-041219

Dedicated to my wife Virginia—my helpmate, mentor, and critic for almost fifty years, and to the thousands of colleagues and students who have helped to shape my thoughts and actions.

Contents

vii

 # Foreword

"I yell so loud because I care," goes a pithy bit of T-shirt graffiti. Once upon a time, capturing Herb White's sporting such costume for an impromptu songfest would have been a natural shot for one of the library glossies' conference shutterbugs. Herbert S. White, emeritus Dean of the School of Library and Information Science and Distinguished Professor at Indiana University is the author of *Librarianship—Quo Vadis? Opportunities and Dangers As We Face the New Millennium*. In addition to selected "White Papers," White's former *Library Journal* column, the present volume also includes conference presentations and monograph chapters. Readers familiar with White's first two collations, *Librarians and the Awakening from Innocence* (Boston: G. K. Hall, 1989) and *At the Crossroads: Librarians on the Information Superhighway* (Englewood, Colo: Libraries Unlimited, 1995) will recognize the author's customary motifs: forging credible relations with management; politicking for funds; feuding between practitioner and educator groups; providing (or not) on-the-job training; hiring, evaluating and retaining subordinates; adhering to unpopular decisions while thriving amidst the fray; and so on. In *Quo Vadis* White articulates a new one: "What is the nature of [the library] profession, what are its opportunities and its dangers, what are its strengths and its shortcomings?"

Self-confessed amateur actor, White has always taken puckish delight in riling up the audience. Even veteran readers may find themselves smarting at such pieces as "Never Mind Being Innovative ... Just Be Nice," "Our Strategy for Saving Libraries—Add Water to Thin Soup," "Planning and Evaluation: The Endless Carousel," and "Lead Me Not into Temptation to Do Good" (after Drucker), and "Who Will Lead the Unsuspecting Lemmings Over the Cliff?" How dare he? Why dare he to proclaim such apostasy? Very simply, Herb White cares. And as his caring grows, so does the decibel level of his matchless baritone. For those who have never heard White whisper, "The Legacy of John Swan" is a must-read. *Library Journal*'s John Berry, author of what is the most gracious published encomium for White to date (November 15, 1999, p.6)—worthy of a foreword to a future *Festschrift*—observed that his adversarial relationship with Herb White had long ago mellowed into a deep and mutual respect. A transformation like that illustrates one of White's own management themes: play hard and fair with your adversaries and you may find yourselves respecting and even liking one another.

Dean White's style—fitted out with plenty of irony, hyperbole, and *reductio ad absurdum* together with broad-brushed exemplifying, occasionally cruel directness, and unrelenting bombast—is more akin to a journalist's than to a basic researcher's. How grievous though, that some, having dismissed his writing as opinion, may have failed to read his pronouncements and exhortations, much less to pay them heed. Yet White's work is empirically derived by a half-century of observation. It is to miss the mark to reduce a *corpus* 50 years in the making to White's 11 management principles, *à la* Fayol's, enumerated specially for list-minded notetakers. Consider, rather, the indelible lessons that his students and disciples carry with them back to the workplace, and his epigrammatic maxims that by now have slipped into the public domain. Although White never began with a theory or set out to test a hypothesis, he has contributed to the body of knowledge as certainly as any 20th-century library management guru; to Veaner, White has fashioned a *gestalt*, "a complete philosophy of modern librarianship."

Survey research never suited Herb White. Nor in spite of his ardor for history is he a historian. Future historians will discover in his work, however, a well-spring of commentary, a chronicle of events sacred and profane: the passing fads of library management (in their 15 minutes of limelight, typically after corporate management has moved on to another in-thing), the author's barbs at antics of professional associations and their leadership, and the eternal struggle to educate for tomorrow.

Before proceeding further, readers must not neglect White's own introduction to this volume. There, for example, he provides context for—although to some his justification may never be complete—his pronouncements about the American Library Association. Next skip ahead to "The Legacy of John Swan." One final portion of advice to the reader is never to forget that Herbert S. White is foremost an advocate of *librarians.* He has been librarians' most outspoken, articulate, and steadfast friend of the past 50 years, perhaps of the past 125 years. Guilty as John Berry charged: "contentious, cantankerous, [and] irreplaceable." Who will be next to don the T-shirt?

Marion Paris, Ph.D.
Associate Professor
School of Library and Information Studies
College of Communication and Information Sciences
The University of Alabama

Introduction

This volume is the third collection of publications and speeches I have generated. It includes primarily my work over the last five years, but because this is undoubtedly my last monograph (I have been officially retired for over five years), I have stretched the dates to include a few things for which I did not have room in the past. Much of this material consists of columns written as "White Papers" for *Library Journal*, and it may be familiar to some readers of this monograph. Other articles and book chapters may not be as familiar, and talks presented to specific groups would only be recalled by those in the audience. However, all of my writings and talks stress one recurrent theme—what is the nature of this profession, what are its opportunities and dangers, what are its strengths and shortcomings? This is particularly true for this third collection because it contains no published research, because I have done none since my official retirement from Indiana University five years ago. Tabular material, carefully stated hypotheses, and the analysis of findings are to be found in my earlier collections but not in this one. However, all of my professional work, including my research, was applied in nature. It was certainly written, at least in part, for academic credit, but it was also written in the hope that practitioners might read it and evaluate its applicability to their own work. The fact that this rarely happens, that educator/researchers and practitioner/managers tend to live in separate worlds with almost no contact and almost no overlap in value systems is one of the problems that weakens both communities, and it is an issue I will address further in this Introduction as well as in some of the material contained in the book. It was not always thus—at one point educators and practitioners understood that they needed each other to confront what can be dramatically called the common enemy, but what is in any case the common indifference and lack of understanding of outsiders.

The first two collections of my papers and talks were entitled *Librarians and the Awakening from Innocence* (G. K. Hall, 1989), and *At the Crossroads: Librarians on the Information Superhighway* (Libraries Unlimited, 1995). In both of these works I attempted to divide the material into subject sections. The first book had four such sections: (1) Education and Training, (2) The Internal and External Political Process, (3) Library Operations and the Library User, and (4) Economic Issues. It didn't work very well, because virtually everything I write and say spills over into several categories. Categorization was therefore often arbitrary and unfortunately misleading.

With the second book I tried again, with three sections: (1) Librarians and Their Role As Defined by Themselves and by Others, (2) Librarians: Their Self-Image and the Perceptions That Define Their Preparation, and (3) Librarians in the Cruel World of Politics and Money. It didn't work any better, and while all those topics are still relevant, this time I didn't try. This material is arranged chronologically, and anyone who seeks to determine what I have written or said about a particular topic or individual will simply have to use the index.

Because there is only one Introduction (the other volumes had one for each section) and because this work represents the culmination of fifty years of professional activity and thinking, I think it is appropriate to write something about what I have done, and particularly how my background and my experiences have helped to shape my thinking. Most individuals, in my observation, become librarians for one of three reasons, or perhaps from a combination of more than one. Some have always loved the libraries they grew up with and hoped to emulate the librarians who were already their mentors and heroes or heroines. Some individuals found themselves working in libraries from a variety of circumstances, and concluded quite pragmatically that if they were going to spend their careers in libraries, proper recognition and higher remuneration required that they obtain the "union card," the library degree. Still a third group, having tried other careers and finding them unfulfilling or objectionable, decided either on their own or from the advice of friends or counselors that librarianship offered a viable second chance. There are certainly other reasons or combinations of reasons, including mothers who needed to wait until their children were older before considering any professional career options.

There is nothing wrong with any of these reasons, but none of them apply to me. Growing up I knew no librarians, and my Brooklyn elementary and junior high schools had no libraries at least of which I was aware. My high school did have a library (I don't know how good or how staffed), but the school operated on separate morning and afternoon sessions, so that morning students had to vacate the premises on schedule, and afternoon students were not allowed in before their time. Use of the library was reserved for either free periods or detention assignments. Neither applied to me, in part because I never got into trouble, and in part because I belonged to clubs and the orchestra, signed up for an extra major, and never had any free time. Nor did any of my assignments require use of the school library. Occasionally I used the main branch of the Brooklyn Public Library, but I found that if I ignored the librarians (or support staff—how can you tell?), they ignored me. I was too intimidated to ask for help, and nobody ever asked me if I needed help. They all looked so busy, and of course, they still do. It did not occur to me until much later that perhaps that was because the penurious municipal budget did not allow for nearly as many of them as were needed. That of course is still true today, as is the fact that librarians take the blame on their own shoulders, rather than posting signs stating that the library is woefully understaffed. Of course, allowing the school library to be used as a detention center is worst of all.

This is certainly not intended as a complaint, only an explanation of why, as an undergraduate, I was able to develop a definition for the library profession in which I wanted to work that had nothing to do with the "real world limitations" with which so many students and their employers are not only fettered, but chained. What I wanted to do was to address a gap I saw between the chemistry students and professors who didn't know how to find anything at the College of the City of New York (CCNY) library when I was an undergraduate, and the humanities and social science-based librarians who didn't understand what we were talking about, and who thought that in particular students shouldn't be so lazy and figure it out for themselves. I never recall a reference librarian finding anything for me, their "help" was limited to telling me how I could find it myself.

My definition of the field in which I wanted to work was therefore unencumbered by "reality." I sought the skills in my library education needed to allow me to do what I wanted to do, and I apparently sufficiently impressed Dean Wharton Miller of the Syracuse University Library School so that he recommended me, without ever having told me, to the Special Recruit Intern Program of the Library of Congress. Either that, or he had a grudge against LC. In any case, as a librarian I have always worked to my own professional standards which were much higher than those mandated by the institution. Some supervisors undoubtedly may have considered me a "difficult" subordinate, but I still insist that this was because of their own weakness. In any case, I had the opportunity to run my own corporate library after only four years, and I found that patrons really liked better and more personalized library service geared to their needs and even more importantly their preferences if you offered it to them. Raised expectations would undoubtedly lead to greater needs for materials and staff, but I made sure that my clients made that point not to me but to my management. I also found that subordinates are allowed to cause trouble if it is perceived that they are worth it. Those supervisors who don't appreciate your innovative ideas don't deserve you. That is the principle I followed in my twenty-five years in operations management, and it is what I have taught in the following twenty-five years. The students I personally recommend are not intended to be anonymous members of consensus-seeking teams. They are intended to be innovative destabilizers. And, of course, I have found that whole generations of managers and management writers from Peter Drucker and Mary Parker Follett to Tom Peters, Gifford Pinchot, and Thomas Watson, Jr. urge that we cherish and empower those wild ducks. It is only in a few fields that being nothing more than inoffensive and anonymous is considered a virtue. I have always listened to the beat of my own drummer, and for me at least that has worked out.

My professional career can be divided into two parts. For the first twenty-five years, from 1950 until 1975, I worked in library operations, which turned to library management, which eventually turned to even larger information operations, such as the NASA Scientific and Technical Information Facility and the Institute for Scientific Information. There is no reason for me to specifically detail my professional career in this Introduction. Those who might be interested can certainly find all of this information in biographical directories. However, some points do need to be stressed in this Introduction. In general, my professional career advanced rapidly, either because of or in spite of the personal characteristics I have described. I have enjoyed and sought out challenges and opportunities, even when these involved some risk of failure, as opportunities usually do. I have also enjoyed the opportunity to manage. Someone has to manage, and while I have stressed to students that nobody should ever accept a management assignment unwillingly, it is also true that librarians work in what are usually highly bureaucratic and hierarchical structures in which they will either be managers or be managed, usually both. Management skills can be taught to prepare adequate if not necessarily superb managers. This is not true for leadership skills which, despite all of the quickie instant leadership workshops offered, remain an inherent personality trait. Drucker has told us this often.

Part of the opportunity for upward mobility came from the fact that I achieved visibility both from writing and professional participation, and I stress to students that they must never allow job pressures to keep them from either a personal or a professional life. I urge them to work hard and effectively, but not only to do what is possible, but also to inform their bosses of what cannot be done, and what it would take to get it done. Because I started as a special librarian, I attended my first Special Libraries Association conference in 1954, when I had just started my job in Dallas. A Texas colleague and I felt so lonely and isolated that week that we went to the movies twice. However, I persisted. In 1957 I ran for the presidency of the SLA Texas Chapter. I lost, but I won in 1958. Ten years after that I was president-elect of the national association, having served as president of a chapter and chair of two subject divisions (science-technology and aerospace) and as a three-year member of the Executive Board. In 1974 I became president of the American Society for Information Science (ASIS), and I subsequently served as Treasurer of the International Federation for Documentation (FID) and as a Board member of the American Federation for Information Processing Societies (AFIPS).

It requires caring and it requires work, but each election makes the next one more possible. It also provides professional prestige and mobility, because even prospective employers who can't evaluate your work understand that if others select you it means you are probably pretty good. If you then make continued professional participation a condition for accepting employment, how can they refuse? Your involvement is what they liked about you in the first place! I have no patience with colleagues who tell me their jobs keep them too busy for professional involvement. They cheat not only themselves, they also cheat their employer. Whether he or she realizes it or not, professional employees should be more than drones. And perhaps if they are only drones they are not really professionals.

It also helps if you have decent and honest bosses. In 1964 I was Program Manager of the IBM Technical Information Center, with a corporate-wide mandate for computerized services and two libraries, and a staff of forty. I was then, quite unexpectedly, offered the directorship of the NASA Scientific and

Technical Information Facility and a vice presidency by the contract operator, Documentation, Inc. I was quite frankly bewildered. Like virtually all IBM employees at the time, I expected to stay until retirement. Fortunately for me, Don Miller, my boss and the Director of Administrative Services, spoke to me honestly when I expressed my concern, because this new job offered not only almost a tenfold increase in managerial responsibility, but also a far greater opportunity, ironically, to work with IBM technology. Don told me that I was doing an excellent job, and they would be sorry to lose me. As an IBM employee, I could expect excellent salary increases and excellent benefits for the rest of my career. At the same time, I was now in the top IBM job available to a librarian. Without expertise in law, engineering, or finance, this in one form or another would be my job until retirement. I was now thirty-seven years old. Would I be willing to settle for that? I am sure he knew my answer when he asked me, but I will always be grateful to him.

Even in a rapidly rising career, mistakes are made, and it is important that I acknowledge mine. Students in particular must understand that making decisions inevitably means making mistakes, but that mistakes need not be fatal if you are well prepared, well known, and highly regarded. While I served as Head of the NASA Facility and was having the time of my life at the cutting edge of library technology and service, my friend and mentor, Mortimer Taube, the founder and board chairman of Documentation, Inc., suddenly died. His replacement, Eugene Miller, asked me to give up the Facility job and come back to Bethesda to help him. I selfishly refused, and he ended up selling the company to a group of financiers who understood the economics of computer leasing but nothing about information, and who complicated that sin of ignorance with the double sin of arrogance and nepotism. They ruined the company, and destroyed the working relationship with NASA by making profitability demands that the agency simply could not meet. I still blame myself for allowing this to happen.

Fortunately for me, I was well enough known so that Eugene Garfield, another of my heroes and mentors, asked me to come to Philadelphia to head the operations of the Institute for Scientific Information (ISI). It was a good relationship, because while I certainly lacked Dr. Garfield's vision of product and service innovation, I was better at managing the balance between cost effectiveness and frill. The relationship worked because of mutual respect. Garfield, who had little instinctive respect for operational and financial managers who did not understand the library and information field, realized that I did. I have since stressed often that any professional relationship must be based on mutual professional respect, and when that is lacking, it may be time to leave. Affection is not a requirement, but perhaps surprisingly respect, even grudging respect, often leads to affection.

I forgot my own injunctions and cautions when, in 1974, I accepted the presidency of a Macmillan subsidiary subscription agency (Stechert Macmillan). I was so besotted by heapings of praise, a high salary, and the title of president, that I failed to notice that corporate management had no real interest in this business venture, and only found it attractive because of its presumed positive and early cash flow. Subscription agents offer no unique monographs or periodicals, only those already published by others. There were only two ways to succeed in such a business, by offering stronger and more useful computerized support software for the customer, or by offering lower service charges than the competition. My bosses had no interest in investing in the first alternative, and there is no long-term future in the second. It was my own fault—I should have investigated beforehand.

The release from my dilemma came from a totally unexpected source. I was contacted by Bernard Fry, Dean of the Graduate Library School at Indiana University, who asked if I might be interested in a position which combined a faculty appointment with the direction of the School's Research Center. I had known Fry only slightly, through professional meetings of the Special Libraries Association and the American Society for Information Science, but I had never, in these first twenty-five years of my professional career, considered the possibility of an academic appointment. I had written and published but never performed research befitting academic rigor. I had lectured but never taught, and most significantly my academic credentials consisted only of my chemistry bachelor's and library master's degrees. Bernard Fry knew all that, but he was confident of both my ability to teach and to undertake meaningful research. He invited me for a visit, and I was favorably impressed. More to the point, I apparently impressed the faculty members and students of the school and the university research and administrative officials who also interviewed me.

I knew nothing about academic procedures, and so I consulted my friend and Philadelphia colleague Charles Meadow, who was a professor at Drexel and yet, as I knew, did not possess a doctorate. Meadow told me that there were three parts to the hiring negotiation process: salary, tenure, and rank of appointment. Salary allowed for some negotiation, and I needed to stress my management and professional society experience. Tenure could not be offered to me because I had no record of academic research, but my new position would not only encourage but demand that I become a proficient researcher. Did I feel confident I could meet that challenge? The most important negotiation, I was advised, involved the initial rank of appointment, because my lack of a doctorate would make later promotion highly unlikely.

It was excellent advice, and I joined the Indiana faculty as an untenured full professor. I make this point because I was told by many people not just that such an appointment combination was rare, but that it was "impossible." I have tended to challenge such a word, and I urge my students to challenge it. What needs to be done almost always can be done, and I recall that generalization along with the one voiced by Peter Drucker: "In the absence of money there is always money for anything that is important enough so that it should be done." It is particularly cogent advice for librarians who accept passively the statement by municipal administrators that "there is no money," when money is later routinely found to deal with what might endanger incumbent reelection.

In any case, Bernard Fry was somehow totally correct in his assessment. I was comfortable as a public speaker, and I had experience with audiences as an amateur actor. That was added to the fact that I insisted on only teaching things I understood: special libraries, management, scientific literature. Teaching is very much like acting. You must interest your audience, and you need to know your lines. Students accepted from the first my credentials, and they appreciated the fact that I was speaking from experience in the "real world."

I also loved doing research, because there were many things about my profession which troubled me, and I have always been curious. One of the marvelous privileges of university faculty is not only that they are allowed the time and resources to perform research, but that they are allowed freedom in selecting the areas they want to explore. I was extremely fortunate in finding doctoral students who shared my interests and curiosity, and together we produced meaningful research and meaningful publications, reprinted in the two earlier volumes of my collected works. Karen Momenee, Marion Paris, and Sarah Mort (now Cron) all went on to significant careers of their own. They helped me, and I think I helped them.

As Charles Meadow and Bernard Fry assumed, I produced enough research and teaching credentials so that I applied for tenure not in the sixth year of my stay but in the fourth. Again, there were those who told me that such early consideration was "impossible," but that only meant that it was unusual, and some managers always assume the unusual is therefore impossible. I countered by noting that I was not in my early 20s but in my early 50s. If for some reason the university was to consider kicking me out, I needed to know as quickly as possible. Part of this thinking came from early management advice I received as a junior administrator at the age of twenty-eight—that managers do no favors for individuals they protect in jobs they cannot do. They only postpone a problem and make it worse. I later became Dean of the School then named Library and Information Science, and in the ten years I served in that capacity I never had a faculty candidate turned down for tenure. That does not mean that all new hires achieved tenure, only that, as necessary, I counseled some individuals that they should leave before facing the trauma of tenure rejection. Managers are supposed to do that when it is necessary.

The fact that I have now spent an almost equal twenty-five years each as a practitioner and as an academician allows me to examine what has become the "struggle" between the two groups with some level of objectivity, and the fact that it has become a dispute helps neither. Practitioners have always had the advantage here, at least in principle, because practitioners in this as in other graduate professional fields (law, medicine) were given accrediting authority by the Council on Post-Secondary Accreditation. It was assumed that practitioners would cherish this tool and take it seriously, as indeed they do in other fields. At one time leading practitioners in our field did this as well. Now, sadly, they have largely abdicated the control process to other educators, and reserved to themselves the privilege of only complaining about the inconvenience for them.

The premise of graduate education, as delineated in our field almost eighty years ago by C. C. Williamson, is that education is not training as our profession was initially defined by Melvil Dewey as the teaching of skills. Indeed, it can be argued that educators should not do what employers can do after hire, or what they can accomplish through training programs and workshops. Educators are supposed to stress principles and options, and most importantly teach their students how to think, and how to recognize and evaluate options. It is a principle accepted in graduate education. When DuPont hires a graduate chemist or Price Waterhouse a graduate accountant, they understand that this individual is educated but not trained to the specific organizational culture, and that this process will not only take time but that it will initially subtract from operational productivity.

Librarians have rarely accepted the premise that newly hired professionals are educated but not trained, and that training them may indeed make them negatively productive initially because other professionals must train them. How many public library administrators have made this point to their Boards, even though many of the members come from fields in which they know this is exactly what happens? If they don't expect posteducational training from librarians, it is only a short step to concluding that librarians are not "really" professionals, even if they have a master's degree.

Much of this, in my observation, comes from the fact that many librarians accept the premise of what Peter Drucker calls *moral imperativism,* that even without adequate support and staffing the library must always be well run, and they must never complain. This not only teaches their bosses that library problems, unlike police problems, don't really have to be addressed, because we will always take the blame, or assure everybody that everything is just fine. The insistence of library employers on individuals who are already trained and immediately productive comes then largely from their unwillingness to demand and fight for a training budget. Their insistence on locally convenient library schools comes largely from the fact that their budgets contain no money for interview and moving expenses—at least not for public and school libraries. Why not?

It was Joseph Raelin, cited in my writings, who noted that true professionals were cosmopolitans who placed responsibility to their profession above responsibility to their employers. Academic faculty (and of course I was one) understand this instinctively. Librarians in the same university often do not. This is why I have now established an annual award for competitive selection at the Indiana University Libraries to support a librarian's proposed research project. There is only one stipulation. The research cannot be directly job-related. If it is, it is the responsibility of the institution to pay for it. In the ten years I served as dean I inevitably undertook fund-raising campaigns, but I faithfully promised the alumni that I would never use their money to let the university and state government off the hook for what they should be funding. Ultimately, my institution would be as good as I could make it, but the primary responsibility was that of my bosses. Librarians train their bosses badly.

Because I still have some credibility with practitioners, I was sometimes asked why we library educators did not simply teach what they wanted us to teach. My response surprised them, because they had never considered it. "What makes you think," I asked them, "that I want my students to turn out like you? My whole point is to turn out new librarians who will be better than you."

If I have problems with the educational expectations of practitioners, I also have difficulties with the value systems of many of my educator colleagues. If they are going to educate rather than train, there is still the requirement that this education have content which will be relevant to the work of librarians. As educators increasingly seek to distance themselves from the profession for which they still prepare perhaps 90 percent of their students, they have loaded their curriculum with courses which may appear impressive but probably have little relevance. More importantly, they have replaced faculty who knew how to educate librarians because they understood what happened in libraries with outside specializations. Those specializations have their role, but they must always be secondary to the primary purpose. Law schools do this much better than we do. They include other specializations on their faculties, but they make it clear to these individuals that the primary purpose is the education of lawyers, and that therefore their research, if it is to count, should have relevance for lawyers and future lawyers.

There is much which must be done to bring the needs of practitioners and the needs of educators into conjunction, because in reality neither can succeed without the other. I see no movement in that direction, indeed I see a further division of priorities. I must, at least at this point, agree with Mercutio's statement in *Romeo and Juliet*, "A Plague O' Both Your Houses."

As I continue to teach, write, and think about my profession, I continue to realize how little we plan for what we want to become and receive credit for being—to the great extent to which we continue to be reactive to the often contradictory priorities of others, and how little we develop and promulgate professional agendas of our own. It is this concern which has caused me to select the title for this book. Where are we going? Do we even give any time to thinking about the future of the organization in which we work and the future of our profession? Or are we too busy scrambling around doing the work that the subordinate staff we do not have should be doing? What will our bosses learn from that, except the realization that a sucker once found will never be released? I will have more to add about the issues which confront us at the end of this Introduction. At this point let me only note some of the basic principles of the management literature, and perhaps librarians should spend more time reading that literature. Authority can be delegated, and should be delegated whenever possible. It can even be abdicated. Responsibility, however, remains at the top. Ultimately it is not you who is responsible for the quality of the library, it is the mayor, or corporate official, or principal, or university president. Make sure that they understand at the very beginning what their options are, and what credit or blame you will make sure they receive based on their decisions. You do not do this in public forums; you first do it in private meetings. Those who have not tried this tactic should not scoff. Once your management understands that librarians can really have a back-bone, and that they have other agenda items besides doing more with less simply because management felt like giving them less, you may earn something from them that you may not now have—professional respect. And without respect, mutual respect, no real management relationship is possible.

This is why, well past my two quarter centuries each in library and infor-mation management practice and in academia, I will continue to speak to profes-sional groups and teach students as long as I am able and invited. It is important, I think, to continue to reach practitioners to explain the options they have of which they may now be "too busy" to be aware. I think it even more important to reach students, perhaps before they are poisoned by their perception of the inevitability of hopelessness.

I now teach a course in "Planning and Evaluation" precisely because I know that in many libraries neither happens. Planning must take place before your management has decided on your budget and your staffing, and your plan-ning must present higher-level bosses with the alternatives, and the implications of those alternatives not only for the library but for them personally. When we "plan" after we have been given the bad news about our budgets and staff, we are not really planning at all. We are simply reacting, trying to put a positive spin on what may be a disaster, a tactic which simply encourages penurious administrators to be penurious the next time. As I tell my students, from my own management experience, nobody ever allocates funds in a competitive environment unless they absolutely have to. And, of course, as Drucker reminds us, there is always money. My simple answer to the boss who tells me he is sympathetic but really has no money is to express my own confidence that he is really a better administrator than that. If I can persuade him, I know he can find the money. All I ask at this point is that he listen to the opportunities and dangers I want to describe.

In lecturing about the characteristics of effective managers, I give my students a list of the eleven I consider most important. These are generic manage-ment traits, and they have nothing to do with how well you catalog or answer ref-erence questions. These are, of course, important, but as you rise in management, it is far more important how well you enable subordinates to perform these tasks. It is important to recognize that it is not cost-effective for us to be doing what a subordinate could do, even if that means first that a subordinate must be hired. However, at this point many librarians are even uncomfortable with the word *subordinate*.

The eleven management characteristics I list for my students (because I know that anything which is numbered will be copied) are:

1. Fairness

2. Consistency which must be balanced against flexibility because sometimes applying the policy makes no sense

3. The ability to grasp new ideas, particularly if they come from somebody else

4. Open-mindedness

5. Ambition, because unless you are ambitious you will frustrate and stall your subordinates

6. The ability to communicate, which includes listening as well as talking and writing

7. Leadership, because all organizations develop leaders, and it would be better if the leader were really the person who is supposed to lead

8. Idealism tempered with pragmatism: what is the long-term objective and what is possible today

9. The ability to set priorities

10. The ability to delegate, allowing subordinates to make decisions and to make mistakes

11. Courage

I tell my students that I consider courage the most important of these characteristics, because without courage none of the others can really be achieved. However, I have come to conclude that an equally important problem, certainly as we address our long-term needs at the national professional society level, is our unwillingness to set priorities. I had been sufficiently active in both the Special Libraries Association and the American Society of Information Science to serve as president of both, something only one other individual had done. However, by 1980, because of my involvement with library education, I was inevitably drawn into the activities of the American Library Association. ALA has some wonderfully caring individuals, but it is unwilling to set priorities, to decide what is most important and what is either not germane or at least less important. I know that John Berry, my long-time editor at *Library Journal*, agrees with my contention that ALA does not work hard enough, or perhaps not at all, at promoting the importance of librarians rather than an undefined but presumably good "thing" called the library. A more controversial contention of mine is that all of this stems, at least in great part, from our unwillingness to separate professional issues from sociopolitical ones.

As a newcomer to ALA who attended his first national conference in Atlantic City in 1969, I became immediately aware of this problem, and I don't know how long it had existed. The conference spent two full days in acrimonious debate about the Vietnam conflict, and none of the discussion involved libraries for military personnel in Vietnam, or even the civilian population. For me the absurdity became most clear when, toward the end of the second day, one of the members said timorously that she wanted to bring up an issue which concerned not Vietnam but libraries. Was this in order? I think we fail to recognize that when we take side excursions of time and energy into questions which concern our relations with Iraq or whether an individual convicted of a crime unrelated to libraries was properly tried and convicted, we weaken our own political concentration and the time and energy we can spend. Most importantly, we fail to prioritize.

In dealing at the national political scene we have now created a situation in which liberal Democrats assume our support and therefore feel no need to give us anything, and conservative Republicans understand that there is nothing to be gained in pleasing librarians because their votes are unattainable. In reality, I suspect (although I have no reason to want to know) that librarians at least ought to be as representative of the political spectrum as the rest of the population. If not, why not? Certainly no credal test occurred to me when I chose this profession, and I suspect that my own voting record defies categorization. The important thing for us to recall is that political leverage is something to use in negotiation, and not something to be given away freely. Even as I disagree with its program, I must admire the single-minded and dogged dedication of the National Rifle Association to its own agenda, to the exclusion of everything else.

The reason the NRA's tactics work and our don't is because of something Peter Drucker noted a long time ago. In the political process, there are no neutrals. People are either for you, which means that your priorities become their priorities, or they are against you. People against you are those who claim that they would be for you if only they had the money, or who state that they will support you as soon as they have finished supporting the "more important" needs. We need to understand that when we send political messages in support of sociopolitical causes, we confuse our listeners. Are we then agreeing that these other priorities are more important than ours? Surely we understand that in a finite overall budget environment we compete for priorities, even as I understood at Indiana University that a large allocation of funds to the Business School lessened my own chances for the School of Library and Information Science.

There is nothing wrong with Round Tables at ALA, or Caucuses as they are called in the Special Libraries Association. We all feel comfortable in the company of people who tend to agree with us. The problem arises when these special interest groups seek to make their agendas action items for the parent bodies, and when they succeed simply because they are dedicated and the rest of the membership is apathetic. That is hardly an exercise in open democracy, only in manipulation. The Special Libraries Association has a Baseball Caucus, and I have been tempted to join, even though my own deep affection for the sport was crushed when the Brooklyn Dodgers fled to the West Coast in search of more money. However, the SLA Baseball Caucus has never sought an Association vote concerning the induction of Pete Rose into the Baseball Hall of Fame. My argument is simply that while, as individuals, we can pursue as many agendas and belong to as many groups as we like, as librarians we should understand what our priorities are, or at least ought to be.

It will not surprise readers to know that, while both my views and my professional activities made me highly visible within ALA, they did not make me universally popular. Perhaps in a way it did surprise me, because I knew from my initial education as a scientist and my familiarity with that literature that disagreements, when expressed with civility, are essential to professional growth. That is not our tradition in librarianship. We convene programs in which we make sure that all of the speakers already agree. We could indeed have some very dynamic programs because there are many issues we could productively discuss. However, we tend to avoid such "unpleasantness," and seek instead a wishy-washy consensus which will probably neither please or offend anyone, but more importantly resolve little if anything, because dynamic breakthroughs don't come from consensus.

In any case, it began to occur to me, after a few years of modest waiting, that despite my visibility no Nominating Committee would ever select me for anything, because my selection might offend somebody. I am not really sure why I decided to become a petition candidate for the ALA Council 1988–92 term. Perhaps I just wanted to see if I could win, and I was of course gratified to be elected by the highest vote total, even edging out a former ALA president. My term was not a particularly happy one, because it confirmed my observation (as indeed that of others) that the ALA Council spent a great deal of time on issues which were either ceremonial or at best tangential, and that we had neither the time nor the will to deal with issues which were central to our profession. No, not just libraries. Librarians. I did volunteer for service on the Planning Committee, because I thought that this committee might differentiate, among the perhaps three dozen things which ALA had over the years committed itself to support, those which were important enough for concentration of our energies and resources from those which, while perhaps admirable, we should stop pretending we would really do anything about. We got as far as prioritizing our list in draft form, but then of course ran into a storm of protests from special interest advocates at our public hearing. When I heard the chairman say soothingly that these definitions of high priorities were not really firm, and that perhaps they could be expanded to include lower priorities, I knew that the necessary will simply was not there. It turned out not to matter in any case, because the Council decided not to deal with such unpleasantness and referred the issue back for "further study." As a long-time administrator, I also understood that this really meant "and don't bring it back." I was eager to see the end of my term, because I was realistic enough to understand that in four years I had spoken often, and perhaps even meaningfully, but that I had really accomplished nothing of substance. Avoiding professional substance is for some people the primary purpose.

After that experience, I am really not sure why I decided to seek the ALA presidency in the spring 1991 election. Obviously I was never nominated, but I became a third and petition candidate in the fall of 1990 after the official slate was announced. What I sought to offer the electorate was a real choice, and a chance to elect a candidate who would really try to change the association's priorities. I aimed my campaign specifically at those members who never voted because they didn't think it made any difference, and that is certainly the largest membership group. I also thought I had a chance to a win. All three of the candidates were library school faculty members, and I expected that we would probably divide the "academic" vote fairly evenly. Where I thought I would have the advantage was with public librarians, who knew me through my writings and the fact that I had by then spoken at numerous state library association conferences.

Election results are not analyzed, so I can't tell what actually happened. However, I was truly surprised at the animosity which my candidacy evoked, from individuals who considered me the Great Satan who would ruin ALA forever. That animosity extended not only to nasty questions about my work in SLA twenty years earlier at the Candidate Open Forum. Nasty questions are perhaps fair game, but it had never happened at earlier ALA forums, and neither of my opponents were similarly assailed. At the last possible moment, the end of the winter conference, a fourth candidate, a public librarian, was suddenly introduced into the contest. In all fairness, I don't believe that this candidate, who finished a weak last, understood that he was really simply being used to draw off public library votes. As a long-term manager, I am used to the rough-and-tumble of the political process, but this bordered, in my judgment, on the inappropriate in a professional society election.

In any case, the tactic worked, and deprived me of being able to claim the unique honor of having been president of three major professional library associations. I finished second by 43 votes, out of a total of 13,000 votes cast. In retrospect I conclude that, even though I would have tried, I would probably have changed very little if anything. A one-year term is very brief, and the structure allows individuals their own hobby horses and does not force them to prioritize anything. I note without venom that all of the ALA presidents I have known have largely simply presided over the ceremonial process, some more eloquently than others. None have sought to tamper with a mechanism which still, at least in my judgment, leaves us largely ineffective and ignored. If you doubt this conclusion, look at recent U.S. presidential appointments in areas which ostensibly require a prestigious librarian. And this comes from an administration with which we at least claim to be friendly. I can only refer back to Drucker's observation that those who are not your friends as a first priority automatically become your enemies. We have never demanded that our "friends" confirm their words with actions.

A few weeks after the election results were announced, I received an honor I consider far more important. At Indiana University "distinguished professor" is the highest rank which can be achieved. It is conferred without the involvement of administrators in a selection by those who are already distinguished professors. My own selection was significant for me for three reasons. First, they selected an individual whose only formal educational qualifications included one bachelor's degree and one master's degree. I know research libraries which will not even consider a junior hiring candidate with such sparse credentials. Secondly, all of my research, while significant in quantity and range, was applied research. I was addressing real problems, and attempting to propose solutions. Thirdly, and perhaps most importantly, they were inviting an individual to join their group who, even though a professor and former dean, had always proudly insisted on being considered a librarian. It indicates what is possible.

At my induction ceremony I was invited to present a brief lecture, before a captive audience including not only my fellow distinguished professors but just about every university administrator. I told them that the obscene and irrational increases in journal prices was something librarians could not control, because publishers dealt with faculty as customers and librarians only as purchasing agents. If there was to be resistance to double-digit inflation, it would have to come from the academic establishment, and also from specific disciplines. If they were half as interested in this problem as the ones caused by the lack of academic priorities for student athletes, they could do something about it. If not, they could simply expect to provide lots more acquisitions money for the library budget, or see their favorite journals canceled. After my talk I had several questions from my professorial colleagues. I had none from administrators, who heard my remarks in stony silence. They obviously did not want to be reminded of their responsibilities. It was certainly easier to blame librarians, particularly when librarians accept the blame, and make filling this bottomless pit their own first priority.

I cannot resist the temptation, at the close of this Introduction and my own professional career, to list the individuals who have influenced my thinking and actions to the greatest degree, even though I realize that there will be omissions I will later regret. The interesting thing, for me, in compiling this alphabetic list is the realization that many of these people had no idea they were talking to a librarian or influencing him. I also realize how few of these individuals who for me are leaders are people whom librarians have elected, presumably to lead rather than follow them. My alphabetical list includes Andrew Abbott, Edmund Burke, Joshua L. Chamberlain, Winston Churchill, Peter Drucker, Mary P. Follett, Bernard Fry, Steve Furth, Gene Garfield, F. W. Lancaster, Hans Peter Luhn, Tom Peters, Gifford Pinchot, Pogo Possum, Joseph Raelin, Hyman Rickover, Mortimer Taube, Margaret Thatcher, Harry Truman, Thomas Watson, and Virginia White. All are individuals willing to lead, willing to innovate, and willing to be at least temporarily unpopular. They did not follow others; they persuaded others to follow them.

As we come to the end of this millennium (either in 2000 or 2001), what are the opportunities and dangers which confront my profession, and demand that we change our priorities, not only for our own sake but for the sake of our clients? Most obviously, we have been affected by technology, which not only allows access to far more information, but also constantly proclaims that through the Internet direct access, and being able to find things, is both fast and easy. Whether or not we agree with such simplistic statements, they will be believed. The role of librarians as would-be teachers is therefore limited, and not just because the so-called real teachers have never accepted us as partners. A whole generation of computer-reared young people insist that they need neither books nor people; everything is already on the Internet. To the extent to which librarians stress their role in providing computer tools for self-service, that convenience may be appreciated, but it is also recognized as a routine and clerical function.

Academic librarians, who have always served their faculty clients not as they ought to be served but as they selfishly wanted to be served, have accepted the premise that only faculty and not they evaluate the importance of information. They have not really provided information, only containers of information. In the new millennium, with huge quantities of information, that is not enough. What is required is a profession which will deal with knowledge rather than information, with quality rather than quantity, and which will pride itself on how little material but of high quality it transmits to its clients.

Will this happen? Of that I am certain. Somebody will do this, because it needs to be done. We see the example in other fields. As complexity has grown, so have new highly specialized service professions which do for us what we cannot do, and what in truth we really don't want to do. Our clients will want to know what part of all of this stuff will help them do what they are paid to do, or are intellectually rewarded for doing.

Will librarians be the ones filling this need? Certainly we are qualified, but I am not confident. Two years ago I evaluated grant applications for the Institute of Museum and Library Service, an institution which, according to the law, is now supposed to be headed by a librarian. Almost all of the applications I reviewed, from academic and public libraries, asked for money with which to acquire technology, either hardware or software. All of these requests were for enhanced end user access. Not a single request was for technology to be used exclusively by librarians, to enhance their effectiveness and prestige. I can think of no other profession which would be so self-effacing.

For us to change our strategies and our priorities, because I certainly now consider both to be suicidal, we must first frankly and openly consider the challenges and opportunities which we face. Doing this will require our best and most courageous minds, from academia, from library operations, from society leadership. In setting the agenda for such conferences we must first establish our priorities, and the first priority, as for any profession, must be to strengthen and empower itself. Many dialogues with user groups and administrators will follow, but it is essential here that these discussions be based on a mutual understanding that it is, in any such setting, the professionals who bring the unique expertise to the table. What we most certainly do not need is a Third White House Conference in which individuals lecture us on what we ought to be doing, after we have patiently told them what the conference is about. Perhaps the very first things we need are pride and self-respect. Respect cannot occur until there is first self-respect. As Eleanor Roosevelt noted so accurately: "Nobody can put you down without your permission."

Look at All Those Beautiful Birds Overhead!

In my last column ("Coalition-Building and the Image of Power," *LJ*, January, pp. 69–70), I argued that our political strategies as a profession were not effective. We make alliances and join coalitions without getting anything in return. We also waste our energies on fighting with each other and calling each other names, when we could certainly find many things on which to agree as professionals.

Our recent fascination with redefining Christopher Columbus as a villain is simply a handy example and points out only that the strong have an unpleasant tendency to brutalize their weaker neighbors. Aztecs and Incas kept slaves and felt no compunction about killing them. Had Columbus not landed, there would certainly have been some other form of barbarism, from another European country, from another continent, or from the "native" residents whose only claim may be that they came earlier to wipe out the inhabitants that they found.

The only useful speculation I see concerns the question of what would have been the world impact of never having had a Declaration of Independence, and the subsequent impact that this document had on future movements for political freedom, including the French Revolution and all of the revolts of 1848.

In any case, for those still young enough and so inclined, I suggest a further opportunity for outrage in 2066, when we can castigate the Normans for what they did to the Saxons. I will cheerfully admit that these heady broadsides are much more fun than discussing our role in the National Research and Education Network (NREN), or the appropriate and inappropriate place of volunteers to disguise the absence of librarians. Dazzling plumage gets more attention than the plain looking birds that waddle at our feet.

Reprinted, with changes, by permission of the author and *Library Journal* 118, no. 3 (February 15, 1993): 143–144. Copyright © 1993 by Cahners Business Information.

1

Nor does either my last or this column suggest that individuals within professional associations don't have the right to try to bend those associations to their political viewpoints on any nonlibrary issue. I just wish they were not so selfish as to do it. Certainly I learned in college politics at the City College of New York (CCNY) that a small handful can always take over any group if they are committed enough to come early, vote late, revote after others have left, and, above all, always run for office.

Analyses of the American Library Association (ALA) Council tells us that members of round tables are five times as likely to be members of the Council as those who don't belong. Perhaps it can be argued that those who belong "only" to chapters and divisions do not have as strong a commitment to the specific issues that define round tables. Nor is there anything I can find wrong in that, except perhaps when that is translated into an attempt to speak for a larger group of members.

Out of Focus

Of course, political activity through Council election is not particularly noticeable for all round tables. The Government Documents Round Table (GODORT) and Map & Geography members exhibit few such stirrings, and one can surmise that these people are interested more in their own professional interchange than in the Middle East. However, as a prime example of one round table that creates much of our societal agenda for us, it is interesting that the Social Responsibilities Round Table (SRRT) represents 2.8 percent of the ALA membership and 16.5 percent of the ALA Council. When these individuals then additionally claim that it is "others" who subvert the will of the majority to their own ends, they are unintentionally humorous. It is they who do it, in speaking with a voice far louder than their own tiny one.

To try to do that is certainly within their rights. If they care more than the rest of us, it may be that we can rationalize that it doesn't really matter what resolutions they pass in our name. That is only partially true. Nobody outside our profession cares, but we agonize over all of this, and that in turn weakens our ability to act on issues that matter professionally and not just personally. I want to stress that these emphases bring only comfort to the agitators and keep us from concentrating on other issues—if only we could find the time and focus. I needed this follow-up column because I see how hard we work to so little professional effect. It may be that some librarians look at self-promotion as the eighth deadly sin. As some are loud and shrill, others are self-effacing to the point of invisibility.

For Better or Worse

Of course, I have a ready example in mind. We have just selected our next theme for National Library Week, and it will cover two years. That theme is "Libraries Change Lives." We assume that others will know that means for the better, but most of all this returns us to the safe stressing of libraries rather than librarians. It should please some of the letter writers who worry that we might be self-serving. Stressing libraries is safer: in the public mind, libraries and librarians are at best vaguely connected, and there is certainly little connection between library, librarian, and money.

The world does love libraries, particularly if the term is as unencumbered by nasty realities as it is in this slogan. People love libraries so much, they will insist they have them even when they don't. Voters like to hear that they have perfectly fine libraries without pain almost as much as they like to hear candidates promise to enhance programs as they cut taxes. Nobody needs to convince college presidents of the importance of their libraries. We can be assured that they will not close them, even as they may decimate the staff.

The beating heart of the university to which Carlyle referred beats as a collection with or without a staff. The good parents and school board members of some California communities are so enamored of "libraries," they take pains to hang onto the name long after all the librarians have been laid off. In that decision, and in the substitution of volunteers for professional librarians, they also define their trivial view of what the former librarians presumably did. However, that warrants fuller discussion in a later column.

My greater concern is not with college presidents and community leaders, because they will certainly love our new painless theme. However, is that our professional objective? Are we too busy excoriating other miscreants in the world to notice what happens to us? Do we simply want something called a library, no matter how sickly or scrawny? Do we have any belief at all in euthanasia for once-were or perhaps never-were pseudolibraries, so that at least we can describe what we are talking about? Are we ever going to be prepared to specify what a library is supposed to achieve if it is to serve all of the constituencies—at the very least, education, information, and perhaps recreation? Are we prepared to stress that at least information is never measured in quantity but in timeliness and specificity? If all libraries are generically equally good, then cost becomes the only factor of significance.

No Pain, No Gain

It is little wonder that our agenda does not grab attention when compared to crime statistics and potholes in the streets. Are there not potholes of the mind? The strategy of stressing holdings for academic libraries and circulation for public libraries as the measure of "goodness" worked to get us money in the

1960s, but anything would have worked then. Neither works today, because political bosses grasp that these measurements of activity are ultimately not as important as their other priorities.

Those who teach and practice management know the difference between goals and objectives. Goals are statements of principles and ideals; they are open-ended and intentionally unquantified. They therefore cannot serve as management measurement tools, and, without implementation mechanisms, they become merely slogans. We have many such slogans, as generated by National Library Week themes and recommendations of the White House Conference on Library and Information Services (WHCLIS) and WHCLIS II. Has anyone else noticed our charming tactic of adopting the roman numerals used to separate Super Bowls, although it will take us a while to reach WHCLIS XXV? Goals and slogans can always be adopted "in principle," because that is certainly cheaper than funding them.

This is why managers understand that goals require translation into objectives, and these contain both time frames and dollar signs. Objectives require the identification of strategies, of plans, and of resources, as well as checkpoints against which progress is measured. If the objective is not being met, one does not automatically rush to revise the objective, nor to drive oneself crazy trying to meet it.

Inadequate funding covers a multitude of excuses and is not just a simple fact of life. If we expect the money to be found, then the process of renouncing or watering down objectives must be made politically visible and very painful—politicians tend to react primarily to pain and gain. Is there any political clout in asking for the support of "libraries" without defining what they are, and, more importantly, what they are not? I doubt it. There is not the slightest chance that California elementary schools will have professional librarians as long as local politicians can continue to pretend that the children still have adequate access to something called a library. And yet all of these deceptions fit quite comfortably into the new National Library Week theme.

Fight the Real Enemy

Our fascination with causes that may attract librarians on any and all sides of a question because they have nothing to do with the profession and our failure of self-discipline in concentrating on what is uniquely ours lead us to become angry at each other rather than at our tormentors, just as my stating this may cause some readers to become angry with me.

Don't waste your energies! I'm not the one who cut your budget. This self-trivialization lost us the opportunity to hear Al Gore speak to us directly about a librarian role in NREN, simply because some selfish and short-sighted protester would rather have him explain his vote on allowing military intervention in Kuwait. It is a fair question, but not at an ALA conference whose attendees deserve more relevance for their registration fees.

Perhaps we could learn something from the single-mindedness of the National Rifle Association (NRA), much as I personally dislike its agenda. Andrew Torok of Northern Illinois University has suggested sardonically that the NRA's phrasing of our National Library Week theme might be "If librarians are not kept on the job, only criminals will have information."

Before you are tempted to reject that thought as absurd, consider that the approach might work better for us than the forgettable themes (Quick! Name the last five.) that we now use. Virginia Wade once commented that playing beautiful tennis was sometimes more important to her than playing winning tennis. She was a talented player, but she didn't win nearly as often as Billie Jean King, whose game was effective but was never described as beautiful. There is also a great sense of beauty and serenity in watching lovely and graceful birds as they soar overhead. Let us not forget there is also danger of an unpleasant fallout if you stand directly under them.

Priorities for the Research Library Budget: A Humble Proposal

My love affair with management now goes back over 40 years. I call it a love affair because over that period of time I have come to realize what a fantastic opportunity for success a well-structured management philosophy represents. That is why I now teach management to neophyte students.

I have, as a private sector and academic administrator and now as a full-time teacher, interacted with a whole range of managers—some wonderful, some terrible, and a lot in between. I have managed large organizations with staffs of more than 300 and with lots of technology. I have supervised in the kinds of small organizations still so frequently found in our field. Finally, I have managed under faculty governance, in which there is very little formal authority, and in which leadership comes from seizing opportunities, filling vacuums, proposing initiatives, never simply reacting, and in impressing, inspiring, and persuading others.

My most recent assignments have allowed me to speak to the staffs of dozens of research libraries in both formal and informal settings. The research library should be a laboratory to test present and potential approaches. It would receive far more academic credit from the faculty colleagues it courts so assiduously if it concentrated more on researching its own options and perhaps less on running the warehouse and just doing what it is told to do.

Reprinted, with changes, by permission of the author and *Library Journal* 118, no. 5 (March 15, 1993): 52–53. Copyright © 1993 by Cahners Business Information.

Research libraries connected to major library schools should be able to do this more easily, because there is much that theory and practice can teach each other. I have been fortunate in being able to participate in a number of such studies: At other times, I have observed academic libraries as one would look into a fishbowl to see what is happening. From this, and my studies of academic library economics, I have come up with this short list of priorities for the research library budget.

1. An adequate student labor force. This first one is easy. In academia, unlike the public, private, and government sectors, student labor is both cheap and plentiful. Furthermore, universities encourage the hiring of students and student spouses. Moreover, what student workers do in the research library—shelve and retrieve materials, answer directional questions, handle routine processes, and make and deliver photocopies for use from the increasingly expensive collection of journals—all optimize the use of a very expensive investment. There are only two alternatives to having enough students, and they are both bad. Things either don't get done at all, with a waste of all that investment in collection, or they get done by the higher paid others who leave their jobs undone.

2. An adequate support staff. We used to call these people clericals or paraprofessionals without intending any insult. However, in a time when garbage collectors have become sanitary engineers, appearance becomes more important than substance. In any case, you know whom I mean. These are full-time people (which differentiates them from the students) and often career employees who perform the duties that do not require professional education and preparation.

Normally, that preparation includes a library degree, sometimes also a subject advanced degree, although it is frequently stipulated without being needed, and occasionally only a subject degree (as perhaps in accounting and systems analysis in the library). Given the stockpiling of talent in academic communities, it is not unlikely that your clerks also may have advanced academic preparation.

However, as we know from wage and salary analysis, if a skill isn't required by the job description, it doesn't count toward evaluation. That does not in any sense suggest that these individuals have trivial roles. Far from it. The tasks that they perform keep the library functioning on a daily basis. If there are not enough staff support people to perform these duties, they don't get done at all. Or, more likely, they are done badly, unwillingly, and expensively by the individuals who should be doing what we define as professional library work.

3. Professional staff. That professional staff then becomes the third in a string of people priorities only emphasizes what I have known for a long time: the quality of any organization is in its people and what they are able to do. Large buildings and collection statistics can be impressive, but they are also misleading. In selecting professionals, the first determination involves both how many and what kind we need.

That, of course, must come from objectives, plans, and strategies we have already presented to university administration for approval and support. It means that professionals don't do the things that students or support staff ought to be doing, hence the order of priorities. This might suggest that we need fewer professionals. In reality, there are numerous professional tasks nobody is doing at all that would make use in a cost-effective manner of the resources already purchased. The difference in the level of reference service provided in a corporate library and the much lower level offered in academia to faculty who may have very similar backgrounds and needs is one obvious example of how more academic library professionals might be useful.

Quantity of activity emerges from the negotiation of budgets with university administrators, with their taking ultimate responsibility for what the library is to do, and what it is not to do. Quality is never negotiable and is more important than quantity. If recruiting and keeping quality means higher pay, that will not surprise the professors of business administration.

It has always disturbed me that one of the main reasons for low librarian salaries is not a specific institutional edict but an attempt by library administrators to get as many people as possible for the money in the budget. If professionals are doing work on a consistent basis that could be done by those with less preparation and skill, something is very wrong. It is easy for this to happen, because libraries are traps in which clerical procedures take precedence over professional activities. Without enough students and support staff, everyone becomes a clerk. Attending lots of meetings is not a substitute.

4. **Education, training, and professional involvement** (as you can see, I am not quite ready to leave the people emphasis). You need all of these both for credit in the institution and for quality and modernity in the workplace, an awareness of changes and options. In the absence of these opportunities for not only your professionals but also for your support staff, you collect drones. The library can't afford drones, especially obsolete ones.

5. **Physical facilities and equipment.** This is purposely vague because these situations will differ so widely. Equipment suggests an increasing number and power of computer terminals—both for staff and end user applications, although end users (including students) should always be able to rely on staff if that is their preference. The library is a self-service institution only for people who prefer one.

However, my categorization also includes a further range of opportunities. Faculty should be encouraged, when possible, to use library materials and access services in the library rather than back in their own offices—a contradiction to many present trends. The reason is simple. If people work in the library rather than simply drag stuff out of it, they think of it as a laboratory rather than a warehouse, and, in the faculty mind-set, laboratory is better for us. It also means that material is more easily accessible for the next requester.

For students, we have to understand that the library has been a place for social congregation for as long as anyone can remember. There is no point battling with students about the "proper" use of a library. We can either accommodate this use along with all the others, or persuade the university administration to provide the students with a better place to hang out. Fighting with students, just as fighting with faculty, is a no-win situation. It is much better to fight with administrators. It is even possible that once students find the library for social contact, they might also discover that it has other possible value. However, first you have to get them there and let them feel welcome.

6. **Access budget.** I have saved this priority for last, in part because it is the one that others will always cultivate as their first priority; there is therefore little point in putting a primary emphasis on something on which others will place their only emphasis. Please note that I have used access and not collection development, because collection development is only one form of access.

All other things being equal, owning something is better than having to acquire it, even when acquisition from off site can be accomplished in two days or less, as it certainly should be. However, ownership does not guarantee access, and estimates as far back as Richard Trueswell put the probability of same-day retrieval from within the collection at no better than 50 percent.

As we have consciously removed duplicate acquisition for heavily used material in order to buy more single copies of little-used material, we have not only trashed everything Samuel Bradford told us but also probably further lessened the probability of same-day delivery, particularly in the absence of students to do the delivering. Whatever the mix, the point is that purchase, interlibrary loan (ILL), telephone and fax use, and database searching followed by terminal ordering are all alternatives that must be evaluated without preconditions, with the decision option in the hands of library management. The bottom line is never to discuss quantitative holdings with the faculty if you can avoid it. Discuss access. Isn't that what really ought to matter?

Where Do We Go from Here?

All right, I'll admit I've rigged the sequence. Collection development is not really the last priority. However, I think we must pretend that it is in order to place some balance into the process. There are faculty and administrators out there for whom collection development is the only priority, given the shortage of funds in academia. When is there enough money with which to buy everything that somebody wants bought? Not yesterday, today, tomorrow, or ever.

If collection development is allowed to be the first priority, it ultimately becomes the only priority. Our other needs can be quantified; this one can't. That is why we must budget everything else first and purchase materials with the money left over. Or at least pretend to. Of course, administrations can always give us more money, and that money might be for materials. Certainly, they will never volunteer money for anything else. We have to make sure that they understand that giving us money specifically earmarked for publisher invoices is an indication of neither support nor largesse, except perhaps for the publishers.

What Do We Give 'Em? And Who Are 'Em?

I have written many book reviews, but never as a part of this column. However, *Give 'Em What They Want!* (*GEWTW*), written by the Baltimore County Public Library (BCPL) Blue Ribbon Committee and published by the American Library Association in 1992, has caught my special attention, if only by its title. I have been aware of the innovative and nontraditional approaches of this library for 30 years, first as a fellow Marylander and vice president of Documentation, Inc., which produced BCPL's book catalog.

The Tale of BCPL

As a library educator, I have heard tales about what may be called the wonderful or terrible—depending on the speaker's viewpoint—operational philosophy of this library. BCPL was also one of the public libraries that chose to forgo earned salary increases in order to buy more books. I have already expressed my feelings that such actions are foolish for the library and set a bad precedent for the rest of us ("The Perilous Allure of Moral Imperativism," *LJ*, September 15, 1992, pp. 44–45).

And then there is the book title, repeated continuously throughout the text. Although the book was written by a committee, it speaks with one voice. If the title was intended to draw attention, it certainly caught mine. Taken at face value, giving people "what they want" resembles a fast food carry-out window. We have seen that simply "giving pleasure" becomes a weak argument for receiving public funds when our competitors put forth more serious justifications.

Reprinted, with changes, by permission of the author and *Library Journal* 118, no. 9 (May 15, 1993): 46–47. Copyright © 1993 by Cahners Business Information.

Libraries:
Important, Yes; Crucial,...?

New York Governor Mario Cuomo's announcement that parks and libraries are important, but they are not as crucial as New York's more urgent priorities, demonstrates that the agendas of public libraries, if he perceives them primarily in the context of providing pleasure or convenience, have not caught his attention. Furthermore, a slogan such as "give 'em what they want" requires the abandonment of marketing simply for the sake of selling something. Giving people what *they* want, rather than what *we* think they ought to want, is certainly crucial to survival. However, marketing also creates an awareness of possibilities as to what people *might* want, once they know there is such an option, and that is something we have to tell them.

A whole new range of telephone services now give us what we presumably want—things we never suspected we wanted until reams of advertising alerted and persuaded us. The telephone marketers knew that if we wanted it badly enough we would find a way to get it. Peter Drucker has told us that in the provision of a service or product that people really want, cost is irrelevant. Conversely, if people don't really care very much about the service or the product, something provided free/cheap will not impress them nor will it save the provider.

The Painful Truth
About Librarians

GEWTW notes that librarians don't read their own literature to any appreciable extent. That is painfully true. If the intent of the title were to get us to buy and read a book we might otherwise have ignored, then the tactic succeeded at least in attaining the second objective. Professors rarely buy books; they urge libraries to buy them. And in this case, that was unnecessary.

The operator of the newspaper kiosk next to the subway station gives people what they want, and his face expresses no reaction to the choice of either *The Racing Form* or the *New York Times*. That discipline is crucial, and a failure to anticipate who wants to read what leads to unhappy customers and a loss of revenue. Is that all librarianship is? Can we expect to take moral stands, hold professional conferences, and try to shape national information policy if that is all we do?

A Monolithic Sense of Purpose

There is much in *GEWTW* to interest and stimulate the reader. The book is not only written well, but written with a passionate dedication to the rightness of its cause. If these BCPL staffers feel attacked by the outside library world, one senses that they relish the attention. Even though composed by a number of authors, the book displays a monolithic sense of purpose and value. One wonders, however, if a price was paid in shaping this unity of vision.

One of the most reassuring characteristics of the American decision process is that we fight and argue and react badly to being told what to think. It is by far the best way to reach good decisions, as our Eastern European friends would now certainly agree.

If there is no sense of friction, of disagreement, or even of the gradual evolution of concepts in this book, perhaps that should not be surprising. BCPL has had the same director and deputy director for 28 years—a long time for two people to manage in one place. I myself sensed, after ten years in the deanship here in Indiana—a decade marked by excitement, growth, and innovation—that I had accomplished all I could, regardless of time frame, and that staying on would simply be marking time. There is often a temptation to stay longer because successors, to establish their own identity, immediately start to unravel what you have knit. However, even BCPL's longtime management team may find this inevitable after retirement.

A Longstanding Administrative Team

Twenty-eight years of a single administrative team outlasts any recalcitrants and breeds a unified mind set. Those who might not have shared the same vision at the outset would have left long ago. Library Director Charles Robinson will cheerfully acknowledge that he has strong opinions, and, in a profession in which too many try to search for a majority view before expressing their own, he is refreshing. However, in a position of authority, what can seem courageous in juniors can become dangerous to the survival of the iconoclasts any organization should cherish, if only to keep it honest.

Moreover, BCPL's own hiring practices seem to be designed to perpetuate the comfortable sense of agreement with existing policy and practice. Ninety-three of the 135 full-time librarians were hired as raw and unspoiled recruits without library degrees and trained internally and by the state. That suggests that more than 60 percent of the professional decision-making staff learned just about all that it knows from those already in a closed system, and that makes all of the unanimity in this book a little suspicious.

BCPL reserves management positions, alone among professional activities, for those holding an MLS degree. That also surprises me: while there may be some sense of agreement that library education programs know how to prepare catalogers, reference librarians, and collection developers, there is far less certainty about our ability to prepare managers, even though some of us try very hard. This insistence that only library degree-holders can manage but the internally trained can do everything else is not explained. The argument that in the 1950s there were not enough degreed librarians to hire sounds a little thin today.

Inbreeding in Libraries

I can't comment on the quality of the BCPL professional staff, but it is much easier to have a collegial group that agrees on fundamental value systems if you raise them yourself. Is there danger in the process of inbreeding? We know what can happen—from pit bulls to race horses. It enhances existing characteristics, both the good and the bad.

Is this dangerous in organizational dynamics? Management writers like Mary Parker Follett tell us that we should encourage disagreement and not suppress it, and that we should not rush to achieve agreement or consensus. That 135 individuals all share the same value system sounds wonderful, but is it? What happened to the others? Were they simply not selected, weeded out, made to feel uncomfortable, or "persuaded"?

One of my observations when traveling in Alaska (and marveling at the scenery and complaining about the weather) is that the residents take the weather in stride. That is, the remaining residents; I assume the complainers left long ago to seek a warmer climate. We used to think that organizations in which everyone agreed—where everyone thought the same way and perhaps even dressed the same way—were the best of all worlds. Now we are not so sure. Look at IBM.

Luck Is Not Enough

Yet, something obviously did work at BCPL for a long time, in community support for both the materials collection and for staff salaries. I take no pleasure in noting that the strategy employed by the library now seems to work no better than it does elsewhere (as attested to by several BCPL budget cuts of millions of dollars). Some of the past success may have resulted from being in what was an affluent community, but luck is not enough. Nor, I suspect, is the single-minded vision displayed in this book. I have no problem with the argument that local geography does not lend itself to the traditional approach of a main library and branches. That changes only mechanisms; it tends to make libraries more labor intensive and expensive even as it makes them more personally responsive.

I also agree with the thesis that a public library is not an academic library, imposing its value system of "good" literature on the public, although academic libraries shouldn't do that, either. Only professors and teachers are allowed that arrogance.

However, I suspect that the leadership and staff at BCPL are also smart enough to know that the users are not monolithic in the other direction, either. *GEWTW* makes the point that the reader who wants *Lancet* is not more important than the child looking for a good story. Agreed, but neither is that reader less important. We do not know if that reader might or might not have other sources for this information (an irrelevant and ugly question to put to a taxpayer). Just be glad the person is there.

Public Libraries Have Diverse Wants

The difficulty for public libraries is the need to serve a wide variety of customers, with a wide variety of needs (or wants, as BCPL insists). Is it possible that BCPL doesn't really give 'em what they want, by first defining who 'em are? I hope not, because it isn't that far from Baltimore to Newark, New Jersey, where John Cotton Dana saw the importance of also stressing service to the business community, large and small.

Libraries must obviously establish priorities, but our patrons have their own very narrow priorities as well. Ultimately, only we can decide what librarians do and what they do not do. Just giving 'em what they want, all of them and everything, is chaos. Arbitrary decisions about who might be worthy of better or any service—a charge levied against academic libraries—are just as bad from public libraries. I still recall being a college student whom my public library wouldn't serve. The library had decided it did not want to serve those citizens who presumably had other access to information. It was an arrogant action that I still have not forgiven, because I had as much right to be served as any other resident.

I suspect the directors of BCPL understand all of this. I also suspect that somebody may be putting us on, for the sake of a better story. It may even be that the decision to sacrifice earned salary increases to buy more books was simply a calculated investment to earn more empathy and support in the future. One step back and two steps forward. Is that what BCPL did? I hope so. However, if satisfying 'em is simply a process of sacrificing salaries to buy more books, then I want the municipal leaders to lead the way, as leaders are supposed to do.

—■—

The Legacy of John Swan

John Swan, library director at Bennington College, Vermont, died on January 26, 1994 at the age of 48. He died of ALS, or what is commonly called Lou Gehrig's disease. John's death saddens me, it angers me, it makes me grateful, and it makes me aware of how unique and courageously principled a librarian he was.

I am saddened because I recognize, in my mid-60s, that 48 is an absurdly young age at which to die. At 48, just about all professionals are at the height of their most productive period, with enthusiasm and energy leavened by experience. I am angry because I am aware how little is being done to find a cure for ALS, a disease whose horrors have been known for a long time.

A Productive Administrator

I am grateful because this disease, horrifying as it is in wasting the body of the victim, does not attack the mind. John Swan was fully productive as an administrator and perhaps more importantly as a true and pure supporter of the principles and not just the conveniences of intellectual freedom until the moment of his death.

One of my treasured possessions is a letter from John, written on January 25, 1994, the day before he died. Much of what I will state in the rest of this column carries his personal endorsement. What matters then is not that what I will posit is my opinion, but that it is also his. It is in his own insistence on the purity of the principles of intellectual freedom, regardless of personal inconvenience and disagreement, that John Swan has left us his greatest legacy. It is the awareness that we have no one to replace him that should cause all of us to reassess what we mean by "principles."

Reprinted, with changes, by permission of the author and *Library Journal* 119, no. 5 (March 15, 1994): 50–51. Copyright © 1994 by Cahners Business Information.

The Freedom to Lie

I became most directly aware of the eloquence, courage, and rightness of John Swan as an upholder of the tenets that characterize our profession when I read *The Freedom to Lie: A Debate About Democracy* (McFarland, 1989). In that book, Swan argued as passionately and as clearly as only he was capable of doing that individuals who wanted to advance the ugly and despicable lie that the Holocaust was just an invention and that it never happened had the right to do so and had the right to rent an advertising booth at an American Library Association (ALA) conference.

The argument that John raised was incredibly and personally painful to me. I was born in Austria and was forced to leave in 1938 (indeed, was fortunate to be able to leave) with my parents, who left all their possessions behind. I lost countless relatives in the ovens and gas chambers of Auschwitz, Maidanek, and Treblinka.

And yet I realized, no matter how much I might twist and rationalize, that John was correct. My considering these to be evil people meant nothing and in particular meant nothing in the consideration of the principles of freedom of expression to which I had sworn allegiance.

Focusing Principles on Librarians

If John Swan taught me this, I could certainly have learned it earlier from a number of eloquent philosophers, including Voltaire. Swan's contribution, for me, was to focus these statements of principles on my own profession and to realize how casually we embrace principles and then fail to apply them.

It is precisely because I remember that the members of the Hitler Youth were fervent in their conviction that they were right that I am not only suspicious but also revolted by members of my own profession who explain their violation of the rights of others by an appeal to some "greater" principle.

There is no greater principle. Certainly convenient adherence to expedience for the sake of "rightness" does not qualify. We are not only tempted but fascinated by the desire to do good, at least good as we personally define it, and never mind the rights of others.

Do we need to be reminded of examples? This is a good column in which to drag them out, because all of them are issues that I discussed in correspondence with John Swan and represent conclusions that he shared. The bittersweet memory for me is that some of his statements came just in the day, or at most days and months, before he died. John Swan was true to his principles.

The Final Swan Publication

In one of my own columns (*LJ*, February 15, 1992, p. 138), I noted my own incredulity that a great majority of UCLA faculty colleagues attacked Donald Case and John Richardson for stating conclusions they had every reason to state and did so in the particularly ugly format of "They of Course Have the Right To Say This, but . . . ." In what may be the last Swan publication to appear before his death, a *Library Quarterly* book review (January, p. 89), Swan independently reaches the same conclusion.

As a four-year member of the ALA Council, and even before that, I witnessed the skirmishes between the groups representing intellectual freedom and those representing international relations about whether we should be fulfilling interlibrary loans for the Republic of South Africa.

However, the question is much larger than the issue of apartheid. How can librarians ever, and under any circumstance given their own backgrounds and value systems, support the withholding of information, to anyone for any reason? As individuals, they can certainly do this and decide to abandon their profession for what they see as a larger and nobler cause. But as librarians, and as an action of a body of ALA? I can't imagine it, and I believe neither could John.

Putting Our Money Where Cincinnati Is

Recently, the ALA board voted unanimously to remove the 1995 Midwinter Meeting from Cincinnati, at an association cost estimated at $200,000. The cost be damned for the moment, in the expression of what principle? I am grateful for John Swan's words here in his January 25 letter to me, so that I can share them with you directly.

There might be some point to it if we were reaching the people we want to punish—say a cabal of homophobic hotel and conference center owners. But even that could only be justified as retaliation, ignoring the trickier question of the constitutional right of a people to make a bad move.

Did that principle of the right to be wrong escape the ALA Executive Board? And yes, that applies to the right of the citizens of Arizona *not* to allow us a day off on Martin Luther King's birthday—even as I might personally disagree.

The citizens of Arizona have the right not to celebrate that holiday without being punished by citizens of Indiana like me, who did decide to celebrate Martin Luther King in a national observance. Fine either way, because what happens in the other 49 states is, according to the Constitution, none of my business.

Upholding Our Self-Righteousness

And yes, that also applies to something we once cared about so passionately but which has faded into the background, because we can only uphold so many self-righteous principles at a time: the ERA boycott. Ratification is an action on a state-by-state basis. Though we never discussed it, I would hope that John would agree that the rest of us have no right to pressure others.

My view here may have cost me the ALA presidency, but when you lose by 43 votes out of more than 13,000, lots of reasons can apply. However, here's one last one about which I do know how John felt.

In his December 1993 *American Libraries* column (p. 1003), Will Manley notes surprise that one of his reference librarians, a staunch opponent of all forms of censorship, supports the removal of an older but heavily borrowed management text that perpetuates sexual stereotypes. I do not yet have Manley's response to my letter, but it was my observation that his reference librarian has been a censor all along but has not until now encountered a fellow censor with whom he or she agreed.

If we must fight ferociously to keep Leslea Newman's *Heather Has Two Mommies* (Alyson, 1989) in the collection, as indeed we should, we must fight equally strenuously to keep all of the sexist literature, particularly if it is sexist simply because it is old and was written before we acquired some much-needed sensitivity. That might even apply to what we may now find as sexist or bigoted in Shakespeare, because John Swan taught us that we librarians provide access to information even if we consider it wrong or personally hurtful. That includes the spoutings of revisionist historians who know exactly what they are doing and of old-time sexist management writers who never had a clue.

John Swan clearly understood all these principles. He also knew that adherence to them, no matter how personally painful—perhaps particularly if personally abhorrent—is what sets us apart as librarians from all else we might be. John, you gave us so very much and for that I am grateful. If it is selfish of me to be sad and angry that you weren't allowed time to give us the so much more that was in you, then I am selfish.

Small Public Libraries—Challenges, Opportunities, and Irrelevancies

As a special librarian for almost 25 years, I am very familiar with small libraries. There are many special libraries with a professional staff of only one, and many of these libraries function quite effectively. In addition to the one professional, the library must also have at least one and preferably two clerks, and that is the low end of my bargaining stance.

Libraries are clerical traps. In the absence of clerical support, the presumed professional librarians not only function as clerks but begin to resemble clerks to their users because they spend their time shelving, date stamping, and collecting overdue fines and interlibrary loan fees.

These are clerical activities and are recognized universally as clerical activities. Except in the case of death or dire disaster, librarians shouldn't be doing these things any more than they should be sweeping floors. Librarians performing clerical tasks negatively affects their personal image as well as the image of the profession. In addition, it is always a waste of money to use someone to do something a less qualified and lower-paid person could do.

Since I moved to library education, I've noticed that the exact same phenomenon exists in public libraries. If it also exists in academic and school libraries (not enough clerks to do the clerical work), then this is the ultimate absurdity. In these settings clerical labor is student labor; student labor is abundant and cheap; and hiring students should be part of the organizational mission. Special and public librarians who find themselves doing clerical work because there are no clerks might have some excuse since obtaining clerical help confronts the dual problems of relatively high salaries and hiring freezes. Academic librarians who do clerical work have no one to blame but themselves.

Smaller Is More Important?

There is one other thing I remember clearly from my special library career and the occasional disputes with corporate personnel officers. The smaller the professional staff, the more important it becomes to select truly excellent professionals. It is the larger libraries that can occasionally endure and hide mediocre professionals. The smaller the staff, the greater the emphasis on excellence because the greater the stakes. If we have to find room for lesser librarians, then let us stash them in major Association of Research Libraries institutions or national libraries where their incompetence can be diffused or hidden.

Mediocrity or worse in the smaller library (be it academic, public, or special) has far more dire results, because our users will accept both mediocrity and incompetence without complaint. This thesis (something along the lines of smaller is more important) flies in the face of the common bureaucratic tools for rewarding size of staff or management responsibility. But forward-looking organizations have begun to develop more flexible evaluation techniques that reward more than number of subordinates; they look at innovation, initiative, and creativity as well.

The Alaska Model and More

I was reminded of all of this as I prepared to speak at a meeting of Alaska librarians, particularly public librarians. Alaska is a very large, sparsely populated state. All of the arguments describing smallness and geographic isolation that are sometimes used to explain away inadequate library services can be applied to Alaska. After all, who would have a better excuse? And yet, such arguments are a sham and a fraud. The development of bibliographic access networks and document delivery mechanisms are such that geographic constraints are largely irrelevant.

Hawaiian television viewers found a way to see professional football games on Sunday when they were played rather than on film on Monday because it was important to them. They use a satellite, and so could we. The planning team for the ill-fated Iranian National Library on which I participated in 1975 recognized that the paucity of roads would make surface delivery of interlibrary loan from the National Library impractical, and so we planned a heliport on the roof. They might not need the heliport now; they might make do with fax machines, portable generators, and a centralized room full of reference librarians with phones and terminals, backed by a large collection.

Librarians Determine Librarianship

All citizens of this country are entitled to minimum levels of library service. It is the job of this profession, through a national week that professionalizes rather than trivializes us, through White House Conferences, and through national commissions, to determine and inform them what that is. Of course, problems of information service for our communities are first of all issues of the library profession, just as quality of medical service begins with the question of whether we have enough doctors, the right kind of doctors, where they are, and how well prepared they are.

Librarians who attempt to provide adequate information services to their communities without the advantage of a large collection in the same building must, all other things being equal, be better librarians than those with the easier jobs of just looking on their own shelves and in their own catalogs. They must be more assertive, more innovative, more people oriented, more caring, more dynamic.

They must fight through the layers of bureaucracy that can smother all of us to get their clients what they need in a reasonable amount of time. Readers of this column already know that what these clients need is not necessarily what they thought they needed, what they asked for, or what they thought you could get for them. Professionals give 'em what they need, in any field.

Certification As Subterfuge

Must these intermediaries in the smallest and most isolated locations, or in other libraries, be professional librarians educated in accredited graduate library education programs? Not necessarily, but they probably should be. While certification at the state level can be used to measure other ways of learning to become a professional, it should not surprise us to learn that certification examinations, if they are going to be properly administered, updated, and graded, will probably cost the state more than simply requiring an accredited MLS.

It may be worth spending more to provide a greater degree of fairness and of options, particularly in states in which accredited education is not easily available. However, if certification is simply a subterfuge for providing communities with cheaper library heads (although it is hard to envisage paying even less than degreed librarians are paid in small public libraries), the library community, and particularly state librarians, should be counted on to fight against this misleading practice. If a state wants to provide nondegree options for the qualification of professional librarians, then this is a laudable goal.

However, the validation of that would be a process that costs more, forcing the state library and the governor to whom it reports to put their money where their principles presumably are. The point, we need to remind ourselves, is better libraries, not cheaper libraries. At least that is the point for the library community and the state library. It should not be surprising, given the brevity of our graduate educational programs, that simply requiring a degree for anyone who is going to head a library is both the simplest and the cheapest option. Can anyone come up with a rationale for pseudolibrarians? Or pseudodoctors?

Cheaper Certainly Isn't Better

Good things can only happen if our profession controls not only what it takes to be a professional librarian, but also what situations and settings demand one. State legislatures cannot do this for us any more than for other professions. Since I have already postulated that small and rural libraries are most in need of innovative and qualified professionals if citizens are not to be shortchanged, then why do we sometimes put the case backwards by agreeing to the very opposite?

However, if funding bodies in the ever-present search for economy are not willing to staff the institution properly, then it becomes our task to point out to the citizens of this community that they don't really have a library and they are being cheated. Perhaps public librarians must be better prepared—not necessarily differently but better—than some others, particularly if they are in a small library. They and special librarians are immediately sent into combat, from the first day on the job.

Training the Pseudolibrarian

Educational program quality is not the only issue. My fellow special librarians can be eloquent in demanding that library educators toe the mark and teach what they are supposed to, but are rather quiet when it comes to disciplining organizations that run pseudolibraries. Instead, we help train the staff and allow them into our clubs. Interlibrary cooperative activities are such clubs. It is a little bizarre when special librarians have to explain interlibrary loan to their new "colleagues."

The club membership qualifications need not be simply educational. There could be equivalencies, and we should probably, at some point, demand more than simple degree credentials. However, it seems that there has to be something. When we rush to "fix" things by creating instant librarians through simple collegiality, we only demean what we have worked to achieve and the most obvious basis of our uniqueness. But of course we also give quick training fixes to White House Conference delegates, so they can then, based on one day's knowledge, make policy for us.

Ultimately, it always comes back to the same thing: Professions control their membership, and they control the credentialing process. If we are not willing to do that, then perhaps we don't deserve to qualify as one, and that, too, has been suggested. A librarian is a librarian is a librarian, as Gertrude Stein undoubtedly meant to say. Librarians need to be prepared educationally, or through whatever approaches we might approve, to be librarians. There can be no such thing as "only" a rural or academic or special or school librarian.

The reason is simple. Library school graduates often work in settings other than those in which they thought they would work. They go where the jobs are, and most employers consider the MLS basic in the hiring process. There is little evidence that they avoid candidates from schools that did not claim a particular specialization. How would they even know? The school doesn't tell them, accreditation doesn't specify, and the graduate is certainly not going to mention it. There is, on the contrary, a good deal of evidence that, except for large academic libraries, employers prefer to hire from a local pool: it is more convenient and it is cheaper.

Libraries Begin with Librarians

If our profession isn't willing to define some common standard that all who claim the title of librarian must meet, then contract administrators, municipal officials, school principals, and corporate personnel officers will gladly define librarian for us. We already know that this definition will fit their own preconceptions and specific scenarios, particularly if they already have someone they want to promote or hire. They will also create definitions in terms of how much they want to spend, and usually that is very little.

Libraries do not start with books but with librarians, particularly in this electronic age in which you can run a very good library without an in-house collection. It is easy to establish pseudolibraries and understand why administrators and politicians would want to foist a pseudolibrary off on an unsuspecting public—pseudolibraries are cheaper. However, why would librarians want to help perpetuate this sham by going along with it? Perhaps only a qualified psychiatrist can answer that. Psychiatrists, unlike librarians, keep a sharp eye out for interlopers.

"Lead Me Not into Temptation to Do Good"

The statement comes from Peter Drucker at the graduation ceremony of a theological seminary. Drucker acknowledged that his advice would not be well received. Nevertheless, he argued that there are only a few things that time and resources allow us to do, and we need to select those carefully. If we opt for all the things that we perceive as needing to be done, we will end up completing none at all, doing the ones with which we are least compatible, or doing everything poorly.

Drucker's advice to theologians has meaning for librarians, because what tempts them certainly also tempts us. Library budgets have fallen under the axe for more than 20 years, giving librarians the reputation of being resourceful and able to cope with any situation. Politicians assume that somehow librarians will always find a way, and that assumption makes meeting our needs less crucial for them than meeting the needs of those who, unless funded, will produce an embarrassing mess. What they think of us is not a compliment, and I hope none of us are naïve enough to think it is.

The Budget/Program Relation

There are, according to management theory, two classic ways of dealing with the relationship between budgets and programs. The first, and certainly preferred by management theorists, is to allow the implementation needs of proposed and then approved programs define the budget.

Reprinted, with changes, by permission of the author and *Library Journal* 119, no. 15 (September 15, 1994): 47–48. Copyright © 1994 by Cahners Business Information.

The second, and more common, process is to specify a budget and then let the budget define the programs. Incredibly, at least for librarians, there is the political perception of a third alternative. Budgets and programs are considered independent, with no relationship to each other.

That is, of course, nonsense, and that is why cost estimates are needed for each of the recommendations of White House Conferences. If not, politicians will embrace the recommendations in principle, they just won't fund them. Will we implement them anyway? We will certainly try. We have become so predictable in this area, we will certainly be given the opportunity to accomplish everything with nothing. If that leads to stress and burnout, that is surely not a politician's concern.

Making a Choice

Drucker states the obvious when he notes that any list of things worth doing might yield 64 items, of which we are able to do perhaps five or six. But which ones? If I translate Drucker's advice to theologians, it requires asking three questions.

1. What is our unique and specific job?

2. What is our unique and specific role in the larger universe in which we function?

3. What are our unique strengths and characteristics? And, by extension of all three questions, what do we do only incidentally and peripherally? Please note the recurrence of the word unique.

Our response should focus on three areas in which we can establish a unique presence: education, information intermediation, and recreation. The last, while perhaps the easiest to achieve and to establish visibility in, is also the most dangerous. In any environment of prioritizing, recreation becomes the most expendable and rightly so.

Education and information intermediation as priority areas offer opportunity potential, because both are recognized as larger societal agenda items. The two are closely related, because a large part of education is the creation of an awareness of information options, from helping yourself to simply being smart enough to find a reference librarian. People don't have to find their own answers if someone else will find them. We call that the development of the service professions, and it provides the most rapidly expanding sector of our economy.

Someone will most certainly be sitting in clover. It ought to be librarians. We should also be able to claim an important role in the educational process, but that requires a negotiation of our role not only with fellow educators but also with the general public, and we have not done this well at all.

We do not set our own priorities within the funding cycle of the U.S. Department of Education, sparse as those funds are, and of course they are always threatened with total extinction. However, even when there are funds, we are expected to respond to priorities that are already handed to us. Our own freedom to set agendas and claim funds in areas of research and education, quite aside from whether or not other educators find them important, simply does not exist.

Step Aside, Librarians

Teachers have become adept at establishing ground rules for feeding time at the power and money trough. The information community, by contrast, didn't exist at all until long after librarians. If it was able to claim a fertile new territory, perhaps it was because we left some lying around unused.

Information people don't really understand our potential contributions any better than the educators do. The one role they do understand is the document supply role, but it takes no foresight to realize that in a routinized and computerized environment, that has importance but not professional importance. It is sad to speculate what we might now be if we had followed the lead of visionaries like John Cotton Dana, who, as head of the Business Branch of the Newark Public Library, NJ, recognized the potential for intermediation. And Dana had no technology.

On the Wrong Track

If we have missed the opportunity to spell out our profession it is because we unknowingly followed the model of the American railroads, which at the turn of the century had lots of money and an open terrain. But they forgot they were in the transportation and not just the railroad business.

For us, the missed opportunity may have come from the insistence, from both inside and outside our profession, that we need to make filling the needs for "doing good" our first priority. If we were to define our unique capabilities in both the areas of education and information intermediation, it would give us plenty to do. I haven't mentioned a role in the areas that seem to fascinate us so much—work with adult illiterates, with latchkey children, with the homeless, and with an ever-growing list of societal problems to which crime and drugs must certainly be added; while we can "do good," we have only our frail bodies and not any unique expertise to throw into this fray.

What Do We Know About Literacy?

It has been suggested that the public library can provide assistance in dealing with adult illiteracy and latchkey children. We could do something, but is using the library in this manner—particularly to the exclusion of tasks such as computer-based or manual reference service, which qualified librarians can perform better than anyone else—a worthwhile effort, either for us or for the nation? Government officials, who certainly know how to establish political priorities, are perfectly willing to preempt our priorities (although we have stressed pitifully few unique priorities) for their own.

We have no unique expertise as reading instructors. And yet adult illiteracy was ordained, of course by nonlibrarians in the federal bureaucracy, as our first priority. Our preoccupation with latchkey children is even more puzzling. What is being asked of us is to be a combination of playground supervisor and babysitter.

Neither is an expertise we possess as a result of our master's degrees nor an expertise worth claiming. However, there are even more intriguing examples of our seizing the opportunity to do good. We read of public library programs that lend construction tools. However, we possess no expertise in the stocking, recommending, and lending of tools.

If such programs are worth having, then they are worth municipal and federal support, with the logical outlets being hardware stores, which have both the tools and the expertise. If your local Ace Hardware Store has not yet leapt at the opportunity to lend its tools to the homeless, perhaps it is because it is not as fascinated by the urge to "do good." Perhaps it also has a clearer understanding of what hardware stores do well and what they do poorly.

Our Fascination with Doing Good

Our fascination with doing good can even lead us into dangerous and glib statements that perhaps we should not make. "A Lesson in Leadership from NLM" (Editorial, *LJ*, February 15, p. 90) congratulates the National Library of Medicine (NLM) on its "courage" in providing free access to its AIDS-related databases. But why only AIDS-related and not any of the others, particularly dealing with such killers as cancer?

Certainly, it is not statistically true that AIDS is the more important medical problem. Indeed, it can be argued that AIDS, for which we have no cure but a great deal of knowledge concerning prevention, cannot begin to approach in importance those diseases for which we have neither. And yet NLM finds a rationale for charging for cancer information and providing AIDS information for free, and *LJ* can find this courageous? It is more likely that what NLM has shown is not courage but rather acquiescence to a better organized political lobby. John Swan, who died of Lou Gehrig's disease earlier this year, complained bitterly about the lack of interest in researching his disease, as did basketball coach Jim Valvano before he died of cancer.

Avoiding Overcommitment

We must be very careful about the implications of what we do and do not support. The need to avoid overcommitment and blurring of unique purpose was Drucker's message to future theologians, and, perhaps, it should be his message to us. When we do things that are not part of our unique list of skills and characteristics, and take on instead the support of issues to which we bring nothing uniquely distinctive, we often stop doing the things we ought to be doing because we are singularly qualified to do them. However, because we rarely mention what we are not doing, no one else notices. When government officials hand us new priorities, they don't know what priorities they just killed.

We need to reread Drucker to remind ourselves that we should establish solid, short, and doable programs that match our priorities and eschew handy and emotional issues that are foisted upon us, invariably without our having been asked. For us the desire to implement the premise of "management by trying to do good" (although MBTTDG is an unworkable acronym) is so prevalent and so disastrous that this issue warrants more attention. To be continued in the next two White Papers.

Our Goals and Our Programs: We're Better at Caring Than at Getting Others to Care

In my last column (September 15, p. 47ff.) I began exploring the trouble we get into when we allow our value systems and priorities to be seduced by the temptation to "do good." Management writers have long made a distinction between goals and objectives. Goals are general statements of principle and intent. They are important, but they come under the heading of motherhood, apple pie, baseball, and waving the flag. Goals cannot be the basis for anything that follows, either for ourselves or for our staffs, without the articulation of objectives.

Objectives deal with the specifics of what is going to be accomplished within a time frame, usually no more than a year. Objectives lead to plans, strategies, and the identification of needed resources. Objectives are articulated by the operating manager (in this case the library director) and then presented to the governing body (usually nonlibrarians) for its concurrence and approval, i.e., a commitment to the needed resources. Without that, we have no achievable objectives, and we need to revise these to represent what our bosses are willing to pay for.

If there is a discrepancy between the old and the new objectives, that difference must be spelled out clearly and publicly articulated. As sage political leaders such as Gov. Otis Bowen of Indiana have told us, politically we can offer our bosses only two options: reward for support and punishment for nonsupport. If that suggests in turn that management is not for the faint of heart, that is hardly news.

Reprinted, with changes, by permission of the author and *Library Journal* 119, no. 17 (October 15, 1994): 38–39. Copyright © 1994 by Cahners Business Information.

Depend on Drucker

Regular readers of this column know of my devotion to the words of my fellow Viennese Peter Drucker, who states options with such marvelous clarity. Drucker has noted repeatedly, as I have, that managers need to understand that their own boss is their most important subordinate and the primary influence on whether they will fail or succeed. In establishing this relationship it is essential that we make our bosses care.

Finally, Drucker reminds us that the essence of management communication is exception reporting—what did not happen and why not. Reporting success is something we will do anyway; if we report only the positive and never the negative it becomes quite clear that we never needed any money in the first place. That principle is so obvious to all of my students, many of whom have never worked in libraries, I wonder why the writers of library annual reports fail to understand it. I also shudder to think about library directors who report that despite budget cuts circulation still went up. Are they being incredibly naïve or suicidal, or both? If budget cuts lead to good things anyway, then what is the problem? We will never catch police chiefs, or even school teachers, making the kinds of political mistakes we make routinely.

Bosses Will Opt for
Fuzzy Vagueness

It should be no surprise that if our bosses are more dedicated to the easier principle of good libraries than to the harder reality of funding them, they will much prefer leaving library communication at goals, rather than moving on to the hard specifics of objectives, plans, strategies, and resources. Our bosses will certainly opt for fuzzy vagueness (we are committed to good libraries but we just don't have any money right now) unless they see the issue of rewards and punishments in terms of their own value systems.

Despite this temptation to keep things vague, more than 40 years ago managers in industry forced their subordinates to move away from a discussion of fuzzy goals to a discussion of specific objectives and resources, in programs called management by objectives (MBO), and later refined into exercises in zero-based budgeting. These emphases on a demand for specifics by the boss have never worked very well for librarians, largely because our bosses see a greater value for them in our being cheap than in our being good, particularly if the goals that we continue to trumpet so loudly repeat a commitment to goodness and virtue—forgetting that the skinflints will never allow us the money with which to implement either goodness or virtue, let alone library programs.

Self-Correcting Mechanism

Presumably in industry but not necessarily in federal, state, or local government, in academia, or in the general not-for-profit sector there is a self-correcting mechanism. In the for-profit sector we can't succeed simply by stirring goals about how we will capture the sneaker market. We have to do it, or stockholders will notice. In these other sectors no one will necessarily notice at all. This is particularly true when the operational managers refuse to blow the whistle, and even more so when they take the blame for any shortcomings on their own stooped and bony shoulders.

It is this difficulty of dealing with the relationship between resources and what does or does not happen outside the for-profit sector that has caused Drucker to announce that he will devote the remainder of his career to management issues in the not-for-profit world. That includes all libraries, even corporate special libraries unless the case can be made that having a good and not just a cheap library makes a difference to the corporate bottom line.

All of this seems so obvious that it continues to puzzle me that many librarians are willing coconspirators in keeping issues at the general level of goals without forcing discussion at the hard-core reward/punishment level. Surely we realize that our present strategies in dealing in generalities have led to fairly consistent declines in library funding since the early 1970s, even as both politicians and public surveys continue to assure us that we are wonderful. Even when it is announced in the media that we have "won," it simply means that we have restored an earlier loss. Rarely do we get bigger, even as the information world we live in does.

The White Example

Perhaps an example of how I apply the teachings of Drucker in managing my boss may be useful here. In 1980 the chancellor of the Bloomington campus was kind enough to offer me the vacant post of dean of the library education program, and I was both flattered and interested. However, before I responded, I asked him a question: Did he want me to run a library school that would contest for being one of the best in the country? For being an average, middle-of-the-road school? For being the cheapest school that could still qualify for accreditation? I told him I would accept only if he selected option number one.

Was there risk in this strategy? Perhaps, but in reality very little, and I was prepared to take that risk. However, at the abstract level of choosing goals, I was reasonably certain that he would choose option one, and, of course, he did. However, striving for that level of quality would take a good deal of work on both our parts. I would do most of the hard work. His job largely consisted of finding money, but only if I could justify my request in terms of the quality to which he had just agreed. How he found that money was certainly not my job; I had plenty of things to do for which I was certain he would evaluate me. I would evaluate him on the basis of whether or not he would find the money to turn to reality the programs with which he agreed in principle.

As I looked at his face, I began to glimpse that perhaps he thought he had agreed to too much. However, he said nothing, because, to an administrator as to a librarian, the suggestion that we might be the best is attractive. Learning that there is a price to pay is part of growing up, even for a university official, mayor, or governor. He could, of course, always change his mind and opt for a second-rate school. I would most certainly then resign, but first of course I would have to inform students and prospective students of the new and diluted goals.

So Let's Play Hardball

I wouldn't mind so much our reluctance to play hardball (Tom Galvin told us that management was a contact sport) if our kinder and gentler strategy produced results, but it doesn't. It is not surprising when the Urban Libraries Council reports that public libraries are pressured to accept keeping the doors open as their primary priority. Neither library boards nor library users may know any better, particularly if we haven't taken control of our objectives, or worse if we don't have any. What I haven't heard is the end of the story. What did those public library directors say in response?

Similar problems arise with emerging strategies in both academic and special libraries that are not meant to become as cost effective as possible but as financially invisible as possible, despite the well-known management dictum that control over how money is spent is the greatest political power in any environment. Such strategies are implemented when we adopt a tactic of hiding costs, by passing them along to user groups where they may never even be identified. I have already heard the suggestion that one of the "advantages" of the virtual library in academia will be our ability to distribute information costs to user departments. Corporate libraries have been doing the same thing for a long time. Why? Because it is more cost effective? Because the users, if charged directly, will spend less? We certainly know better.

The cost of information is, where necessary, trivial and nonnegotiable. If we don't provide needed information service because we can't "afford" it, someone else will afford it, at a greater cost to the organization and at a tremendous cost to our prestige and status. As a special librarian, I understand that there are times when the immediate supervisor might prefer a cheap library, no matter what its total costs. That might be that supervisor's value system in terms of a narrow interpretation of personal objectives, but those value systems don't count. The chief executive or the chief financial officer will make it quite clear that spending more money by hiding costs is not an acceptable strategy. Our purpose must always be to be useful, not to be cheap.

Sticking with fuzzy goals is certainly a temptation for those above us who prefer to have cheapness while pretending an adherence to caring about quality. Why we go along with all of this is something I never quite understand, unless we have a professional preference for "doing good" rather than "doing effective." As I noted in the first of this three-part series, Drucker suggested that danger to theologians. Are librarians any more immune? In the last part of this trilogy, I will talk about a great warm fuzzy "good" that has been allowed to distort program priorities. It is only an example. There are others.

The Politics of Reinventing Government Libraries

There are good managers and bad managers, but all managers with even the slightest interest in survival know that to succeed they have to be noticed. That means that they have to solve problems and avert crises, even if they first have to invent the crisis in order to be able to solve it. They also understand that nothing is gained by protecting the status quo, because organizations which remain the same in an otherwise changing environment, even when this requires Herculean efforts, automatically get worse. If you have succeeded in renewing every one of the periodical subscriptions in your library for next year, I congratulate you on what must truly have been a massive effort, but I also have some bad news for you. Your library is now automatically worse than it was.

Managers also understand that clamoring for attention means that there have to be problems. If there are no problems which keep your bosses tossing in their sleep at night, you are boring, and boring is the worst crime any manager can commit. The process of growing while everything about you appears to be getting smaller requires that you create an awareness of crises important enough to make you an exception from the norm. Law enforcement officers understand this; librarians often do not. We try to spare our bosses their deserved responsibility of worrying about the library, deserved because worrying about their

Speech Presented at the 38th Military Librarians Workshop, Huntsville, Alabama—
November 15, 1994.

39

subordinates is what they get paid to do. At the same time we get no credit for being boringly competent. A Vice President for Research in a corporation said to me during a consulting assignment that he was certain that his organization was spending too much money on the library, because nobody was complaining about it. Marion Paris, in her dissertation on the reasons for the closing of library schools, found that administrators closed library education programs because "they never seemed to want anything." They simply couldn't understand that, and they didn't have enough interest to investigate, and so they closed the school. James Matarazzo, in his study on the closing of corporate libraries in the 1970s, found exactly the same thing. Libraries were closed in large part as an act of euthanasia, since they had already been cut so badly that the final cut was in fact merciful. Nobody understands how much they should spend in support of libraries. There are no management guidebooks to tell them anywhere except in academia, and here we are largely talking only about number of volumes, and that has no usefulness for corporate or government libraries.

Almost all managers understand that cries of poverty are automatic, whether or not they are real. They also understand that in the absence of money there is always money for things for which money must be found. The city of Chicago somehow found money to pump the water out of its basements, and the state of California cannot and does not ignore what happens when an earthquake destroys the highways. The federal government always deals with unexpected costs—Cuban and Haitian refugees, continuing problems in Bosnia and Rwanda, an offer of funds to deal with floods and droughts, usually in the same year. Where does this money come from? Who cares? If it is necessary to spend the money we spend it, and worry about the impact later. The federal government has a technique called "out of budget expenditures." Corporations can't do that, but they do what they must. They recall products, they settle damage claims. Look at poor Exxon (and I use "poor" only because I see them as victims), whose crime was hiring an employee who had a drinking problem. However, if they had tried to fire him for that, some of the same people who now vilify Exxon would have complained.

I need not tell you that library budgets are in serious difficulty, but why is that? Does anyone notice that the same officials in both the government and corporate worlds who swear fidelity to the information superhighway then allow library budgets to be cut? How does this all add up? The answer is that it doesn't. The point is that we are wonderful workers, we are terrible in the political process. We keep trying to be cheap when there is no virtue in being cheap. There is only virtue in being effective if others know you are.

Organizations in government or in the corporate sector must swear fidelity to the process of both effectiveness and cost reduction, because that is required. However, nobody really knows how to do this, and therefore in the process some prosper and some suffer. Librarians have never been very good at this game. When Californians passed Proposition 13, they made an arbitrary decision to curtail government expenditures because they had concluded that only in that way could they reduce their taxes, and that process worked. By doing this, they abdicated the decisions on how those cuts were to be implemented. To a great extent, libraries suffered. In a conversation with Howard Jarvis, one of the founders of the movement, I heard him say that while the proponents of tax cutting wanted to reduce government fat, they didn't really have libraries in mind, because libraries were not and never have been examples of fat government waste. Jarvis and his friends succeeded in reducing their taxes, but they did not really eliminate the programs they thought were wasteful because they were too well politically entrenched. They ended up brutalizing libraries. When I pointed this out to Jarvis, he replied that this was our problem of political skill and not his. I've thought about that many times since, and I have to conclude, with regret, that he is absolutely correct.

We still don't know how to play this game. While the American Library Association complains bitterly about the inadequacy of library budgets, it also announces that its surveys indicate that 90 percent of the public is satisfied with their libraries, and 70 percent think they are wonderful. What that suggests to any politician is exactly what it suggested to the Vice President for Research—that the budget can be cut some more, until people complain. What other message can they take from this? When public libraries report proudly that, despite staff and budget cuts, circulation continued to increase, the clear message is that the budget cut was valid, that it caused no problems, and that it is time for another one. In the simplistic manner of budget assessments about which I will speak more later, the message is no longer "If it ain't broke, don't fix it." It is "if it ain't broke, cut its budget until it breaks, and only then let's find out if anyone cares." At the 1994 Atlanta SLA conference there was a program devoted to how libraries should deal with the results of downsizing. I was not able to attend the program, because I only arrived on the last day for the SLA Banquet in which people were nice enough to install me into the Hall of Fame. However, I can see no useful purpose in such a program, because once the budget is cut, it is too late. The money has been reallocated and is almost impossible to get back. If the strategy then becomes one of trying to continue to offer superb service with a smaller staff, all you have done is validate the budget cut and prepare the next one. If the strategy is to pass along more jobs to either contractors or to the ultimate user, is this really a savings or just a cosmetic savings? Don't misunderstand me, cosmetics are very important, and they have always been. When I worked at IBM more than 30 years ago I observed, quite accurately although not to the pleasure of my management, "we're going to have economy no matter how much it costs." It was true then; it is true today. The appropriate topic for an SLA program is not how to survive a budget cut. It is how to avoid one. How can your budget be increased while all other budgets are being cut? More specifically, why should your budget be increased precisely so that other budgets can be cut? Think about that one, because I will come back to it.

In the corporate sector there is great and continuing pressure to reduce staff, and that process will continue, so nobody should really be surprised. Sometimes that makes sense, sometimes it doesn't. We do have far too many managers who do very little except get in the way of their subordinates and cause trouble. Perhaps, by empowering subordinates in a corporate environment we can get rid of managers we didn't need in the first place. In government that can't be done, because in a downsizing process the people who did little or nothing have seniority, and they will simply replace some of the people who really did something. What this leads to is slaughter of the innocent, and that can happen in corporations, too, when library budgets are cut because their managers have not sufficiently scared the hell out of their bosses as to what would happen if they were dumb enough to cut the library. What would presumably happen is that the bosses would get fired, and even the slightest possibility of that is enough to cause them to pick on somebody else.

Much of the process is not real, but rather cosmetic, certainly in the government sector. Where it is real, as it can be in the corporate sector, it could be done effectively and carefully, but it almost never is. Managers don't know what to cut, and so they cut across the board. When that can't be done politically they cut the overhead, because nobody has suggested that in cutting overhead you shift work to the direct sector if the work still has to be done. And of course, in cutting overhead they always cut libraries. And yet, they have sworn that information is important, that stupidity is unacceptable. How does any of this make sense, and why do we let them get away with doing something so totally nonsensical?

Let's tackle government first. My first observation is that government grows and that government programs become more complex, and there is nothing that any administration can do about it. The fault is not with the government. It is rather with the citizens, who constantly demand more government services from their representatives in the legislative process who in turn institute more control procedures which must be monitored and reported. Some of these are instituted at the federal level for implementation at that level; some at the federal level for implementation in the states or locally. It is beyond the scope of this paper to argue whether or not these programs are necessary and worthwhile, although undoubtedly some are and some are not. The main point, however, is that the citizen who insists on all of these services does not want to hear any mention of the suggestion that they need to be paid for, and that they should be the ones doing the paying. The last national political candidate who suggested that taxes needed to be raised, not for "them" (whoever they are) but for all of us was Governor Bruce Babbitt of Arizona in the 1988 primaries, and he disappeared immediately from sight thereafter. He is now serving as a cabinet secretary, and he didn't have to run for that office. Indeed, his disappearance was so sudden that his campaign manager wrote a tongue-in-cheek book entitled "The Dog Ate My Candidate."

Since growth is inevitable and ordained, regardless of who wins the election, but every candidate must argue that he will cut the federal payroll if elected, and then claim he did it to be reelected, there is a great deal of emphasis on style and wordage rather than substance. This is not said with malice toward any politician, but government constantly reinvents itself at the behest of the public, by getting larger. There is really no answer for this process as long as the complexity of the political process requires that we subsidize both cancer treatment and tobacco production. I suspect that government librarians know all of this, and have learned to take all of the verbiage with a grain of salt.

That doesn't mean that the federal actual payroll is not sometimes cut, because it is, usually through attrition. Sometimes that process can even be accelerated by early buyouts, a stupid process of pay now and also pay later when you realize you have just shipped into early retirement your most productive people, and this is something that government learned from industry. When the cutbacks are made, are the savings real? It depends on what happens to the programs. If the programs totally disappear, perhaps, but government programs do not disappear. Do we still need a Department of Agriculture at all, when there are far fewer farmers who still produce more than we need and are taught to produce more surplus which must then also be stored and paid for? Of course we do, because farmers vote, and because studies in my state of Indiana indicate a lot of people who haven't worked on farms at all for the last 25 years, but who wear International Harvester caps to work at the automotive assembly line, think of themselves as farmers.

Sometimes what happens to the government programs when individuals disappear but the program must be kept is that we contract it out. Does that save money? Sometimes yes, but I suspect, frequently no. I worked in Washington in the mid-1960s, and when I now return, I find a whole range of industrial organizations charmingly called Beltway Bandits who do what government employees used to do. Better? Cheaper? The assumption is yes, the answer is we don't know. However for government libraries there is a greater danger. Instead of keeping government libraries or contracting, we do neither. What happens then, particularly in the face of the other reality that information is crucial and vital for the work of the institution? We pretend that the users, at no real cost, will do this work themselves in their "spare" time. If anyone believes this, it is simply because we librarians have made no effort to disprove this absurd lie, obvious to any trained accountant, and our strange reluctance to blow the whistle continues to puzzle me, unless it is because, as librarians, we truly believe that self-service is good and that helping people is somehow immoral and supportive of sloth. That's the librarian as educator, but special and government librarians, with very rare exceptions, aren't supposed to be educators. They are supposed to be information providers. Perhaps it makes sense to get rid of librarians in carrying out a commitment to ignorance and stupidity. But does it make sense to get rid of librarians and replace them with end users, who don't know how to do it, do it badly, and who get paid three times as much? Do they do it in their spare time, or instead of doing what they ought to be doing? If you begin to get the glimmer of the idea that the way to cut costs and staff is by hiring more librarians and getting the dilettante end users away from the search terminals and back to what they were hired to do, stay with me. There will be more.

As I have already suggested, industry can decide, well or badly, whom to terminate, but government doesn't even have that option, and I recall one article in our own literature that reported, twenty years ago, that Library of Congress subject specialists (not librarians) were shelving books, and shelving them badly and incorrectly as well as expensively, because no shelvers were being hired, or because the shelvers with low seniority had been terminated, and yet somebody had to shelve. A similar thing happened at the Applied Physics Laboratory of Johns Hopkins University, a then totally government funded agency, which somehow budget froze itself out of virtually all secretarial and clerical staff. Ph.D. research physicists were doing the collating of technical reports. Would you like to guess whether they did it well or badly?

There is a movement to downsize the federal government by 200,000 people, and the process may even at some point yield a level of proof which will be offered on the altar of public opinion, but we know that it will involve either the wrong people, or cause unqualified and overpriced people to start doing what they can't do, or hiring contractors without knowing how well they will work, only what they cost. When this process does work it is because the agency has kept enough of its own professionals to write criteria, and to monitor the work of the contractors. When the evaluation is being done by the contracting officer, forget it!

Just to show how simple it would be to really eliminate 200,000 jobs, and also how impossible it would be, let me pose the following scenario. The president (any president) goes on TV on Monday to announce the elimination of 200,000 federal jobs. It was done over the weekend, and the termination notices have been delivered. We undertook a computer search for every employee who had the word coordinator or facilitator in his or her job title, because we all know that coordinators and facilitators produce no useful work, they only cause trouble for others. Can't be done, can it?

In industry the process could proceed more logically, if indeed anybody knew how to do it. Instead, we begin by offering or demanding early retirement from people who are just in the prime of their work career, and of course the ones most anxious to accept are the ones smart enough to know that they are good enough to get other jobs after they retire, perhaps with competitors. If you are going to get rid of people, get rid of the worst ones, and get rid of the ones whose jobs can be left undone. However, since nobody will ever admit that his or her job is anything but crucial, nobody knows what jobs can be left undone. Except, I am afraid to tell you, for librarians, whose work can be done by the end users, presumably at no cost to the organization. Sounds absurd, doesn't it? Then why don't we make the case, long before the layoffs begin? Stay with me.

In 1976 Bo Hedberg, writing in *Administrative Sciences Quarterly*, accurately predicted that organizations might indeed get smaller. He did not argue whether this was a good or a bad idea, only that we should not lie about the process. Most specifically, he argued prophetically that management would suggest that somehow this work could now be absorbed by everyone working harder. Hedberg noted that the argument that people should work harder was a bankrupt strategy, because it required a self-indictment that we had been goof-offs all along. Perhaps we can work harder, but we will never admit it. Except perhaps librarians, who have conference sessions which deal not with how to punish the people who cut our staffs but how to validate their action. Please note that neither Hedberg nor

I argue that budgets can't be cut, because obviously they can. However, when budgets are cut, programs must be modified, and the modification of the program must be openly and loudly announced. It may just be possible that the cut is unacceptable to people who are important enough to cause a change. If so, the money will be found. Corporate librarians don't spend enough to make a difference. The cuts are made because they are symbolic and because they are easy. We don't even wiggle on the chopping block. Sometimes we help guide the ax.

    I am about to launch into the political strategies that are required of us, but before I do I need to make just one more point about how cosmetic this process is. What of course it represents, in the corporate sector, is a process of bloodletting, of reducing costs and worrying about the impact later, at least in part by trying to bludgeon people into believing that "they" can still do all of that work if they just apply themselves. I also notice, at the same time, that while this goes on the executive officers fiercely protect the people who make their lives comfortable. The people gotten rid of are your clerks, your professional colleagues, your librarians. If the chief executive depended on a daily library fix, you would be spared. However, librarians spend a good deal of their time serving the junior people and ignoring the senior decision makers, simply because they don't ask us anything. So tell them anyway! One final point before I let go of the process of demonstrating how totally illogical and unscientific these decisions are, because the desired result is simply cutting costs. What happens as a result of those cut costs is rarely discussed, and almost never discussed when it comes to service and overhead areas. What we're doing, ostensibly, is squeezing out the fat. There's obviously got to be fat. One would hope that in anticipation of this library managers stashed away a lot of fat for the lean years, but somehow I doubt it. The process in industry is called downsizing, and I can live with that. However, when it is called "rightsizing" it really makes me gag. If we are now rightsizing, then how are we punishing the executives who tolerated wrongsizing in the past?

    All right, the point is that we are dealing with a very amorphous process which is political far more than it is substantive, which deals with appearance, and which rewards the noisy and punishes the cooperative submissive, as indeed it always did. There are two tactics for dealing with this process, and I stress again it is too late after the budget has been cut. You must anticipate and head off the cut, and surely you already know what is in the wind. The process is, for everyone, cosmetic, and it must also be so for librarians. However, for us it can also be substantive. We are cheap, we are cost effective, and we deal in that most precious of all commodities, information, as against the "ignoramus lobby," those who favor stupidity as a virtue.

    One of the things I have developed in my spare time is a list of politically correct terms, and I mean politically correct in the internal management structure. I have lots more, but let me just share a small number with you. I am sure you will recognize them. In alphabetic order, these are: balanced, broader mission, compatible, cost effective, flexible, forward looking, functional, integrated, mobile, needs oriented, optimal, payoff, quality assurance, responsive, synchronous, systematized, total, user friendly, value driven, virtual, and vision. All of these terms must constantly appear in your memos, in your proposals, and in your reports, and I will offer a special prize to the first person who can use all of these terms in one sentence. You will notice that there are some terms that are missing from my list, and they include library, backlog, circulation, book, report, and journal. All of these terms are internal to your organization, and they make no difference to anyone else. One of my saddest experiences in teaching my course in special librarianship was the guest speaker who reported that she had been informed that there was an office betting pool on the monthly size of her backlog. That indicates how trivial the statistic was perceived to be. What your reports need to deal with, in using all of the right "in" language, is the impact on the announced objectives of the parent organization. I assume you know what those are, because that impact, particularly if you can frighten people enough, is really all that matters. It is when they are frightened of the potential consequences for them, personally, that they will think twice before they cut your budget. If you "absorb" the cut like a good soldier, you will only be cut again. In order to be effective you must learn to be selfish. Run your library or information center as though it were a private business. If you run it well you are doing what they hired you for, although they may have forgotten. Let the chief financial officer worry about the money; financial officers get paid a lot more than you. Having told you about a depressing guest speaker, let me tell you about what an exhilarating one said, "Don't be afraid to overspend your budget or exceed your authority if you have a good reason, and the alternative would have been worse. You will be forgiven."

The approach to style is important, and you must learn that your management needs for you to communicate, even if they don't expect it from you. However, librarians have a more tangible strategy, and we need to spend the rest of this talk on that topic.

Any basic management text will tell you that power comes in large part from the ability to control spending, and in particular to control discretionary spending. That suggests that your budget should not be as small as possible, it should be as large as possible as long as that means that others will not spend the money. Let me illustrate with an example:

In a corporate consulting assignment I began with a meeting with the Vice President for Research. That individual had not personally selected me, but I suppose he wanted some idea of what he was paying for. After looking through his notes, he stated that he was pleased that I had been contracted to evaluate the cost effectiveness of his library. I told him that I didn't really think that was why I was here. He looked puzzled, and so I continued by pointing out that I could certainly limit myself by evaluating the library, but that it seemed to me that the larger question was the effectiveness with which the organization acquired and assimilated information, an essential process of which the library was an important part but only a part. I told him that I doubted that he was interested only in the library, if for example that meant that saving money on the library meant that more money would be spent overall. I assumed he was interested in total corporate effectiveness, and not just library effectiveness. He quickly assured me that this was what he had really meant to say. However, my point to you is that is not what he had initially meant. He only stated the larger objective when I challenged him to do so, because it would be absurd for him to argue in favor of library savings and overall cost increases. And it is precisely that larger point you need to make. Don't allow yourself to be entrapped into talking about the library. Talk about the organization's information needs, which are formidable and which nobody will downgrade or deny.

As a service and overhead organization we still have some advantages that other overhead groups, such as the cafeteria services, would be very grateful to have. We need not make the point that information is important, and that ignorance is politically unacceptable. We need only spell out and document our own crucial role in this process. It should not be difficult to do, but only if we are assertive enough. Pledge loyalty to the information superhighway while we decrease the size of our libraries? There must be a joke here somewhere—explain it to me.

We can and must make the case that, if information is important, we are preferable to any of the alternatives. There are only three alternatives. 1. We can opt for ignorance. 2. We can transfer all or as many of the information acquisition costs as possible from librarians to end users. 3. We can contract with outsiders to avoid having to pay insiders.

The first alternative, I need not elaborate, makes no sense. The second makes no sense, either, if we simply examine the economics. Do end users, who get paid a great deal more on the average, and who search less efficiently, make a good investment in the process? Only if we are unwilling to make the point that a hidden cost is still a cost, and while hiding costs may be politically attractive to some of our supervisors, in particular perhaps our most immediate supervisor, it is totally unacceptable to the people responsible for overall financial decisions. However, they will only know if they are told. A number of years ago I heard a talk at an SLA conference by a West Coast bank librarian, and I wouldn't have been rude enough to ask my question except for the fact that she was enjoying herself too much. She noted that her own supervisor had edicted a cut in library staffing, and an emphasis on end user searching. As a result the end users were now doing terrible searches, wasting their own time and access costs, asking the wrong questions, and generally coming up with garbage. I asked her what she saw as her professional responsibility, even if perhaps at some risk to herself, to inform top management of this squandering of resources? She said only that it was a difficult and painful question.

I sometimes ask medical librarians how many of them think that doctors can do complex information searches on Medline three times as rapidly, or three times as well as we can. There are no hands raised. Why then, I ask, is the National Library of Medicine consciously and willfully wasting my taxpayer money in stressing end user search training, and, even worse, why are some medical librarians accessories in this ripoff? I am told that the given reason is that not all doctors have access to a medical librarian, and I can only respond that I am not surprised when medical librarians are laid off as doctors are trained. But isn't the obvious cost effective solution to get more medical librarians? Has anyone pointed out to Hillary Rodham Clinton that one of the reasons for unsatisfactory medical care is that doctors are spending too much time doing what they shouldn't be doing? Doesn't the same scenario apply throughout the corporate and government world?

The third option, of hiring outsiders either to do the same work we could have done, or perhaps to do the work that is so specialized that we could not do it, may have some validity. In the first instance it may be, as I have mentioned, that the appearance of economy is more important than economy itself. That, unfortunately, can be the case with government programs, and it is the fault of the voters and taxpayers. Appearance of economy should never be an acceptable reason in the corporate sector. Whom are we fooling, our own bosses? Our own stockholders? Tell somebody—quickly. There is no doubt that the use of contractors is increasing, and at least in part this is because of phony economics. I have already mentioned the Beltway Bandits, who may or may not do a better job than government employees would have done, but at least we should keep honest records. In industry the need to appear to downsize (even as we perhaps spend more money) gives rise to what the British journal *The Economist* has called the Meatware Industry, as contrasted to hardware and software. Meatware people use the hardware and software created for our use, either because there aren't enough of us left to use it, or because we don't want to use it. When it makes sense to do so, fine. However, I know of no science called economic cosmetology.

Even when the use of outside contractors is either desirable or necessary (such as in a hiring freeze that is not a spending freeze), we must make sure that we continue to control the process. We select, we control, we monitor the contractors, because we are the experts. Certainly no contracting officer can monitor them, because contracting officers have no understanding of the information world. That's OK, they don't need to have it. They need only be willing to understand that they have no understanding. Similarly, if there is a heavy use of outside contractors, it is essential that the end users still come through you, and that the contact is between you and your contractors. If end users can negotiate for their purchases of either materials or of information searches, your own unique turf control is gone. Purchasing agents, who insist that all requests must come through them for processing, understand the concept of political turf far better than we do. And, yet, without political unique turf you have nothing at all.

Our consistent unwillingness to insist on controlling our own turf, both for our benefit and that of the parent organization, always puzzles me. One of the obvious manifestations of turf is control over money, and a wag has suggested that the golden rule means that those with the gold make the rules. And yet we constantly try to hide the true information costs—not to be cheap but to appear to be cheap. Why? Libraries often try to get user groups to pay for books and journal subscriptions. It is the same parent organizational money, and what has been given away is the professional assessment of whether it needs to be bought at all. How many *Wall Street Journals* and how many *Official Airline Guides* do we really need for information?

Charge-back mechanisms represent another example I do not understand, although I encounter it in my consulting assignments. If it is assumed that being asked to sign a form authorizing a charge to the requesting department for the book, photocopy or interlibrary loan somehow decreases the number of requests received, there is not a shred of evidence that this is true. If it were true, it would certainly not be true for the senior requesters whose demands are more likely to be both expensive and outrageous, but more likely for the junior individuals perhaps afraid to ask their bosses, and yet it is those individuals we need to protect. What does occur in such a bureaucratic maze of approvals is not only an increased cost mechanism which far outstrips any savings that might be achieved, but also two other side results that can be devastating. First, it is assumed by many users (and I know because they have told me) that the implementation of this approval procedure is the library's own idea. After all, don't librarians love forms and paperwork? The second reason is the total loss of control over what little money you do spend. If you have to ask permission or get someone else to be willing to pay, what control do you have over either your budget or your decisions? And, no, it is not true that the users know better what needs to be purchased than the librarians, because their decisions are made within a much narrower framework of the alternatives of which they are aware, and because they cannot rank order their priorities against those of another group. Only we can do that.

If cost allocation of the library budget is to be undertaken, then I much prefer a system which allocates not on the basis of actual use, but on the basis of presumed use. Presumed use can be based on almost any kind of formula, and the records kept by the Personnel Department, which report that group A has 27.3 percent of the professionals in the organization, will do just fine. Group A is then charged 27.3 percent of the total library budget. The advantages are clear. We have a rationale for allocation, it is a logical rationale, and it requires no record keeping. More importantly, it penalizes not use but rather non-use. Since you are paying for it anyway you might as well encourage your subordinates to use the service. Finally, it allows library service programs to seek and achieve their own valid level. If service activity declines even without financial constraints then obviously that might be a reason for cutting the budget. However, if demand increases, the justification for expansion is already built in.

Administrators are nervous about such an approach because they somehow believe that, without constraints and controls, people will overwhelm the library with trivial requests just for the fun of it, but there is not one shred of evidence that this is true. Individuals are not looking for more information. They are looking for as little information as possible, in as efficient a time setting as possible, so that they can get on to what they are really expected to do and will be measured against. The individual who argues that he or she got nothing accomplished because they read so much in the library simply does not exist. Management is protecting itself against a non-problem, in part because it doesn't have a clue, in part because when it doesn't have a clue it instinctively makes things smaller, but most importantly because we have failed to make the case.

The problem for us and for the workplace is in fact the reverse. Given both the growth of information and its growing interdisciplinary complexity, the emerging ground rules which encourage more communication may well mean that individuals will spend all day at the terminal trying to sift through all the garbage (and every user defines garbage personally) to find what is needed. That will most certainly happen unless somebody, and I obviously hope that will be librarians, protect them against information trash. We are already beginning to see articles about e-mail trivia and Internet overload, and the avalanche is just starting to rumble down the mountain.

The far greater risk for all organizations is that individuals, badgered into greater accountability by staff cuts and overwhelmed by mountains of information, will opt for pretending that they don't need information at all because getting it is too much trouble. What is the organizational cost and danger in that, particularly since nobody will even know? Is ignorance bliss in the management process? Hardly. This is the point you have to make, because no upper manager will risk overall success of any major project for as trivial a cost as an inadequate library or an inadequate information service. You need to make that point. You need to worry and frighten them.

This means that you need to destabilize your environment, and that is how marketing works. You don't want satisfied users, you want users dissatisfied in the awareness of what they are not getting because you are not allowed to give it to them. That also simply means that both credit and blame are ultimately passed along to upper management. Credit is better, but blame also has its uses. In doing all of this you must move your strategies beyond the vision of your immediate supervisor, who may not really care what happens as long as he or she looks good. There is always danger in a larger sphere of communication, but librarians because of what they do have access to any and all levels within the organization.

Don't be surprised if the financial people, whom librarians always consider their archenemies, turn out to be your best friends, if you can phrase the questions properly. I have already noted that it is generally agreed that better information is an assumed virtue in any organization. How is this best accomplished? By end user searching? By contracting out? By having an adequate and competent in-house staff? Don't be afraid to recommend, or even demand, a cost effectiveness study of the alternatives. It is the financial managers who are most likely to keep honest books.

Finally, the drive for downsizing leads to another temptingly delicious possibility. You can point out to your management that the optimum information gathering and evaluation environment is one in which the trained specialists in the library and information center free the users from as much distraction as possible, and makes it possible for them to spend their time more effectively in the pursuit of the assignments given to them, and for which information is an essential but still fuzzy input.

It is even possible that, by strengthening the library or information center staff it might be feasible to operate with fewer library users. Even a tradeoff of one more librarian for one less user would be financially attractive. However, if end users do library work as ineffectively as they appear to, a ratio of 2 or 3 former users for one more librarian might be possible. In other words, if you want to continue to downsize the organization, increasing the library staff might be a very effective tactic. You can indeed make that point, and don't be afraid to make it. However, I would suggest that you make it quietly in discrete communications to upper management, and not to your users.

That, I believe, will be our future if we are to have a future. We must seize control of the information access process, and in doing this you may have to deal with hardware and software people in your own organizations, with database vendors who insist that everything is "easy," perhaps even with your own supervisor who may care only about the appearance of economy. These are formidable adversaries. However, you do have potential allies. These include the higher levels of management, levels which worry about both adequacy of information access and control over costs, and which are also concerned that employees are using terminals effectively, and not playing computer games. Your potential allies include financial management, because they are paid to keep honest books and have no hidden agenda. They even include end users, who for the most part don't really want to spend their time doing what database vendors insist they love to do. The key question is whether they can trust you to do this, so that they can do something more important for their own careers.

Fairy Tales from the Wonderful World of Library Politics

At its most recent conference, the national organization of police chiefs and other law enforcement administrators announced some wonderful news. According to a just completed survey, 90 percent of the American people believe that law enforcement is between good and excellent, and 70 percent think it is wonderful. Obviously heartened by this news, the President and Congressional leaders of both parties announced that, while law enforcement was obviously in very good shape, they would transfer $30 billion from other priorities to law enforcement, just to show their appreciation.

You won't buy that story? I understand. Professional library leaders announced publicly that, according to a just completed survey, 90 percent of the American public believe that library service is between good and excellent, and 70 percent think it is wonderful. Obviously heartened by this news, the President, Congressional leaders of both parties, the National Governor's Conference, and the National Conference of Mayors all announced simultaneously that, while libraries were obviously in very good shape and didn't need any money, they would transfer a lot of money from other priorities to library programs, just to show their appreciation.

Reprinted, with changes, by permission of the author and *Library Journal* 120, no. 1 (January 1995): 59–60. Copyright © 1995 by Cahners Business Information.

User Satisfaction
Isn't Money

I'm sorry if you won't believe that story, either. I was tempted to put the figure of $30 billion in there as well, but I know that librarians would laugh. We don't think in billions, only in thousands and occasionally in a heady million or two. Nevertheless, the first step in the process is honestly assessing what is wrong and needs to be fixed.

If you don't accept the premise that reporting user satisfaction would get us more money, you are in agreement with 100 percent of my management students.

Then the obvious question remains: If it is so destructive to report that customers are happy, why do we do it all the time? Peter Drucker, who has so much to teach us about management politics, put it quite simply many years ago when he noted that the essence of management communication is exception reporting. Telling people what we do well is something we are inclined to do in any case; after a while such self-praise becomes both distasteful and boring. Boring is the worst thing any manager can be. The statement that the best managers make the most trouble for their own bosses but are worth it is at least as old as the Industrial Revolution.

Will Libraries Always
Be Wonderful?

How is it possible that as library service is downgraded as budgets are downgraded, as reference service all but disappears in public libraries and is replaced by the simpler objective to just keep the doors open, people will still think of libraries as wonderful? Is it possible that people will still consider their libraries wonderful ten years after those libraries are closed, as an expression of the faith that even a closed library generates waves of goodness?

As the police chiefs understand and we appear not to, the management strategy for getting more money involves: 1) telling people what is wrong and why that hurts them; 2) telling them what could be right if only we had money and staff; and 3) pointing them in the direction of the nearest political action strategy. That we do not do any of these can be seen from just a few simple examples:

- We make no threats against the groups that almost categorically oppose our budget requests (that includes the senior citizen group I will soon join). Instead, we continue to reward those whose actions punish us. It is therefore simple to conclude that, when it comes to library programs, money doesn't matter. If circulation is the only valid criterion, and circulation continues to rise in the face of budget cuts, then presumably money really doesn't matter.

- We have steadfastly refused to tell people what libraries could do but are not doing. Instead, the library service that we do offer becomes the library service that individuals expect us to offer, and even the worst library becomes a "good" library when there is no basis for comparison. Even when higher management and library staff agree that the library is inadequate (and how often does that happen?), library users continue to insist that the library is just fine. Why should that surprise us? They have no way of knowing what reference services might be possible. We presumably do, but we refuse to tell patrons. As a result, citizens who use the library and citizens who don't are equally "happy" with their libraries, and politically that is the most destructive statistic of all. "If it ain't broke, don't fix it" is now an obsolete management maxim. It has been replaced by "If it ain't broke, cut its budget until it breaks." That's the only way we can tell that perhaps we shouldn't cut it any more.

Trivializing Ourselves

We need look no further for examples of self-trivialization than the annual process of urging people to "read." I could understand booksellers adopting that slogan, although "buy something to read" would be better. But for librarians, is that all there is? No wonder academic administrators fail to understand the need for a graduate education program. It is one of the basic tenets of marketing to create a craving for a product or service on the premise that if it is not available, pressure will demand that it become available, and that tactic works.

It would work for us as well, except that we refuse to play. We don't market, we advertise what we have to sell, except when selling creates a demand we cannot satisfy. That is of course a good problem and not a bad one, and three-hour lines at the reference desk should be photographed, with the names of the individuals in line furnished to the media.

Perhaps the simplest encapsulation of our problem comes from librarians who protest in letters to the editor that they run exactly the kind of library their users want. But is that all their job involves? Or should they perhaps educate their users about options and opportunities they have never even dreamed of to see if they might like them? If they like them, we then have a reason to try to get the money for implementation. Marketing is a process of destabilizing, of creating an awareness of need. Telephone companies understand the need to make customers dissatisfied and then address the unhappiness they have just created. Would we have available to us all of the multiple telephone options if the phone companies had waited for us to ask? Indeed, our marketing job should be easier, because what we offer is much easier to justify.

However, we just won't do it. Instead, we brag about increases in circulation and user euphoria in the face of budget cuts. What message do we think that sends? Would it not be better for the American Library Association (ALA) to report that 90 percent of Americans are not only upset about the deterioration of library services but are getting mad enough to do something about it politically? Does anyone see the connection between this approach and the $30 billion earmarked (at least in small part from libraries) for fighting crime? That money is not being made available because crime fighters have done a good job but rather because they have done such a bad job. However, there are two political requirements: The first is that people have to be told whom they should blame, and the second is that we have to get them to care.

Raising Citizens' Expectations

Getting people to care about libraries should be simple enough, but only if we raise their expectations. Some public librarians have begun to complain bitterly that the public sees only the library's recreational uses, overlooking its educational role. That is true enough, but if that is to change, we have to change it. Emphasis on the educational, crucial nature of libraries and librarians will never be initiated by educators themselves, whether located in the public school system or the U.S. Department of Education. When things get tight—and they are certainly tight for educators—we look first to protecting our own. And "our own," for both the principals and the teacher's union, refers to classroom teachers in preference to school librarians, or media educators as we sometimes prefer to call ourselves in the hope that changing the nomenclature might help us survive. It won't.

However, if the educational role of librarians is not clearly understood and stressed, our more promising role as information intermediaries providing safe conduct through the rock-strewn shallows and torrents is not even considered—sometimes not even by us. How else can we explain the simultaneous actions of pledging fidelity to the information superhighway while slashing library budgets, as practiced in academia, corporations, and government agencies? Have we pointed out the enormous waste that such an action guarantees? Have we posited to management committees that if there is a serious commitment to cutting costs though a greater reliance on information, such economy is certainly possible but only if the organization first strengthens its information organization, its library?

All of this requires preemptive initiative. When the Special Libraries Association (SLA) discusses, as it did in its 1994 conference, how to protect quality library service after the budget has been cut, it is already much too late. Surely the likelihood of a budget cut is known well before it actually happens. It is then, in support of the proposed economy, that the library organization must grow. Tell the corporate gurus that for every librarian they add they should be able to lay off ten other employees. But you might want to tell them privately.

No Relief in San Francisco

The reported budgetary difficulties of the San Francisco Public Library are certainly not a cause of satisfaction for me, but there is a superb irony in all of this. San Francisco, or "Baghdad by the Bay," has always prided itself, perhaps arrogantly, on its cultural superiority. What are we to conclude about a mayor who professes his love for libraries while he stubbornly opposes all attempts to increase their funding? What would he propose if he didn't love us so much?

Suggesting that ALA refuse to meet in San Francisco until adequate library funding is restored is a suggestion that won't work. ALA does move conferences but only for nonlibrary reasons and certainly not for anything so crass as expressing support for our own profession. What appeals to my sense of the absurd most of all is the organization of a relief campaign to provide reading materials for the destitute, ignorant, and knowledge-starved citizens of San Francisco. Perhaps the far more fortunate and affluent burghers of Oakland might want to take a leading role in this relief effort for their less fortunate and less affluent friends across the water.

Is Anyone Still Training the Circus Animals?

Let me begin by stating I am not a Luddite. I worked at IBM in a corporate information management setting for more than five years. I directed NASA's Scientific and Technical Information Facility and served as senior vice president for operations for the Institute for Scientific Information, both at the cutting edge of providing computer-supported information products and services.

I consider systems analysts, programmers, and hardware managers as valuable allies. They are capable of doing wonderful things but only when and if they work to the direction of specified outcomes; since the outcomes we need do not really stretch the capability of a technology that can modify the reentry trajectory of a space vehicle, everything should be fine. It is not fine because we have forgotten to train the beautiful and strong animals we have brought to perform in our circus. Instead, we have turned them loose to eat the members of the audience.

I served for six years as a member of the Board of Directors of the American Federation of Information Processing Societies (AFIPS). The experience convinced me that the Association of Computing Machinery (ACM), Data Processing Management Association (DPMA), and Institute of Electrical and Electronic Engineers Computer Society (IEEE-CM) members with whom I interacted were remarkable in what they were able to do and explain about their machines.

Reprinted, with changes, by permission of the author and *Library Journal* 120, no. 3 (February 15, 1995): 135–36. Copyright © 1995 by Cahners Business Information.

However, their knowledge base is very narrow and very specialized. Allowing these finely honed specialists out of their cages to perform their tricks without our having our whips and chairs handy causes the risk that they will start dining on the customers, which in this case is the information-using public. One thing of which I am totally convinced is that neither these information technologists nor the general public have the vaguest idea about what is happening or is about to happen. I can't really blame them, particularly the second group. I can blame our profession, because we presumably do know, or at least ought to know.

Technology's Giddy Promise

The giddy promise for the future is that technology will provide us all with more information, under the premise that more means better. Doesn't anyone notice that there is no clamor for more information? The real wish is for less information but more relevant information in a more rapid and assured environment. That requires that we protect ourselves, and our clients, from the garbage.

Gresham's Law of Economics, which predicates that bad money will drive out good money, also works for information. Bad information will drive out good information for a variety of reasons. It is more plentiful, it is getting easier to disseminate, and self-publicizing through electronic messaging is an attractive promotional ploy. Individuals fortunate enough to belong to the Invisible College (an informal communications mechanism) understood that one of the great advantages was in keeping out the riff-raff. Because, as we surely (and probably nobody else) understand, the definition of bad as opposed to good information rests in the hands of the recipient and not the transmitter. And, yet, in the systems now being foisted on us, we have no way to "punish" the transgressor who insists on giving us what we don't want. We librarians, who are information users as well as disseminators, certainly know this. Our clients—who certainly could expect that we protect them, but unfortunately we don't—sense that as they receive more quantity, the process of finding what they want gets more difficult.

Terminology Over Substance

In large part we are losing the war to help assess what information delivery systems should or should not do because we do not understand that the terminology is more important than the substance. There are 14 terms and phrases that need to be included in all of our future management documents. Never mind what they mean, because no one else knows, either. My list includes balanced, compatible, cost-effective, forward-looking, functional, incremental, integrated, needs-oriented, optimal, responsive, synchronous, user-friendly, value driven, and virtual. A special prize will be offered to the first individual who can use them all in one sentence.

It is precisely when we know least what we are doing that we adopt slogans. Information superhighway is a silly term, deserving of all the limp metaphors (potholes, detours, speed traps, semitrailers with failed brakes) now being made about it. Do any of you notice that when we don't have a clue we invent a slogan: wiping out illiteracy, eliminating poverty, reinventing government? Don't blame those who coin the slogans. The pollsters tell them that we prefer slogans to painful solutions; solutions might cost money, so we get slogans.

Certainly unfettered access to information is crucial. However (and it would startle the systems people to hear this), information access is not an end in itself; it is a means to an end. Operations research people have known for a long time that the ideal information system is the one that contains what is wanted and needed and nothing else. Large libraries are harder to use than small libraries, because all of the garbage gets in the way. It is each user who personally gets to define the word garbage. That might explain why the academic users of megalibraries immediately haul the stuff to their own offices. Most of us, and certainly in this field, instinctively and correctly support any initiative that will widen access and facilitate delivery, but those instincts can get us into trouble.

Communications Improvements

More than 30 years ago in an era that was technological but not yet online, my IBM colleague Hans Peter Luhn suggested a modification in corporate policy to facilitate communication among engineers and scientists. Individuals would be permitted and indeed encouraged to post technical messages to any and all of their colleagues through computer bulletin boards, without having to get permission from their more bureaucratically inclined bosses. Corporate management approved enthusiastically, because the opportunity to speed and improve communication was obvious.

Indeed, the system worked from the first day, but it worked too well. Individuals with preliminary ideas learned quickly that this was not an effective tool for them: they not only ran the risk of being pestered by inquiries that would keep them from their work, they also risked having their ideas stolen. On the other hand, individuals with nothing to say made sure they said something at least weekly, sometimes daily. Luhn's system, which was totally permissive and totally nonjudgmental, was ultimately buried in its own trivia. Any Internet system that places no responsibility for relevance on the communicator, and exacts no fee for posting messages to hundreds of people, ultimately passes the cost along to the unsuspecting recipient, because the cost in time spent is real enough.

Communications Overkill

My own experience might be atypical, but when I return now from having been away for a week I find in excess of 100 electronic messages. Perhaps five are important, and perhaps another five are interesting even if unessential gossip. The other 90 I purge as fast as I can, but it takes me an hour or more to do it. How can I get the right five or ten and avoid getting the wrong 90 (remembering that right and wrong are mine to judge)?

Discussions about technophobia are rapidly becoming the nonissues they deserve to me, as more students who are comfortable with terminals in their homes and offices graduate. However, the computer is neither a toy nor a god: It is a tool. At least that is how people ought to be urged to look at it. That of course is why, in our academic programs, technologists should be the specialist teachers but never the administrators in our schools of library management and information assessment.

It does not take a great deal of perception to realize that while individuals fear losing out on what they need to know, they also already feel totally swamped. When I tell individuals in a corporate consulting setting that the library or information center will provide access to more databases, looks of terror come into their eyes. More stuff to read! How many of our users now cross their names off circulation lists, pretending they have read what we have sent them so as not to offend us?

Information Sanitary Engineers

The issue for the next century will not be one of format. We will use all sorts of formats, and they will matter only to the extent to which they are the most useful. The issue will be one of protecting the client against garbage. As we begin to define the virtual library (another undefined nonsense phrase) in terms of simply channeling more information to users' home or office terminals, do we really think that is what they want? We certainly should know better, because when we provide end user search training, surrogates, frequently secretaries, are often sent. Users vary, but if we provide them with more information we won't be helping them. We should certainly be aware of the infinite variety of end user preferences from the many options used in SDI (Selective Dissemination of Information) profiles to suppress what would otherwise be a hit (unavailability in full-size print, foreign language, etc.).

In addition to hindering our users by simply dumping more stuff on them, we certainly don't help ourselves. In discussing unionization with many management students, I point out the power of the threat of a strike is the intolerable inconvenience caused by one's absence. If the librarians in a "virtual" library go on strike, will anyone even notice? Not as long as there is still plenty to "read," in print and on terminals, and we continue to stress that reading "something" is what matters.

And Now Onto the Highway

The "information superhighway" is such a totally undefined concept that it clearly promises us, as individuals, both pleasure and grief. For librarians that reaction will be doubled, because we are not only ultimate beneficiaries or victims like everyone else, we are also supposed to serve as facilitators for our clients, and from them the message is "better, not more." Do we have a clue as to how to do this? If we do, our status is safe for the next 50 years. Tom Peters certainly understands the point. In his January 26, 1994 syndicated column he wrote, "A Flood of Information May Be the Enemy of Intelligence." Should we carve that over the entrance to the library?

After a lecture, Norbert Wiener, the father of cybernetics, was asked about whether he was concerned that computers might take over our lives. That was over 25 years ago, but people had just seen a film in which a computer kills an astronaut (*2001: A Space Odyssey*), and at least the questioner was worried. Wiener was reassuring. He doubted that this would happen, but if he feared it might, he would simply pull out the plug.

I'm not suggesting that, but I realize that technology is not an automatic benefit or improvement. Voice mail, which now allows me to punch telephone digits as instructed, is cheaper for those I am trying to reach, but I know I was better off when a human operator (since laid off) answered the phone. Are we prepared to protect quality of access for our clients, or do we just want to teach them to push buttons? If so, that's bad for them and worse for us. It is much worse because clients will find someone else to do what we stubbornly refuse to do: tell them what not to read since they don't have enough time to read everything. And reading includes terminal access, too.

Information Intermediation: A Fancy Name for Reference Work

Of our profession's three potential niches—recreation, education, and intermediation—the last is the one that shows the greatest promise. Our role in recreation, which mayors and some public library boards still see as our most important focus (give them what they want, never mind what they need), is the easiest to justify, though politically the weakest.

As funding priorities are evaluated and rank ordered, recreation simply does not stack up against more urgent priorities, no matter how pleasant a place the library may be. We will increasingly be told to find our own sources of funds from generous donors. And, faced with the unthinkable alternative of not being able to buy books at all, we will revert to the mendicant role with which many librarians already feel comfortable.

Our Role in Education Is Flawed

Our role in education could be important, except for two crucial flaws. First, education, considered so important to the public as a priority in the 1960s and early 1970s, has slipped badly, and certainly both school systems administrators and university presidents are well aware of this problem. Secondly, this dilemma for educators causes them to turn on librarians, their tolerance for them directly proportional to their ability to afford them.

Reprinted, with changes, by permission of the author and *Library Journal* 120, no. 5 (March 15, 1995): 44–45. Copyright © 1995 by Cahners Business Information.

If you question our status as Cinderella when it comes time to dress for the ball, you need note only that eliminating librarians will always precede, in a troubled school system, eliminating classroom teachers. In California, that simplistic value system even suggests that school teachers outrank public librarians. If any of you still have delusions about our equality in this process, try floating the trial balloon of having the federal agency renamed the U.S. Department of Education and Librarianship, with the two professions alternating the cabinet post. We can't even get an assistant directorship.

A Fancy Name
for Reference Work

The one area that has historically been ours has been information intermediation, which is really just a fancy name for reference work. It is the one thing we do singularly well from both a qualitative and a cost standpoint; as a validation of the money already spent on collection development, it can be demonstrated without too much difficulty to the most hard-bitten cost accountant. If you buy reference materials and don't have the staff to use them, what is the point?

The only difference between the more fanciful information intermediation and the more prosaic reference work is that the former defines itself in the amount of effort and energy it requires. The amount of time needed to deal with an inquiry can range from 30 seconds to several weeks, with the only issue worth addressing being whether the question is worth answering at all. Those who fund libraries might be willing to tackle that one, but librarians are not. All inquiries are important; we do not judge our patrons.

Only in corporate libraries, and indeed only in *some* corporate libraries, is the process allowed to seek its own level. In public libraries, the process is usually rigged by assessing a time limit on the inquiry. It is doubtful that reference librarians use an alarm clock, or that supervisors call "time's up" as might be done in a quiz contest. Still, the intent is inevitably to make sure that the true needs for reference services are never allowed to develop to the point where they might suggest something rational to those who fund public libraries and who appear to think that opening the front door and turning on the lights is all that librarians really have to do. We hide the problem of inadequate reference staffs by adapting it to the budget. In that way, and since there are no huge lines of waiting patrons at the reference desk, no one knows what reference service could have been and what reference staffing should have been.

Academicians and Reference

For the last 20 years, academic librarians have appeared reluctant to do reference work at all, and by that I do not mean the heroic reference librarians but rather those who make policy and assign funding priorities. It may be that the desperate attempt to appear to be full-fledged educators leads to an insistence that academic users ought to do their own information searching; perhaps with students we can get away with that—at least until they graduate. However, faculty and, in particular, academic administrators have many alternatives to doing their own information searching, including giving the task to a graduate student or a secretary, and, most significantly, pretending that they didn't need to know in the first place.

If we reach that decision, it is unlikely that anyone else will ever know our guilty secret, and the economic pressures that are growing in all sectors are likely to increase this pretense to information. Academic librarians stubbornly refuse to act as special librarian intermediaries for the administrators who used to be researchers but no longer think or work like them. Thus, it should not surprise academic librarians when these administrators give short shrift to the funding requests of those who never offer to help them in their own daily struggles.

Healthcare and Librarians

The argument that information is growing in size and complexity, that having current and up-to-date information is something to which all of us at least pretend to pledge allegiance, and that therefore the desperate search for more effective ways to deal with this dilemma should ideally serve reference librarian wannabes has been made before and need not be elaborated upon. If we who are better educationally prepared for information searching and who keep up-to-date with information options cannot easily demonstrate that end users should not be undertaking searches that librarians could undertake on their behalf so that they can do other things, then something is indeed very wrong.

The National Library of Medicine (NLM) argues that end user physicians need to be trained for complex database searches because some do not have access to medical librarians. That argument is self-perpetuating until it is pointed out that the nation would be better served if one of its top health priorities were for more medical librarians, because then either physicians and medical researchers would use their time more effectively, or perhaps we would need fewer doctors.

I don't expect doctors to make a case for more librarians instead of more doctors any more than I expect school administrators to make a case for more school librarians instead of teachers. But where are our presumed advocates such as the NLM, whose first responsibility should be to its fellow librarians? Shouldn't somebody tell Mrs. Clinton where one possible reduction in healthcare costs lies?

End User Searching Inevitable?

What is most upsetting is the rising suggestion in academic librarianship, in special librarianship, and in the shifting programs of our library and information schools that somehow the changes in technology, the development of the so-called "virtual library," will make end user searching not only possible but also inevitable and even desirable.

The last straw in what I consider this suicidal mania comes from a group that should certainly know better. The Fall 1994 issue of *Special Libraries* is devoted almost entirely to tactics of enabling and empowering end users. To leave us doing what? I do not expect to find in the literature of purchasing managers how-to manuals for teaching their users to do their own buying so that all purchasing agents can be laid off.

The strategy of purchasing managers has always been to insist that while you could do it, you shouldn't, because the parent organization will be better served if you stick to what you do well. Does that same argument not hold for us? Am I the only one who notices that while organizations swear eternal fidelity to information access, they decrease the staffing of their libraries? Do the people who write these articles in our own literature understand their own part in this process?

Technologists on the March

Part of the fascination with end user searching undoubtedly comes from the premise that if something can be done technologically it therefore should be. That is of course the mantra of the technologists, who always seem offended when the world decides not to do something simply because although it is possible, it is not comfortable.

I thought we might have learned that lesson from the predictions of a paperless society. It could have happened but didn't, because people still like paper, as a security blanket if nothing else. That is why terminals are attached to printers and why the filing cabinet industry is still thriving.

We are about to make this same mistake again, in believing that just because end users *could* do all of this work themselves, they will want to. For a few that may be true, but for the vast majority there are even more reasons for disbelieving this myth. Still, the technologists will continue to insist that if people can do their own information searching they will want to. Many managers, who believe that advanced technology is the self-evident proof of managerial genius, will continue to believe them.

Librarians Should Know Better

It is particularly disturbing when librarians, who certainly do know better, join the howling mob. What do librarians so bent on enabling online end user searching think they will be doing? Fortunately, it will never happen, but that will not necessarily help us or our employers.

It will not happen because for almost all end users the search for information is a means to an end and not an end in itself. While they need to know "something" to validate their actions and decisions, that process is difficult if not impossible to trace for their own bosses, who do know what they are measuring their subordinates against.

Except in law firms, where clients can be billed on an hourly basis for search time no matter how sloppily done, time spent on a terminal is not only a means to a larger end, it is a means for which workers get no credit and arouse only the suspicion of their bosses.

Nor do many professionals consider this work very satisfying, compared to the final result of making a presentation or writing an article. What end users will do, even when confronted by the new technology, is exactly what they have always done: that which best suits them.

Beware the Lemmings

In the information process, if and when the reference librarians have disappeared, we can contract to vendors (it's expensive, but it doesn't involve head count), we can give the task to a secretary or clerk, or, most fortuitously, we can pretend we didn't need to know. That is a thicket into which no one can follow us.

In other words, you can lead an end user to a database, but you can't make him or her search it, let alone search it well. Better give the job to someone who does it well and wants to. It is the fascination with head count, with downsizing, and with the appearance of economy—whether or not it is real—that dooms the strategy promulgated by academic librarians to recast themselves as advisors and consultants.

If there is one thing we should see in this downsizing frenzy, it is the concentration on keeping people who *do* things specifically and getting rid of all of the others. Middle manager, facilitator, and coordinator are all fatal titles. And so are consultant and advisor, when they clutter up our own head count. We might still occasionally hire a consultant, but that is a temporary decision without long-term implications; consultants are not on the permanent payroll.

Our ability to do information searching better and cheaper than anyone else should play to the downsizing agenda. If you keep more of us, you might be able to get by with fewer end users, perhaps at a ratio of three to one. In this shift in emphasis toward preparing our students for a nonexistent future "empowering" end users by asking these users what they want us to do, we forget that they don't really know and may become angry at being embarrassed. When focusing on the training of end users to make them the experts in the information process takes over library school curricula, I can suggest a title to replace the "L" word from which some educators are trying so hard to distance themselves. They might become School of Lemmingism. Same initial for ease of filing.

Library Studies or Information Management—What's in a Name?

A Spring 1994 issue of *Library Hotline* brought us the news that the Berkeley School of Library and Information Studies would be reborn from the ashes as the School of Information Management and Systems. This represented a heroic achievement for Nancy Van House and those who worked with her, and I offer my genuine congratulations.

Berkeley administrators tried very hard to close this school. It was subjected to study after study of committee after committee, despite the "annoying" (i.e., to administrators) conclusion of earlier committees that the school was fine, that it should be retained, and that it should be more generously supported.

University administrators countered with a strategy that is unique to academia in its indirect ugliness; corporate and even government sector people would be more direct. The school was forbidden to search for a new dean, and Van House was forced to serve with all of the workload and none of the political advantages of being an "acting" dean. Faculty vacancies, as they arose, were frozen. Money could be spent, but tenured or tenure track people could not be hired.

Finally came the strategy of strangulation. The admission of new students was suspended. This is not an unusual tactic when an administration has the will but not the power to close a program. Our field also saw it at Case Western Reserve University. When enrollment eventually disappears, the school has closed itself. There are names for such tactics. I prefer calling it management without the guts to take responsibility for its own actions. As a teacher of management, I find it despicable.

The Berkeley Debacle

With all this as background, the ability of Berkeley to survive is a real tribute to the dogged determination of its administrator. What then has changed? Most obviously, the name. The Berkeley school—after the reconstitution, the selection of a dean, the hiring of faculty, and the cutting of the velvet cord so that students can once again enter—will have a new name in which the word information remains but little else.

A purist might argue that management and systems represent a lesser academic emphasis than studies, but this would be a needless quibble. The major change is that we have rid ourselves of the dreaded "L" word. If I perceive a slight hypocrisy here, it is only that Berkeley has not yet changed the name of the institution that schools such as this have historically served. It is not yet the University of California Emporium of Information Management and Systems. It will probably still be the University Library. How is this possible? Lawyers but no law school, doctors but no medical school, librarians but no library school?

Much Will Change—Good and Bad

I know I am being petty. Undoubtedly much will change in both the curriculum and faculty mix, and I am sure that a great deal of this will also be to the good. There is no doubt that our educational programs must change. If that suggests a changed emphasis from training to education, even as some employers might prefer training for instant job effectiveness, then you know I support such a broadening of the curriculum.

I am certainly no apologist for the status quo; it is only my observation that the profession changes by expansion and not by massive shifts of tectonic plates. Any university, and in particular a public university, must pay attention to the educational skills demanded by employers in its state, balancing them with the school's own ivy-clustered assessment of its mission. It is an intriguing conjecture that the librarians at Berkeley might consider their school's own graduates as unqualified and might refuse to hire them. It won't happen, but it might make the chancellor think.

Managing Info Isn't New

Will this school now educate information managers *instead* of librarians? Having spent much of my operational career as executive director of the NASA Scientific and Technical Information Facility, as program manager of the IBM Corporate Technical Information Center, and in a variety of similar posts, I am confused. What I was doing way back in the 1960s was managing information, with a staff of reprographic specialists, systems analysts, and programmers to support me. Cost effectiveness, cost benefit, and total quality management (we used different terms then, but the concept is very old) were all part of the management strategy. And yet, the information facility I was managing was clearly a library.

What qualified me to do all this was my background as a librarian, supplemented by other skills. There is clearly a mixture of capabilities involved here—some can't even really be taught—but one of my attributes as an information manager was my training as a librarian. The systems people were individuals I hired—and I tried very hard to hire good ones—but they didn't have a clue about overall purpose and direction.

Is It a Library?

What I am saying is that throughout my career I have never been able to differentiate between a library and an information management facility, because a well-run library *is* an information management facility. The nomenclature can be confusing. There are institutions with the humble title of library that are superbly proactive and anticipatory information facilities. There are things called information centers, information facilities, information systems complexes, and other exotic titles. It has been my rule of thumb that the more incompetent the organization, the more it must strive for heady nomenclature. Nowhere is this truer than in academia where style is infinitely more important than substance.

The Berkeley announcement assures us that the school will still be preparing librarians, and that decision is certainly prudent. For the long foreseeable future the students who matriculate will still wander off into jobs called librarian, even as the school title pretends there is no such thing. Schools that have already changed their names to eliminate the "L" word know this. Fortunately for them, there are no truth-in-labeling statutes to which they need to adhere.

Teaching the Good Ol' Stuff

It is wonderful news that Berkeley will continue to educate librarians. Lest anyone fail to notice, there is not exactly a glut of library education programs in our most populous state. There are more accredited education programs in the New York metropolitan area or in the state of North Carolina than in California, even with the saving of Berkeley. California, which may soon have more major league hockey teams than library education programs, barely edges out the city of Denton, Texas.

What is not certain, since no faculty have been recruited and no dean search criteria have been established, is what the Berkeley school plans to teach prospective librarians. Presumably all of the good new stuff. Probably at least some of the nonsensical new stuff, because there are a lot of people now wandering around wrapped in the shimmering information mantle who don't have the vaguest idea what an information question negotiation is. One hopes some of the good old stuff will be taught, because competent information managing librarians know many things that some of the johnny-come-latelies have yet to discover.

If this column seems to have an angry tone it is because I am angry. Not at the people who struggled to save what they could at UC-Berkeley and succeeded admirably. Not even at the library school administrators who are taking actions they see essential to the survival of their programs. My anger is directed at a profession of practitioners that sometimes allows itself to be easily distracted, easily appeased, and at times appears to lack any clue as to the forces that surround and threaten to engulf us.

Diluting the "L" Word

Let me clarify for those who see happy portents everywhere. Libraries are fine. Libraries will always be fine. They will be defined and redefined by individuals who insist politically on having libraries even as they destroy them financially; they may ultimately simply define our institutions as something or other with open doors. Cut the budget, cut the staff, cut the services, but don't close the branches, so that administrators can pretend they haven't really done anything bad.

It is this continuing diluted definition of libraries, a dilution in which we unfortunately acquiesce all too willingly, which means that the profession of librarianship is in trouble. There is no doubt that no profession deserves turf for which it is unwilling to fight. What is a library? What is *not* a library? What is a librarian? What is *not* a librarian?—and therefore, we as a profession demand you stop calling yourself one?

I find myself in rather uncomfortable agreement with those who note that we should not be teaching library *science*. What we should be teaching is librarianship, and that term should have been expanded long ago to include everything that now goes on electronically, because it simply is the furnishing of more and better tools. It is up to us to evaluate and decide.

It's Time to Define Ourselves

Libraries are institutions designed and described by librarians for service to their users, and while user input is always valuable, it cannot be decisive here any more than in a doctor's office. It is probably therefore not a good idea to invite me to the decennial love feast called White House Conferences, because I would tell the lay delegates to go home and clamor for better professionally staffed institutions as their most useful contribution. As football coach Biggie Munn told Michigan State alumni, "We will appreciate your support but not your advice."

Perhaps it is too late to save both the term library and the term librarian from decades of trivialization under the guise of budget shortages. We are not very good poker players, and everyone knows it. At this point, no one would believe that we would be willing to block the entrances of our own public libraries, stage sitdown strikes, or picket the Library of Congress.

Those with whom we deal know that we will ultimately accept "libraries" on any terms, with any budgets, and with any staffs. Perhaps our most immediate fault has been in placing library ahead of librarian, although that's not the way it is ordered in the dictionary. For me the Berkeley name change is backwards. Librarianship is not a part of information management. Information management is a part of librarianship. However, I understand why they did it. And I don't blame them; I blame the rest of us.

Preparing for Library Work

Perhaps the educators who are prepared to jump ship are correct, although I cling stubbornly to my heritage. I could be wrong. If the word library and the word librarian are beyond saving, then we had better call a conference involving both practitioners and educators to decide what to call ourselves and how to put teeth into the decision.

Among the many uncertainties to which I admit, there is something of which I am sure: Without educational programs at major academic institutions that proudly prepare people for work in our profession and that use a consistent terminology with the practitioners, we will most certainly lose what is left of our profession.

We will lose it to pseudolibrarians, both the uneducated and the miseducated. The arguments about budget shortages are spurious, no matter how real they appear. And the excuses about a lack of money will never end and are therefore irrelevant. If anything is to change, it won't be because of a healthier economy, or because of some new glowing government initiative. It will be because we changed it. And that is a very big *if*.

Technology in Libraries—A Continuous Process

We can't be certain, but some of the cave drawings we now discover may have been attempts to preserve and communicate information, and that would have made them libraries. So, of course, was the later development of communication through stone tablets, which, depending on the size of the stones, could perhaps be made available for circulation, although we have no record of that. Nor do we have information about overdue fine policies. By the time of the great Alexandrian Library, rather casually even if accidentally destroyed by fire during a Roman assault, we had a very large collection which very much resembles the libraries we think of today. The point is that their development of technology—and make no mistake about the fact that it was a technological development—still required each copy to be individually produced. In Alexandria it was papyrus scrolls.

The great technological change, perhaps even greater in magnitude than even what we face today, came in the invention of the printing press, and now we are only several hundred years from the present. This permitted the making of copies, and of rapid dissemination of information to many people in a simultaneous environment. Our present technology really allows libraries to do the same thing—better, faster, and cheaper.

Talk Presented to the 63rd Annual Meeting, Quebec Library Association, Montreal, Quebec, Canada, May 13, 1995.

If we think that we moved directly from the printing press to modern day computers, we ignore the technological craze which dominated the first half of the 20th century, and particularly the 1930s and 1940s—microforms. I will not get into specific differentiations between such forms as microfilm and microfiche, except to note that even as these technologies gained acceptance and converts, there were skeptics and critics. Some of the highly emotional reactions involved the refusal of some library patrons to work with microforms at all, and it can be admitted that some of the initial equipment for utilizing microforms was rudimentary. Improvements, here as with any technology, comes from standardization and a broadening of the customer base. I recall my own heavy involvement in microfiche as a government information distribution program in the United States in the early 1960s. The agency with which I worked was NASA, and the Atomic Energy Commission, Department of Defense, and Department of Commerce all had their own programs. The same occurred in Canada at just about the same time. The primary problem was that each agency had its own standards, not only for size but also for material (silver or diazo), and most annoyingly in a failure to agree on reduction ratios. It was only when equipment manufacturers such as Bell and Howell pointed out that they had no incentive to produce microfilm and microfiche readers in large quantity and at low cost until they could be assured that this equipment could handle all microform products that agreement on specifications was painfully and reluctantly reached. I mention this because the same problem has had to be solved in the computer age—we need systems that are compatible and that can be upgraded. That was not true at the very beginning.

Even then, there has been and to some extent continues an emotional negative reaction to technology. Harold Wooster of the National Library of Medicine commented in his own charming humorous approach that microfiche readers would never really be popular until we could use them in bed, and urged manufacturers to develop cuddly equipment. On a more serious note, prominent writers such as Kurt Vonnegut have made computers the villains of their work. You probably all remember the villainous computer HAL in *2001: A Space Odyssey*, but you may not have noted that HAL is exactly one set of letters removed from IBM.

Libraries were not only slow to adapt to computers—well into the 1960s the Library of Congress subject heading was still Calculators, Electric—but libraries were even reluctant to utilize typewriters, let alone electric typewriters. If you want to have a little enjoyment look up some of the turn of the century literature in which writers fretted that the elimination of hand written catalog cards would destroy much of the pleasure which came from using libraries. When I enrolled in library school in 1949, Syracuse University had only recently eliminated the course called "library hand," a course in handwriting for librarians. This was fortunate for me, because I doubt that I would have graduated.

Returning to early computers, even as the Library of Congress called them electric calculators, the most immediate application was for the production, storage, and retrieval of clerical records. Libraries are very suitable for this purpose. We create a record when we order a book, another when we receive it, and we keep reproducing that same record in catalog cards, in circulation systems, in bibliographies, and in overdue notices. The fact that most of the early computers were installed for accounting and inventory functions explains not only why they usually reported to the Chief Financial Officer, but also why systems designed for inventory control, accounts payable and accounts receivable, bank transactions and insurance policies worked so well in libraries. Indeed, my early IBM colleague Al Warheit, hired to develop library systems, was quickly transferred to business applications when it was noted that his knowledge was just as applicable there, and of course a great deal more money could be made.

The validation of technology for clerical and repetitive operations no longer needs any defense to any group, including librarians. At this point we don't know how we would function without them. The other use of technology, for the rapid and cheap dissemination of information and its content, is where the advantages become most clear. Make no mistake, applying technology has a cost, and that cost will increase the operational budget of your libraries (you must immediately disabuse your bosses of the thought that this is not so), but technology, when properly used, is tremendously cost effective, and that benefit extends to both unit cost and unit size. Computers have become steadily smaller and also steadily cheaper, certainly as compared to unit cost of performance. One financial analyst suggested (and I don't know if this is completely true but it is certainly provocative) that if the advances in cost reduction and miniaturization found in computers had been applied to the automobile industry, we would now be driving cars that weighed two ounces and cost three cents.

Information technology takes advantage of the fact that information is not used up as it is used, as for example a hot dog is. It can be used over and over again. For libraries, this simply means that any library, even in the most far-flung locations like northern Quebec, has the potential for access, rapidly and easily, to the holdings of the world's greatest libraries. It can be accessed electronically, and it can be delivered electronically. I need not remind you that you don't have to wait until tomorrow to see a film of the game between the Montreal Canadiens hockey team and the Los Angeles Kings. You can see the game live, if need be via one of the many satellites which now circles the earth. The process works!

Of course it has a cost, but the question is whether or not it is worth it. If rapidity of information is important to hockey fans, is it equally or more important to library users who need the information to do something else? Have you attempted to present the case? Generally speaking we have not made the case. Our tremendous electronic capabilities in bibliographic access stand in stark contrast to the fact that we still tend to do document delivery the way we have always done it, through the postal system. It is disturbing that, to a large extent the very business and government officials who do use rapid document access for themselves fail to understand that they also need to provide it for us.

As technology clearly provides us with the opportunity to mechanize our clerical and document acquisition functions, it also provides both opportunities and dangers as we address the larger issue, and of course the reason why people bother to do this—the content of the document and its usefulness for a variety of reasons—recreation, education, and information which can involve national security on the one hand and saving lives on the other. The great freedom we now have is that, as we are able to delegate or abdicate routine clerical work, we can now do more information work—applying the contents of our collections as the needs arise.

It puzzles me that many librarians don't want to do information work, and prefer that the end user do this work without us. I won't even bother to explain why this makes no economic sense for society as a whole—ignoring competent professionals who are (unfortunately) poorly paid in favor of having this work done badly, more slowly, and more inaccurately by people who often earn more than we do. This is a case you should certainly be able to make without difficulty to the financial managers who increasingly control decisions in government, business, and academia.

What puzzles me even more is our frequent failure to understand that, as technology takes over our clerical routines, professional responsibilities will really be the only ones available. The routines will only require a few clerks. Others have noted that the advent of technology will not only permit but demand the development of a new profession of information intermediaries who will filter and interpret the huge volumes of information for users who are unable and frequently also unwilling to do this for themselves. The argument that people (perhaps except for web-surfing teenagers) like to spend time looking for information is a myth, even if it is a myth perpetuated by organizations to whose advantage it is that end users search expensively and sloppily. Most individuals would rather delegate the process, if they can find a person to whom to delegate. The University of Alberta Library in Edmonton found that its offer for end user search training was routinely referred by the faculty members contacted to graduate assistants and even secretaries. Peter Drucker has predicted that the most important profession of the next century will be the profession of knowledge workers, individuals who help us find the truly useful from huge and increasing volumes which contain, for most of us, largely trivia. Others have taken up Drucker's prediction. We not only have a large and growing information for a fee service, which should put to rest the often stated argument that "there is no money." We also have the development of new academic disciplines which style themselves as "information something or other." The exact title doesn't matter, but they are careful to avoid the word library in their job descriptions. They help perpetuate the perception that librarians do only clerical and routine things. So, unfortunately, do many librarians. The unfortunate reality, however, is that it is precisely clerical and routine things which will be done by computers far better than we can do them. For that purpose alone we won't need librarians.

The opportunity and danger are both there for us. Technology changes jobs, and even eliminates some jobs. It is rapidly eliminating the work of telephone operators and bank tellers. It does not need to eliminate our jobs, at least not the jobs we need to be doing. I began by pointing out that technology has been a continuum which has always been with us. The rate of change has become more rapid, and will of course continue. Libraries have always changed, and will continue to change. The advice to those being overtaken by an avalanche is to try to stay on top of the snow. It applies to us as well.

Educating for the Now and Future Profession

These are not easy times in which to be an academic administrator. Public disenchantment with higher education—coupled with continuing pressures to fund other priorities without raising additional funds and even cutting taxes—is bad news for public universities as well as for public libraries.

In both the public and academic environment, throats are being slit, but in academia it is done delicately enough so that all bleeding is internal, because style is far more important than substance in the academic value system. It is understandable that library and information science deans and directors might be tempted to rush to revise their curricula, perhaps in the hope of making them more relevant for students.

Primarily, though, it is done to impress higher-level administrators with the appearance of a newly found academic rigor. The tactic may be understandable, but what is unforgivable is when it is carried out unilaterally and intramurally by its administrators and faculty. The process cannot be forgiven because such arrogance ignores the primary responsibility of any educator, which is not to the university but to its students. Students are our customers, and they pay our salaries.

Reprinted, with changes, by permission of the author and *Library Journal* 120, no. 9 (May 15, 1995): 44–46. Copyright © 1995 by Cahners Business Information.

The Whims of Educators

Peter Drucker noted long ago that the content of curriculum in graduate education was far too important to be left exclusively to the whims of educators, who would simply make the process longer and more expensive without any tangible results. Using nursing as an example, Drucker observed that students learned less and less about patient care because faculty and administrators increasingly consisted of individuals who had never provided any patient care. Since they did not know how to teach it, they simply decided it wasn't worth teaching.

The decision of the Council on Post-Secondary Accreditation (COPA) to place accreditation authority into the hands of practitioners and not educators to a great extent confirms Drucker's assertion. It is the American Library Association (ALA) and not the Association for Library and Information Science Education (ALISE) that is accountable for the quality of accredited education programs in our profession.

It has become fashionable for some educational administrators to ridicule the process of accreditation—it does not work as well as it should—but that is largely because practitioners, who presumably feel they have enough problems of their own, have abdicated their assigned role back to the educators. Drucker might liken that to putting the fox in charge of the chicken coop. If library administrators took their responsibility seriously, not only for the quality of hires for their own institutions but also for the protection of students who have no one else to protect them, there presumably would be no problem.

Dampening Our Ardor

Educational administrators may indeed want to impress their academic colleagues by demonstrating how unlike librarians they really are. Yet even these schools must pay attention to student enrollment and the increasing dollar share of academic costs that students are asked to pay. *If* accreditation were rigidly monitored by practitioners (as indeed it is supposed to be), and *if* prospective students understood that without this approval by their future bosses there would be no jobs after graduation, the fear of losing enrollment would quickly dampen the ardor for change for appearance sake.

The process of educating students is a delicate balance between preparing them for a productive job in tomorrow's marketplace and a career in whatever the profession turns out to be ten or 20 years down the road. The implication is that we imbue them with value systems and aptitudes for future learning, far more than with specific job training programs, because all training becomes almost immediately obsolete. That ongoing process of training can be handled by supervisors or vendors.

What do students want from their educational experience, and, perhaps more importantly, what do students need? They need both preparation for tomorrow's job interview and the next decade's career; to prepare them for one without the other would be irresponsible. We know a great deal more about the first than the second. Much of the present job market is pretty much like yesterday's job market, except for the increasing emphasis on the use of technology and the application of systems—but those are only tools in how we serve our customers.

Educational administrators understand that they must give at least verbal recognition to the first requirement for an immediate job even as they might ignore it in practice. The schools that have surgically removed the word "library" from their names understand that the great majority of the students they need to attract will enroll with the intent of becoming librarians. They therefore rush to assure these prospective students, the so-called "cash cows," that they are still welcome. Certainly their tuition money is welcome.

Students First Need a Job

Students who seek a career, first need a job, and they are not very good at predicting what that job will be. The study that Sarah Mort and I reported in the July 1990 *Library Quarterly* showed clearly that ten years after graduation, half of the students were doing something completely different from the specializations for which they had prepared themselves, and the reasons were clear: Graduates need *a* job—much as they might prefer *the* job—and they will accept what is offered.

Employers, with the primary exception of academic libraries, hire from a local applicant pool, largely because they are willing to pay neither interview nor relocation expenses. Furthermore, graduates overwhelmingly reported, and indeed earlier studies confirm, that employers were far less concerned with specific courses taken than with the overall impression created by the interview. That might be good news, but only if the interview is properly weighted to measure unique potential and not just feel-good team collegiality.

Being Prepared for All Futures

All of this suggests that students must not only be prepared for the job market they will enter the day after graduation, but also prepared generically rather than specifically. No one knows what they will end up doing—not the students and certainly not faculty members who have never been there. What we insist that all students learn is far more important than the range of electives being offered, particularly if the elective courses have no relationship to the general thrust of the curriculum.

Certainly, our profession is undergoing change, and employers should hire individuals who threaten to become uncomfortable iconoclasts in leading that change in their institutions. However, fragmenting the curriculum into tracks is a disservice to students, because although we know there will be change, the specifics are much harder to predict. It takes no genius to predict generally more technology, greater quantities of information, and a heavier reliance on systems of international as well as national and local dimensions. However, these simply enlarge the options for how we best serve our clients. They change nothing fundamental.

Our Unpredictable Future

What about the "new" opportunities for students in graduate programs with such catchy names as information analysis, information utilization, and information management? Job opportunities for the graduates of the undergraduate programs that sprang up more than a decade ago were easy to forecast and were indeed realized. However, after more than ten years we still cannot be sure whether these graduates with bachelor's degrees filled positions that might otherwise have been given to clerks, or whether they became cheaper candidates for posts that might otherwise have gone to librarians.

For the graduate market there are now lots of predictions but almost no hard facts. We know about the opportunities for librarians to become entrepreneurs running their own businesses armed with a phone, a fax, and a terminal, but is there a "new" field here for today's graduates (and ten years from now is too iffy a prospect to count because graduates can't wait ten years)? Or, stubbornly even if perhaps incorrectly, will employers continue to insist on the MBA, or the business school's totally undefined MIS? The one attempt at making an assessment of the future job market for our programs, the fall 1993 *Library Trends* study authored by Indiana University's Blaise Cronin, Michael Stiffler, and Dorothy Day, produced results sufficiently vague so that the first two authors can disagree on their meaning.

With all of this uncertainty, some things appear quite clear. What our educational programs produce will be the key to whatever professional future we have: thus, practitioners need to care about what is taught far more than they do now. I suspect COPA understands this quite clearly, for all fields and not just ours. If accreditation now works badly it is not because it is oppressive, but rather because it stresses the obscure and the trivial. It could be significant but only if the accreditation process emphasized the one thing only professionals can assess— the quality of the educational programs—and did not make sidetrips into society-wide issues already dealt with in every university. It might be easier if the accreditors thought of themselves primarily as advocates for students.

The process of curriculum development and change must come from the joint efforts of practitioners and educators, because if it comes only from educators it is both contrived and irrelevant, as Drucker has warned us. This places a responsibility on educators to listen once in a while. It places a responsibility on practitioners to deal with issues besides the eradication of the backlog.

The Self-Confident Librarian

Most of all, if this field is to shape a curriculum to serve the future we want to create, we have to spend some time determining what we want and what our strategies for fighting for it are. More importantly, we must develop a sense of self-confidence and self-worth. It is vital that we continue to hear and assess what others have to tell us, but we should be reluctant to give others authority over our educational programs simply because they profess a so-called virtue of being unencumbered by the past. Those administrators and educators who now seek to lead our profession must understand the opportunities and challenges of the future. However, they must also acknowledge both a respect for and understanding of our past. In the current vernacular, if they want to "talk the talk," can they also "walk the walk?" Talking is always much easier.

Ironically, leaders in graduate education, through the Holmes Group, insist that those who educate teachers must demonstrate an understanding of what happens in the classroom. At the same time, our profession, which never had this problem, is moving stubbornly in the opposite direction. We not only seem to seek out those who know little if anything about what happens in libraries, we sometimes agree when they argue that this ignorance of the past is really a virtue.

All of this is part of the continual professional self-abasement of librarians, reminiscent of Eleanor Roosevelt's comment that no one could be put down without his or her permission. I still fail to understand why we grant this permission. Since we control the hiring process in our own institutions, we could still at least significantly influence the educational process. A decision to react with economic power might or might not impress our new self-appointed messiahs, but it would certainly be noticed by their own bosses in academia, who spend a great deal of time poring over the financial ledgers that increasingly control academic policy.

The Cost of Knowledge and the Cost of Ignorance

Many of you have seen the beautiful American Library Association poster featuring a landscape and the caption "Knowledge Is Free." The picture is lovely, but if I had not recently written about and strongly agreed with the late John Swan's commitment to freedom of information access regardless of the personal pique it might arouse, I would be tempted to embark on a campaign to destroy these misleading and destructive messages. I would state the following:

- Knowledge is not free. It is brought to taxpayers at great expense and considerable inconvenience by people who studied long and hard in school to create it, by others who took the trouble to record and reproduce it, and by overworked and underpaid librarians who, after many years of special education and training, ultimately present it to you, the taxpayer.

- We hope you appreciate it and the trouble it entailed. Because the point for you to remember is that knowledge is valuable, important, and the key to success and contentment. If this message persuades you, it might even impel you to concentrate some of the 12 years you are forced to spend in school to seize the opportunity both to learn how to read and then to read, rather than waste your time hanging around malls and video game parlors.

- Knowledge often comes to us in the form of information: a wonderful, renewable resource that is not consumed in its use, as a hot dog is. Information is nevertheless expensive but well worth the cost and certainly preferable to any alternative. As a taxpayer, you will ultimately end up paying for this information, as you pay for anything else, one way or another. Since you will be paying for it anyway, go ahead and use it. Why get cheated?

Reprinted, with changes, by permission of the author and *Library Journal* 120, no. 11 (June 15, 1995): 48–49. Copyright © 1995 by Cahners Business Information.

Not Free, But "Valuable"

These statements are definitely not part of the common currency of our profession. Instead, we insist that all of this stuff is free. If funds are not provided by others, we will still supply it; to do otherwise would be our fault. We perpetuate all this with signs inscribed over doorways announcing that this is the "free" public library. Of course it is not free, and in perpetuating this misconception we only trivialize what we do. How about "valuable" public library?

The most important thing in dealing with the cost of information is that we keep accurate accounts in order to make informed recommendations to those who make the painful choices of where money is to be spent or not spent. Because technology brings us bibliographic access, whether or not that ever leads us to document delivery, library budgets will increasingly have to deal with the reality that, to serve their own patrons, they will have to tap into the holdings of other libraries.

Of course, the larger and more complete the library, the more likely it will be the tappee rather than the tapper. However, all libraries will be increasingly constrained to justify the priority decisions that managers must make. Service to your own community comes light years ahead of service to those who never contributed to your budget. It is still permissible to use the phrase "charity begins at home."

Costing Out ILL

We don't need to reinvent the accounting profession. The process of supplying a document from library A to library B has a cost. Part of that is the direct cost of actually receiving the request, making the copy, forwarding it, paying the mail or fax charge, and paying the people who do all this. Part if it is the indirect cost—the amortization of the initial purchase cost that someone else is now sharing, the cost of the building and its upkeep, and the cost of management.

There are a variety of ways to distribute the cost. It can be charged to the library, which, because it does not own everything, must tap outside resources to satisfy customer demand. It can be billed to the customer directly, although there are ethical problems in doing this. The client did not get to decide what the library owns or does not own. If, as a result of the decision not to purchase, the institution is now forced to rely on the resources of another supplier, that is hardly the individual requester's fault.

Finally, of course, the cost of supporting this transaction may be borne by a level of government, certainly the one responsible for the operation of the requesting library, perhaps an even higher level of government that is responsible for both the requester and the supplier. It is not difficult to explain why encouraging and supporting this process for a responsible agency is cheaper and more cost-effective than either of the two alternatives—replicating everything or telling the customers, "Tough luck because this is a library funded by cheapskates."

Who Pays, Tapper or Tappee?

Although there are a variety of options for paying for this process, the one most obviously unavailable is to ask the organization supplying the document to pick up part of the cost, in addition to dealing with the inconvenience. That option has always been absurd, but it becomes recklessly absurd as we move increasingly into an era of validating our expenses and our decisions. The explanation that we ran out of money for serving our own clientele because we spent it on someone else's will be about as convincing as the explanation that we used the money to buy a car for a cousin.

And yet we stubbornly cling to the belief that somehow the exchange of information is a "common good" in which we all share equally. As long ago as April 1959 Samuel Sass argued in an article in *Special Libraries* that special libraries should increase the process of lending more to the academic libraries from which they borrow so much rather than be parasites in the process of ILL. The argument made little sense to me then and makes even less today. ILL is a labor-intensive activity, and special libraries have a great deal of difficulty in getting staff in a corporate setting.

Special libraries do, however, still have an easier time getting money than people. By contrast, academic libraries could easily hire cheap, part-time student labor *if only* they weren't chronically short of funds. The most beneficial relationship for both institutions is simple: special librarians, or their corporate employers, should furnish the university libraries with money in return for service. Many corporations already supply tax-deductible dollars to universities, but that doesn't count. The money must be specifically earmarked for library discretionary spending or we will see none of it.

Service Doesn't Come Cheap

Our present arcane and contrived practices for dealing with ILL lead, not surprisingly, to poor levels of service, because the supplier has no incentive for lending at all, let alone lending more by providing superlative service. Under present ground rules, supplying documents for another library is a low priority, indeed, a much lower priority than serving everyone in our own constituency first. And that is absolutely correct. The resulting poor response rates for ILL (should anything today ever take more than 48 hours?) has opened plenty of opportunities for commercial vendors. That solves the problem for some but not for those who have no other financial alternatives, the very individuals for whom public library service was created.

If document supply from alternative sources (the other alternative being to buy it ourselves) will most assuredly be an increasing requirement, then it becomes incumbent on us to inform everyone of the quality and not the cheapness of what is being offered, and why it is essential that it be offered. That is why harping on the "freeness" of what we do is so counterproductive. "Keep the doors open" is the ultimate statement of a library trasher who wants it all politically, preferably at no cost. Unless we respond vigorously to such suggestions, they will be repeated. We have seen the example of the San Francisco mayor who fired his own library board because library funding was pitiful but he didn't want to be blamed for branch closings.

Tell the Truth About Costs

If the buy-or-borrow decision allows a true selection among alternatives, we need accurate information about what these choices cost. We have that information for purchase; we try desperately not to know for borrowing. When that happens, we take all honesty out of the process and allow politicians to randomly select a public library access fee for nonresidents because, while perhaps wrong and inadequate, it feels politically safe. Has it occurred to the politicians to make up the difference?

It was refreshing to learn of a Research Libraries Group (RLG) study completed by Marilyn Roche in 1991 that found that the cost of supplying a document from library A to library B was $29.55. That sounds plausible, and it can serve as a basis for management decisions. Perhaps that number was generally known, but I had to wait for a 1993 report from the Council on Library Resources (CLR) to find out. I would have thought all academic and public libraries would have grabbed those numbers and run with them to their own funding agencies.

What is still disturbing in the Roche report is the news that $10.93 of the transaction cost (37%) was absorbed by the supplying library. The cost means there is absolutely no management justification for doing it at all, let alone well. If we assume that the cost in 1995 is $36, the supplier must be given all of that. I have an even better idea. Let's give the supplier $40. That way supplying libraries have an incentive to do this work, money to hire students, and a management tool with which to castigate subordinates when demand—and income—drops. Does anyone recognize the mechanism for quality enhancement? It will also help borrowers be better managers, because it clarifies whether to spend the money on purchasing or on borrowing.

I can hear the complaints already. We don't have the money; all our board and our mayor want us to do is keep the doors open. There is no simple solution. We can ask Congress to allow us to print money. Or we can tell our bosses what our clients need, why they need it, and what terrible and embarrassing things will happen if we don't get the money.

How Many Priorities Are We Allowed to Have—And Who Sets Them?

I try not to pick fights with the Department of Education (DOE) Office of Library Programs (or if DOE goes under the knife, with whatever its successor is). It's a group of hard-working people who don't control their own agenda. Librarians have no role in federal education policy-making. In commenting that the appearance of progress is more important than the substance, I indict no particular party. If anything, I indict a public that has long taught its servants that generalizations are safer than painful facts. That is why government programs are replete with unachievable goals that will in time be replaced by even newer and shinier goals. It is always silly season in Washington.

In a brochure entitled "Public Libraries Serving Communities: Education Is Job #1," the Office of Educational Research and Improvement draws that theme from its analysis of a study undertaken by George D'Elia of the University of Minnesota. The study does indeed identify the support of education as libraries' top priority, and public librarians should be grateful for that at least. The brochure does not say, "Buying Books Is Job One," "Creating a Fun Place Is Job One," or "Keeping the Doors Open Is Job One." However, the study identifies many other priorities designated by the public at least as critical as numerous non-library programs the government chooses to fund when it recognizes public support for spending money. I would have titled the brochure, "Education Is One of the Public Library's Many Priorities Which Needs to Be Supported by Government at All Levels." I know, the title needs work.

Reprinted, with changes, by permission of the author and *Library Journal* 120, no. 13 (August 1995): 50–51. Copyright © 1995 by Cahners Business Information.

Even a cursory reading of the tables in the brochure shows that the public has identified not one priority, but at least ten that, for the respondents as a whole or for at least one or more politically significant subgroup, attracted majority support.

DOE's Self-Serving Choice

It is certainly true that the three highest vote-getters, lumped by DOE in a self-serving priority number one (self-serving because it just happens to coincide with the programs that the DOE has agreed to fund even if at minimal levels) drew the highest affirmative vote totals, generally exceeding 80 and even 90 percent. However, the survey respondents also suggested a role for the public library as a center for information about the community by a margin of two to one and as a research center for scholars and researchers by a clear majority not only in total but also by every subgroup.

The role of the public library as information center for community businesses drew a majority response from the general public and overwhelming support from blacks and Hispanics. If we accept DOE's lumping of the top three vote-getters as priority number one, its list still suggests *at least* eight other priorities worth supporting, and that means worth funding.

I say at least because as honest as the survey methodology undoubtedly was, it may not have asked all of the questions. For example, with regard to the much-ballyhooed information superhighway, a positive majority could have been elicited had the respondents been asked, "Do you see an important role for the public library in protecting you from being overwhelmed by information in which you have no interest?" That will probably turn out to be the most important role of information professionals in the 21st century—filtering and discarding to protect the swamped information user. If we librarians aren't interested in doing this, we can be certain that someone else will be.

We Have More Than One Priority

Why all this fascination with establishing what is priority number one? In tennis we get two serves, in baseball three strikes, in football four downs. The Secretary of State would never identify Bosnia, or China, or the Middle East, or Haiti as our first foreign policy objective because it would send a clear message that all of the other countries are considered to be trivial. Many surveys have told us that the general public considers the economy to be the most important issue of national concern. Does this suggest that the President will go on television to announce that all of the other initiatives of his administration (including healthcare reform, the war against drugs, law and order, etc.) are being abandoned? We know better than that.

Labeling something as priority number one may not be intended to trivialize everything else, but that is the clear result. My November 15, 1993 column ("Would You Like to Rank Order the Importance of Your Children?") castigated the State Library and Library Association of Oregon for trading a few dollars for their own pronouncement that service to children was the greatest priority for the public librarians of Oregon.

That's an even narrower focus than what the DOE would impose. It infers that nothing else matters enough to be worth funding. The state librarian of Oregon responded with a letter that argued that this was not the intent and that it was not true. However, I suspect he knows better. At least as a practitioner in the political setting, I hope he knows better.

Getting Trapped by the Shell Game

We become victims of the same shell game when we allow our federal education officials to stress the fight against illiteracy, which Barbara Bush handed us—without bothering to ask—as our own first priority. Do we understand that such a rank ordering negatively affects public library service to children, never mind what else we might want to do? What happens in this sort of mindset to the priority of the public library as a center for information about the community, endorsed by 65.6 percent of all respondents, and 85.6 percent of blacks and 85.3 percent of Hispanics? What happens to the public library's role as an information center for business, endorsed by 55.1 percent of the general public, 78.9 percent of blacks, and 72.7 percent of Hispanics? Is 55.1 considered too low a level of endorsement? Are all of the officials elected with 55.1 percent of the vote prepared to resign because they don't consider their mandate strong enough?

Of course not. The result of priority ranking for Oregon librarians may have been accidental, but the tactic within the federal bureaucracy is completely intentional. We know the feds have no intention of spending much money on library programs. By lumping all priorities into one, the federal government can keep the funding down, curtailing what is spent on even that one. The employees of the Office of Library Programs know all of this. However, they are subordinates and are not allowed to speak the truth. They are only allowed to ask for what they are told to ask for, and then they must testify that this is really plenty. I know state librarians who keep their jobs by that same act of self-abasement.

Meeting All Their Needs

The study by D'Elia could have been very useful because it identifies what citizens want that public libraries do not offer. Certainly anything with the support of at least one group of 75 percent or more becomes part of priority number one. We could even extend that list of unmet needs by asking respondents about the desirability of services they don't even know libraries could provide. That is called marketing: creating an awareness of an unmet and often an unsuspected need.

The federal government, state governments, and local governments should be interested in knowing what unmet and even unidentified needs there might be. When it suits their political agendas, sometimes they are interested. For libraries, that is never the case. The basic strategy is: 1) express love and support, 2) provide as few funds as possible, and 3) make no commitments except in the generalities of unachievable and even unmeasurable goals. We are told by the media that when the President was asked to increase his support for library funding, he expressed sympathy but made no commitments. Politically, what that represents is a flat turndown. I am not picking on this incumbent President; he is only doing what every one of his predecessors did.

It's Only Words

We can only engender change in government attitudes toward us by political organization, and political organization operates on the well-understood principle of rewarding support and punishing opposition. Lest we misunderstand how this works, support "in principle" with funding to come perhaps "when things are more affordable" is the same as opposition. We should understand that as long as the leaders of the Public Library Association, the American Library Association, and our counterpart organizations in states and localities thank incumbent politicians for their kind words, words are all we will get.

My suggested strategies for dealing with all of this are simple, even as their implementation requires major change in what we expect from ourselves and, more importantly, in getting others to take us seriously. First of all, government bureaucrats at all levels need to understand that they do not tell us what our priorities are. We are the professional experts, and they are the servants we pay. We tell them. Then the question at least becomes substantive: What are they going to do about what we have just told them? The operative verb is "do," not "say."

Secondly, we need to make the support of public library funding and the implementation of the many first priorities a matter of national urgency. Priorities are measured in terms of funding commitment. We should start with a level of $20 billion, an amount large enough to get attention and yet small enough to make no difference, when we recognize that $20 billion is less than the level of accuracy with which federal deficits can be predicted. And, of course, it is less than what the administration and Congress are enthusiastically planning to spend to put "more police on the street." I do not object to this because there is more than one first priority.

The $20 billion would be just the federal share of this program. We would make this available to states and localities based on a matching grant formula, and the fear of losing money grants would make even the most penurious of states somehow cough up the money. Why do I think this would work, and why does it all look so familiar? Simply because that is the strategy for highway repair funding, and without such a strategy there would never be any money for fixing bridges until after they had fallen down. It could be argued that our priority is at least as great; certainly our wellspring of public support is much greater. What we have not learned, unlike the organizations of road contractors, is how to make people give us the money. Instead, we accept platitudes.

Block Grants Won't Cut It

Can the federal government afford to support libraries? Despite all of the anguished rhetoric, it is clear that the government keeps what it wants to keep and eliminates what it wants to eliminate, always pleading poverty in the process. The next time your representative or senator pleads that there is no money for libraries, ask him or her why there is money to allow the U.S. Naval Academy to operate a dairy farm. Is that part of midshipman training? (The answer turns out to be that about 80 years ago the farm was established to protect future officers from the danger of tainted milk.) As long as silly excesses such as these (and there are thousands of them) remain unchallenged, we will continue to get platitudes about "maybe more money when times get better." We get them because we accept them and even act grateful. The new Republican tactic of block grants, which shifts responsibility for decisions from the federal government to the states, doesn't make a difference for librarians because we get platitudes and vague promises from everyone.

Never Mind Being Innovative and Effective—Just Be Nice

When I last wrote about our fascination with the formation of teams, regardless of how well they did or did not work ("The Tyranny of the 'Team,'" *LJ*, April 15, 1989, pp. 54–55), the reaction was so underwhelming I thought it might be time to try the question again. It seems that our fascination with teams for the sake of teams has not abated.

When I first meet my classes I explain that there will be no group projects with shared grades. In all of my years as a teacher I have never been able to figure out who did what part of the shared assignment, except to suspect that the contributions are never totally equal. For all these people to share one grade is unfair to all but particularly to those who did the bulk of the work.

I watch the faces of the students, and I find that those who smile and nod their agreement almost always turn out to be the best, the brightest, and the most articulate students. They are also the ones who face the frustration and difficulty of getting jobs. The difficulty for them is that they contribute more good ideas than those with whom they work. This becomes a particular problem when those others, especially those with seniority, become aware of this. I know of at least a dozen examples of what I would consider our best and brightest who, after a couple of years of frustration, have chosen to enter another profession. Don't feel sorry for them; they have done just fine. Feel sorry for the rest of us, because we systematically crush the spirit out of those with potential by insisting that, far more important than being productive or innovative, they be "collegial."

A Stubborn Search for Conformity

Team building, as we practice it, is a conscious and stubborn search for conformity and therefore mediocrity. Both Mary Parker Follet and Peter Drucker have warned us against a search for an easily achieved consensus, because that suggests that those with contrary (and perhaps better) ideas have been bludgeoned into silence.

These management writers urge that bosses send their subordinates out to fight some more. Quickly reached consensus is easy precisely because it is unimaginative and boring. Thomas Watson Jr., the late IBM board chair, constantly urged his own executives to protect the "wild ducks," those individuals who insisted on seeing what others did not see. It was, of course, possible that people who appeared obnoxious were simply that without a redeeming quality.

However, it was just as possible that they appeared obnoxious because they were smarter and because they were right. Watson's point was that no organization, and certainly not IBM, could allow itself to become so immersed in the comfort of genial agreement that all new ideas become trivialized. History has shown us that Watson was well advised to fear—and Louis Gerstner, the current president of IBM, to try to erase—this arrogance.

The June 5, 1995 issue of *Time* reports that Bill Gates, founder and chair of Microsoft, practices a management style called "armed truce," in which employees are encouraged to challenge everyone, including the chair. We are told that conflict is at the heart of every decision in a company constantly at war with not only outsiders but also with itself.

Since Gates has a net worth that may exceed the combined worth of the entire American Library Association (ALA) membership, perhaps he knows something we don't. If collegial comfort and the absence of healthy ideological battles tend to define U.S. libraries, it is hard to figure out why, because we have very little to be smug about. Perhaps we treat each other so nicely as a form of compensation, because others treat us so rudely. However, we treat even those who routinely kick us in the teeth nicely, whether they be patrons or administrators.

Appropriate Committees

We need to remember that committees have never really accomplished anything worth remembering, including *AACR2*, and the old joke that a camel is a horse designed by a committee reminds us that others know it, too. The *Mona Lisa* was not painted by committee, nor was the *Eroica Symphony* composed by one. There are, of course, perfectly appropriate uses for both committees and consensus, but the misuses as a pleasant way to avoid responsibility have become legion. The musical *How to Succeed in Business Without Really Trying* includes a song entitled "No Matter Whom They Fire I Will Still Be Here," and we should all know what that means. It means be pleasant, be collegial, be a "team player" even if it means running to the wrong end of the field. Above all it means never call attention to yourself and your opinions. First find out what everyone else thinks and then agree. What a horrible price to pay in wasting the human mind, for such a small creature comfort return!

Don't Investigate, Just Apologize?

In the final exam of my management course I present my students with an "In Basket" exercise, in which they are directors of a major academic library. One of the memos on their desks is from a chemistry professor who complains that the chemistry branch librarian has been rude to him, and he demands an apology from the library.

That is all the information provided, but perhaps ten percent of the students immediately write the demanded apology, without even knowing for what they are apologizing. When I point out that perhaps investigation might show that the librarian was right, that perhaps the dispute resulted from the demand that the branch librarian violate the copyright law, or a demand for sexual favors, students begin to squirm.

How many of today's administrators would simply apologize? But isn't the customer always right? Not when the customer is dead wrong. You owe it to your subordinates to find out and, if appropriate, to defend and protect them. If not, what exactly is your job?

Does Being Nice Mean Gaining Power?

Why this fascination with being nice, or really with being obsequious? Is it because we think that by writing apologies on demand to any faculty member, that faculty member is more likely to accept us as a professional equal? Do we think that this is the appropriate tactic with which to gain respect, money, power, prestige? From anyone? Is this our strategy for saving library education?

If libraries are heavily bogged down in bureaucratic models, that is not totally our fault. Patrons, in their insistence on the good old library as they remember it—as opposed perhaps to how it really was—are far more reluctant to change than even the most reluctant librarians. However, change we must if we are to remain relevant, and the impetus for that change will not come from library users. However, when librarians operate the kinds of libraries "their users want," even when they know those libraries are inadequate, the continued silence is simply a total abdication of all professional responsibility.

Sometimes the process of glorifying the "good old library" turns to maudlin sentimentality. In an article in the April 4, 1994 issue of *The New Yorker*, Nicholson Baker laments the great loss suffered in the transfer from card to computerized catalogs. Like all writers for this magazine, Baker writes well, even passionately, but his eloquence cannot hide his lack of knowledge about his subject. Does he realize, for example, that only a tiny fraction of the library's content is represented in the card catalog? Does he realize that multiple-term Boolean searching, heretofore impossible, can now be done? In other words, even with all of the current problems, does he know what a step forward this represents?

Change Comes from Annoying Individuals

We can be certain that what change does come will not come from the collegial team or committee process, which will ferociously protect its members, particularly those it likes. If change comes, it is usually from the shrill insistence of annoying individuals that unpleasant facts must be faced, and some of the people who are annoying may be so because they are right. We need to protect our wild ducks from the tyranny of the team, and if we don't understand that this is also part of diversity, then our definitions are much too narrow.

It is perhaps possible that some library administrators think that they should encourage management-directed teams because that is what management writings urge them to do. If so, such managers are ten years out of date. Such ideas have faded not because they were bad, but because they were simplistic, as just about all management "solutions" are. The new management literature, perhaps equally simplistic, stresses teams, but these are very different teams. It begins with the process of selecting and hiring the best possible people, as few of them as possible, paying them well, giving them the understanding of what needs to be done and the tools with which to do it, and then walking away and leaving them alone.

Voluntarily Formed Teams

It is little wonder that this management concept requires far fewer bosses. These people—individually empowered, individually judged, and individually rewarded—may well decide to organize themselves into teams for their own reasons. However, they will be voluntarily formed teams of mutual convenience, and it is not only assumed but also hoped that they will kick out those who fail to contribute their share: the pleasant incompetents. Getting rid of pleasant incompetents is something managers have never been able or willing to do very well and not just in libraries. We prefer to get rid of the unpleasant competents. Voluntary teams will be selfish, they will be temporary, and they will have the smallest possible membership.

As women finally and belatedly begin to achieve top administrative positions in this predominantly female profession, there may yet be another reason for librarians to be specifically concerned. I have always insisted on teaching management values as a totally gender-neutral process, arguing that the manager's gender has nothing to do with what it takes to be a good manager.

At the 1995 conference of the American Psychological Society, University of Minnesota researcher Laurie Rudman reported that her studies indicated that while both male and female bosses had a tendency to prefer meek to assertive female subordinates, the tendency to avoid confident and articulate subordinates was far more predominant among women bosses. These are the female subordinates least likely to be willing to sublimate themselves in teams, although "teams" that never compete to win against either set objectives or other teams surely become a contrived semantic game that fools none of the "members." If the Rudman study is valid, it sends warning signals to women executives in libraries not to allow what might be an inherent preference for pleasant team collegiality to get in the way of carrying out their responsibilities as managers.

There may be readers who consider my insistence that some workers are more valued than others and should be treated accordingly as elitism. The label does not bother me, although I prefer to think of my value as the meritocracy. However, there is nothing wrong with an elite as long as it is a genuine elite, open to all based on individual merit. Surely we should recognize that the very appropriate emphasis on diversity must move beyond casual political definitions to include a diversity based on values that not everyone sees perhaps because they are not smart enough. We desperately need diversity in libraries, but an insistence on collegial teams as the first priority probably gets in the way of protecting the wild ducks who are an essential part of both diversity and quality.

Smearing with a Broad Brush

In my last column ("Never Mind Being Innovative and Effective—Just Be Nice," *LJ*, September 15, pp. 47–48), I began to make the point that if diversity means that we accept the contributions of individuals from backgrounds and frameworks that might differ from the expected "norms," then tolerance for diversity must also include cherishing those who are different simply because they are quicker, brighter, and smarter.

Tolerance is really not the right term, anyway. Managers should encourage all sorts of diversity because they are paid to be selfish and to develop the best possible organization that limited resources can buy. An insistence on comfortable mediocrity in the name of consensus for the middle-of-the-road "team" can be dangerous for both fairness and quality. Teams cannot be allowed to become cruel destroyers of dissent, even for the sake of comfort. A workplace is not a club, and even for clubs there are laws.

Can We Be Sports About Teams?

The use of the term "team" comes, as so many things do, from our fascination with sports, and we forget that in a team concept the objective is understood, but individual contributions differ. In football, the quarterbacks have to inspire confidence and be able to assess the significance of shifting defenses. It also helps if they can throw the ball.

Running backs must have power and speed, as well as be able to catch the ball. We even know the difference between offensive and defensive linemen

Reprinted, with changes, by permission of the author and *Library Journal* 120, no. 17 (October 15, 1995): 41–42. Copyright © 1995 by Cahners Business Information.

as largely one between cunning and technique on the one hand and sheer brute power on the other. Putting 11 players on the field who are exactly alike will not work in football, and it will not work in libraries. And, of course, teams must be able to compete against other teams or at least specific objectives, because the point is to win.

If we cherish the difference, as indeed we should in stressing diversity of background and approach, it is precisely because two different people can contribute more than two people who are exactly the same. That does not mean that we change the objectives that govern our direction to make people feel more comfortable. It means that we use flexibility in determining what individuals can contribute, and not just what makes others feel comfortable. We expect you to work professionally with other individuals. If you like them that helps, but it is not essential. And, of course, you are always free to quit if you don't like it here.

Elitism Is a Broad Term

I suggested in my last column that my comments might expose me to charges of elitism, and elitism is a word so smeared with a broad brush of evil that we have lost the ability to distinguish what it might mean. If it means making preconceived judgments about individuals we do not know based on some sort of general description (race, age, sex, school affiliation), it is immoral and wasteful of our national resource of talent.

If it means the simple observation that some individuals turn out to be harder working, more courageous, smarter, or quicker to learn, then ignoring that simple fact in favor of a group generalization becomes in itself an act of bigotry. One of the things that makes management both difficult and fun is that people are not turned out with cookie cutters. If the people with all of these virtues turn out to be pleasant and congenial, so much the better. But don't be surprised if they aren't.

Just as elitism has become a dirty word, egalitarianism has developed a positive image. Treating everyone exactly the same somehow seems fair. It isn't. It is unfair because when you treat everyone exactly the same (with the same promotion ladders and salary increases), you reward the people who deserve no such rewards, and you do it by punishing the people who do deserve them.

Of course I know why we do it: egalitarianism is easy, and the decisions don't have to be explained or defended. However, whoever suggested that management was supposed to be easy? We should understand that egalitarianism is a downward weeding process. Your best people will leave, or they will resent the unfairness if geographic constraints or investment in retirement benefits force them to stay. Your worst people will never leave. Why on earth should they? And none of this has anything to do with characteristics of either race or sex. It affects us all. If anything, women have become greater victims of egalitarianism, because if they are perceived as the less-important family wage earner, they are not as likely to have the option of relocating for another, better-paying job.

The Ugliness of the Team

Let me give you an example of what ugliness can occur in the search for team comfort above all else, when that process becomes more important than quality of work. I will draw my example from outside the library field, because these issues are generic.

Even back in the 1950s, Admiral Hyman Rickover, the father of the nuclear submarine, didn't fit conventional models. He drove himself, his subordinates, and his contractors ruthlessly, generating respect and admiration but perhaps less love. He knew that for a manager, being loved does not matter. The other reactions do. Rickover refused to consider consensus committee reports and insisted that each individual furnish him with a signed copy of what he or she personally believed. He wanted to know whom to praise and whom to blame. Rickover was, beyond all else, hugely successful in meeting his assigned task of developing a nuclear-powered submarine.

The Navy tried its best to force him to retire, over and over again, and only Congressional involvement saved him. He may have been good, but he didn't fit the acceptable model of naval officers, particularly admirals, and the Navy certainly understood, for the sake of its own "morale," what was more important.

Forty years later the same Navy (and I am not a basher of the military because it could have happened in any corporation or any library) faced the embarrassment of the Tailhook scandal, in which drunken naval aviators groped and assaulted women in a Las Vegas hotel. What happened took place in plain view of hundreds, but no perpetrator has been convicted because no witnesses ever stepped forward. After all, it is better to have drunken swine who are "members of the team" than a successful admiral who is not.

I don't think the comparison to the fuzzy warmth that some are trying to instill into library management is farfetched, and the results of stressing the wrong values will be just as disastrous. Nobody tends to know what an incompetent library is, because certainly the users don't, just as nobody knows how bad things get in the Navy until it is time to fight. With luck we'll never know for the Navy, and it might not hurt us. What we don't know or practice about library management comes back to haunt us on a daily basis.

Our Still Basic Wants

What people "want" hasn't changed at all for a long time. They want to be treated as individuals and with fairness. They want to be properly paid, properly evaluated, and properly rewarded and recognized when they do something commendable. They want to be given assignments that can be accomplished within the prescribed time frame, with the tools and resources to make success at least possible. They want to be protected against insult and indignity from fellow workers, from outsiders, and from patrons. The development of a sense of self-worth is not a group exercise, it is an individual exercise.

If they are treated fairly, good people will stay. If they are treated fairly, incompetents might leave, but what is wrong with that? Most of all, individuals should be given the freedom to function in their own comfortable way, as long as the results are acceptable. How the supervisor might do it is really irrelevant because that doesn't count. That, and not fuzzy warmth, is the management lesson of the latter 1990s. And yes, individuals might well form themselves into groups to the extent to which they personally perceive that there is some advantage in it for them. And that's probably good for the library, too.

It is fascinating that managers interfere where they have no reason to interfere and at the same time refuse to do what they are supposed to do. One of the things that managers are supposed to do is select the best qualified people, based on valid criteria, for which congeniality ranks fairly low. Managers need to take responsibility for whom they hire because it is only fair that their own bosses then hold them responsible for their results. You don't let the "team" decide on whom to hire, any more than you let the team decide on whom to lynch. They'll get rid of all the Rickovers and keep all their drunken buddies—although you'll have to translate that into library issues yourself. Trust me, it happens in libraries, too.

Diversity Is Essential

Let me bring this two-part column to closure by returning to the theme with which I began. A belief in diversity and not defrauding ourselves of the talents of individuals who might differ from our own characteristics and our own comfortable expectations is essential for all of society and specifically for libraries.

However, we also need to expand our definition of diversity from its current narrow, sociopolitical boundaries to include those who are different because they resemble the wild ducks at IBM whom I wrote about in my previous column. We need to include those who don't want to be dragged down into a faceless and creditless team because they think they have more to offer than their colleagues. They might or might not be right, but can we accept the discomfort of dealing with people who are "different," because of race, ethnic background, sex, age, height, weight, physical limitations, political views, or even brains? Can we tolerate the diversity that all potential leaders bring to the workplace, or do we perhaps think we can create leaders with collegial warm fuzzy cookie cutters? And if the whole point of diversity is to create a new and improved unity, how do we define and measure that? More on that in the next column.

The Role of Information Intermediaries and the Superhighway: Crucial, Important, Trivial, or Non-Existent?

Abstract

Politicians have a habit of inventing terminology that is at once exciting and promising, and at the same time vague and nonspecific. The phrase "information superhighway" is such terminology. We have all learned of the wonders of the Autobahn, which allows us to get from place to place and with a minimum of discomfort. Information superhighway suggests a similarly happy scenario.

However, the comparison rapidly disintegrates from that point forward. Travelers enter a highway at their own volition, and precisely because using that highway allows them to get to wherever they want to get, for their own reasons and at their own schedule. If they like, they can ignore every other vehicle on the same road. Passing is easy, and they can always get off.

Reprinted, with changes, by permission of the author and the Essen University Library, from *Information Superhighway: The Role of Librarians, Information Scientists, and Intermediaries*. 17th International Essen Symposium, October 24–27, 1995, pp. 47–60, edited by Ahmed H. Helal and Joachim W. Weiss. Copyright © 1995 Essen University Library, Germany.

Information seekers travel their own highways for the same reasons, to get to some place, and to achieve an ultimate objective for which information is crucial but nevertheless secondary. However, the information superhighway promises no possibility of privacy, and no ability to regulate the traffic interaction with others. What information users already face, and what they will increasingly face, is the problem of tremendous volumes of information—some of it crucial, some of it interesting, most of it irrelevant and annoying. At the same time, the amount of effort that end users will be able and willing to spend on the information process will continue to be very limited, because information remains a means to an end, and not an end in itself. And there are many ends.

Acting as screeners of this information, to make sure that the "good" material gets through and that the irrelevant never bothers the client, will require a new profession of information traffic policeman, individuals who can be respected and trusted. Someone will certainly fill that role. By preparation and experience, it should be librarians, but only if they stop focusing on sheer volume and start concentrating on what the client considers quality.

No one in this audience needs to be persuaded about the growth in information. That growth is demonstrated, and amply documented, both in the amount generated through research, through analysis, and through expository pronouncements, but perhaps even more through the ability, with the aid of technology, to disseminate this information far and wide. Nor do I need to persuade any of you that society has become increasingly aware of the importance of information. Ignorance has never been an acceptable rationale, and certainly it is widely held that it is the information power base on which decisions can be made that holds the key to success in the governmental, industrial, and academic sectors.

It is certainly also true that individuals, as they emerge in particular from our school systems, are far more comfortable in using computers, and are becoming literate in understanding how to make them work. In a relatively short twenty years, in my own university's academic program for the education of librarians, we have moved from the assumption that the arriving students knew little if anything, to the realization that while this is still true for some, most of our students not only feel comfortable using computers for what we call computer applications, but also in their application as writing machines. At this point perhaps 75 percent of the assignments that are turned in to my classes, none of which have to be done on computer printers, are done on computer printers.

However, the fact that individuals are no longer computer phobic and reluctant to use machines as that use is appropriate, does not necessarily mean that being able to sit down at a computer terminal is their greatest aspiration, and the one thing they want to do above all others. Drinking beer might rank higher, and you can use your own imagination to identify other priorities. For most of my students, and for my former students who are now professionals, and indeed for virtually all of my professional colleagues, the computer terminal is now a tool to be used when and as it is appropriate to do so. The emotional hatred and fear has disappeared, but it has not been replaced with a new value system that somehow ranks sitting at a terminal as a virtue in and of itself.

I believe that this pragmatic approach is completely appropriate. Technology is, and must always be, our servant, and never our master. Occasionally, technologists wonder why a certain technology, the elegance and power of which is certainly impressive, is not used to anywhere near the extent to which it appears to the technologists that it ought to be used. The answer is very simple. People use what they want to use, and they ignore what they want to ignore. The process is emotional far more than it is rational, but we always have the ability to justify our own decisions to our own satisfaction. Thus, for example, I continue to use both the computers and electric typewriters, and I use the latter almost exclusively for creating papers such as this one. Why? Because the great virtue in having this stored in a computer is the ability to move paragraphs and phrases around, to rewrite and edit online. I don't write that way. I write front to back, and I change very little. Given that, I find a typewriter keyboard much more forgiving for the heavy handed way in which I hammer keys. In other words, for me, for certain applications, the typewriter is easier, faster, and more comfortable. That doesn't make me a Luddite or an old barnacle. It simple makes me selfish. I do what works best, and most comfortably for me. I think it is important that all of us who are in the information business remember that our clients will always do what they think is best for them, regardless of what the so-called experts think and say.

I find that thought comfortable, and my recollections go back all the way to hearing a talk by Norbert Wiener, the father of cybernetics. Wiener was asked, perhaps by someone who had just seen the film *2001—A Space Odyssey*, in which a computer kills an astronaut, whether or not we had anything to fear from computers telling us what to do. Wiener was reassuring. He doubted that this could or would happen. However, if he feared that possibility, he would simply pull the plug out of the wall socket. I tell this story largely because I served for six years as a member of the Board of the American Federation of Information Processing Societies (AFIPS). AFIPS included representatives from the computer professionals—the Association of Computing Machinery (ACM), the Institute of Electrical and Electronic Engineers Computer Society (IEEE-CS), and the Data Processing Management Association (DPMA). It also contained representatives from a whole range of user societies—educators, historians, biologists, political scientists, and of course librarians. The key disputes, always argued pleasantly and courteously, centered on whether machines should adapt to people, or people to the efficiency of machines. I also recall virtually my first day as Executive Director of the NASA Scientific and Technical Information Facility, when I found editors trying to work with computer produced data that seemed to me to be very inconveniently arranged. I was assured that this was indeed the case, but that the material had to be arranged in that way. The programmer had told them so. I called the chief programmer, who fortunately reported to me (and there is a lesson in this on who should be whose boss), and told him that I had no interest in discussing programming intricacies. However, I was certainly sure that the information could be reformatted for the convenience of the people who had to use it. It might take more effort, it might even be inconvenient for the system, but it was certainly worth it.

These are old war stories, and I know that we have come a long way in developing what are now called "user-friendly" systems. Then why don't I always find them so friendly? "Invalid instruction" is a rude response made by a human being, it is an even more rude response made by an inanimate object. If that computer doesn't shape up, I may just pull the plug. Am I alone in thinking that the concept of voice mail, in which I am not greeted by a human being but by a series of push button options which can leave me hanging out to dry after I have already invested in making the connection, is for me a degradation of quality, even if perhaps the organization that installed the voice mail system thinks it saves it money? Perhaps it does, but it does so at my expense. Whenever the recorded menu includes the option of speaking to a representative, I always choose that option, because I almost always have more than one question. Don't they know that? Unfortunately, I am punished for daring to demand a human interaction by being forced to wait for 15 minutes while recorded music plays in my ear. Does anyone still want to suggest that this is an improvement?

Unfortunately, I sense a growing hypnotic preference for buzz phrases, and without attempting to be critical of the planners of this conference, certainly information superhighway is a buzz phrase. Just exactly what does it mean? And what does virtual library mean? Are any of us willing to demand that our planners stop talking gibberish and speak to us in plain terminology, or do we simply acknowledge our commitment to these great new virtues, without knowing what we are committing to? As I speak to various groups in the United States, I give them a list of terms that should always be included in all management communications. They are valuable because they sound so expert, and are yet so meaningless. Let me just share a part of that list with you. The terms include: balanced, compatible, functional, integrated, optimal, responsive, synchronous, systematized, total, user-friendly, virtual, forward looking, cost effective, flexible, mobile, needs oriented, broader mission, payoff, quality assurance, value driven and vision. I will offer a special prize to the first person who can use all of these terms in one sentence.

If we can ever dehypnotize ourselves from all of the verbiage which suggests that we are about to be launched into some sort of new and utopian age, perhaps we can recall why it is that individuals want information, assuming that they do want it. They want it so that they can do something else with it. That means, quite clearly, that they want what they think they need, and they don't want what gets in the way of their understanding and using what they really do want. Operations research people have known for some time that the ideal information collection is the one that contains everything I want, and nothing else. Large libraries are harder to use than small libraries, and their only possible virtue is in the assumption that, by being larger, they also contain more of the things I think I want to see. Librarians have seen this phenomenon many times when users take material out of the library to keep in their own offices. They do this, and of course I do it, too, because a library in my office that anticipates most of my questions is the perfect size, and the material is always available. And, of course, as we have worked with selective dissemination of information, SDI profile reactions have also told us this. Some users don't mind the garbage along with the good stuff.

Certainly newspaper readers have developed a great deal of tolerance for information that does not interest them. Other of our clients get very angry when we tell them anything at all that does not interest them. Different people have different reactions, but in general researchers have a greater tolerance than executives and decision makers. Can we design generic systems for the satisfaction of all of these people? Any reference librarian knows better.

However, there is a great danger in concepts of the information superhighway as it is being designed for us. There will be lots of information on our terminals, and it will get there very rapidly. However, the decision of what is transmitted is being left to the disseminator, and his reasons for generating something may not be the same as mine for receiving it. In fact, they are almost certain to be different. The great attraction of the invisible college, for those who were members, was that the information being transmitted was small in amount and important in content, because the quality control mechanism was membership in the invisible college. These were people who thought as we did, and we trusted them. If they betrayed that trust, we simply kicked them out of the club.

The problem of trying to protect ourselves against too much information goes back, in my own personal recollection, more than 30 years, and if getting too much information was a problem then, it is certainly a problem now. In the early 1960s my then IBM colleague Hans Peter Luhn proposed a concept which would allow scientists and other researchers to bypass the slow and strangling management approval process and communicate their ideas, research findings, and questions directly by computer to their colleagues in the far-flung international IBM empire. This was, of course, before online access, but the concept of electronic messaging was certainly workable. Management liked the idea, approved it, and it was implemented. Technically, it worked beautifully. However, it failed, and it failed because of people. It quickly became apparent that those with really good new ideas should not put semi-developed concepts into the network. At best they were deluged by questions and visitors that kept them from their work. At worst, their ideas were stolen. On the other hand, many people with absolutely nothing to report proceeded to report that nothing on a regular basis, sometimes daily. Posting messages became an exercise in self-promotion. Can we be sure that anything now dumped into our computer systems has passed some sort of value judgment? Who will impose that test? The originator? Management writers such as Tom Peters understand the problem. Peters has written, "A flood of information may be the enemy of intelligence." Are we communicating intelligence, or at least information for a purpose, or are we communicating a flood of information that we measure by the bucket?

I know from my own consulting assignments that library and information systems users are desperately afraid of drowning in information, even as they are afraid they might miss something if they turned off the spigot. As I tell information users in my consulting assignments that we plan to add more databases, for access on their own terminals, I can see terror in their eyes. They are not using what we give them now, simply because their own boss insists that they do something beside just access information. Their bosses want them to create something. Should any of this really be all that strange to us? Surely those of us who distribute material with routing lists know that some users simply cross their name off the list and pass it on, pretending they have read it so as not to offend us. I know I do it all the time with material I get from administrative offices or the school library.

Many librarians I know are still fascinated with the opportunity to provide our users with more information. This process began with the reporting of increased circulation as a virtue rather than an admission that we don't know what to give them so we give them more. Perhaps the simple reporting of the size of a library in terms of holdings, without any analysis of what needs we are meeting, is part of that same generalization. I know that many of our own bosses measure us by the statistics of circulation and holdings, but that is only because we have never given them anything better with which to measure our contribution.

Users, of course, treat a library or information system far differently. To use the term coined before World War I, they balkanize it. There is no library as such, there is only their library. If it contains what they want that is good, if not but it contains 2,000,000 other things, that is hardly a substitute. Nor is it a consolation to be told that we own it but you can't have it, for any of a number of reasons all of which make sense to us but don't matter at all to the client.

Information users, as I suggested earlier, have long learned to protect themselves, and to make the system work for them. They do this by pretending they have read it, or pretending that they don't need it. What they want is not more information, but more useful information out of a pile of certainly no more and hopefully less information. And they certainly don't want to spend any more time on the information process. Nor do they appreciate being told by a machine that they are stupid.

I have no real sense that the designers of the information superhighways, who certainly do understand machines and what they can do, understand people anywhere nearly as well as we do. And yet, even as we do presumably understand the problem and what ought to happen to be able to solve it, we stubbornly cling to obsolete and outmoded concepts. We insist that information users, certainly students but indeed also everyone else, not only ought to do their own information work but that they ought to want to. In doing this, we place a moral value system on the entire process that is totally irrelevant to the issue. I will give you further examples of this, but let me simply state at this point that there are conflicting values between wanting to be teachers, to be moralist preachers, or information professionals who earn their keep and the undying gratitude of others for doing for them what they do badly, and what they don't really want to do in the first place.

It is time for examples. At one major Canadian university at which I have taught, the library embarked on a massive program of faculty end user training, so that the faculty would be able to find what they needed, in their own offices, without the need to come to the library. I understand that many faculty don't want to come to the library, and just perhaps they even enjoy spending at least some time in their own offices (depending perhaps on how comfortable the furniture is), but what makes us think that they really want to have the opportunity to sit at terminals receiving error messages? Certainly, they would like the ability to do specific, direct, and simple item lookups, or even to order a book from the library, but that is very different from a complex and time consuming search the outcome of which is quite problematical.

When there is fear that there is something we don't really know how to do, the preferred reaction is to insist that we don't need to do it. (Don't forget, I teach management). Of close to 1,000 faculty members offered the opportunity for end user search training, perhaps 25 responded. Six took the course, the others sent their graduate assistants or their secretaries. And that is the elite group which responded at all. Don't think of them unkindly. They have a lot of things to do for which they will get measured. If necessary, information searching is something about which they can pretend to themselves, and to others.

If there are clear indications of an opportunity and a need, it continues to puzzle me that librarians are so reluctant to assume that role. If we try to assess reference service in an academic library in terms of any sort of a model of number of clients per reference librarian established in a corporate environment, we find that reference service has a very low priority and a low visibility. In public libraries, at least in the United States, reference service is just about the first thing to be eliminated, in the insistence that above all else the doors must be kept open. To do what? And how do these strategies and perceptions of the library as a place for low-key self service relate to the new parameters of rapid and up-to-date information, in huge quantities, brought to us over what is called the information superhighway?

We already have a superhighway of sorts, in the identification of options for acquiring material from other institutions, as their holdings are displayed for us in online systems. That electronic superhighway leads to a rutted two lane dirt road called document delivery. We still talk here in terms of weeks and sometimes months, to deliver what we have identified and located in a fraction of the time. And yet, of course, the chain is only as strong as its weakest link.

In talks at this symposium during earlier years, and in a large number of articles, prominent academic library administrators have described their vision of what is called the virtual library. It involves transferring from the library to the terminal in the user's office direct access to all (or at least much) of the information that is contained in the library. All of that material? And without any filtering? Are we certain that this is what our clients want or prefer? Have we asked them, and described alternatives? Or is this, as I fear, simply an attempt to hide information costs by distributing them to the accounts of end users? The result may well be a greater overall cost, but the library will not be blamed. Is this good for the end user? Is it good for the organization that supports both of us? Is it even good for us, politically? Certainly I know enough about politics to understand it is unwise to give away your power base. Money represents one of the most obvious of power bases. If the end user wants something, is it not wiser as well as cheaper overall to have him come to the librarian, who controls the money and makes the decisions?

In my management class I use the example of this proposed virtual library scenario in talking about library unionization. The ultimate power of any union in its negotiation with management is the threat of a strike, and the presumed fear that the withholding of services generates in the minds of those who are being asked to fund us. In a so-called virtual library, with all material deposited directly to the user's terminal, if the librarians go out on strike will anyone even notice?

However, the larger question than the political implications for librarians in their decision of whether they want to be information intermediaries, or simply road sign painters, is still the preference of the end user. There is a growing industrial endeavor which recognizes the need for information intermediaries, and in an article in the British journal *The Economist* in July 1993 this enterprise was given an intriguing name. It was called *meatware*, and the term can be understood directly, in relation to the other two information service terms, hardware and software. Hardware and software supply us with tools, but those tools suggest that we then use them. For a whole variety of reasons already suggested, some individuals would prefer that somebody else uses those tools as their surrogates. This then is the meatware, the human bodies that complement the hardware and the software. The premise of meatware specialists is so attractive that, according to the journal article, a thriving industry of selling such interpretive services is already in existence. I have talked to users in a number of organizations that have contracts with meatware supplying organizations, and the response is mixed. They certainly appreciate the service, without which they would be lost. At the same time, they wish that the meatware specialists, with whom they communicate via telephone, fax, or e-mail, had a better understanding of what the clients were doing and why they were doing it. This obviously suggests that the far better alternative would be an in-house information intermediary. However, that is rarely mentioned in personal conversations unless I bring it up first, and it is not mentioned at all in the article in *The Economist*. The article implies that meatware specialists are the only alternative to nothing at all. Whatever happened to reference librarians?

Part of an understanding of why this happens comes from a recognition of the business reality that an appearance of economy is more important than economy itself. Thus government leaders point proudly to the fact that there are now 5,000 or 10,000 fewer employees in an agency, and the same justifications are used in the corporate and academic sectors. What is not mentioned is that these 5,000 former employees have now been replaced by service contracts that cost twice as much. The fact that the appearance of economy is sometimes considered more important than economy itself is sometimes encapsulated in the nonsensical yet true statement "we are going to have economy no matter what it costs."

Nevertheless, in all of this playing of games to hide and disguise costs, we should be able to count on the accountants to tell the truth, and I have suggested on many occasions that the financial people are, at least, potentially, the library's greatest allies. Because we should certainly be able to demonstrate, without half trying, that qualified information intermediaries are far more cost effective than any alternative. That requires, first of all, that we speak the truth, and that we demand that others speak the truth. When an organization fervently pledges its commitment to the information superhighway and then cuts its library budget, it is committing the ultimate act of folly. Has anyone mentioned the fact that hooking onto the information superhighway will be very expensive, not only in hardware and software costs, but particularly in end user time commitments? It may be that users will spend so much time becoming informed, given the tremendous amount of information that somebody who thinks it is valuable will now send them electronically, that they will have no time to do anything with what they have learned. I see nothing in the description of technological options that will act as any sort of form of birth control for the information generators and transmitters. The reliance on meatware specialists is one alternative, but it would seem to me that there are better ones already in place.

At last year's conference a vendor described a software package aimed at making the work of doctors searching the National Library of Medicine database easier, and reported glowingly that physicians reported in large numbers that this tool had helped them get exactly what they needed. However, how do they know what they could have had, and whether or not there would have been better alternatives?

When I speak to medical librarians I ask for a show of hands of those who think that doctors perform online searches three times as well, or three times as rapidly, or with only a third the computer access costs. There are no hands raised. I use the concept of three times the quality or three times the economy because it is fairly obvious that, conservatively, doctors earn three times as much as librarians, and their time is therefore three times as valuable. If their own access to databases does not meet that test, then it seems obvious, at least to me, that they shouldn't be wasting time and money doing detailed searches at all. They should be doing what they do best, and allow medical information intermediaries, often still called medical librarians, to do this work. Ah, I am reminded, many doctors do not have access to medical librarians. However, that is an easy problem to solve. All we need is more medical librarians, and we must hook them to physicians through terminal access systems we already have. The result is both an improvement in quality and in cost effectiveness. The problem is that some would rather hide the cost, or pretend it does not exist.

As we move toward implementation of the information superhighway, which largely means an uncontrolled flood of information rolling down on us from the hillside—primarily because nobody has made the generator responsible for what he takes the opportunity to tell me, it is not difficult to predict that application of the system will be imperfect. We already know that the ultimate user will do what is most convenient and most comfortable for him. He always has, and he will continue to. In dealing with information, we are not dealing with exact phenomena that can be measured. Just as the user is free to cross his name off a routing list and pretend that he has read the material, he is free to delete all of his computer messages if he has a headache, or feels particularly swamped. As the users of Hans Peter Luhn's system at IBM learned very quickly, the odds of finding something useful is not in their favor. What they will do then will be totally selfish, and oriented toward their own survival. However, that is not necessarily good for the organization that has paid both his salary, and for the computer access hardware and software.

When I return to my office from having been away for a period of about two weeks, I will find on my e-mail system perhaps 250 messages. They will not be rank ordered in any way, they will be chronological. Of these, I guess that perhaps 10 to 15 will be of significance to me, another 10 to 15 will contain interesting but not crucial tidbits of gossip and speculation. The remaining 90 percent will be, for me at least, the garbage that somebody else dumped on me, for a variety of reasons about which I can only speculate.

I am probably not ready, as Norbert Wiener suggested, to pull the plug, but I will be sorely tempted. As I move toward a formal retirement in which my value system becomes much more selfish, I may unhook the machine completely. Those who reach me by phone, fax, or letter, must make an effort and pay a price, and perhaps that is a good control process, after all. However, what I would really like is an individual, in whom I had absolute trust (neither a secretary or a meatware specialist 1,000 miles away whom I have never met), who will tell me that, based on a complete knowledge of what I am working on and what I care about, he or she has deleted 225 of the 250 messages, and left me with the 25 important ones. That, of course, is what SDI systems have always done. There is nothing new in this.

The development of information intermediaries not only meets a crucial need, it also fits in completely with the shift, as countries develop, from a production and agricultural economy to a service economy. We want people to help us to cope with the flood of information that the hardware and software specialists, because of their brilliance and energy in doing what they do best, are in the process of unleashing on us. We want this intermediation service, we need this intermediation service, and we will be certainly prepared—as a nation, a corporation, a university—to pay for it. Not only because the alternatives are more expensive, but also because they are more uncomfortable. Hardly any talk of mine is complete without a quote from Peter Drucker. "In the provision of a product or service that individuals consider essential to their own value system, cost becomes irrelevant." Both librarians and publishers learned that as early as the 1970s, when studies which Bernard Fry and I undertook for the National Science Foundation showed clearly that the average price of canceled journals was considerably smaller than the average cost of retained journals. When it comes to a contest between money and value, at least in the professional setting, value will win every time. And certainly we should be pleased at this, but only if we know how to use that piece of knowledge.

If there is going to be a large profession of meatware specialists—of information intermediaries, as I am certain there is going to be, who will these people be? Certainly success here ought to be based on subject understanding, on an understanding of the user and his preference for working, and on an understanding of the technology and the options it presents. However, it requires more than that. It requires political and marketing skills; it requires an ability to talk not about absolute costs but about alternative costs and the implications of various options for the prediction of success of the larger enterprise. Perhaps most of all, it requires the ability to generate confidence in our own skills and our own abilities, and getting others to believe it must start with believing it ourselves. That may be the greatest challenge of all.

Nothing I have said should be taken in any sense to be the suggestion of a Luddite attitude. I am neither for nor against technology, because technology is a tool, which is sometimes useful and beneficial, and sometimes not. Certainly the potential for benefit is overwhelming, and indeed it can be argued that without the judicious evaluation of the technological options, and the adapting of those that meet our needs, we will accomplish nothing at all. The question whether we use technology is not germane at this stage. The question of how we use it, how we manage it and control it, and how we make it serve us, is very much germane.

The hardware and software specialists who design new products and services for us will certainly continue to do a superb job—there are enough of them. At the same time, I think that we can continue to assume that they will deal in the efficiency of the system, and that is measured quantitatively. We, by contrast, are the intermediaries for end users whose interest has always been qualitative, and never quantitative. And that describes our job, and explains why it is so crucial.

Unity Through Diversity: We Need to Define Some Terms

Over the past several years, but increasingly over the past several months, we have seen articles, conferences, and workshops devoted to the need for diversity. Frequently it is stressed that diversity will have a strengthening effect for all of us and that it will lead to unity. It is the term unity that I have seen no attempt to define; it is essential that we come to some sort of consensus with regard to what we mean.

Support of diversity for me is a no-brainer. I am a direct beneficiary of the diversity that has always characterized this country, although when we now speak of diversity we appear to have an agenda that defines the term narrowly rather than broadly. Given my own background of fleeing to the United States from Austria at the age of 11, knowing no English, and being a victim of direct religious persecution, I am not only proof that diversity works—certainly not perfectly but at least better than in any other country I know—I also qualify as a minority in every library category save race.

In addition, I have been told by many that my approach to my profession is neither traditional nor comfortable, and I take that as a compliment to my own role in introducing diversity into the workplace. Readers of this column already know that for me diversity includes not only differences of cultural and racial background but also the diversity brought by those who are simply smarter or more courageous. When the argument is raised by some that women will be different managers, and perhaps even better managers, that becomes part of the same continuum.

Reprinted, with changes, by permission of the author and *Library Journal* 120, no. 19 (November 15, 1995): 43–44. Copyright © 1995 by Cahners Business Information.

Warning: Integration

Our national dependence on diversity is certainly not new. As we now acknowledge, perhaps with 20-20 hindsight, essential contributions have been made to this country by the integration into our cultural fabric of successive waves of immigrants as well as African Americans and Native Americans. Why would growth through diversity ever be thought to end?

I have used the term integration, which sends up warning signals. It didn't used to. Integration into a totally color-blind school system was the objective of *Brown v. Board of Education*. Along with a lot of other people I fought for integration in the Texas of the mid-1950s. I fought these battles because I believed then, and continue to believe, that everyone must be afforded opportunities in housing, education, jobs, and respect, based on a society that measures only individual merit.

As an avid student of U.S. history (why would I want to study the Hapsburg dynasty?), I learned that what allowed this country to succeed more than any other nation for over 100 years was that we built a new and different nation through all of our contributions. I thought that melting pot was a very good, non-pejorative term because just by being there I changed the makeup of what the pot contained. So did everyone else. I am now reminded that melting pot is no longer an acceptable term, and even integration is out of fashion. Do we want to go back to separate but equal? We should certainly remember from the 1960s that separate can never be equal.

Differences As an Additive

We can and should stress our differences as an additive but never as an end result because that leads only to suspicion and hatred. We tend to mistrust the people with whom we never have any contact. Of course, all of us bring different backgrounds and that explains the intense loyalty we feel toward the country of our ancestors, even if we have never been there.

However, that allegiance is more sentimental than substantive, precisely because people have no basis for any sort of substantive understanding of this "romantic" history, which upon close scrutiny is probably not romantic at all. It is probably because I lived through this that my own priorities are now so fiercely American. Those who did not achieve their nationality easily often appreciate it more.

Why would I not expect the same sense of passionate loyalty from Mexicans and Southeast Asians who came a few decades after I came from Europe? Or from blacks, forced to fight so hard for what many whites were unwilling to give them as an automatic right? I stubbornly claim to understand these issues of diversity far better than those other Americans who are members of the British-based WASP majority, no longer a majority in any case. Europe is itself very diverse, with lots of national superstitions and hatreds, as is Africa.

What Do We Mean by Unity?

If I can dispose quite comfortably of diversity as a problem and see it as a strength, I am left with the question of what we mean by unity, what is it that defines us as Americans as contrasted to any other nationality? I tried to raise that issue most specifically in my keynote address to the 1991 Washington State Library Association conference in Spokane. To a conference theme that celebrated diversity without really examining what it was or was not (as I believe so many of today's speeches and articles continue to do), I argued that diversity could not be allowed to evolve into fragmentation, that it required us to build a new and stronger whole out of many parts.

In my talk I referred to the comments of Jesse Jackson, who had noted at the 1988 Democratic National Convention that America is not a blanket woven from one thread, one color, or one cloth. He was absolutely correct, but if you want to end up with a blanket for warmth and protection it must be woven, and weaving requires a good deal of discipline. Loose threads, no matter how colorful, will not keep out the cold.

Today's More Complex Issues

What then is the definition of the unity that is always used in conjunction with diversity but which authors and speakers never get around to? What is it that makes us all uniquely and specifically Americans, regardless of our background? I can answer the question for myself, because when I now visit Vienna I come as an American tourist who can still speak the language but whom no one would take for Austrian.

Perhaps the issues have become more complex since I arrived in 1938, and they have certainly become more convoluted and more selfishly contrived. Yet one of the things I understood immediately as an 11-year-old who spoke no English is that I had to learn it fast if I had any hope of becoming a part of a "unity" I understood even if I couldn't define it. I had to learn it because I planned to live here. I understood that one speaks English in New York as one speaks German in Vienna and Spanish in Mexico City, and even now I always try my best when I get there.

Favoring Bilingualism?

I am thoroughly in favor of bilingualism and multilingualism. However, both mean more than one, and here "one" must be English. I also understood back then, as I later learned, what Berlitz has always understood, that the only way to really learn a language is by total immersion, as you study math, history, and social studies, as you buy groceries and play on the playgrounds.

We all have studied "foreign" languages one period a day in school, and so we know what a contrived and exotic exercise that is. To really speak a language you must think in that language, particularly in understanding the idioms. In the 1930s nobody offered me an easy choice, and although that made it more difficult, I am deeply grateful. I learned English because I understood that this was now my first and primary task. My parents learned English because their 11-year-old son refused to answer when addressed German. Eventually they came to appreciate it. I get angry at the cruelties we perpetuate economically on individuals whom we allow, after 30 years of living in this country, to get away with not learning proper English. Proper English, without the emotional garbage, is simply the English spoken and written in the business and academic communities at any given time. Waiving that requirement simply sentences the victims to a lifetime of hardship and low-paying jobs in hotels and restaurants. The assumption that somehow they can't learn is the ultimate putdown.

Libraries Promoting Unity

Libraries can play a significant leadership role in promoting unity in the way they define their own objectives, measurable targets, and rewards. However, libraries can also play a significant role in weaving the blanket of U.S. nationality of which Jesse Jackson spoke so eloquently. Unless we can define and stress what unites us as Americans, we run the risk of becoming separate enclaves of individuals who never even speak to those from outside their narrow little groups. Do I see this as a potential danger for our national future, as well as a potential opportunity? Indeed I do. I see an emphasis on groups based solely on commonality of race or national origin and nothing else. That is not unity, it is fragmentation.

As *de jure* segregation was always immoral and, finally, illegal, self-segregation is sad because it is so pointless and counterproductive. For libraries, if diversity leads to unity it must ultimately be reflected in an increased quality. I have long been selfish enough to want for myself the best reference librarian I could find, and if that individual chooses to wear a dashiki, a turban, or a yarmulke, it is irrelevant to me.

Despite the hardship in learning to write and speak English, librarians from countries as dissimilar as Germany and Japan have made the effort, because the reality is that English has become the world's lingua franca. When German and Japanese computer scientists meet in Stuttgart or in Tokyo, they converse in English. If we routinely expect an understanding of English from others, is it unreasonable to expect it from ourselves?

The Search for Terminology

In the search for a terminology that does not offend even at the cost of becoming fuzzier, it is now fashionable to argue that we have replaced the melting pot with a salad bowl. I understand enough about metallurgy to remember that iron is strong but brittle and to produce a more useful metal we need to blend in other elements and alloys. That to me is what made the melting pot so easy to understand and explain. What, by contrast, is the tensile strength of a mixed salad and what can you erect from a pile of lettuce, tomatoes, and cucumbers?

In any case, if unity is to be a tangible outcome and not just a glib slogan, we must agree to tests for measuring it. If we don't do this, we will be forced to repeat the history of countless countries, including the Roman Empire, whose inevitable destruction began when it split into two empires, one east and one west, and when it was no longer possible to remember what it was that made Roman citizenship prized and unique.

Blaming the Victim— The Academic Library Version

I have visited the OK Corral University Library in this column on two previous occasions (September 1, 1987, November 15, 1989) to comment on our inability to exert any leverage on the process of determining the relationship between the publishers of scholarly journals and the research libraries that are their primary customers. I have noted in these writings and in other articles and speeches, some of them to publisher groups, that I perceive the primary reason for this lack of success to be the publisher perception that librarians are not customers but simply purchasing agents who act at the direction of the "real" customers. Publisher prices will increase by large amounts each year, and whether or not the increase is a catastrophic 22 percent or a more "modest" 8 percent is still a decision in which we are not allowed to participate. All of this happens while economists tell us that inflation has slowed to 1 percent and less. That affects our salaries and our budgets but not journal prices. Why not?

This leads to other, rather strange side effects. Publishers like to blame the price increase on growth in the number of pages, forgetting that we never asked them to print more pages. They also tie the price of overseas journals to the conversion rate of the U.S. dollar. Thus, a recent notice from a publisher advisory service, while certainly intending to be helpful, produced some rather strange language. Dollar prices *might* decrease if the dollar strengthened; they *would* increase if the dollar weakened. Heads I win, tails I'm not sure what happens. The

---

This article was written with the intent to publish it as a "White Paper" in *Library Journal* in 1995. It was never submitted for publication because of space limitations.

extent to which librarians have bought into this rationale was expressed by a recommendation passed by the ALA Council that urged the federal government to keep the dollar from weakening because of the difficulties this caused us in buying overseas journals. Fortunately, nobody in Washington noticed. Dollar pricing policy results from much larger strategies than this. A weak dollar, which we once sought as a matter of national policy, although now we prefer a stable dollar, was designed to assist U.S. exports and to curtail U.S. imports by making import prices less attractive. This should lead to a narrowing of the trade deficit. The strategy worked only in part because those who sell to Americans, and particularly Japanese auto makers, responded by either lowering their preconverted prices or by shifting production to this country. In any case, they at least recognized that a weakened dollar was not the customer's problem but the vendor's. International publishers continue to see this as our problem. Some of them have even expressed sympathy for *our* dilemma, and an article in LOGOS (vol. 1, no. 4, 1990) congratulated us on our ability to keep finding additional funds with which to match price increases.

In earlier writings I also noted that there appeared to be little help and support for us from either university administrators or the research faculty who wear the multiple hats of author, editor, reviewer, reader, and academic credit dispenser. I opined that not much would happen until one or both of these university groups began to recognize their own need to deal with this problem. At that point it would be solved quickly enough. This has not happened, at least in part because of our inability or unwillingness to get their attention through the fairly traditional even if risky management tactic of exacerbating rather than ameliorating a crisis. There may be several reasons for this. It is possible that some librarians really believe that their collections are more important than they are, even in the face of resource sharing and bibliographic network developments. After all, the statement "We will be remembered not for the service we gave but for the collection we left behind us" still hangs over us like a dark cloud, but at least that pronouncement preceded and could not anticipate some of the other options we now have. It is also possible that some academic library administrators perceive taking a stand on this issue as a likely way to get fired. They may be right, and in my management seminars I stress that I cannot make strategy alternative decisions for the student, only point out the implications of the options. It bothers me when some librarians stoop to such tactics as urging faculty to "adopt a journal," particularly when I notice with horror that the tactic might work. It is reported that Cornell mathematics professors have started teaching extra courses, donating their earnings to the library materials budget for mathematics journals. I can only wonder why anyone, particularly mathematicians, would accept the premise of price increases well beyond the range of inflation so uncritically, and rush to assuage it. Did we teach the professors this, or did they think of it all by themselves? If I were to demean myself to the point of asking individual faculty to think of the library as a worthwhile charity, it might as well be to enhance my small salary.

What has happened recently in a number of major research libraries confirms our worst nightmares—at least mine and hopefully yours. Universities in both the public and private sectors have been confronted by enormous economic problems, and solutions both real and imaginary (such as closing library schools) abound. Nevertheless, the problems are real enough. Among the recently most favored tactics is that of splitting the library budget into component parts, and mandating an increase for the materials budget, while freezing or decreasing everything else, including professional positions, clerical support, student labor, automation, travel, client services, etc.

As a long-time manager, I am outraged. This is a direct intrusion into the authority of any manager to establish priorities within an overall framework. The essence of management is the ability to make decisions, and if that authority is taken away, we really become purchasing agents, as some publishers now perceive us. The power of any position is not in total spending. The Treasurer of the United States has her signature on every bill of currency but nobody knows her name. Power comes from *discretionary* spending, and I have thought that all managers have always understood this. Is a good salary and a nice office without decision authority worth it? I can only answer the question for myself. Other library directors might want to modify the old Johnny Paycheck hit record into "Take This Budget and Shove It!"

However, quite aside from the issues of power and turf I am always so fond of stressing, the strategy of giving the materials budget primacy simply because the faculty said so is a stupid strategy from the overall interests of the institution, and while perhaps faculty don't know that, we certainly should. What then is our responsibility for telling them? There are many reasons, but as usual in this column I am running out of space, so I will restrict myself to three examples.

1. Simply scraping up funds to meet ever-increasing publisher prices does not provide any solution to this problem; it simply assures its perpetuation. Why would anyone want to tamper with a mechanism that works so well? Would it not be simpler, instead of waiting for publisher invoices, to inform them that we are prepared to offer a 3 percent increase for all of our present periodical subscriptions from each of them, and that we assume they will find this acceptable? Three percent is fair, and is often more than we get. If they don't agree, and since we have plenty of journals on our waiting list, we will automatically cancel all journals with an increase greater than 3 percent. There might be some temporary inconvenience for faculty, but only until authors refigured what journals to now select for their article submittals. Even this need not happen if publishers think we're not bluffing. And, of course, faculty must understand why they need to be supportive, presumably because the president urged them to be for the sake of the school.

2. Shifting funds out of professional activities, out of staff, automation, and networking helps destroy what may be the only meaningful opportunity for communication, cooperation, and resource sharing. All of these have start-up and operating costs, but they are not the bottomless pits of the acquisitions budget. It might even be better to shift money from the acquisitions budget into

the exploration of the newly emerging potential alternatives for getting what we don't own, and in that case the 3 percent increase offer to the publishers might have to be withdrawn. Our own research has long told us that just because we own something doesn't give the next requester a great shot at getting it within a reasonable time frame. In other words, ownership means only that, and not access. I know that faculty and administrators don't read our literature, but don't even we remember?

3. Cuts in the student staffing budget appear the most insane strategy of all. Student labor in colleges and universities is cheap, and it is plentiful. It is in the school's interest to provide job opportunities for students and student spouses. When the student labor source in academic libraries is constrained or strangled, either that work now gets done by others who then don't do what they are supposed to do, or mechanisms for improving or facilitating the ability to use this expensive collection, sometimes simply by making photocopies and putting them into the campus mail, are ignored or lost. Would any department store spend a great deal of money on merchandise, without caring about customer access and the ability to find a sales clerk?

I have the idea for a screenplay, entitled "It's a Wonderful Academic Library." In the final scene, to background music from the last movement of Mahler's Third Symphony, the university president apologizes abjectly to the library director for lack of vision, lack of trust, and interferences, and swears to the dawning of a new era.

She or he (that casting option is open although the librarian's role is reserved for Glenn Close if she wants it), promises that never again will administration or faculty meddle with regard to library decisions they are unqualified to make, and that henceforth the professionals in the library will be accorded exactly the same courtesy and freedom in establishing priorities already in place for any of the academic disciplines. There are parts in this movie for both Jimmy Stewart and Donna Reed, although box office pressures demand they be supporting roles. Unfortunately, Frank Capra, who told us that in the absence of faith and hope terrible things like becoming a librarian could happen to you (it's not clear from the flashback in *It's a Wonderful Life* where Donna Reed earned her MLS), is no longer available to atone by directing.

There is a glimmer of hope. Academic library directors like Maureen Pastine at SMU have persuaded faculty groups to endorse the premise that not only will the library cancel the journals with the most obscene price increases—regardless of rationale or even of claimed quality—but also that the faculty pledge not to submit articles to such journals for publication. I can promise you that this last threat is the most serious for greedy publishers of all. They can survive for a while with a decline in library subscriptions. They can't survive for more than an issue or two without authors. Let's hope that the strategy catches on. It is the authors/readers who control how responsible publishers will be in their pricing, and blaming librarians becomes the most bitter irony of all. How long before we tell them off?

The Perilous But Also Opportune Future for Special Librarians

What follows is primarily intended for special librarians, although others—particularly academic librarians—may find it appropriate. I have worked as a special librarian and then taught special and other librarians for all of my adult life. It is my view that the present strategies of this profession, and indeed of the many academic librarians who work in cost accountability environments no longer limited to corporations, are based on three disastrously wrong assumptions.

1. "Special Librarians and the Developers of Databases and Hardware Are Always on the Same Side." There is certainly room for cooperation. Developers should understand, however, that librarians could be important customers who should be listened to once in a while. Developers seem to be deluded into thinking that because end users could do their own searching, it suggests that librarians are no longer necessary. We have seen employers pick up on that suggestion by downsizing their libraries in favor of end user searching. The strategy does not surprise me. What does surprise me are the many articles in our own journals that stress the "virtues" of end user searching. I understand why this might be attractive for the hardware and database people. End users search more expensively and sloppily. But why is this attractive for us?

Reprinted, with changes, by permission of the author and *Library Journal* 121, no. 1 (January 1996): 59–60. Copyright © 1996 by Cahners Business Information.

"Searching" for Cost Savings

2. "End User Searching Will Be Cost Effective for the Employer, and Will Even Save Money." Some employers, but certainly astute writers such as Tom Peters, Mike Royko, Dave Barry, and Russell Baker, have begun to realize the absurdity of the premise that taking people away from their work and placing them at search terminals will save money. Other employers will catch on eventually, but by then it may be too late for us because, as the aboriginal information workers, we will be gone.

It is certainly possible, through the powerful terminal in everyone's office, to access valuable information, assuming that people know how to do it and, more importantly, want to do it. It is likely that they will drown in obsolete and useless information, particularly if end users don't know how to filter out the garbage.

It is even more likely that the terminal will provide a superb opportunity to do things other than search for information. Windows 95 has already generated ads about how many more games we and our children will be able to play, and a Hewlett-Packard TV ad shows a presumably hard-working executive really playing a simulated round of golf. Employers, who have even been suspicious of the time their staffs spend in the library, at least in the corporate world, are not going to ignore that potentially far greater time waster. However, that realization may come too late to help us.

Parenting the Parents

3. "There Is a Future in Becoming the Parent Organization's Information Advisors and Information Consultants." That sounds so attractive that even research librarians, and public librarians who constantly urge their users to do their own information searching, find it attractive. However, that dream has no chance of coming true. Few think of librarians as professional colleagues in either industry or academia. Any opportunity for claiming a role as advisors that might have existed has been destroyed by the present and continuing wave of downsizing, a process that stresses keeping people only to the extent they can prove they contribute directly to the objectives of the parent organization.

Middle manager, facilitator, advisor, and consultant are job titles that are highly suspect, and individuals unlucky enough to hold these titles are being terminated as this is being read. There might be an occasional reason to contract with an outside consultant, but that is a short-term and controlled investment; consultants are never put on the payroll. Indeed, we have seen cases where terminated librarians have been hired as contract or temporary employees, without security benefits.

Our strategy for dealing with this phenomenon ought to be obvious, but we are ignoring the opportunity here. Professional conference programs now deal with how to maintain the quality of a downsized library, in corporate as well as in academic and public settings. All that does is protect and validate an incorrect management decision.

In the recognition that downsizing is now a continuous process, the strategy ought to be an unsolicited approach to top management to point out the dangers and expenses of unmonitored searching or game-playing by untrained and money-wasting end users. Library managers need to stress that, if the objective is indeed downsizing, it can be most effectively accomplished by increasing the number and authority of librarian information intermediaries and decreasing the number of end users.

Death and Downsizing

In March 1995, Baker & McKenzie, which claims to be the world's largest law firm, closed the library of its Chicago office, laying off all staff. It is not the first time well-established corporate libraries have simply disappeared at the stroke of a management pen. I congratulate the Chicago law librarians who have refused to provide any sort of help for this incredibly short-sighted organization.

However, this experience raises a larger question. The decision to close the library was based on the recommendation of a management consultant firm, a company that employs many professional librarians. What is the future for the librarians in this consulting firm? What sort of image have they been creating for their own clients, clients who presumably include the consultants who suggested that a law library was unnecessary? Most directly, have these librarians sufficiently recognized the enemy to accuse these consultants of incompetence and to demand that they be fired?

Management by Objectives

The emerging management tactics that stress direct contribution to overall objectives should suit us beautifully. After all, we contribute a great deal, and we contribute it cost effectively. We are a tremendous bargain. Perhaps if Baker & McKenzie is really interested in saving money it might examine its need for as many lawyers to do what librarians can do better, its need to accept consultants' bad advice, and its need for administrators who hire such consultants and are swayed by them.

These points suggest the futility of what has long been the justification by special librarians of "proving" their value to the users of these services in lower ranks of the organization, with whom they have really always competed but with whom they particularly compete in the 1990s, in clamoring for scarce support and funding.

A variety of studies have sought to "prove" the value of the information provided by asking end users what the help proffered to them might be worth in dollar amounts, and sometimes the responses are flattering.

However, corporate financial officers are not as easily seduced by these honeyed words as we are, because clients never volunteer to give up any of their own budget in recognition of the value of the library. In other words, the "savings" are based on the bogus notion that in the absence of a library the end user's budget would have been increased, and certainly financial officers know this is nonsense. If users were forced to choose between keeping librarians and keeping their own subordinates or even themselves, we know what the answer would be.

What special librarians need to understand is that their clients are not only their customers but also their rivals, and academic librarians need to understand this as well. It is this reality of management decision mechanisms that argues that, rather than make our clients independent of us, we need to make them totally dependent on us. It is this train of thought that then leads to the understandable conclusion that with more and better librarians the employer should need fewer and more expensive end users. It is a premise that obviously the Baker & McKenzie corporate management never considered. Its problem is not too many librarians but probably too few librarians and too many lawyers working as second-rate librarians.

Closing Arguments

In closing, I'll pose two questions to my readers.

1. Which do you think is greater, the number of computer and technology specialists invited to speak at meetings of professional library associations, or the number of librarians invited to impart their knowledge at meetings of computer specialists?

2. Which do you think is greater, the number of doctors invited to lecture to medical librarians, or the number of medical librarians invited to speak at the meetings of the American Medical Association?

Special librarians who attended the 1995 conference in Montreal will have an advantage in answering my two questions. That conference included a program discussing how we might get along better with the computer systems people. Does anyone think that computer systems people, or teachers, or professors, purchasing agents, or government officials have meetings on how to get along better with librarians?

The strategies espoused in our literature have an incessant drumbeat in urging us to get along better with end users and fellow service professionals. However, when we fail to recognize that these individuals are our rivals in seeking the support of a higher management looking for ways to cut staff and cost, then those strategies become at best simplistic.

When we depend on end users, and not on our professionally qualified arguments, to make the case for our "value" to top management in industry and universities, but most particularly when we train end users so they can presumably function without us, those strategies are disastrous. Our bosses will love us when we save them money and make them look good. End users will love us when they understand that without us they will probably fail and be fired. And only then.

Managing Within Change—Or Helping to Shape the Management of Change

The only thing which can be said about change is that it will occur. Indeed, it is important that this happens. While not all change is for good, all good comes from change. Theological library managers, like all managers, must understand that there is no benefit to be gained from the status quo. Doing things this year as you did them last year is certain to make your library worse, even if somehow you managed to renew all of the periodical subscriptions. The reason your library will be worse is that the environment in which your library functions will have changed, and at least in some ways, improved. Staying the same is the same thing as standing still in a race.

The forces of change can be assumed, from a study completed by the Eli Lilly Endowment, to take two directions:

1. There will be greater management accountability in all institutions, not just corporate ones. The process will most certainly extend to academia, and even to academic theological institutions. We see examples of this greater management concern in downsizing, either through the direct process of terminating employees, or in what is considered the less cruel approach of waiting for an employee to retire, leave, or die, and then eliminating the position as an "opportunity." While this approach is considered more gentle, from a management standpoint it is really worse. It makes all change the result of happenstance, and permits no planning whatsoever. The other impact of greater management accountability

Talk presented at a meeting of the American Theological Library Association, Chicago, Illinois, January 18, 1996.

leads to the demand that each unit, and each employee, prove what contribution is being made to the parent organization's objectives. Some librarians are terrified at even thinking about this process, but it really represents an opportunity.

2. The second dramatic change comes, not surprisingly, from the growth of technology, which will have a significant impact, hopefully for the good, but certainly not automatically so. The basic question with which all of us, including you theological librarians, must deal is the one of whether technology will enable you to expand and then fulfill your own plans and objectives, or whether technology, as the master rather than the servant, will determine what you do simply because you, or more likely your management or clients, see that changes are possible, and therefore automatically assume that they are desirable.

These changes, in both of the areas mentioned, may come more slowly to academic institutions than the corporate for-profit sector, but they will most certainly come, at least in time, to theological libraries as well. You may have a little more time to prepare, but your scenario is really no different from that of any other library, and your patrons are really not different from other institutions. What do we want to do? How can we do it most cost effectively? Who is best qualified to do what needs to be done? These are still the operational questions.

We have certainly been deluged with writings about the importance of information, and the impact of these opportunities on our value systems. Daniel Bell was perhaps the first to examine these issues seriously, and he was then followed by the Tofflers. However, in addition to serious analysis, we are also getting a good deal of catchy sloganeering. The most obvious examples, and political leaders are probably most guilty of using these catch phrases without substance, are the references to the information superhighway (with the inevitable jokes about traffic jams, detours, and flat tires), and the assumption that somehow technology will "reinvent" how we work. It is important to remember that, as Peter Drucker has cautioned us, people will still fight to work as they feel like working. The truth of that observation can be seen in the bitter complaints from some technological product and systems developers that, for some inexplicable reason, nobody is using their "wonderful" system. The reason is quite simple. People don't use what they don't want to use. Thank goodness for that window of sanity, because it still insists, as Drucker urges us to insist, that human beings must be the bosses and machines the servants. At the same time, when I see the tortuous protocols being imposed on us when we call an 800 number for service—sequential instruction menus which sometimes exceed 20 in number—I wonder how we are supposed to be benefiting. Weren't we better off when we could talk to an operator, a human being who would transfer our call or relay a message?

However, even without examining these issues in detail, it has become obvious that access to information is considered the key to success. Indeed, that premise has no enemies. There is no anti-information or pro-ignorance lobby. No administrator, in the corporate, government, or academic sector, is in favor of stupidity. Then why doesn't this seem to work for librarians—really for all librarians—but specifically for you? Why, when millions are being spent in our parent institutions on technological information enhancements, when Microsoft is still the hottest commodity in the marketplace and Bill Gates may have a net worth greater than that of all librarians combined, doesn't it occur to anyone that perhaps library budgets need to increase as a part of this natural process?

There are a lot of people we can blame, but perhaps we need to start with ourselves and our pitifully low expectations. Why do we declare "victories" when our budgets are cut less than originally proposed, or even if our budgets remain the same? Don't forget that a failure to do new things and to innovate is a defeat. Basic management theory tells us that when things stay the same, they automatically get worse.

Although there are many other possible explanations for our failure to capitalize on the growing importance of information in the modern world, let me posit only two. First, our clients do not understand that "information" has anything to do with libraries. On airplane flights I frequently encounter individuals who are puzzled at my argument that the two are connected. Their argument is that librarians deal only with the physical containers of information, and not information itself. If they have come to that conclusion, it is primarily because we have concentrated on numbers of and the movement of containers, to the exclusion of the information content. As one library educator asked by comparison, "Does Budweiser consider itself to be in the beer business or the beer bottle business?" Certainly our insistent emphasis on some formats in preference to others suggests that our emphasis may be misplaced, and that the general public may indeed have interpreted correctly.

The second reason may come from Peter Drucker's assessment of service professionals, and while he does not mention us by name, we certainly fit within his definition. Service professionals, Drucker argues, accept the moral imperative. Somehow, with or without staff, with or without money, with or without support, they take full responsibility for doing what they are supposed to do, and if they fail, they consider it their own fault. Drucker adds, almost unnecessarily, that other fields place clear responsibility on higher management, and points out that when management understands that some subordinates will never blame them but only themselves, then they have those subordinates exactly where they want them. Why would any manager provide additional funds when there is absolutely no risk of being blamed for failing to furnish them?

In addition, of course, librarians are uncertain about their roles and their priorities. For public librarians these usually include recreation, education, and information, and often in that sequence. For academic librarians recreation falls from the scene, but the priority issue involves either education or information. That they have, almost without being pressured, chosen education over information is suggested as a priority for academic librarians in the fascination for encouraging end user searching, and, in conjunction with this, the decline in reference librarians and the provision of reference service. Totally left out of the equation are the needs of university administrators, who hold ultimate power over librarians, and who, if not provided information intermediation services, are very unlikely to consider finding their own information a priority. They will make decisions both good and bad based on instinct, and certainly we get no credit in the process.

On a much larger scale, librarians tend to misunderstand and dislike the political process; indeed I often find library science students reluctant to deal with political issues. They somehow consider such concerns as beneath their dignity, and insist that management should support us because we deserve it. They find it difficult to believe that politics is not a dirty word. It is simply a normal political process of deciding how scarce resources are to be allocated. It is generally the losers, or those who refuse to participate, who consider this most normal of processes as somehow evil.

Otis Bowen, who changed from a family physician to becoming governor of the state of Indiana, certainly understands the political process, and he is puzzled at our failure to understand it. In a message to the conference of the Indiana Library Association, he noted that librarians have generally failed in the process of rewarding their friends and punishing their enemies. Enemies, both he and Drucker have noted, are not necessarily people who hate you. They are simply individuals who fail to support you, either because they prefer to support something or someone else, or because they simply don't want to spend the money. Enemies can be guilty of indifference and not just hatred.

I like to present my students with a list of management communication terms, with the suggestion that as many of these terms as possible should appear in their management memoranda and proposals. These terms, in no particular order, include: balanced, compatible, functional, integrated, optimal, responsive, synchronous, systematized, total, user friendly, virtual, forward looking, cost effective, flexible, mobile, needs oriented, broader mission, payoff, quality assurance, value driven, and vision. I point out to my students that the words *circulation, holdings*, and *collection* appear nowhere on this list. These terms simply have no meaning for non-librarians. All right, you have a backlog! What difference should that make to me? Drucker, whom of necessity I quote a great deal, points out that the essence of management communication is not the reporting of accomplishments. We will report these in any case. The essence of management communication is exception reporting. What has gone wrong, how does that failure endanger bosses and the parent organization, and what can be done to repair the damage? It is these things which must be reported to management. Although they are not likely to ask, these are things they need to know.

In returning to the issues of technological advancements and their integration into our agenda, I suggest that we make four classic mistakes:

1. We note that the "information superhighway" will provide more information for everyone. Assuming that this is true, is it necessarily good? Management guru Tom Peters is not the first writer to note that we are drowning in information overload.

2. End user searching is cost effective. Given the fact that end users, particularly in academia, are more highly paid and search more sloppily, do we really mean that? Or is our point simply that the cost, while high, will be hidden and not a part of the library budget?

3. We contend that people *want* to do their own information searching. This is certainly true for a few adults, and certainly for children who love to surf the Net because it beats doing homework, but it is decidedly not true for those busy people who want the correct piece of information *so that they can do something else with it.* Information is not an end in itself for these people; it is a means to an end. These individuals have always looked for others to whom they could delegate work, and it is no coincidence that service professionals—those who do for us what we cannot do for ourselves or would rather not do for ourselves—are the most rapidly growing industrial sector. The British journal *The Economist* has noted the rise of the new "meatware" industry. Meatware are the human beings who use the hardware and software on our behalf. Isn't that what reference librarians do?

4. Perhaps the most mischievous and flawed suggestion is the argument that librarians have a future as information advisors, information consultants, or information gurus. Even if this were a potentially valid argument, it flies directly into the reality of budget cuts and downsizing. Downsizing decisions are made on the basis of *perceived* direct contributions. Consultants and advisors, facilitators and enablers, have been the first to go. We can protect our jobs best by pointing out that we are so effective that, by keeping us, they can perhaps get rid of some end users.

If information is important, and it is—if service sectors are the most rapidly growing, and they are—then our own strategies for dealing with what is both an opportunity and a danger should certainly be clear from everything I have said today. I would stress only that this applies to all sectors of librarianship, and certainly no less to theological librarians and their institutions. Your bosses represent the same mix of personality characteristics found anywhere.

The Politics of Reinventing Special Libraries

Introduction

Baseball fans will recognize that "Tinker to Evers to Chance" is memorialized as the best double-play combination of all time. Statistically, this is clearly untrue, yet the myth persists. Similarly, we embrace the myth that the future role of special librarians rests in moving beyond the long held role of information providers and becoming information relayers, information advisors, and information consultants, leaving the majority of the work to the end user. Such a strategy would shift our time honored motto of "Putting Knowledge to Work" to something more like "Dumping Knowledge Onto the Laps and Terminals of End Users." That premise, like the baseball premise, needs to be critically examined, because for us, the stakes are far higher than they are for baseball fans.

This journal has devoted several articles—indeed entire issues—to the argument that the future lies in end user searching, and that we must adapt our strategies to the inevitability of this. We need to remember that some of these articles have been written by database vendors, and that database vendors, quite correctly, prefer end user searching due to the time and money an end user will spend on a search. It does not matter to the vendors if this time and money was wasted due to poor searching skills. However, such an approach certainly does not serve us, nor does it serve our employers. Database vendors should not be faulted for writing to their own priorities. Rather, as special librarians, we should learn from their successes and begin writing more zealously about our own convictions.

Reprinted, with changes, by permission of the author and *Special Libraries* 87, no. 1 (Winter 1996): 59–62. Copyright © by Special Libraries Association, www.sla.org

The Financial Impact of End User Searching

There is no doubt that end users can now conduct the searches we do for them without us, but does that mean that they want to or that they should? In general, the answer to both questions—with the exception of looking up specific and simple facts—is no. As librarians, we know that we can search databases better and far more cost-effectively than our clients. Why then should end users do what librarians can and should do, thereby squandering both their time and the employer's money?

I am keenly aware of the absence of specific studies proving what we know instinctively to be true—that librarian searching is far more cost effective than end user searching. My question is, "Why are there no such studies?" I would think that every special librarian faced with the danger of end user searching over librarian searching—both in corporations and in academia—would insist that such studies be done, with those in financial management being the first to agree. Is it that we like end user searching because it protects us by hiding our costs? We should certainly understand by now that there is no safety in being cheap because we will never be cheap enough. Our safety lies in being essential.

Do end users want to spend their time searching for information on terminals? Perhaps a few, but not many. Information searching is a means to an end and not an end in itself. The end users realize that credit from their managers will not come from what they have learned, but rather, from how they have utilized it. Most end users would prefer intermediaries to do the information work for them. Where librarians are not available, end users look for other alternatives. This may include assigning the task to secretaries, clerks, or other assistants. It may involve hiring contractors to do, at a greater cost, what librarians are either no longer willing or no longer able to do.

The Meatware Industry

In 1994, the British journal the *Economist* reported the emergence of a new industry, with the suggestion that readers might invest in this growth sector. The *Economist* referred to it as the "meatware" industry. The title is both accurate and clever. The suggestion is that users already know about hardware and software and that they hire "meatware" to avoid having to use this hardware and software themselves. In doing this, people do what they have always done—not what others tell them they ought to want to do—but rather what feels most comfortable for them. However, there is yet another option for the end user, this one being most dangerous for the employer. When end users have neither enough time nor inclination to do information work and are unable to find someone else to do it, they can always pretend they didn't need the information. This ignorance does not have to be admitted, and herein lies the danger.

Does management want end users to do their own information searching? It might appear so, but this is only because they might not be informed of costs and options. With the current fascination for downsizing, these decisions may be based on the appearance of economy—librarians have a visible cost, while costs for end user searching are somehow not seen. This concept is at least as inaccurate as the misconception that there is no cost in maintaining a card catalog if one files all of the cards personally.

Too Much Information, Too Many Diversions

However, there is also evidence that the initial euphoric assumption of "the most information becomes the best information" has passed its peak. Tom Peters has written that a surfeit of information may be the enemy of intelligence, and keen-eyed humorists such as Dave Barry, Mike Royko, and Russell Baker have noted that being buried in information is not nearly as much fun as we keep hearing it is supposed to be.

It is also becoming noticed that terminals can be used for other purposes, particularly for playing games. Indeed, hardware and software vendors ranging from Hewlett-Packard to Microsoft have subtly suggested in their ads how much fun we, as well as our children, might have with their products. Do we think that managers who worry constantly about subordinates using time efficiently, even to the extent of being concerned that they might "waste" time in the library, won't notice this far greater potential for wasting time behind closed doors? They will notice, but by that time, the aboriginal information workers called librarians may all be gone.

The Trouble with Consulting, Advising, and Downsizing

It has been suggested that one future role for special and academic librarians will be to serve as information consultants and advisors. This may have been a viable option in the past, but certainly not now with what we can expect in the next 10 years. The fascination with downsizing has swept out everyone who is not directly involved in maximizing productivity and profits. This includes multiple layers of middle-managers who are now accused of having done very little shy of shuffling papers and interfering. It includes those who hold job titles like "facilitator" and "coordinator," because it is now assumed that facilitators don't facilitate and coordinators don't coordinate. It also includes "consultants" and "advisors," because it is assumed they don't really *do* anything either. Organizations may contract these people for work a day at a time, but they have no place for them on the permanent payroll. The emphasis now is on people who *do* things, which should make this an ideal time to be a special librarian. "Putting Knowledge to Work" would appear to be the perfect slogan for the 1990s.

So why hasn't it worked? One of the reasons that top executive and financial managers don't understand what ought to be obvious is that the people to whom librarians report directly are often more concerned with survival than effectiveness. If special libraries report to bosses who are dynamic, innovative, and ambitious, they are lucky—but such bosses are also rare.

People with such talents are infrequently given the responsibility of supervising a library. The task will more likely be given to people who have outgrown their usefulness to the organization. These people are given jobs that appear significant but expose the parent organization to minimal risk. Office service organizations, mail rooms, cafeterias, and libraries appear to be ideal candidates for such supervisors because these people don't interact with customers and sell nothing to outsiders. In my consulting assignments, I have found that it is often the managers directly over the library who block top management from any real evaluation of accomplishments or potential alternatives. If their own perceived value system is not effectiveness but safety, that can most easily be done by making the library seem inexpensive.

Equal Access to Information

Every few years it seems, an article will appear in our own professional literature which notes the "virtues" of charging end users for the services our libraries provide. The assumption is that this provides control and validation for what the library does. In actuality, all that happens when we charge end users directly is that some of the junior staff members—the ones who need information the most—will no longer receive that information because they have no money to spend. Senior management will never cut anything it finds convenient, including personal copies of the *Wall Street Journal* or the *Official Airline Guide*. From my own consulting assignments I also know that special librarians are fully aware that routing lists, particularly those with 10 or more names, are a very inefficient way of communicating information. Those at the bottom of the list know this as well. However, top management believes in the value of routing lists because they always get the information first. Has it occurred to any of us to randomize these lists so that management will understand what an incompetent system this happens to be for the rest of the staff? They will never know if we shield them from the truth.

Some Disturbing News

Most disturbing is the news that special libraries are being suddenly and arbitrarily closed, without any discussion or consultation with either librarians or users. These library closings stem from recommendations made by consultants who understand that they must recommend something that will have an immediate impact on cost reduction in order to validate their own fee. Some consultants simply suggest that organizations no longer need libraries or librarians, undoubtedly persuaded by the literature that argues the virtues of end user searching. The assumption is that end users can do this work without any impact on their other assignments—in other words, without any cost. Special librarians know otherwise, but they are not consulted. However, judging by the articles in our own literature which praise the "virtues" of end user searching, maybe special librarians actually do agree with the consultants on this matter.

However, this issue raises an even more intriguing question. The consultants who recommended the closure of the most recent and visible victim, a law firm library in Chicago, come from an organization which has a significant number of members listed in SLA's membership directory. Just what sort of message were these librarians sending to the colleagues that recommended closing the library, and to the senior management that allowed such recommendations to be made?

Conclusion

For special librarians, the solution to the dilemma seems clear. Since the organizations that employ special librarians are committed to cost-effectiveness and downsizing, presentations must be made to senior management that stress the need for keeping librarians, rather than having end users do the work more slowly, more carelessly, and more expensively. Moreover, there are clear indications that most users would prefer not to do this work, as long as they can delegate it to someone they trust. The top management proposal really almost writes itself. By having the correct number of qualified librarians, it will be possible to reduce both cost and staffing by eliminating excess end users, since the remaining end users will now be fully productive and not distracted by having to do the librarians' work. This strategy may be more easily applied in the corporate sector than in academia, where there is a higher level of job security through tenure. However, one caution needs to be noted. Unless the librarian's immediate boss is exceptionally supportive, the proposal should not be made to lower management through the normal chain of command. Lower managers will most likely be more concerned with protective camouflage than with sharing your proposal. The proposal should be made directly to top executive and financial management, because it is these individuals who will be interested in the economic solution you are offering. Special librarians know who these top executives are, but it would certainly help if these people also know who the librarians are.

In 1988, Peter Drucker made an accurate prediction of these current events. He foresaw downsizing, stating it would come in the form of eliminating staff and support people whose contributions to the ultimate goals were not obvious. He also stated that individuals who did clerical or routine work would be targeted, because even if these jobs were found to be necessary, they could be handled by temporary employees or outsourced to contractors. Drucker noted that the one group of individuals whose jobs seemed most secure were the knowledge workers, those who position themselves to provide the only possible approach to the knowledge crucial to the organization's survival. Is it our strategy to be knowledge workers? That, I had always thought, was the thinking behind "Putting Knowledge to Work." If the strategy has shifted to making others put knowledge to work, we will need a new motto. If Drucker is correct, and he usually is, we will also need new jobs in some other profession.

Our Strategy for Saving Libraries: Add Water to the Thin Soup

With all the bad news that now engulfs us—from library education programs that disappear or hide their identity by disavowing their name to the sweeping attack on all social service programs including those like ours that actually accomplish a great deal—it is probably uncharitable to challenge the happy news as reported in the pages of this journal that some libraries have escaped being closed.

At the same time, given the observation that library budgets and so-called information budgets are now on express funding trains headed in opposite directions, what exactly is it we are saving and is it worth the price?

We Cope, We Survive

The examples of our endless patience as copers and survivors are all around us. They begin with public library staffs who voluntarily give up their wage increase entitlements so that more books can be bought. We can be sure that the higher paid executives who cut our budgets have given up none of their own earnings for us. In academic libraries, we find that faculty members, who only know what a big library is and wouldn't recognize a good library if it fell on them, insist that the materials budget must have priority even as we slash everything else. We certainly know that in the latter 1990s that is the ultimate strategic absurdity. We should know from our own literature that not only does ownership not even begin to assure access but access through improved announcement and delivery systems is the one place where technology can really help us.

Reprinted, with changes, by permission of the author and *Library Journal* 121, no. 3 (February 15, 1996): 126–27. Copyright © 1996 by Cahners Business Information.

We should be stockpiling our money in ways to assure access for what we don't own; of course, as budgets decline and the literature grows we will own less and less. We should certainly know that holdings are not a significant statistic for an academic library any more than circulation really means anything in a public library. All these numbers indicate is a level of size and activity; they never say anything about who we are and what we uniquely do, or at least could do if allowed the opportunity.

The Quality of Reference

There might be the potential of political support here for us, but we not only fail to mobilize it, we ruthlessly suppress the "troublemakers" who might ask us to do reference work of an hour or more for any given question. In academia we insist that faculty members really want to do their own information searching (or at least ought to want to), even as the evidence around us grows that what we refuse to do is not done at all, is handed over to graduate assistants and secretaries, or is shipped to expensive but at least willing outside contractors. Unfortunately, it is my impression that we don't even try to do substantial reference work. We are just as happy not providing information services of a professional nature. In order to do what, you might ask? That is, in addition to paying inflated journal invoices?

A Chilling Childers Study

There are parallels here for public libraries. A study by Tom Childers, reported in *LJ*, April 15, 1994, p. 32–35, informs us that the demands for public library reference increase even as professional staffing is cut. This phenomenon will hardly be a surprise to people who still work in the public library reference trenches.

However, the study ends with a whimper by asking what *we* can do about this. It is the wrong question. The correct question is what are *they* going to do about it, they being the elected public officials now faced with the user wrath we have presumably so carefully orchestrated.

We find in at least one major California public library a mechanism for selling information services to industry. Industry can of course find public libraries useful, but industry, or for that matter anyone with money, has other options. What about those who can't afford to pay? An "executive" of this library has a simple solution. They can come in and do the work themselves.

Be Nice to
Paraprofessionals

In the editorial pages of *LJ* we are occasionally urged not to be mean to nonprofessionals, who do important work in our institutions. Of course they do, but where is the evidence of our rudeness? Or is the suggestion simply that we ought to allow nonprofessionals to do professional work because they are nice? When the argument is made that we need nonprofessionals to do more professional work because we haven't been allowed to hire professionals, or because the nearby library school has closed, it is a circular argument that eventually becomes a death spiral. Are we concerned that in the absence of enough professional librarians something bad might happen? In the absence of enough professional librarians something bad *better* happen!

Those of us who follow the concept of "market factors" as a distortion to wage and salary administration understand that shortages in a particular skill increase competition and drive up salaries. However, this only happens if employers continue to insist on the stated requirements, and that explains why professors of business administration earn more than professors of comparative literature. There is a shortage of the first, and a surplus of the second, and business schools will not hire anyone they don't find qualified.

The same market factors could have worked for children's librarians in the 1980s when there was a genuine shortage. However, all of this requires the discipline of keeping positions unfilled if qualified people can't be found at the salary offered. It all disintegrates if we hire whomever we can get at what we are willing to pay.

Nonpartisanism and Libraries

Our nation is currently experiencing a fundamental shift away from centralized government and federal social programs. There are partisan differences here, but the general trend is so pervasive that it has been embraced by both parties. Only the details are at issue. Whether we applaud or abhor this change doesn't really matter to us as a profession, although some people can't differentiate their professional from their personal values.

The individual most identified with this shift is Speaker of the House of Representatives Newt Gingrich. While some librarians might instinctively recoil from Gingrich as some sort of reincarnation of the devil, some interesting observations nevertheless can be made. An individual who strongly opposes many of our current social programs, Gingrich has never said anything unkind about libraries and librarians. Indeed, he spoke at the American Library Association (ALA) conference in Atlanta in 1991 long before he achieved the national spotlight, when he had little to gain in the process.

Of course, we can argue about his intellectual credentials, as we can about those of anyone with whom we disagree, but the Tofflers have yet to ask me to write an introduction to any of their books. Gingrich brings a unique point of view. How does that relate to librarians? How does he really feel about us? Perhaps he hasn't really thought about it.

Information Cliffhanging

Managers must be pragmatists even as they must also be idealists. Our profession cannot retain a foothold on the slippery slope of the new information world if our only strategy is an attempt to hang on to some part of our present funding, some part of our present status, and some part of our present educational programs. Staying the same makes you automatically worse in a dynamic environment, and we certainly live in a dynamic environment today. We need to scrap the strategy of hanging on by our fingernails.

Are our own professional needs and interests (distinguished from the myriad other causes and interests that some people bring to their library political agenda) better served by continuing to cultivate political leaders who insist that they love us but who unfortunately have a long list of priorities and never have enough money to get all the way down to us? That is support in principle but not in reality. It is worth nothing, perhaps less than nothing, but many of us seem willing to settle for it.

The Priority Short List

Or might our political interests perhaps be better served in alliances with individuals who have a much shorter list of priorities, if we can get on their priority lists? The great enemy of library funding over the last 25 years, in both academia and the public sector, has been the emergence and growth of other programs that have elbowed their way ahead of us in line. Sometimes that has even occurred with our enthusiastic agreement that they are indeed more worthy than we are. The nation has spent a lot of money, but it hasn't spent it on us. And yet we bear much of the brunt of the present backlash.

We haven't done at all well in the past, and we need some new strategies, not just for keeping our present money but for getting a lot of the new money we never got during the good times. Might we be better off at a smaller trough, if there is also a smaller number of invited diners? It occurs to all of my management instincts to find out, but I am retired and living in Arizona. I can only hope that it occurs to the present batch of elected ALA leaders and to the ALA Washington office.

Traditional Leaders = Nothing

Both mainstream California Republican (some Republicans think he's too liberal) Governor Pete Wilson and Democratic President Bill Clinton support Internet access for all public schools, no matter the cost, but neither has said a word about assuring the existence of a library in every public school.

We can continue to expect nothing from the traditional leaders of both parties. Perhaps we have a greater opportunity for success in an environment in which political reassessment eliminates some of the programs that now compete with us if these decision-makers consider what we do to be the most cost-effective and worthwhile. That is a very big "IF," but we need to find out. We can learn something about prioritizing from 19th-century British Prime Minister Lord Palmerston, who observed that his country had no permanent allies, only permanent interests.

Perhaps it is time to invite Gingrich and all those who aspire to the presidency to an ALA conference to tell us how we might fit onto their lists of priorities. Not in glittering generalities, but in specific dollars for specific activities. However, if we do, how do we keep from having them shouted down? How do we keep from being embarrassed and humiliated by the same gang of the arrogantly self-righteous who pestered Al Gore when he came to talk to us about his vision of information technology because he also had views on Iraq of which they disapproved. He wasn't even going to talk about Iraq.

We have some very loud and very rude people at ALA conferences. However, the concern is larger than that. If we are willing to restrict access to our meetings to speakers who say nice things even as they give us nothing, then this "don't worry, be happy" sort of attitude will continue to cost us in the real world. And, of course, the same thing applies in the pages of our journals, if we content ourselves with messages that sound sweet but have little substance.

Focusing on the Trivial Is Certainly More Fun

C. Northcote Parkinson reminded us a long time ago that the time spent on any particular decision was inversely proportional to its importance. What Parkinson noted turns out to be true: important issues are frequently also unpleasant ones, and to protect our mental health, we may pretend things are really not as bad as they appear. While restoration of half an enacted budget cut may be hailed as a "victory," in the dynamics of management structure, even holding your own represents a loss.

At the 1995 American Library Association (ALA) annual conference, the report of a task force that, after several years of study, recommended restructuring by type of library organization was puffballed to death. This first took place in a membership meeting of interest to so few that no quorum could be achieved. Next a Council vote rejected the report. Then Council sought to expiate its possible guilt at having trivialized so much hard work by giving the primary presenter a standing ovation. In the musical *1776*, the New York delegation, on having it reported by the clerk that it had abstained, insists on stressing that it had abstained courteously. Style is sometimes more important than substance.

Reprinted, with changes, by permission of the author and *Library Journal* 121, no. 5 (March 15, 1996): 47–48. Copyright © 1996 by Cahners Business Information.

It's Easier to Go National

The same ALA Council meeting that could not come to grips with the complexity of a multiyear study of organizational structure had no difficulty in passing resolutions urging the federal government to spend more money, because that is easier than dealing by name with the states and cities that have decimated their library service. The late Speaker of the House of Representatives, Tip O'Neill, who spoke at ALA in New Orleans, is best remembered for the wise observation that all politics is really local, not national. What we might do to laud or criticize and punish municipalities and universities is far more important than the messages we send so readily to Washington.

I wonder at our batting average for these heady and easy resolutions. Are Congressional committees really waiting anxiously to hear us tell them that more money needs to be spent? Can I expect, if I watch C-SPAN long enough, to find business on the floor of the House or Senate interrupted by a clerk who rushes in to read the latest resolutions from ALA?

In fact, the library profession restructured itself by type of library almost 100 years ago, when medical, special, law, and other librarians all packed up and left ALA. That division by type of library has continued, as can be seen by anyone who attends "state library association" meetings. Rarely do school, academic, or corporate librarians or even library educators attend them. They are important meetings, or at least they could be, but they primarily represent the interests and needs of public librarians. Some of the people who hated the Structure Task Force report are trying to forget that what they dislike so much took place many years ago.

Managers Must Manage

It is the job of managers to make decisions, or at least to see to it that needed decisions are made and needed actions taken, and the ALA Council has management responsibilities. We know that in the dynamics of the process good decisions are of course preferable, but even a bad decision is better than referring something back for "further study"—what I mean by puffballing. Parkinson would have clearly understood the attractiveness of avoiding tough choices.

In 1969, when I was president of the Special Libraries Association and the late Joe Becker was president of the American Society for Information Science, we were both living in Bethesda, MD, and had the occasional lunch together. We noticed that not only did many individuals belong to both organizations, but, even more significantly, there was a greater overlap in the elected leaderships of the two societies. We therefore proposed that the two consider merging, and a task force was appointed to explore that possibility.

That was the easy part. The report, which found that a merger had advantages, was received with a good deal of hostility and anger, largely because of concerns about what the new name would be. Specifically, if the phrases "special library" and "information science" were both going to be in the title, which would come first? The point that any name selected was temporary, because any group can change its name whenever it wishes, was totally ignored. Here was a small and trivial issue, but it was clearly defined and wonderfully emotional. Parkinson would have understood immediately.

Subsumed by Special Interests

I have long been a manager and enjoyed the process of management decisions, and for that reason I sought election to the ALA Council in 1988. I was gratified to be selected with the highest vote total of any Council candidate, but four years later I was counting the days until I finished my term. I found it difficult to understand how so many hardworking and caring people could allow their agendas and priorities to be so totally subsumed by narrow and special interests, to the exclusion of any issues for which our actions might really mean something. The only exceptions were intellectual freedom and censorship, although sometimes we even waffled here to conclude that some forms of censorship and boycotts might be all right.

I was pleased to be named to the Planning Committee, because one of ALA's problems then (as indeed now) was the need for discipline in deciding which myriad priorities on the books through many casual Council votes should be retained and stressed and which should be assigned to the trash heap—courteously, of course. The committee did a very good job of prioritizing and weeding, but then it all unraveled at the first public hearing when one of my colleagues suggested that an item not on our high-priority list might be subsumed and included by redefining the others. In that way, all priorities could be retained, and presumably no one would be offended.

What we were apparently doing was rearranging deck chairs, and I have no interest in furniture layout. I was relieved to be removed from the committee for my failure to attend special meetings at ALA headquarters, because I could see no justification in spending the association's money for airfare and lodging.

It is possible that those who feel that organization structure doesn't matter enough to warrant their attention, as long as they can still find a meeting they want to attend, an exhibit they want to visit, or a restaurant they want to try, are ultimately correct. However, the lost opportunity to function effectively as a unified profession, which we started to fritter away almost a century ago, is nevertheless a great loss. It is sad that we can only react to such tough issues by ignoring one committee and stalling for time by appointing yet another one. Obviously telling Congress what to do is more fun and much easier.

Meeting in Comfort

If members must be ultimately allowed to do what they want to do, then we should understand that one of the things they want is meetings that are personally comfortable for them, e.g., groups large enough to include those who share their concerns and interests but not really any larger than that. Why should we fight for restaurant reservations with people we don't even know? Record attendance should please those with financial responsibility, but why should the rest of us always be expected to applaud? I try to avoid an airline that has the highest seat occupancy rate. I prefer an empty seat next to me.

To a great extent meeting in groups that share our interests and concerns means "type of library" meetings—at a minimum, that means more divisional conferences. We have seen the growth in terms of both attendance and professional content, and that trend must certainly be allowed to continue.

It takes no futurist to predict annual conferences for public, academic, and school librarians. If medical, special, and law librarians do it, why not these others? There are models for us in the conferences of the member societies of the American Federation of Information Processing Societies and the American Institute of Physics, which meet separately as well as jointly. The joint meetings concentrate on attracting exhibitors or those who visit exhibits, those looking for a job or looking to fill one, and those who enjoy committee meetings. Most of the technical papers of consequence are presented at the smaller meetings.

If we are able to accept such flexibility, then ALA can avoid repeating the mistakes that drove what may be half of the profession away almost a century ago. If so, then perhaps the reports of structure task forces don't matter all that much. The important thing is to respond to and relieve pressures as they build up. Unrelieved pressure ultimately causes earthquakes. It is unclear what more frequent divisional meetings would do to the financial viability of either the parent body or the children (including the grown children who have already left home), to dues structures, or to exhibitor participation. There should be lots of history here from other organizations that have faced the same issues.

However, as unpleasant as all of this may be for some, it will have to be faced. Individuals will, and indeed should, retain for themselves the right to do what works best for them. It is perhaps because of this that they ignore membership meetings and the pontifications of the Council. When it comes right down to it, this spurning may represent the purest expression of popular democracy.

Dealing with the trivial issues is much more enjoyable than tackling the really serious ones. It is easier to make a sweeping demand to Washington that we know will be ignored than to deal with a state or local issue for which our actions might really mean something. If this is true—Parkinson would certainly think so—then what topic of great emotional but little substantive impact shall I tackle in my next column? How about where ALA should never hold its conferences and why?

Correction

In the January White Papers (p. 59), I stated that law firm Baker & McKenzie had closed the library of its Chicago office, laying off all staff. Though the library staff was let go, the library has remained open. However, I would suggest to semanticists that what defines a library is its properly trained staff and that little else matters for the quality of work in a law firm.

Selecting Conference Sites for ALA

In my last column ("Focusing on the Trivial Is Certainly More Fun," *LJ*, March 15, pp. 47–48), I argued that the business agendas of the American Library Association (ALA) Council were a classic validation of C. Northcote Parkinson's observation that it is much easier to deal with small issues than with large ones. The Council dismissed quite casually a recommendation to restructure the association along type-of-library lines, ignoring the reality that this reorganization had already occurred almost a century ago when perhaps half of the profession left because of their desire to organize by type of library, whether this be special, law, or medical. And, of course, that fragmentation exists at the local level as well. State library associations are primarily state associations of public librarians. Academic, corporate, and school librarians rarely attend, and medical and law librarians come not at all. Even library education is poorly represented. Shouldn't all faculty consider it their obligation to attend? If they and others don't, it is because they don't consider it "their" meeting.

Sweeping Resolutions

Instead, we pass sweeping resolutions demanding Congressional action but fail to postulate, monitor, and enforce expectations for levels of service, levels of support, levels of status, and levels of salaries at the local level. Opting for "community standards" becomes a thinly veiled rationalization for allowing every community to pay for whatever it feels like paying for, because that is what community standards inevitably turn out to be.

Reprinted, with changes, by permission of the author and *Library Journal* 121, no. 7 (April 15, 1996): 57–58. Copyright © 1996 by Cahners Business Information.

Our power to censure, to sanction, and to bar inadequate libraries from professional participation and the sharing of cooperative resources is admittedly limited and is probably only effective to the extent to which negative publicity can embarrass a community and its elected officials.

Our power to withhold and cancel our meetings in states and cities that do not meet our expectations for library support (and remember that lack of money is always an excuse and never a reason) is a tactic we might use but never do, although we boycott and cancel for other reasons that have nothing to do with support for libraries and librarians.

Site Selection

Selecting a location for an ALA annual conference or Midwinter Meeting is really a very serious matter, as long as the association budget is as heavily dependent on achieving revenue projections from attendees and exhibitors. We can all understand with 20-20 hindsight why a summer conference in Miami turned out to be a financial disaster, and those responsible for making governance decisions were correct to worry that the same thing might happen at a summer conference in Orlando.

Choosing New York pleases some individuals and not others, but New York has that effect on people. You love it or you hate it, and it is number one on both lists. Putting the Javits Center on the extreme midtown west side, without also building a monorail, was a monumental piece of political and bureaucratic stupidity. There are no hotels near the center, and in Manhattan the phrase weekday midtown traffic is an oxymoron, because the word "traffic" suggests movement. However, at least it can be assumed that a New York conference will draw attendees, exhibitors, and money. If the issue were simply one of meeting where income would be greatest, selecting conference locations would be easy to do.

However, the process is much more complicated than that. One of the issues is economic. Since our salaries are low and many employers fail to support conference participation, we validate that reality by meeting when no one else wants to come. That explains summer meetings in Miami and Las Vegas, it explains meetings that run over the Fourth of July, and it explains why I have now spoken at four state conferences at ski resorts but never when there was any snow. I would be hard pressed to think of another society that would agree to meet over a national holiday. Since the primary beneficiaries of our conference attendance are our employers, is it not reasonable that they provide both the money and the time off from work? At least the latter! Or haven't we told them how lucky the library is to have its librarians attend meetings, learn about new options and new technologies, and build communications bridges?

There are even further complications. Finding beds to host a conference of up to 20,000 attendees is no problem for any major city. However, ALA's 18,000 attendees also need space for 2,000 meetings. It would be difficult to explain to a visitor from another planet why, given the ease of telephone calls, e-mail, and fax machines, any society needs one meeting for every nine attendees. To suggest that ALA is overstructured is as obvious as mentioning that Wisconsin has cheese. We could announce that only the first 500 requested meetings would be scheduled, and after that number was reached anyone else seeking a meeting would have to stake out a bar.

However, that won't happen, and it explains our frequent difficulty with hotel rooms in one part of town and a conference center an hour away. Hotel managers learned long ago that they don't make money on meeting rooms, only sleeping rooms. If we insist on 2,000 meetings in New York, we can be certain that there will be transportation snafus.

Holding Us Hostage

We face at least one other issue. There are lots of groups that see nothing wrong in holding the choice of a conference location hostage for reasons that have nothing to do either with money or professional convenience. Thus, the Association of College and Research Libraries left Arizona because that state had not yet decided to allow everybody a day off in January to sleep late, stay home from work and school, and go to the mall for some shopping. There can be no questions that legally Arizona had that right, but the state was shown the "error of its judgment" by economic pressure. No, not a library conference, but the threatened loss of the Super Bowl. My neighbor city of Tucson closes schools each year so that students can attend a rodeo. I don't agree, but I don't live or vote there and it is therefore none of my business. Still, it might be better to keep schools open on special occasions so that the person or event being celebrated can be discussed. Declaring holidays is the easy and popular approach but also the most expensive.

Similarly, we rushed to abandon Cincinnati because it had repealed a law that many of the locations in which we do meet had never enacted in the first place. Had we waited a few months, we would have learned that a judge had overturned the civic action and made Cincinnati "wholesome" again. As long as such issues become yet another factor that affects our selection of a conference site, we may yet find the ALA Executive Board faced by two petitions—one that threatens a boycott unless the conference is moved and another that threatens a boycott if it is moved.

Chicago, Always Chicago

All of this leads to a simple suggestion of where ALA should meet for its annual summer conference. Let's meet in Chicago, each and every year. Chicago is large enough, it is centrally located, the late June weather is bearable, and, for the moment at least, Chicago is politically acceptable. It wasn't always.

If we meet in Chicago every summer, there is also a corollary requirement that we never meet there in the winter. Orlando might be nice for a winter conference, or even Miami. However, the most obvious reason for meeting in Chicago is that such a meeting is cheapest for the association. This is where the organization's headquarters are located, where the files are, and where the staff live. Many with family responsibilities might even prefer the opportunity to live at home during the conference.

What are the objections? It would exhaust the local conference planning committee to have to work every year? Not if the headquarters staff did most of the planning. That already happens in many professional associations. It would be boring to come to the same city each year? A city with the size and cultural, culinary, and entertainment diversity of Chicago is not likely to become boring for anyone making an annual visit, and many members don't come each year. Nor should such an argument really matter for a professional group with a professional agenda. Exhibitors might like the certainty of knowing where they will be, and if we can schedule far enough in advance we can make sure never to meet over the Fourth of July. There is even one more advantage. *LJ* and *American Libraries* can stop printing annual lists of restaurants.

If serious arguments won't persuade you, let's get silly—librarians should refuse to meet in any city or state that does not recognize the contributions of Benjamin Franklin through the traditional closing of schools and banks, stopping mail service, and having gigantic sales at the mall. For librarians the contributions made by Franklin extend beyond those recognized by all citizens. Franklin started a subscription library service in 1731 and stressed throughout his life the importance of libraries for the Colonies and the nation. He was the driving force behind the formation of the American Philosophical Society, and he was directly responsible for what is now the University of Pennsylvania. Unfortunately, recent historical writings and the lusty performance by Robert Preston in *Ben Franklin in Paris* create the impression of a hard-drinking, elderly skirt-chaser. There are all sorts of groups within ALA that might be offended.

There is an alternate candidate for our requirement that we only meet in places that celebrate his birthday—Thomas Jefferson. Jefferson was a scholar, reader, writer, and collector of books. Indeed, there is now some historical evidence that he was doing these things when, as governor of Virginia or Ambassador to France, he should have been doing more of the things he was supposed to be doing.

However, none of that affects us as librarians. Jefferson also can claim a university, the University of Virginia. It was his private collection that formed the nucleus of the Library of Congress after it was burned in the War of 1812, and after selling his library he immediately started collecting another one. What could be more admirable for librarians than that? Of course, we might have ALA groups concerned, pro or con, about Jefferson's possible relationship with his slave Sally Hemmings. Do you begin to see how much fun we could have with the conference site selection process?

Research Library Directors and the Squandered Opportunity to Lead

Some research library directors are not only among my closest professional friends but are also among those whose writings and speeches I truly admire. The sweeping generalization of the title might appear to indict them all, and for that I am sorry. Perhaps by the time they have finished reading this column they will know whether or not they are included. Still, I cling to the generalization.

Library directors of major research institutions have had—and perhaps still have—the opportunity to create a positive image for this profession that will be recognized by the general public. Why? They command significant resources in both dollars and staffing. Also, they work in institutions where professionals recognize they cannot fully understand each others' qualifications, and the less they understand, the more important those colleagues must be. If Association of Research Library (ARL) directors have failed as a group, it is first because they failed to exercise the most important management prerogative—the right to prioritize how they will spend their own budgets. Without that right, their power becomes trivial. If ARL directors spend a great deal of money only as instructed, they are not managers at all but simply purchasing agents sitting in plush offices.

Reprinted, with changes, by permission of the author and *Library Journal* 121, no. 11 (June 15, 1996): 43–44. Copyright © 1996 by Cahners Business Information.

Turf Wars

It is important, particularly in academia, to establish the "turf" of what we know and what others agree they do not know. In the late 1970s, when I was a faculty member at Indiana but not yet a dean, I had a conversation with Frank Franz, a high-energy physicist and the dean of faculties, our version of vice president for academic affairs. I pointed out that we had one characteristic in common and one in which we differed fundamentally. First, neither of us knew anything about the other's discipline: I knew nothing about high-energy physics, and he knew nothing about what it took to run a library. Second, I was smart enough to recognize that I knew nothing about high-energy physics.

Franz went on to become provost at West Virginia University and then president of the University of Alabama at Huntsville. I know he learned from our conversation because he has quoted it to librarians with whom he has since worked, and they have reported it to me. I feel that I have helped academic librarians develop a relationship of professional respect with at least this one administrator.

Paralyzed on Pricing

Research library administrators who watch rising periodicals prices with the same paralyzed horror as children who see the incoming tide about to destroy their sand castles are certainly not unique in our profession. This same sort of hand-wringing is evident from public library directors who bemoan their fate while city budgets decline and the general public continues to demand better library service.

The solution to both problems is obvious to anyone who has studied even a bit of management. The people who *are* responsible must *take* responsibility. However, what happens in our research institutions has greater impact on all of us.

At my Indiana University distinguished professor installation dinner, I had the opportunity to speak for 20 minutes about anything I chose to a captive audience of university administrators. I mentioned the continuing increase in journal subscription prices. This happened, I noted, because publishers understood that while librarians paid the bills, they couldn't cancel subscriptions and "punish" major transgressors because faculty wouldn't allow it. Power over journal publishers lay in the hands of university presidents, who might jointly deal with this issue as they dealt with academic qualifications for varsity athletes, something they considered worthy of their attention.

Alternatively, scholars in that journal's discipline could respond by refusing to submit articles for publication. Journals can exist much longer without library subscribers than they can without authors. Since neither the administrators nor the faculty seemed to care, I suggested that librarians also not care. They should spend as much money as the administration gave them, ensuring that they never allowed renewal pressures to become a priority over staffing and other alternatives.

I also noted that the university continued to face a choice between ownership and access, and that access was much better. If the university wanted to face the issue of access from its own collection it needed to face the reality that many faculty used the library simply as a free bookstore, and I was just as guilty as my new colleagues at this dinner. Books that head straight from cataloging to the office of the requester, never to return except by special solicitation, are not "accessible."

Access Vs. Ownership

Access was certainly a better strategy than ownership, I noted, because of the growth of information, the rapid increase in prices, and the improvements in both bibliographic access and document delivery. The ownership game, now a disastrous strategy for all of us, was one we librarians had long endorsed, calling everyone's attention to the Clapp-Jordan formula (see "Quantitative Criteria for Adequacy of Academic Library Collections," *CRL*, September 1965, pp. 371–380). We used this tactic in the 1960s to increase funding for library collection development, but back then even falling down a flight of stairs might have been a successful tactic to get money for library purchases.

I hoped for some level of argument or denial from my audience, but I was only asked by one distinguished colleague why, if the issues and alternatives that librarians faced were indeed so complex, library administrators had not insisted that their research budget be a higher priority than their acquisitions budget? I still have no answer for this question that I am willing to share with someone outside of our field, because it would be too embarrassing in spotlighting our profession's strangely inverted priorities. Instead, we continue to try to minimize conflict by making do and by appearing nonconfrontational and collegial.

Outside the System

Several years ago, I was contacted by the chair of a search committee seeking candidates to direct a major ARL library. After disabusing him of the possibility of my own candidacy, I suggested that the "normal" pattern for selecting an ARL director—looking within the "family" for a director of a smaller academic library or the assistant director of a larger one—would simply perpetuate the present value system and make his library a comfortable copy of all others. If that prospect disturbed him, the committee might expand its search to look for candidates who understood both research and administration but who were not necessarily weighed down by having grown up in the present system.

My response intrigued the committee chair, who called twice to ask for an elaboration of my ideas. However, he was either unwilling or unable to persuade his colleagues on the search committee, because I know whom they finally hired.

The point for all library administrators is that many university administrators and faculty colleagues "don't know what it is they don't know." Telling them this might be dangerous, because, unlike Frank Franz, they may be more egocentric than intelligent. And yet they must be told.

Fighting Back

As I write, I have just read the latest projected price increases for scholarly journals. The increases once again will be high, certainly well beyond the rate of inflation; the justification given for European journals is the weakness of the U.S. dollar against Western European currencies, when added to an increase of "worthy" publication candidates. In their recent *LJ* article ("Setting the Record Straight on Journal Publishing," March 15, 1996, pp. 32–35), Carol Tenopir and Don King even suggest that there are plausible explanations for these price increases.

That may all be true, but it should also be totally irrelevant. If the dollar is now weak, that is a problem for publishers with stronger currencies that seek to sell to us, because they should recognize that customers won't buy if the price is too high. As the dollar plunged against the Japanese yen, car manufacturers slashed their prices and profit margins to make sure they didn't lose American customers, even to the point where it might be cheaper to buy a Japanese-made car in the United States than in Japan.

If the same does not hold true for our foreign scholarly journals—if Dutch and German periodicals still cost more here than in Amsterdam and Berlin— it is simply because these publishers understand that they have nothing to fear from us.

They perceive that we buy what faculty members tell us to buy and pay what the publisher tells us to pay. We know from studies as far back as the 1970s that titles are not canceled because of their high prices unless they are already candidates for cancellation. A study we did at Indiana University for the National Science Foundation showed that the average cost of canceled journals was lower than that of retained journals once the duplicate subscriptions had been cut. The publishers who make it their business to understand how their market operates believe that political pressure affects retention/cancellation decisions far more than does obscenity of price increase. And, of course, they are correct.

There have been some glimmers of activity by library directors attempting to involve faculty members in the fight against price increases that defy all recognition of the economic realities faced by the university and its library. Southern Methodist University and Dick Dougherty at the University of Michigan immediately come to mind. However, most faculty still don't consider the economics of scholarly communication their problem. They consider it ours. And our ultimate response in cutting subscriptions is then something for which faculty blame neither publishers nor themselves. They blame us.

Would some of my friends and colleagues who head research libraries explain to me how they, and by extension the rest of the profession, sank to this condition of powerlessness? Or have we always been powerless, but as long as there was lots of money no one noticed?

Do We Want to Be Knowledge Workers?

The answer to the question is not so deceptively easy as you might assume, because it involves some real choices and, more importantly, significant changes in our behavior and in our strategies. One of our leaders, with apparently a full sense of confidence, recently "described" what librarians do. Our job, we were told, is to identify, collect, and organize the world's information so that others can use it.

I am not sure where that limited perception first arose, but I am certain it is taught today in many library schools. More importantly, I am confident that it drives the thinking of university administrators, public library boards, school superintendents, and corporate officials who rule us. Obviously, how well they let us do our job is open to question and should be open to negotiation. However, when the definition of our role is that narrow, I think we can't win.

I recall no recent professional meetings in which we discussed our fundamental role and mission. Indeed, as I review the literature of our field in preparation for course assignments, I become aware of a subtle but definite shift from a discussion of principles toward a narrower focus on problem-solving. Now, of course, most of our problems deal with money, or really the lack of it.

This preoccupation with immediate and urgent issues is understandable, but it may also help explain what seems to be a growing rift, in meetings and in our literature, between practitioners and educators. Because I still have a foot in both camps, I am perhaps more sensitive to that declining sense of relevance in how we view each other.

Perhaps the correct phrase is not lack of relevance but rather lack of patience. Beset as we find ourselves, we have no time for anyone who doesn't offer specific, helpful suggestions. I first became aware of this when, more than a decade ago, I served on a panel that was supposed to develop a research agenda for federal educational library programs. Instead, we spent most of our time on tactics to allow us to continue to "run our libraries good," even without money.

Broadening Our Self-Image

Before I go further, I must interpose my objection to the narrowness of the definition mentioned in the opening paragraph. Perhaps because I had no background in library work when I attended library school over 45 years ago, my definition was always much broader. I was a neophyte chemist who wanted to become a librarian because I could see that scientists had neither preparation nor inclination to find what they needed.

That problem has not gone away; it has gotten much larger, because the piles of information are no longer restricted to paper. End users now have their own computer terminals, but not necessarily just for the acquisition and assessment of information. They understand that information is not an end in itself but simply a means to an end. Also, they're reminded by hardware and software manufacturers that, along with information, computers can be used to play games.

Because this does not pretend to be a scholarly article, I won't provide you with citations from Daniel Bell and the Tofflers about the growth of information and the need to develop organized approaches to deal with such growth—in its assessment and use, not in its arrangement.

They perceive, quite correctly, that computer technology deals very efficiently with organizing and arranging. So do clerks and their now-suspect bureaucratic bosses. Their concern is allowing people to use information as a tool. Another concern—as diverse commentators such as management writer Tom Peters and humorist Dave Barry have noted—is to prevent being buried by irrelevant information. Unfortunately, they are vague in identifying who will give us what we need and guard us from what we don't need.

New Knowledge Workers

However, Peter Drucker is quite clear on the subject. About ten years ago, he accurately predicted the downsizing frenzy in which we are now engaged, and he also described the criteria that would be used. Organizations would ruthlessly cut as many of their clerks as possible, assuming that they either were not needed, or that their work could be contracted to cheaper temporary employees; these would receive no benefits and not affect headcount ceilings. They would also eliminate the jobs of middle managers and others who did what might be dismissed as paper shuffling, because their work could not be directly related to organizational objectives.

Drucker further predicted that a new profession of knowledge workers would grow and prosper, not only because management recognized their contribution, but also because what they did could not be done as effectively (or at all) by others, Drucker understands, as we should, that technology has not only changed the way in which information is accessed and used. Technology has also made it impossible, despite vendor protestations, for end users to deal with information completely on their own. They will need lots of help.

Drucker did not specify those who would need knowledge workers, but to me they include lawyers in law firms, professors at universities, and the public library's reference clientele. If they try to do knowledge work, they will do it badly and expensively, as long as decisionmakers keep honest financial books.

However, that honesty is often lacking. As budgets get tight, administrators in government, academia, and business narrow the definition of library activity away from knowledge work, if they ever considered it. Now they focus on acquisition, arrangement, and housekeeping—activities that turn the library into a self-service unit.

Examples are obvious, but I will restrict myself to three. When the Chicago law firm Baker & McKenzie decided it could do without a professional library staff, what did it perceive that staff did? Was their perceived role simply one of acquisition, arrangement, and housekeeping? Had anyone argued that the librarians did knowledge work that lawyers were not competent to do, or that the profitability of the law firm demanded that they be told not to attempt to do it?

A similar situation applies in academia, because the university must increasingly function under economic pressure. Should faculty members do end user searching instead of librarians? Why, because professors are already too plentiful and have nothing to do? Don't expect that to be admitted.

The politically more acceptable argument would be that there are too few faculty members and that librarians are needed to free faculty from information searching and to allow them to work on research and teaching. In other words, increasing the knowledge workers in the university library protects academic values at the lowest possible cost. And yet I know of academic librarians who perceive a reduction in reference demand as some sort of vindication for their strategy. Where does that lead them?

Self-Service Libraries

For public libraries the situation is a little trickier, because while in the corporation and university a demonstrated lack of knowledge poses too great a risk, in public settings politicians become quite adept at the use of smoke and mirrors—and libraries are obvious victims.

No one can pretend to have picked up your garbage or filled your potholes when it hasn't been done, but can't a public library be redefined as something or other with open doors available for self-service? Of course it can, but only if we suicidally go along quietly. It is easy for a politician seeking credit to so label the local library and get the public to believe it, but only we know what still needs to be done to make it really "wonderful."

And, given the real and growing need for public library information service, I know of no great "wonderful" public libraries now, because all of them do less than they used to do and far less than they should. Some cities and towns do have nicer and newer buildings, but that is only important to the politicians who seek easy credit. What is important to us and our patrons is what happens inside those buildings.

Nondiluted Quality

We must constantly address two issues. Firstly, we must protect our users from dilution in the quality of library service, while politicians argue that such dilution does no real harm, or that it is financially "necessary." Communities and political bodies will always afford what they choose.

Secondly, we must recognize that our future depends not on being perceived as handy clerks, arrangers, babysitters, or even the purchasers of books that the faculty and the general public would rather not buy themselves. Those are not necessarily unreasonable activities, but they will not protect us in the new cost-cutting frenzy. Only by having unique skills and knowledge that are both essential and cannot be replicated as cost-effectively (or at all) by others, including end users, will we be protected. Hang on to that phrase "cost effective." Repeat it frequently, and point out that it is far more important than cheapness. Sometimes cheapness costs dearly.

Most of us have become familiar with Health Maintenance Organizations. While many positive things can be said about HMOs, one clear negative is that doctors are now treated as employees and are expected to meet production standards. How much "free" time will they now have to search the literature online, a future for which both the National Library of Medicine and many medical librarians insist on preparing them? Would they perhaps be better served if they could reach a medical information knowledge worker, via e-mail, fax, or a toll-free telephone number staffed at all hours, as American Express now staffs its telephones?

Can we not predict a similar future for the "joys" of end user searching in corporations and universities in this era of downsizing, particularly if we remember that the admission of ignorance is the first thing that can be abandoned under pressure?

A Bright Future—For Us?

Perhaps it was this scenario that prompted Drucker to forecast such a bright future for knowledge workers. Indeed, we need look no further than the recent growth of commercial information analysis and interpretation organizations, which contract to our corporate, medical, and academic employers what these purchasers insist they can't afford to pay us to do.

Shouldn't this also prompt public librarians to argue that providing adequate and full reference service is the most important thing the public library does, and that this must be protected even if other things are cut? Sometimes outsiders, quite unexpectedly, can see the obvious. Recently, IBM Senior Vice President for Research Paul M. Horn said he saw a crucial role for librarians as mediators who find specific information for their users in the proliferation of options (News, *LJ*, May 15, p. 12).

Do we really want to be the knowledge workers of the future and fight for that title? Or will we settle for the role of identifiers, collectors, and organizers for other knowledge workers? I argued against such a narrow definition when I was a library student, and I continue to make that argument today, perhaps still with little success. However, the crisis has become far more acute, because of the growing public perception that identifying, collecting, and organizing is something that computers can do quite well on their own, without the annoying and expensive need for people. That perception is at least partially correct. Our future lies in doing what computers cannot do.

Economic and Political Issues in Determining the Future of the Professionally Managed Library Over the Next Ten Years

Library management strategy has been based on two premises. First, we argued that we were really teachers or professors, with the job of enabling individuals to learn to use information for their own life-long benefit, both personal and professional. Second, we postulated that our unique task was the identification, acquisition, and organization of information so that others would be able to use it. In one sense, the two strategies meshed.

As a mechanism for achieving professional recognition, status, and pay, the first has been doomed to failure from its very inception, simply because our "fellow" teachers and professors have never acknowledged or accepted us as equals or as partners. The second strategy now runs headlong into two sweeping generalizations—the first that organizations need to downsize by eliminating those positions that do not contribute directly and immediately to organizational objectives. The second generalization, which feeds

Reprinted, with changes, by permission of the author and Essen University Library, from *Towards a Worldwide Library. A Ten Year Forecast*. 19th International Essen Symposium, September 23–26, 1996, pp. 1–12, edited by Ahmed H. Helal and Joachim W. Weiss. Copyright © 1997 Essen University Library, Germany.

the first, is that identifying, acquiring, and organizing material so that others can use it is something that computers can do very well, with minimal instruction and control.

The one thing that computers clearly cannot do is to aid swamped and deluged end users to decide what should be read and what can be safely ignored.

Management writers such as Tom Peters and Peter Drucker understand this problem. Drucker postulated almost ten years ago that the profession with the brightest future was that of knowledge workers, individuals who would channel individuals to the information they needed, and protect them from what they should not bother to read. If we can assume that knowledge workers have a bright future, do we want to be knowledge workers?

I have set ten years as the limits for the predictions in this paper, because futurists tell us repeatedly that ten years is just about as far as we can see. They argue that we tend to exaggerate what will happen in the next one or two years, because the normal bureaucratic processes, including committee meetings, study groups, and unreturned phone calls and unanswered letters slow the process down. We tend to underestimate what will happen in the longer term future because our predictions are largely based on what we know or expect, and we can't factor in what will happen about which we have no clue. Certainly libraries had no ideas at the start of the 1960s what changes would be brought about by the ability to search online the files located across a continent or a planet. It has revolutionized banking and travel reservations, and quite incidentally in the minds of systems engineers it has revolutionized libraries, and all because systems designers began to realize that one central processing unit could handle the messages from many input/output devices. We may well face such traumatic changes in the distant future, but I can't talk about them. Moreover, if I did nobody would remember or care whether my predictions were accurate 15 years from now, least of all I. Let me restrict myself then to talking about what is already happening, and what we can see quite clearly in the short term future.

Let me begin with three presumably unrelated stories, all true. You will probably see the connection, but in any case I will connect them for you.

1. For more than two decades, a bank in the northwestern United States had an excellent library, respected by all of its users. The librarian was well paid, and promoted to the rank of a bank officer. Then, about five years ago, as part of the merger mania that grips the banking industry, that bank was acquired by a large banking system hundreds of miles away. Decisions came from there, and the local professionals became simply distant employees. Finally, a new chief executive officer was appointed, and that individual had spent the last four years in Thailand. One

of his immediate decisions was to close the library, since it was his assumption that all needed information could now be accessed online by the bank employees concerned. Furthermore, since there was no longer a need for a collection of printed library materials, he offered the entire collection to the local public library.

2. More recently, the midwest office of what claims to be the world's largest law firm called in its totally unsuspecting library staff one Friday afternoon and fired all of them. A consultant report had recommended that librarians were no longer necessary. In this case, the library would be maintained, with material ordered and filed by contract clerks. However, it was clearly understood that the firm's lawyers could find whatever they needed to find on their own, on their terminals and if necessary on the shelves.

3. In an article this spring, the American national newspaper *USA Today* listed ten occupations which, in the judgment of the editors, had a bright future, and ten occupations which they saw as having at best a dim but probably no future. The first list was heavily spiced with computer skills, such as computer animation for anyone who might hope to work for Walt Disney Films. The second list, of occupations which had no future, included bank teller, telephone operator, and librarian.

All right, let me start putting these pieces together, and let me start with the third. What bank teller, telephone operator, and librarian share, at least in the view of the editors, is that they are all jobs which involve clerical and repetitive routines, which have been and will increasingly be taken over by computers. Cash ATM machines instead of tellers, voice mail instead of operators, and easy to access and incredibly friendly and complete computer terminals instead of librarians.

If this last assumption surprises you, you haven't been watching the incessant ads from those who want to sell us online services and terminals. Obviously, bank and law firm officials had been watching those ads, and believing them. Let me restrict myself to two, and I am sure that their equivalents exist in Europe as well. In an America Online ad, an individual who is about to miss a basketball game because he has to go to the library is assured that going to the library is totally unnecessary because all he needs to know is available from America Online. And indeed, as the commercial unfolds, the printer spits out all of the needed information, and he leaves happily for the basketball game, something it is assumed that he would rather do than go to the library.

In the second ad, an off camera voice ushers us into the office of an obviously hard working executive. We know he is hard working because it is late at night. After brushing off interruptions while he is hard at work on his Hewlett Packard computer, the executive suddenly cries out in anguish. It turns out that he has hooked his golf tee shot into the lake. The message here is equally clear. Computer usage is fun, and the Hewlett Packard marketing people understand that it is fun and not just business applications that sell computers. Just ask your children if you are not sure. Of course, all of this creates great temptations to waste time on corporate and university computers by playing games instead of working, and we know that this is indeed happening. However, the marketing approaches are far much too subtle for us to notice.

The premise that end user computer access will suffice for all needed information, obviously accepted by both bank and law firm officials, plays right into the agenda of those concerned by the desire to downsize. Peter Drucker, way back in 1989, predicted the current frenzy of downsizing, and described it quite accurately. The immediate targets would be middle managers, facilitators, coordinators, teachers and guides—in other words the people who didn't really do anything to further organizational goals. They did not produce profits in the corporate sector, or generate tuition dollars in the academic one. The second downsizing wave would target all those who did clerical work. Perhaps it did not have to be done at all. At worst we could replace regular employees who had status and benefits with temporary or contract personnel who might cost less, but who in any case could be easily disposed of. Drucker went on to predict that none of this would really work. Downsizing would not increase efficiency, or improve profits. However, he noted that this would not be admitted. The failure of downsizing to achieve its objectives would simply lead to the conclusion that we needed to downsize some more. We need look no further than the stock market to understand how all of this works. When a corporation announces that it will get rid of several thousand people, its stock immediately goes up in price. Nobody on Wall Street asks who those people will be, what they did, and who will do it in their absence.

One of the dangers for librarians then obviously is this numbers game, and the failure of the individuals who make these decisions to understand what librarians do and why it is important. That failure should not surprise us, because librarians go to great extremes, in both the corporate and academic environments, never to serve the officials who will make decisions about our future. Did the senior law firm partners and the corporate officials several hundred miles away really understand what the library did? It is not likely, because they probably never had any direct contact with the library. Does the president of the university really understand what the library does? What does it do for him—and remember he is not doing research but dealing with administrative choices, like any corporate administrator?

Part of the problem I have already mentioned. It comes from the incessant and highly funded advertising campaign that stresses both the ease and fun of end user searching. We obviously know better than that, and I don't need to elaborate in talking to this audience. Computers are incredibly rude. Invalid instruction is simply not something one says to a distinguished professor. Voice mail systems, of course, are even worse. Frequently I am answered by a recording which informs me that I have reached an invalid number, and tells me to look in the directory for the correct number—when in fact I obtained the incorrect number from the directory in the first place. Voice mail message menus are worse. I must endure a whole list of options, and when I finally select one I may get a busy signal. Fortunately, these systems still have not learned to cope with dial phones as opposed to push button phones. I pretend to be able to use none of these options, and I eventually get an operator.

How many users would prefer to reach a reference librarian? If we allow the downsizing frenzy to reduce the number of reference librarians, and then most disastrously if we adapt the level of service to the reduced capability rather than carefully orchestrating a crisis of service deprivation which we then present to our management as its problem, we end up not only validating the staff cut but preparing the way for the next one.

Librarians, then, are an obvious and easy target for those seeking to downsize organizations, and much of the publicity from computer and database vendors suggests that this is a valid approach, particularly for individuals who 1) don't really know what librarians do because those librarians never serve them directly, and 2) have an innate suspicion of anyone assumed to simply manipulate files without really doing anything.

Consultants, who have the responsibility of recommending some sort of cost savings to justify their own fees, will follow that same course of least resistance. I must emphasize that none of this is really aimed directly at librarians. There is no anti-library lobby. Rather, it is aimed at particularly handy and certainly powerless victims. We want to eliminate people, and these people are handy and presumably unnecessary. Certainly nobody else will fight for them at the risk of their own jobs.

However, the greatest justification for eliminating librarians in a time of downsizing really comes from librarians themselves, and academic and public librarians on the one hand, and corporate librarians on the other, are equally guilty, but for very different reasons.

Academic and public librarians have always seen themselves primarily as educators, even as our fellow educators spurn us as full and equal partners. The premise of much of librarianship is teaching our users to be able to find for themselves in an information environment. End user training and bibliographic instruction are all approaches designed to teach others what we know, so that they can then function on their own. However, once they can function on their own, where is the need for us? It begins to look very much like a self-selected role of facilitator, coordinator, and lifetime teacher, all job titles which are very much under suspicion in the present environment. Job security comes most simply and directly from doing something that: 1) needs to be done because the requirement is urgent, and 2) nobody else knows how to do.

Plumbers and automobile mechanics understand this process much better than we do. I know of no workshops or training programs in end user plumbing or end user carburetor repair. If your car breaks down or your pipes burst you are helpless, and that is exactly what they had in mind. I could make a nonselfish argument that our end users, confronted by an endless array of options and gigantic increases in the amount of garbage (and garbage is defined by any one user as something he or she did not want to waste time having to look at), need information access instructors far less than they need information life-guards. Such an argument would quite comfortably serve both our users and us. However, even if that argument does not appeal to you, are we supposed to be so altruistic as to educate ourselves out of our jobs, abetted as we already are by a whole publicity campaign that already argues that what we teach is easily self taught and fun as well?

Special librarians (and I have been a special librarian as a practitioner and teacher just about all my adult life) have not accepted the premise that they should primarily be teachers. After all, the motto of the Special Libraries Association has been since the 1920s, and remains, "Putting Knowledge to Work," and that does not mean putting knowledge on the end user's terminal, or dumping it in endless piles on the user's desk. There has, in the last decade, been a considerable backing away from that rather straightforward philosophy in the pages of the official journal of the Special Libraries Association. We are now urged to embrace end user searching both as a foregone conclusion and as a virtue. Apparently, some librarians have been watching these ads as well. Instead, it is suggested, special librarians (and the movement has its parallel in academic libraries) are urged to embrace the role of information advisors or information gurus. It is an interesting concept, at least hypothetically. However, in the present fervor for downsizing the gurus and advisors will be eliminated right after the middle managers, or perhaps even ahead of the middle managers.

However, the issue is far more dangerous than that for us. I know that the librarians at the bank and the law firm I just mentioned did an excellent job of serving their clients, as I am sure some university libraries do an excellent job of responding to the demands of faculty, and perhaps even occasionally listening to a student. However, in the present management scenario, serving your clients well is not enough. In an era of downsizing your users, who do not generally make overall management decisions, become your rivals. We are going to downsize—do we keep researchers or librarians?—is not going to be answered to our satisfaction by any researchers, no matter how fond they are of the library or satisfied with its services. I am told that in both the bank and law firm lots of users came by to express their regrets. However, none of them volunteered to have their jobs eliminated in place of the librarians.

What special librarians failed abysmally to do (and I will broaden the discussion to academic and other librarians in a moment) is reach higher level management (the ones who never use the library personally because librarians don't seek out higher level management to address its needs) with a very simple message. The message is that keeping librarians is cost effective, because librarians can do, more accurately and more cheaply, what end users are now being urged to do. In other words, if you want to downsize and save money, add to the number of librarians, and lay off end users by the simple message of ordering end users not to do what librarians can do. As we all know from our studies of management, any job should be done by the lowest paid employee qualified to do it. Anything else is waste.

Would it really be that difficult to make that point, discretely of course? Does any law librarian doubt that he or she can do literature searching as well as lawyers, or medical librarians as well as doctors? It is not even necessary to be as good. If we can be only half as good, the fact that we are paid one third as much should make us more cost effective. And cost effective, I want to remind all in this audience, is a more important concept than cheap.

In an academic library the issue is a little more complex, but really the same. Academic libraries, certainly the ones I know, are also in great difficulty. Here librarians have allowed themselves to be maneuvered into an even weaker role. We are judged by the faculty not by what we do but by the collections we amass, and several decades ago a distinguished academic librarian like Robert Downs could argue that we would be judged not by the service we gave but for the collection we left behind us. Perhaps, but at best that was then, and this is now. More recently Robert Munn pointed out that the academic library was seen by the administration as a bottomless pit—the more you pour into it the emptier it appears. Certainly that observation is far more with us today.

But how and why did this happen? And more importantly, why have we allowed it to continue when it all became a disaster twenty years ago? Academic librarians in this audience know that the price of scientific and scholarly journals has increased at rates far beyond that of any inflation growth. Why these prices have increased does not matter, or at least it should not matter to us. Price increases beyond the norm are a problem for the vendor, assuming that the customer cares. The vendor can find cheaper ways to produce, make the product smaller by tightening acceptance standards, or by going out of business and leaving fewer vendors.

However, that is only if the customer cares. Here, the customers, who are university administrators and faculty, don't seem to care at all. Librarians of course do care, but librarians are not perceived as customers. They are perceived as purchasing agents. And so librarians try to survive in this absurd environment by eliminating subscriptions, but primarily by avoiding this process as long as possible:

1. by transferring money from monographs to journals;

2. by canceling the duplicate subscriptions to retain one of everything, even though we certainly know from our own literate about Bradford's distribution. However, it is the students who primarily need the duplicates;

3. by accepting poison pill budgets which give us more money for material but not for professional staff and continuing education.

Despite all of this, of course, collections continue to shrink, except in a very few libraries, and perhaps they should shrink in those as well (depending on what the other priorities are). And when collections shrink, the faculty become angry at us, and the administrators, whose only perception of the role of the library is that it not be a source of irritation for the faculty, then become annoyed at us.

The picture I am attempting to paint for academia suggests that, in a time of critical financial decisions and downsizing, we have as little a power base as corporate libraries. What then must our strategies be? Cynics might argue that academic administration is really an oxymoron, but at some point even here decisions must be made. What then is here the role of academic librarians in demonstrating their cost effectiveness—which really means simply that they are preferable to any alternative? I will have to begin with issues of ownership versus access, something we should understand quite well from our literature, but something which nonlibrarians do not understand at all. We can no longer own everything we need, although some major universities will try longer than others, and will succeed longer than others. However, given the rate of publication growth and the rate of price increase, even these will ultimately fail, and it might be more prudent to cut their losses early.

We also understand that ownership does not equate to access, because many of the things we do presumably own cannot be produced on demand—they are charged out and not due back, they are lost or misshelved, they are at the bindery which may really mean they are in the back room ready to go to the bindery. For us all of these excuses may be important, but for the requester they do not matter. For the requester the impact is binary—either I get the material or I don't. During my last ten years at Indiana University I began undertaking sort of an informal survey among faculty colleagues. I will admit that my survey is flawed, because all of the individuals I asked were serious and intelligent people with a view of the larger world. None of them were petulant babies who knew a great deal about one little thing and nothing about anything else. I asked them simply this: "If a librarian can guarantee to you that 95 percent of the things you requested would reach you within 48 hours, does it matter to you where the material comes from? And if the answer to the first question is no, is it then any of your business what I initially buy and what I decide to obtain through other techniques—AS LONG AS YOU GET IT?" My survey response was very encouraging, although I admit my response population was flawed.

However, at some point the issue of ownership versus access will have to be addressed by the administrators who are responsible for our universities. When that happens, I hope that the recognized experts in making alternative recommendations are librarians. When (and I don't say if) access is finally taken seriously, there is no doubt that copyright laws will once again have to be addressed. I'm not remotely worried about that because, fairly or unfairly, revision in a political arena will certainly protect the interests of the larger body, the users. Still, I hope it is fair. I also believe that for anything to be done which individuals truly believe to be essential, cost becomes irrelevant, and that belief is also articulated by Peter Drucker.

What then of the second academic issue, the one that most parallels the corporate alternative? Are faculty doing things that librarians could do more cost effectively? Are they doing it at all? There is a mystique in the academia I inhabited for over twenty years that faculty spend a great deal of time doing research. It is certainly true for a few, but not for very many. Ladd and Lipseth have reported that the average number of annual scholarly publications per faculty number is less than one. I found a surprising congregation of faculty colleagues during Christmas breaks heading for that most important of all research locations, cruises and warm weather beach resorts. When the University of Alberta Library offered online search training for faculty members, only a handful enrolled. A larger number enrolled secretaries and graduate assistants.

However, quite aside from whether or not faculty do information research, should they, like their corporate colleagues, do what reference librarians could do more cost effectively? What is the responsibility of the university president to see that this does not happen? Unless of course, the university already has too many faculty, and they have nothing to do anyway. Don't expect anyone to admit this. However, even if it were true, what an opportunity to downsize faculty by adding librarians and saving some real money!

Only in public libraries does the economic model on which I have so heavily relied because it is the one on which management increasingly relies become more complex. Work not done by professional librarians is presumably not done at all, or it is done by the citizens, whose own labors presumably cost government nothing. Here the strategy must be to raise the public expectation for what government must provide, even as we try to cut taxes and expenditures. That public outcry demanding better services works for police protection, it works for garbage collection, and it works for repairing the holes in the highway. If the public outcry has not demanded more professional librarian intermediaries, it may be because we have not orchestrated that demand. Of course, public librarians at least in the United States demonstrate the suicidal tactics one could otherwise only ascribe to lemmings. We accept Microsoft equipment from Bill Gates to help wean and train his future end users for him. Gates is a multi-billionaire, and I understand why this is a good deal for him. The computers he gives us are a good investment, and a tax write-off to boot. But what is in it for us? What else are we going to get?

Let me close by returning to Peter Drucker's accurate prediction of downsizing and the mechanisms for implementing and evaluating the process. At the same time he made these predictions, Drucker also predicted that the most glorious and important profession of the future would be that of knowledge workers. Quite simply, knowledge workers would be crucial because what they did would be essential, and because nobody else could do it. It almost sounds as though Drucker was talking about plumbers.

Do we have any desire to claim the role of knowledge workers? I have seen little indication of it, and certainly the editors of *USA Today* who equate librarians with telephone operators and bank tellers have not seen it, either. That is the fork in the road I see in front of us, and I wish I could be more optimistic about our choices and our strategies to accomplish what I think we could still accomplish, but not without a major reassessment.

Book Review

Troubled Times for American Higher Education. The 1990s and Beyond, by Clark Kerr in association with Marion L. Gade and Maureen Kawaoka. State University of New York Press, 1994. 189 pp., index. Softcover. ISBN 0-7914-1706-9. $18.95. Hardcover. ISBN 0-7914-1705-0.

As President Emeritus of the University of California, Berkeley; as former chair of the Carnegie Commission on Higher Education, and as the former chair and director of the National Commission on Strengthening Presidential Leadership under the auspices of the Association of Governing Boards of Universities and Colleges, Clark Kerr is at least as qualified as anyone else to speculate about the future of American higher education. The author of a number of books about higher education and the role of universities, Kerr has written this book as the second of three volumes, all published by the State University of New York Press.

The work consists of essays originally presented to other audiences, as well as of chapters and introductions written specifically for this book. It is arranged in three sections: 1. Approaching the twenty-first century. 2. Higher Education and the Economy, and 3. The 1990s and Beyond: Some Special Perplexities. Thirteen chapters of between 10 and 20 pages are distributed into these three areas, with each area also having its own separate introduction. Each chapter includes a fully annotated set of notes, which also serve as a useful bibliography. Finally, there is a three-page index to individuals and organizations, but not by subject.

Reprinted, with changes, by permission of the author and *Publishing Research Quarterly*, Fall 1996.

Kerr dedicates the book to his colleague Howard Bowen, the author, along with Jack Schuster, of the 1986 "American Professors: A National Resource Imperiled." Kerr acknowledges that, along with Bowen, he has recently tended toward pessimism in his outlook on American higher education. However, unlike the Bowen and Schuster work, which cited voluminous statistics and concluded that professors were unjustly unloved and unappreciated, Kerr's work shows a much more balanced approach. In the middle of the pessimism there are also strands of hope and of opportunity.

The author makes far too many points to allow all of them to be included in this review. I will restrict myself to only nine, and some are simply repeated without elaboration.

1. The author notes, and not without some concern, the steady advancement in the curriculum of specialized and vocational courses, and the growing supremacy of the labor market in enrollment trends.

2. He quotes Henry Rosovsky in noting that academia (particularly faculties of arts and sciences) has become a society without rules, or more specifically one in which tenured faculty members make their own rules. The perceived responsibility toward "faculty citizenship" is seen to be declining.

3. Higher education will need to strengthen its decision-making processes to remain dynamic, and must learn to subtract programs as well as to add them.

4. The U.S. academic institutions, despite all of the naysayers, still play a dominant role on the international scene, particularly in the sciences. In these fields Americans have received 58 percent of the prestigious international awards, and contribute 37 percent of the articles to the literature, which in turn receive an even higher 51 percent of citations. While much is wrong, much is also right.

5. Kerr considers the growing conflict between the desire to achieve equality, and the desire to reward merit, as the crucial issue emerging in the latter 1990s. The insistence on achieving equality of results based on numerical proportionality will, in Kerr's view, intensify. He does not consider the two objectives as necessarily contradictory, but I would agree that they must be carefully balanced, particularly at a time when some minority groups increasingly stress their uniqueness and difference, rather than seek integration into a unified whole.

6. Kerr comments on both the briefer tenure and more difficult tasks of the university president. For a president's evaluation, eight areas with a grade of A and one area with a grade of F totals an overall grade of F.

7. Is the main purpose of the university, and in particular the public university, one of serving the economy? Kerr notes that this is increasingly the view, particularly as governors and state legislatures take a growing role in spelling out the missions for their universities. He makes a spirited defense for the multiple roles of the university, but it occurs to this reviewer that many universities play into this single-track validation by concentrating on "proving" what they contribute to the economy. Kerr considers such single strategies unwise, and argues that in any case the charge that the university has failed to support the economy is simply untrue.

8. The United States may place an unfair and unwarranted emphasis on higher education as the "solution" to all of our problems. Germany, by contrast, relies far more on apprenticeships, and Japan on a combination of secondary education and job training. I agree, but it occurs to me that during the 1970s and into the 1980s higher education did nothing to discourage, and indeed welcomed, the assumption that education was the key solution to all of society's problems.

9. Kerr indicts the much-heralded quest for enhancing the quality of undergraduate education as far more rhetoric than performance.

These are just tidbits and samples from a very thoughtful, provocative, and informative book, one that is well worth reading. Despite his acknowledgment of many problems, his growing pessimism, and the frank observation that solutions for all are not readily in view, Kerr remains upbeat. Yes, there are problems, but there is also a tremendous reservoir of talent. What is required is the will.

Faculty Status for Academic Librarians: The Search for the Holy Grail

A great deal has been written in the literature of academic librarianship about faculty status. Some writers brag that they have it, others insist that they neither want nor need it. One reason to covet faculty status is easy to understand. It carries rewards and privileges, including higher salaries, eligibility for sabbaticals, and almost always a process of tenure under which termination becomes difficult, even for senility. Faculty almost always get more fringe benefits than the unwashed rest of university inhabitants.

Tenure was initially established to protect faculty from dismissal based on the controversiality or unpopularity of their views, and it could be argued that this protection is no longer needed. However, tenure represents a valuable piece of turf, and faculty would be foolish to give it up. Since it is valuable, it becomes just as important for librarians. Do academic librarians want the financial benefits and security that accrue to faculty? They would be unwise if they didn't. The financial package is important not just for what it will buy, but because it represents proof that you are valued. Talk is cheap. If we are told that we are loved and appreciated, then we should ask for proof in our pay.

The second reason to demand faculty status is more emotional, and it cannot be undermined even with bribes of money, unlikely as that is for librarians these days. Faculty status is important because it carries with it recognition as a "member of the club." The *right* to lunch in the faculty club is more important than whether we *want* to do so.

Gaining Respect

Equal treatment can be demanded, but respect only comes voluntarily. It's simplistic for librarians to believe that faculty status or faculty equivalence also earns automatic collegial respect. Individual librarians can and do earn that respect. They may work as subject specialists in close contact with other specialists who teach and conduct research. When this happens, their expertise is acknowledged by those with whom they interact, frequently by the conferral of additional faculty rank. I wouldn't go so far as to suggest that collegial acceptance is granted *despite* their being librarians. However, along with many of you, I have been paid the dubious compliment that I don't "act like a librarian."

Some who work behind the scenes in academic libraries do not have the same opportunity to earn collegial awareness and recognition, simply because faculty do not know who they are and what they do. We sometimes go to great pains to make sure no one knows our work and its importance. It would not be a problem if respect were granted simply on the assumption that an individual must be qualified if so deemed by his or her peers. Universities make such assumptions, as I've seen on university-wide promotion and tenure committees. Physicists and classical scholars cannot really evaluate one another's dossiers because they cannot understand them. But they will respect and accept each other after relying on those presumably qualified to judge and to recommend.

Aping Faculty

Real displacement of value systems and of work priorities can occur when librarians try to resemble faculty members or, even worse, when their tenure dossiers are evaluated by faculty who have no idea what professional librarians do and simply insist that librarians ought to look like them.

Librarians work under rules far different from those of professors. The latter, if they have a teaching load of two, three, or four courses, are committed to a specific schedule that requires only between five and ten formal class hours per week. They need time for lecture preparation (unless this is the 14th time they have taught the course), for exam grading (unless this is done by graduate assistants or optical scanners), and for student counseling. However, all teaching faculty have at their disposal a lot of unstructured time. It is assumed that they use some or perhaps all of this for research and for writing, and if they are still untenured they had better do so. Some of it is also available for the lengthy and repeated meetings for which faculty are notorious.

No "Free" Time

The point is that when faculty attend meetings they do so on their own "free" time, and their general use of that time is not monitored. When faculty show up at the office at noon, it must be assumed that they were doing research or writing all morning. Sometimes they really were, but in any case that is no one's business. Faculty are judged by results, not by time clocks.

It is a nice system for faculty, but unfortunately it is not available for academic librarians, who tend to work regular work schedules starting at 8 or 9 a.m., and whose regular job duties, which have nothing to do with either writing or research, reflect this. Librarians don't get away with failing to show up for reference desk duties because they were fascinated by their research, unlike some teaching faculty. When librarians immerse themselves in meetings, they may be aping professorial style, but they will not be forgiven any of their other assigned duties. Moreover, they insist on these meetings not because of any importance to the library but because they are trying to emulate the process of "faculty governance," which is based on an unstructured environment, not a library hierarchical one.

It is for this reason that, as dean of a library school, I insisted on paying directly those librarians who taught as adjuncts rather than "buying" their services from the university library. The library would happily take the money but would never forgive the librarians—particularly those with supervisory responsibilities—any of their other duties.

Doing It Our Way

It is difficult to understand why librarians who try so hard to look like faculty would want to start forming teams for both work and decisionmaking, with shared responsibilities and shared or blurred credit. Faculty structures are based on a rugged individualism; rewards are given for specific accomplishments and never for what the team or the committee does. Faculty care far more about national and international reputations, and if individuals turn out to be more highly regarded than their colleagues, then they become the "stars" who must be paid whatever it takes to keep them.

Who, by contrast, are the universally acknowledged stars in the library? Why, if we want to emulate and impress faculty who are really the purest bastions of entrepreneurship (*my* book, *my* award, *my* grant), would we want to use a system they despise as unworthy of the academic process? Even when faculty form teams for research and writing, each participant is identified by name in any public recognition that ensues. Why do we do our best to make ourselves anonymous—to other librarians and, more importantly, to faculty?

Research Outranks Teaching

The preoccupation with being characterized as teachers so as to resemble faculty is also dangerous: faculty in research institutions, despite all assurances to the contrary, will not value teaching as highly as research and scholarship. Being considered *only* an excellent teacher unfortunately may not even earn tenure. Research continues to outrank teaching, if only because the first will impress a far more prestigious constituency. University administrator Clark Kerr made this point in 1994, as Logan Wilson had made it in 1940. Good teaching impresses primarily students, and students are only transients. Nothing has changed, nor is it likely to, in this value system.

Do librarians get credit for all of the unique things they do and the time they spend doing it? It should be obvious that our schedules cannot produce the same volume of research and publication without limiting our formal job assignments to between five and ten hours per week. Since that won't happen, we must stress to faculty that judging us by their standards is absurdly unfair. Instead, we should emphasize that we are entitled to all of their benefits and all of their status, not because we are exactly like them, but because what we do is just as important and our contributions are just as significant. Unless we can lay claim to a specific level of unique expertise, we will be on very shaky ground.

Fortunately, the recognition and acceptance of specializations is the very premise for the existence of the "multiversity." Shakespearean scholars, physicists, and librarians of high quality are not interchangeable. However, specialists in all three areas are essential for the success of the institution. In academia, it is those whose work is so esoteric that the rest of us don't understand it who are assumed to be brilliant.

Changing Perceptions

In the anniversary issue of *LJ* ("Academic Libraries: 2000 and Beyond," *LJ*, July, p. 74–76), Jim Neal makes a number of predictions about the future of academic librarianship. I have no reason to challenge any of them, but at least two disturb me. He predicts that tenure for librarians will once again be questioned. If so, I suggest it is not because administrators are wicked, but simply because the faculty will not rise to fight for us as they would for themselves. The lack of collegiality can also be seen in the recent UCLA administrative suggestion that librarians receive smaller salary increases than faculty on the assumption that faculty would not mind having librarians receive smaller raises, if this might protect their own increases.

Neal's second disturbing prediction is that the number of librarians in academia will decline. In my last column ("Do We Want to Be Knowledge Workers?" *LJ*, September 15, p. 41–42, I suggested that lowering demand for reference services by teaching faculty to be self-sufficient was disastrous for the institution but particularly for us. The threat of losing tenure and the threat of losing our jobs are very much related to the larger issue of how important we are perceived to be to the university. Not the library—everyone knows the library is important. How important are the librarians? Is it somehow assumed that a large, high-quality library and a large staff of high-quality librarians are independent variables? Would anyone suggest something so absurd in a discussion of academic departments?

Adapting Commercial Strategies to Managing Government Libraries

I will begin this talk by defining four of the terms heavily used in the commercial sector. These terms are (1) *overhead*, (2) *downsizing*, (3) *outsourcing*, and (4) *marketing*. All of these terms are, of course, also used in the federal sector, although perhaps with slightly different definitions and perhaps even significantly different intent. However, the federal government insists that it is trying to operate as though it were a business. In any case, these definitions and perceptions particularly affect, and often particularly endanger, libraries in all sectors.

Overhead organizations are those which do not contribute directly to the primary objective of the organization. In the corporate world, this is frequently the production and sale of products for profit. In the government sector, it is usually defined as not being directly involved with the primary mission of the parent organization, which might be to protect the environment in one case, or to safeguard the nation from air attack in another. The definitions are not rigid, for example, sales is sometimes considered a direct cost, sometimes not. In any case, however, the organizations categorized as overhead are not necessarily unimportant or powerless. They include, for example, the entire executive staff, from the chief executive on down through the staff assistants. They include personnel or, as it is now called to make it appear more important, human resources. They include accounting, and they include public relations. And, of course, they include

Talk presented to the Federal Library and Information Center Committee Meeting, Library of Congress, Washington, D.C., December 10, 1996.

199

general service organizations such as libraries. I make this point to stress that, while all overhead organizations are automatically suspect of being perhaps less necessary or even unnecessary, some of your partners in this pool are far more capable of defending themselves against cuts than others. This is important because the overhead budget is usually determined initially not on a case-by-case basis, but as a total related to the direct budget, usually by percentages. While shifts in the allocation of the overhead budget are not only possible but likely, the overall total usually remains unchanged. The battles for reallocations, therefore, usually occur between overhead organizations, and not with direct organizations. Production people usually have little input and less concern about things such as the library budget, because it does not affect them financially. That is, they will not care unless they feel that an inadequate library affects them more directly than, for example, an inadequate cafeteria. This then automatically suggests the strategies in protecting and enlarging your own part of the overhead budget. It also suggests the difficulty if you report to an executive who also supervises other, and perhaps for him or her, more endearing parts of the overhead budget, such as Research and Development. While librarians generally like reporting to researchers because they are articulate and well educated, in a budget battle, they may be your rivals.

Your success in protecting or enlarging your share of the overhead dollar pot depends less on actual contributions (because these are difficult to quantify) than on a *perception* of contribution, and this point must be clarified. An end use department manager may well agree that the services of the library has "saved" his department the work of two researchers, but what does that mean? Does it mean that the manager will now reduce the staff by two researchers? That is not likely. Or does it mean that the manager will now not require two additional researchers? Financial managers may well counter that these would never have been authorized in the first place, and therefore, the saving is not real.

Nevertheless, the best tactic in protecting against downsizing is in doing much of the work which clearly must be done if the organization is to succeed. This means that, rather than encouraging end user searching, you should take over as many of these information-gathering tasks as possible, precisely because they must be done.

If the end users really do all of their own work, then what remains to the librarians is housekeeping and record keeping, and these are truly perceived as trivial and therefore expendable. The obvious strategy in avoiding downsizing is never in being cheap, because you will never be cheap enough. The strategy is one of being crucial, essential, and irreplaceable. How do you make the point that you can do professional work more cost effectively than end users, and, of course, you usually can? By undertaking on your own, or by demanding studies to examine the most cost-effective approach. There are still individuals, perhaps not in your immediate management but certainly at top management and financial management, who are interested in cost effectiveness and not simply appearance. Since these are the people who will in any case determine your budget (almost always in meetings at which you will not be present), these are the people you must impress.

Did you hear me suggest that it is more important to impress top management than your direct users? Yes, you did, although obviously it is important to serve your users effectively. However, if your users are in the same leaky overhead boat as you are, they cannot really help you.

Downsizing was a process which was predicted by Peter Drucker in the late 1980s, and he noted that while we obviously want to eliminate those people who don't really do anything useful, when it becomes simply a numerical game, it will not work. As usual, Drucker was correct. Unfortunately, here as with overhead budgets, we are dealing largely with perceptions, and the perception is that downsizing *always* saves money, although obviously sometimes it causes a disaster. Thus, when AT&T announces that it will reduce its labor force by 20,000, the stock market reacts favorably. Nobody knows what those 20,000 did, perhaps not even the people who are making the budget cuts. It is simply assumed that they did nothing worthwhile. It is precisely the downsizing frenzy which may place you into direct competition with your end users. When it becomes necessary to nominate candidates for the chopping block, any head is preferable to our own. To avoid downsizing you must not only demonstrate that what you do is crucial, but even to create the subtle impression that, if the organization assigned more work to the library, it might be able to reduce the number of direct employees. Here, then, as in all strategies for all libraries, corporate or federal, the classic strategy must be not simply in pleasing your clients, but even more importantly, to reach the top administrators who will decide. Effective library managers must develop strategies for doing this, because contact with top management is, for most of us, not automatic. Yes, of course, they need information, but it is usually not the information we have been "chartered" to provide. You therefore need to expand your charter to serve the people you need to impress, whether they ask you or not. This is not, I should stress, a silly wasteful game. They really do have information needs, and you can help them. You simply cannot wait to be asked.

Outsourcing comes in two varieties: the legitimate and the cosmetic game. Outsourcing is legitimate when, because of economies of scale, outside organizations can do work more economically, and things like large microfilming projects come immediately to mind. Contractors have the staff, they have advanced equipment. Contracting, which is really simply the other name for outsourcing, also makes sense when the contractor possesses skills not available in your own organization. It might involve a consulting assignment, it might involve a specific systems analysis or programming task. Finally, outsourcing makes sense when the work is so simple or routine that it can literally be done by anyone, with minimal preparation or training. Since headcount ceilings will always be important, we should not waste precious staff on work which might be routine, or perhaps even temporary. Libraries which purchase their books so that the contractor pastes in the pockets are doing exactly the right thing.

Outsourcing becomes an ugly game when the intent is not economy but the appearance of economy, and I am afraid that the federal government is most vulnerable to this charge. The elimination of 200,000 federal jobs makes little sense if they are replaced by 400,000 contractors, and just driving around the Washington Beltway leads me to suspect that this may be exactly what is happening. Where did all those contractors come from in the years since I last lived in Washington, particularly in an environment in which the federal government is presumably shrinking? Of course, we all know that the federal government is not shrinking, and in fact, cannot shrink. That is not your fault, it is the fault of those of us who live in the rest of the country. There are more of us, and we constantly want more services. However, who is going to confront us with that truth?

Outsourcing also becomes ugly when we look for presumed economy which is not cost effective but only cheap. Cheap can turn out to be very expensive. Unfortunately, libraries are vulnerable to the danger of being contracted to the lowest bidder, because there are no standards as to what a library is supposed to do. When contracting officers preside over the process, they usually write the contract terms as number of books processed or number of reference questions answered. However, what books, how well processed, how well answered? Contracting officers cannot answer these questions. Therefore, at a minimum, when the operation of a federal library is to be contracted, the agency must retain at least enough of a high-level professional staff to assure that the contract specifications are properly written and properly administered. All too often, this does not happen. If I repeat a theme here, it is because it is relevant. The best way to avoid having your own position outsourced is to make the point, to key executives well in advance of the decision, that what you *personally* contribute cannot be replicated. I made this point in talking to Air Force librarians. While Air Force libraries are routinely outsourced, the flying of our fighter planes will never be outsourced. Why not? I'm certain we can find former Russian MIG pilots who might be just as capable, and who would undoubtedly be cheaper, considering what is happening in Russia. This obviously cannot be considered, because who flies our fighter planes is far too important to entrust to just anyone. How important are Air Force libraries?

Let me stress again that outsourcing is not necessarily bad; it is bad only when the intent is cosmetic, without concern either for real cost or the maintenance of quality. In 1964 I directed what was one of the earliest contracted government operations, the NASA Scientific and Technical Information Facility. Mel Day and the rest of the NASA team chose a contractor not because they thought this would be cheaper, but because they thought it would improve performance. From my own biased viewpoint, I think they were correct. However, Day and his team did not just trust us. They kept a high-level team of NASA professionals who wrote detailed contract specifications, and who monitored our performance literally on a daily basis. Finally, just to make sure, there were performance clauses in the contract. The better (not the cheaper) we did, the more we would earn.

The issue of *marketing* concerns not just what we do but also what we are supposed to do. Determining what that is requires a proactive approach, which involves not simply asking people what they want, but also asking them whether they might like something we do not presently provide. Marketing is then a process of destabilizing the environment, by creating the awareness of an unmet need. Marketing is not simply the process of offering what you have been authorized to offer, it is a process of creating instability. It is unfortunate that marketing is frequently confused, in our literature, with selling, when in fact, they are almost oppositives. Selling depends on satisfied customers, marketing depends on dissatisfied customers, which then allows you to propose to your management tactics for meeting this genuine but heretofore unrealized need. Don't be afraid that in doing this, you will manipulate your clients. You can't do that. If they don't want what you are suggesting, they will tell you. However, frequently, their lack of awareness may come either from not knowing that what you are suggesting is even possible, or that the library could do such things. When, in my own consulting assignments, I am asked to determine what needs the library ought to address, I begin by asking a cross-section of organizational professionals (not necessarily heavy library users) to tell me what they wish an ideal library or information center would do for them. They protest that doing this is silly, but I tell them that, whether they get what they dream about or not, our knowing what it is becomes the first step.

I hope it is clear from what I have said that I consider the issues of overhead, downsizing, outsourcing, and marketing to be interrelated. All of them require librarians to be assertive and proactive. If you simply sit back and wait for bad things to happen to you, I can assure you that they will.

Our Failure to Seek, Much Less Achieve, Funding and Management Support

In the years in which I have taught courses on management to prospective librarians at Indiana University and other places, I have frequently been asked why such courses are even necessary. After all, the business school teaches management in an entirely different setting, and with an entirely different set of assumptions about its students. Students in the M.B.A. program have accepted all of the premises that guide management values and decisions. There are, I suggest, very few if any anarchists in the M.B.A. program. By contrast, it is my observation that there are a considerable number of anarchists or would-be anarchists enrolled in library school. Why do we need management at all? Why can't we all just get along? Why can't we cooperate in simply doing what is best for the library and its users? I did not go to library school to become a manager, I came here because I want to help people.

It is the subject of my very first and perhaps traumatic lecture to note that perhaps guidance counselors and friends have cruelly misled them. Librarianship is not a profession of things or even of books, it is a profession of people. People use many tools, including books, but the most significant tool in their potential success will be other people. Of course we all believe in cooperation, but one of the reasons cooperation works much better in principle than in practice is that we all define cooperation in terms of our own value system and preconceptions. "Why can't you be more cooperative?" is frequently heard. "Why can't I be more cooperative" is never stated. I am already as cooperative as I can possibly get. The problem is you.

Politics, I tell my students, is not a dirty word. It is a normal process of making difficult decisions in the allocation of resources which will always be too small to meet the demand. No matter how much money there is, there will never be enough, and others will want the money which, if they are successful, will not come to you. Those "others" are not just the industrial military establishment, they include the school system, police protection, road repair, health care, and support for the homeless. We may consider some of these to be "good" causes and others to be "bad" causes, but in a political sense they are all bad for us. The amount of total funding is limited, although certainly not unalterable. Who gets money and who does not is the process of politics. It is a normal and perhaps even healthy process. Those who consider it evil or unfair are usually the ones who do not know how to compete or, even worse, do not want to compete. In most fields such individuals rapidly fall aside. In libraries they may progress to becoming directors, primarily responsible for the one task they do not want to perform and do not know how to perform.

Astute management writers such as Peter Drucker have recognized this problem, although in a much larger setting than librarianship. Drucker has noted that the for-profit sector has its own weeding mechanisms for eliminating, through the political process, managers who cannot succeed in doing their jobs.[1] The not-for-profit sector has no such easy management tools as profitability. How does one determine whether a not-for-profit organization is being managed effectively or not? It is this fascination and this challenge which have impelled Drucker to plan to spend the remainder of his professional career in studying and writing about the not-for-profit sector. That sector of course includes libraries, even libraries in the for-profit sector since these institutions are not perceived as playing a direct role. That of course suggests a new strategy for such library directors, as perhaps it even does for public and academic library directors, in looking for ways to demonstrate how the library activities *directly* and not just peripherally affect the crucial activities of the parent body. Drucker does not write directly about libraries; indeed except for one article in *College and Research Libraries*[2], he disavows any understanding of what it is we do. Nevertheless, his generalized assessment of political difficulties for the not-for-profit sector certainly applies to librarians.

Drucker notes three frequently fatal political characteristics for not-for-profit service professionals. First, they are measured not in terms of what they accomplish but rather in terms of how much they spend. When budgets drive programs, rather than programs driving budgets, the management decision process has been reversed, and probably what results will not be very effective. I suspect that not even Drucker could have imagined the library variant to his first principle, one in which budgets and programs are considered independent variables. "Do everything with nothing" is supposed to be a cartoon joke, not a real management strategy.

His second point, that agendas for not-for-profit service institutions are set not by the managers but by various groups of outsiders, who frequently have different and even contradictory goals, requires very little elaboration. Certainly those who fund us, and those who demand service from us, both do much to set our agendas, and their value systems are very different.

Drucker's third point, which in large part explains the reason the first two are even possible, is that service professionals accept the premise of the "moral imperative," that somehow—without funds, without staff, without equipment—they are personally responsible for everything that has to happen. If it fails to happen it will be their own personal fault. Drucker notes that once it is understood by upper management in the political process that management will never be blamed, the decision to give resources to those who do threaten to point fingers and distribute blame becomes absurdly simple.

Almost two decades ago Bo Hedberg accurately predicted the coming period of declining rather than increasing resources for such service fields as education, and warned against possible pitfalls in developing a management strategy for what he considered an inevitable trend for management in general.[3] Hedberg noted that declining budgets would in all probability be first presented as a "temporary" aberration, soon to be reversed, or at least to be reversed as soon as times got better some time in the future. Hedberg argued that in most instances there was no validity for such a suggestion, because declining budgets usually served as the harbingers of further budget declines. The strategy of suggesting that the problem is temporary is often only a tactic for avoiding an unpleasant discussion, and the need to make unpleasant choices.

The second stage in Hedberg's scenario finally recognizes the finality or at least long term status of the budget cut, but argues that programs should be left unaffected by a decline particularly in staff, and that such cuts should be absorbed by "working harder." It may be that this strategy is designed to flush out the moral imperativists in the institution, who will sacrifice not only themselves but their staffs for the "ultimate good." Hedberg has little patience with this second step, noting that while the absorption of more work might indeed be possible, it can never be admitted, simply because such an admission would involve the confession of having been a wastrel or a goof-off in the past. Not only is this unacceptable for managers, Hedberg argues, it is particularly unacceptable for staff members, and the suggestion when coming from higher management represents a betrayal of the unwritten agreement so carefully if unofficially crafted: we will pay you X dollars, in return for which you will accomplish a Y quantity of work.

Hedberg's third step, which certainly appears reasonable and is echoed by many of today's management writers, argues that only when this stage is reached can the budget cut be properly dealt with. A change in resources means a change in the program—in what is done, in the way it is done, and most specifically in what will now no longer happen. That decision of program change caused by a resources change (which of course could at least theoretically be an increase as well as a decrease) must be carefully negotiated, carefully spelled out, and approved by the people who cut the budget. Many libraries, as we all know, get stuck on step two and never even reach step three.

Drucker made exactly the same point when he noted, in a short article in the August 1, 1986, *Wall Street Journal,*[4] that it was essential that any manager and his or her own boss be on the same side of any dispute, against "them." The reason is obvious. Your own management has more power and more authority than you do. But how do we co-opt our bosses into our programs? Through a regular and continuing process of communication, which ties library programs to their own programs and their own objectives. Through a reliance on exception reporting, in stressing in our reports and news conferences not just what went well (we will probably do this in any case) but rather by stressing what went badly or did not happen at all. This is of course not a new management reporting strategy, it may only be new to some librarians. Exception reporting is the backbone of all sorts of management "fix" theories, ranging from management by objectives (MBO) to total quality management (TQM). It is when subordinates are able to shape their management communication in terms of what has and what has not happened, and why this is important to management's priorities, that Drucker is able to postulate that your own boss becomes your most important subordinate.

Other political leaders have also made these obvious points of political negotiation, usually in the general management literature (we certainly can read Tom Peters if we want to) and sometimes even directly to librarians. Otis Bowen, a family physician and superb politician who had become an immensely popular governor of Indiana, noted in a message to the annual conference of the Indiana Library Association that it seemed to him that librarians had not figured out ways to reward their friends and punish their enemies. An enemy, we should understand, does not spew hatred of libraries. That would make them easy to spot, but there really are no such people. Everyone insists they favor libraries. An enemy is someone who would rather not fund them, would rather fund something else, or would rather simply cut government expenditures. It comes out to the same thing.

Our failure to document and report crises is reported almost daily in our literature. Instead, our public libraries report the "good" news that despite budget cuts, circulation continues to increase, and I have noted that strange management strategy in a number of my own *Library Journal* columns.[5]

I have also noted our failure to establish any sort of professional agenda that defines what librarians do, or that differentiates between the library as a building and the library as a professional institution managed and staffed by qualified professionals. Doctors would never permit the term hospital to be used so casually. I need not spell out to the reader that all libraries, in the development of their own objectives and priorities, deal with at least three distinct roles. The first and most obvious is the support of recreation. It is embraced most readily by public libraries, although even academic and school libraries have recreational reading opportunities built into their programs. Only special libraries tend not to embrace this objective. Recreational reading is, as stated, the most obvious and easiest to demonstrate. It is, for many public libraries that provide simply the services "their users demand," perhaps the only real and certainly often the only perceived priority. However, it is also the most dangerous, because in times of budget cuts and prioritizing by government officials it becomes the easiest to dispense with because of a greater lack of urgency. Libraries in this context are frequently lumped together with parks.

The second library role, in support of education, should be relatively easy to justify, and it is the role that librarians most commonly choose for themselves. Education is still considered important as a public priority, although perhaps not as great a perceived priority as in the 1960s and early 1970s. In part, this is because of the growth of other problem areas, and in part because the education community has lost much of its credibility, probably by promising more than it could deliver. Nevertheless, education is seen by both the general public and certainly by virtually all public, academic, and school librarians as their greatest mission. Why this has not worked very well for us either in securing funding support or even in an understanding that our role is as important as we claim it to be is something that will be discussed in later sections of this chapter.

The third area, that of information intermediation, is the newest and at least potentially the most significant. This is because others have already decided, without our help, that information is crucial to success in achieving just about anything, and that ignorance is not an acceptable alternative. However, the library role in this process is not clearly understood, and there are several reasons. The first is that computer professionals are now suggesting that information access will be a self service process, ignoring the fact that information is growing at tremendous rates, that finding the right information while shielding yourself from being buried in irrelevant information is a complex process that will most certainly become more complex and more expensive, even as giddy promises to the contrary are made.

The second reason is the growth of an aggressive and savvy information intermediation industry in the private sector. These "meatware" specialists (to differentiate what they do from the hardware and software that end users would just as soon let someone else use on their behalf—a secretary, a graduate assistant or someone we contract with) ignore the existence of libraries in their own literature and justifications.[6] If pressed, they will argue that this activity of providing answers to specific questions is something that librarians do not do, that librarians cannot do, or even that librarians do not want to do.

There may even be some truth in the assertion, because some librarians see a conflict between their role as perceived educators (teach people to help themselves so that they can be independent of librarians) and the role of providing information to individuals who would rather not do their own information searching. That conflict is most sharply etched in dealing with schoolchildren, but some librarians in both public and academic settings carry it over to working with adults, postulating that individuals do want to do this work themselves, or that in any case they should want to. If we recognize the growth of the service professions as a general phenomenon for fields as diverse as automotive repair and travel reservations, it is not difficult to see that if we not only fail to fight for the role of information intermediaries but even more significantly choose to consider it something we do not want to do, we place severe crimps on our political outreach opportunities. This is particularly true because we have not been very successful in getting others to see the crucial role we claim to play in education, and the ones we have most significantly failed to persuade are our "fellow" educators.

It might be a more rational solution if we allowed the user to decide on whether he or she preferred service or self service. If there is a moral issue here it is for teachers and not librarians to make that case. However, that would require that, in bibliographic instruction, we teach students not only how to find their own information, but also how to demand service from reference librarians, and that we not place a value ranking on these options. I am not at all sure we are ready for such a step, but I am sure that in failing to fight for the role of information intermediaries in an environment in which needed information will increasingly become more complex, more interdisciplinary and more important, we cede almost without a struggle what could become our most important political and funding turf. Certainly someone will do this work, and it will be funded. As Drucker has noted, in the provision of information that the user considers crucially important, cost becomes not only secondary but even irrelevant. That case can hardly be made for the library's recreational role, and in our educational role both classroom teachers and professors have insisted that we get into line behind them.

Whatever agendas (and there needs to be a range of them for any library) we choose for ourselves, it is my own observation that we have not done a very good job in identifying and articulating our own specific priority rankings, certainly not to the individuals on whom we depend for both support and funding. Several examples come immediately to mind. We fail to establish an agenda, and control over that agenda, which is exclusively ours on the basis of knowledge and educational preparation, something that doctors and lawyers automatically do. Indeed, it is one of the definitions of any profession that it controls the interaction between itself and its clients. We concentrate instead on promulgating the need for "the library." However, our failure to define what constitutes a library, and more importantly to specify what is *not* a library, allows others to define the term for us, and we always accept their definitions. It is not difficult to predict that those definitions will frequently mean smaller (except in academia), usually mean fewer or no professional staff members, inevitably a narrower common denominator based both on user control and self service ("keep the doors open" is a classic example of this simplistic philosophy), and certainly cheaper libraries. We refuse steadfastly to blow the whistle on this process by labeling what might result as a nonlibrary or a pseudolibrary. Instead, we concentrate our energies, in the annual exercise of self-trivialization we call National Library Week, on urging people to "read." It is certainly a worthwhile slogan, unless it is a nice day outside and "go for a walk" might be more appropriate. However, it is a slogan that can certainly be implemented without financial support, without objectives and strategies, and most certainly without us.

Our failure to assert our unique expertise is certainly a problem if we ever expect to be able to distribute credit and blame to those who either support us or fail to do so. The medical profession has seen the importance of controlling its credentialing process. Much younger than librarianship, because surgery used to be performed by barbers, the medical field has now established such complete control that, if you call yourself a doctor without the profession's permission, you go to jail, and how good a "doctor" you were does not matter. By contrast, we are even reluctant to support the academic credentialing process which we control, as shown in the Merwine case, where ALA refused to support the importance of its own accreditation procedures.[7]

We complain bitterly when our salaries are consistently lower than those of other professionals with equivalent qualifications, and outsiders explain to us patiently and tutorially that these inequities result from "market factors." However, even when the shortage-surplus game could be turned to our advantage, we fail to grasp the significance. One obvious example will suffice.

During much of the 1980s, when I served as a library education program dean, there was a chronic shortage of qualified children's librarians to work in public libraries. The economic workings of the market factor game should have meant that starting salaries for children's librarians rose dramatically. However, market factors only work when management insists on the specified qualifications. One of the reasons professors of business administration are paid more than professors of comparative linguistics is because people with doctorates in linguistics, who are plentiful, are not allowed to teach business administration, where qualified candidates are both scarce and expensive. To extend the model to public libraries, it would have required that directors unable to find a qualified candidate at the salary posted keep the position unfilled, perhaps for years if necessary, until the Board, beset by angry parents, found the necessary money. That is what happens in academia. It does not happen if, when confronted by the realization that we cannot meet the requirements at the salary offered, we adapt the requirements to the salary we are prepared to pay.

Management writers such as Roma Harris[8] and James Carmichael[9] have, from very different perspectives, described what happens to both men and women who work in a feminized profession. It is certainly true that the problems are real, because our managers expect us to behave in certain ways. However, that does not require that we behave as expected. Female former students in corporate environments have reported to me that their most annoying problem comes from being trivialized by older male bosses, not because these are evil people, but rather because they are "nice" people trying to protect the librarian who is assumed to be naïve and helpless. There is only one way to deal with this, we have to tell them that their assumptions are wrong. Tell them nicely, at least at first, but tell them: Treat us as meanly as you treat everyone else! Don't patronize us!

And yet there are plentiful examples that suggest, indeed as I suspect with my neophyte students, that librarians often lack the ability or the will to use the political process to reward or punish. The problem the entire profession then faces is that when many librarians do not use these perfectly normal management tactics in dealing with their bosses, it is assumed that none of us will. The process would not be nearly as dangerous or appear nearly as strange if librarians were routinely expected to behave as other managers behave. A few examples from a range of library disciplines will illustrate my point.

Public libraries. A recent report by Thomas Childers[10] indicates that in the state of California, in which public library reference service has been decimated by budget cuts, user demand for such service continues to increase. However, the study does not suggest ways to turn this finding into political pressure on those who cut the funds by channeling the anger of those now being deprived. Instead, there is examination of how libraries can provide adequate reference service, or at least acceptable reference service, in spite of budget cuts. What is the political reward and punishment in such a strategy?

We are informed in a number of ongoing media articles of financial problems for the San Francisco Public Library, for which the mayor, desirous of having his cake and eating it, too, fired his own library board for having made the perfectly reasonable decision to cut branch hours in the face of budget cuts. Presumably such actions would have made the mayor look bad. Later that same mayor, while he insisted he "supported" libraries, expressed his displeasure at voter action to restore some of the cut funds, insisting that the library did not need the money. The specific action is not unusual here. What is perhaps surprising, from the political standpoint, is that nobody within the ALA hierarchy, which moves conferences from various cities to punish them for presumed malefactions against nonlibrarians, has suggested that perhaps we might threaten to move the conference scheduled for San Francisco, even if only as a bluff.

A number of years ago the media reported the actions of two public libraries, one on the East and one on the West Coast, which voluntarily gave up scheduled salary increases so that the library could buy more books in offsetting mandated budget cuts. The media reported these actions fully, because they represent the sort of "man bites dog" story that both amazes and amuses us all. Trade unionists could only shake their heads at examples of such stupidity. There has been no sort of move from any of the library associations to repudiate or condemn these actions, which obviously endanger all of our salaries. Who would do such a thing except people who are either stupid or overpaid?

The Urban Libraries Council reports both that public libraries are pressured to "just keep the doors open" in the face of budget cuts, and that funding for staff training and continuing education has been severely cut. There has been no report on how public library directors, individually or collectively, have reacted to such suicidal suggestions. Recognition of our need for continuing education (certainly the doctors and lawyers on library boards understand this need for themselves) is at the root of professional recognition, and thereby an essential if our salaries are ever to become competitive. And yet I have seen no linkage of these issues.

School libraries. The state of California, which appears to be a well-spring of such good news, also informs us through the media[11] of effort by well-meaning parents to keep the doors of school libraries open through the use of volunteers although there are no longer any school librarians. Of course this removal of the last of the school librarians (and classroom teachers would much rather lay off librarians than themselves) already follows a long trail in which we moved from one librarian for each school library to one librarian for two and perhaps three or more school libraries, a sort of post of traveling itinerant librarian. I would not expect the parents to understand the degradation in quality of school library service, and I certainly would never expect school systems administrators to suggest it, but why have we remained silent? It is difficult for isolated school librarians to do something, but is there not a professional role on a national level in alerting parents to the permanent harm being done to their children?

The decision to dump school librarians as the easiest budget cutting approach taken by a conspiracy of school administrators and classroom teachers is perhaps easily understood in the contest of long standing policies in some school district in using the school library as a detention center. When assignment to the library is perceived by the student not as a reward but as a punishment, how likely is any other strategy implemented by well-meaning librarians to work? Perhaps we need to work on the political leverage issues before we concentrate on the lesson plan.

Academic libraries. I have commented in a number of articles[12,13] that academic library materials prices, particularly serials, rise at a rate much larger than either the growth of the literature or the increase in inflation, and I have noted that the primary reason for this phenomenon is that publishers understand that librarians fill the role of purchasing agents, but that the real power rests in the faculty, which have no financial responsibility, but which the administration expects library directors to please. I have noted that it is certainly the right of university officials to decide to continue to go along with this exorbitant rate of increase, but then it also becomes their responsibility to find the money to pay for it.

What seems strange to me is the willingness of academic librarians to accept responsibility for something they cannot control. They might suggest that university presidents (1) unify to put a stop to these price increases, or (2) continue to come up with additional funds. However, librarians accept this problem as their own by either (1) transferring funds from other priorities to the price of materials, (2) taking the blame and acrimony for whatever cancellations are caused by the abdicative acts of others, or (3) gratefully accepting money earmarked specifically to deal with the problem, as though it were a favor being done them. This money, we should understand, is not ours. We simply pass it along to publishers, and it is they who should be grateful. In this process academic librarians also abdicate whatever professional priorities they might have, in return for funds for material purchase. Reference services, continuing education, and all of the other activities and characteristics which define a profession end up being shelved by individuals who really give us little or nothing while believing that they support us generously. What lies at the heart of this problem is the common academic perception that, as defined by Thomas Carlyle, it is the library and not its staff which is the "heart" of the university.

In concert with this tactic of appeasement to avoid making administrators take responsibility is the practice of attempting to hide costs by passing them along to other units within the same larger body. Thus, faculty and alumni are urged to "adopt a journal," and what is now perceived as one of the presumed advantages of the so-called virtual library is that the costs, although they might increase, will be distributed to the budgets of the user populations. The same phenomenon exists for corporate and government libraries, and will be described below. These administrators do not realize that control over the budget and over decisions about how money is going to be spent or not spent is the ultimate power base in any political environment. As an anonymous wag put it so aptly, the Golden Rule in the political environment means that those who control the gold make the rules. Librarians in academic but also in other kinds of libraries fail to understand that the decision over expenditure levels is the ultimate power base. This means, quite simply, that we do not want to hide our expenses by making ourselves look as cheap as possible. It means spotlighting both the expenses and the value derived from the expenditure of funds. And, of course, as elaborated earlier, this means stressing, through exception reporting, what will not happen if the funds are not there. If the funds are available, but are channeled through other power brokers, not only is no money really saved, but in fact money can be wasted. There is no gain in such cosmetic savings, and politically that point must be made.

The political games of the appearance of economy are not uncommon, but we gain nothing in agreeing to play these games. As I once stated in a corporate setting, "We are going to have economy no matter how much it costs." Drucker has noted quite accurately not only that our clients are willing to pay for whatever they consider to be worthwhile, but also that they are suspicious of the quality of anything that is offered free of charge or cheaply. As he puts it, "Any con man can tell you that it is easier to sell the Brooklyn Bridge than give it away."[14]

Government and corporate libraries. I have already suggested the large problem, not only in loss of control and prestige but also in loss of organizational economy, which is created when attempts are made to "hide" legitimate library costs by passing them along to user groups. The argument is frequently made that users, if faced with the need to pay for library materials, will make more prudent requests, but there is no evidence that this is true, certainly not for the high level executives who inevitably make the most wasteful demands. If the process of approval discourages anyone, it is the junior library users who should be encouraged rather than discouraged. A better approach to allocation, in those instances in which allocation is required, is to allocate to user groups not on the basis of actual use (which discourages use) but rather on the basis of presumed use (perhaps based on the percentage of the total population that a specific subgroup represents). This tactic, which is much easier to administer because it requires no detailed record keeping, penalizes nonuse rather than use. The group is paying for the service, it might as well utilize it. This approach also provides, through use statistics, direct and compelling evidence for a need to increase the total library budget, and therefore also the allocations.

What is particularly difficult to understand in any library setting in which the users spend the same parent organization's money (and this would include academic faculty as well as corporate and government employees) is the practice of encouraging end user searching to make the library appear cheaper, through the process of making things more expensive for the user group. If we can assume that these individuals do not do information searching just for the fun of it, but rather as a means to doing something else, it only makes sense to delegate this process away from the library to the end user if it can be postulated that the user can do this work more efficiently, more rapidly, or more cheaply.

I would hope that librarians have enough self-confidence in their own special expertise to reject the first two possibilities (more efficiently, more rapidly) out of hand. The third (more cheaply) is even more absurd when we recognize how much more, in general, end users are paid than librarians. Do doctors do information searches three times as effectively as medical librarians (and I use that relationship because doctors are paid at least three times as much)? If not, then why are we training them (through concentrated efforts of the National Library of Medicine) to do what medical librarians could do more effectively? Has nobody noticed that as medical research increases, medical libraries are being closed, and does this make sense for anyone, most particularly the nation? If it is true that at present there are not enough medical librarians to meet all the doctors' needs, is the simplest solution not just to get some more? It is a political solution that makes sense for everyone.

And Yet...

The preceding sections of this chapter have set a pessimistic tone, and while pessimism may not yet seem warranted, discouragement at the many missed and lost opportunities does not suggest enthusiasm. At the same time, it is still not too late to turn this process around. If we as a profession are willing to play political hardball, in recognition of Thomas Galvin's observation that management is a contact sport, we are very fortunate in the opportunities that are still available to us.

First, and most obviously, we have no enemies dedicated to our obliteration, only enemies in the Druckerian sense of people who are not willing to place us first on their list of priorities, at least yet. There is no organized lobby committed to the elimination of libraries and the extinction of librarians. In general terms the population thinks we are decent, hardworking people who do worthwhile things. We are respected and liked even if not perhaps admired. The individuals who, in state after state, campaign for voter tax relief against what they consider "government waste," do not immediately have libraries and librarians in mind, even if, as a result of the lack of our political experience I have detailed, they end up hurting or destroying libraries in the process. Sometimes they even regret what has happened to us, and seek to assure us that we were not their intended targets.[15]

Secondly, there is no anti-information or pro-ignorance lobby. Those who cut our budgets in a political environment (and that includes corporations and universities) still insist that they favor knowledge and information. They even favor libraries, at least in principle. This then suggests a very obvious strategy, one of documenting that a support of the principle of education and knowledge requires the support of libraries and librarians; otherwise such claimed support is nothing but a lie. Taking such a stance obviously requires political courage, but it is not that difficult to demonstrate. Were political leaders to come out in favor of ignorance for their states, their communities, their school districts, their universities and their corporations, the process obviously would be far more difficult. As it stands, it requires "only" the willingness to play political hardball, to reward your friends and punish your enemies. It also requires an ability to differentiate between real support and lip service.

Third, if we can assume that nobody would publicly favor the alternative of "we don't know anything but we don't care," it becomes necessary only to demonstrate that we are most cost effective (and "cost effective" is an appropriate term in today's management literature—far more useful than "cheaper") than the alternatives. Is end user searching an effective alternative? Not when the end users' salaries are paid from the same general funds as our own (universities, corporations) or when the end users represent the general public that pays for everything (public libraries). End user searching suggests that end users do searches more rapidly, more economically, and with better search results than reference librarians. If we believe this, it is time for some self-love training sessions. If we do not believe it, why do we allow politicians to implement it, particularly on the premise that this represents an "economy?" The National Library of Medicine spends a great deal of money and effort, unfortunately with the help of quislings[16] who work in medical libraries to teach doctors how to do their own database searches. Why? Because they do it better than librarians do? Because they are paid less than librarians? Because they have nothing else to do? Usually the argument is that many doctors now do not have access to qualified medical librarians. Is that really such a difficult problem for society to fix?[17]

One thing we should certainly remember is that, on the question of information delivery, while we vacillate, others voted a long time ago. A great deal of money will be channeled into the support of information intermediation work. The only question will be whether a little bit of money will go to libraries, or a lot of money to others, on the premise that the little bit cannot be afforded. If that seems ludicrous, remember that in the management communication process, style is frequently more important than substance. The hard reality is that economy exists in its *appearance*, and perhaps that suggests that we need to concentrate just a little bit less on being good and a lot more on appearing good.

What Must We Do?

To a considerable extent, strategies that I am about to suggest are implicit from the analysis of problems in previous sections of this work. Nevertheless, a specific enumeration is probably useful:

1. We must understand that in the reality of the political process, there are no neutrals, only supporters and enemies. This is because there is no public outcry, and there is not likely to be, for an increase in taxes. If taxes are ever increased, it will not be to fund libraries, although specific local initiatives are certainly possible. They will not work on the national or state level. The only way for us to get money is for it to be allocated to us instead of to someone else. Peter Drucker has noted that in the management decision process there are no neutrals.[18] People are for you or they are against you. To be for you "in principle," when and if there is money, is no support at all. Support comes in placing your priorities ahead of *all other* priorities. In that harsh context it is not difficult to see how few friends we have.

This is not only difficult for those who profess to support us, it is even difficult for us, because it means a bitter and totally focused concentration on our own agenda, as opposed to all other agendas. That does not require that we actively oppose all else as a profession, merely that we ignore it. I realize how difficult all of this is. We can, as a generally liberal profession, easily come out in favor of diverting funds from the "military-industrial complex" to libraries. However, it is far more difficult for us to argue that library programs are more important than health care, housing for the homeless, or AIDS research. In fact, actions by our own professional governing bodies, both in resolutions and invitations to speakers, suggest that we agree that some of these other priorities are more important than our own. We need to understand that there is no such thing as leftover money. If we do not even believe that our priorities come first, how can we ever persuade anyone else? I agree that this does not pose very pleasant scenarios for us, but managers in the pursuit of political objectives must be tenacious and single minded.

2. We must recognize that the argument that there is no money is a fraudulent argument. It is certainly true that there are environments in which money is more plentiful than at other times. However, the economic situation is never so healthy that money will be volunteered to you, and the argument that there is no money will be made to you in all situations, whether there really is money or not. By contrast, money will always be found for the things that politically become essential for the decisionmaker's success and survival. It is not the librarian's job to find money. That is the task of higher management. It's the librarian's job to make a case that becomes too risky to ignore.

3. We must stress the value of what we do, and not its cheapness or freeness. It may be lamentable, but there is a natural public perception that what is free or cheap cannot be worth very much. The fact that video games and rock concert tickets cost money has never been a deterrent to public demand. By contrast, the advertising industry has long understood that it is not tactically desirable to

stress that your product is cheaper. It is far better to stress that you should feel ashamed if you do not spend the money. Take a look at some of the advertisements for pet food, and bear in mind that in most countries there is no pet food industry. Pets thrive on leftovers. Guilt sells.

4. We must not only learn to reward support and punish nonsupport (and here our undying loyalty to the senior citizen groups who routinely vote against all library initiatives comes to mind), but we must also learn how to organize our supporters for political effectiveness. Marilyn Gell Mason, who as a public library director clearly understands the political process, pointed out some of these options in a talk to Indiana University library school students;[19] two examples from her wealth of strategies will make the point. If it is considered desirable to have the results of public library board meetings reported on the 11 P.M. evening news, it is important that the Board meeting begin at 6 P.M. so that the reporters can be back in the studio with their copy and film (you will be lucky if you get one minute) before 9 P.M. If the meeting runs later than that, the board decisions will be too late for that evening's newscast. They will not be covered the following evening, because by that time what happened is no longer news. Secondly, Mason suggests the rigid discipline of mobilizing "friends of the library" groups so that they can not only pack public budgetary hearings, but if necessary disrupt them. If all of this seems strange to public librarians, it may explain why we have such political difficulty, despite the fact that survey after survey indicates that the public "likes" us. We have many advantages and assets, we simply do not capitalize on them.

5. We need to simplify our agenda. The first two White House Conferences on Library and Information Services produced a list of about a hundred recommendations. No administration, no matter how positively inclined toward library priorities, can deal with that many unranked priorities. Indeed, we were urged by the Carter Administration during White House Conference I to limit the recommendations to perhaps five or six. When the agenda and decisions are in the hands of lay delegates with narrow and specific priorities, that process becomes impossible. However, I am not at all certain that a group of librarians would have been able to agree on such a priority ranking.

6. We need to understand principles of marketing, and recognize that marketing is a destabilizing process that creates patron dissatisfaction rather than patron satisfaction by making individuals aware of what products and services are *not* being provided, and why they might be important. When librarians report proudly that the public thinks that libraries are wonderful, they also inadvertently convey the message that they are at least adequately funded and perhaps overfunded. Additional funds are being thrown at the problem of crime in the streets not because such a good job is being done, but rather because such an inadequate job is being done. Perhaps the most obvious example of marketing comes from the telephone systems, which have made us aware and made us want options and equipment about which we never even knew.

The greatest problem with running any sort of organization that is considered satisfactory for the needs of its constituency comes, however, from the fact that such a perception of satisfaction is boring, and being boring is perhaps the greatest crime any manager can commit. An obvious example comes from the research of Marion Paris, who examined the closing of four library schools.[20] She found, in interviews with the administrators who closed these programs, that the primary reason was not a lack of money, although that became the excuse. The real reason was the perception that these schools did not contribute toward the overall mission of the university, that they never did anything innovative, and that "they never wanted anything." Good managers are expected to pressure their bosses, and to apply all of the political leverage they can muster to encourage or force the correct decision.

7. And finally, we need to take risks, particularly when it comes to economic initiatives. If we raise funds from outside sources, they must always be for activities and programs outside of and in addition to those being funded by the parent and responsible body. If we offset a funding shortfall by begging for donations, all we have done is validate the budget cut, and lead the way to the next one. If budgets are cut, it is essential both that services really do get worse, and that users not only become aware of this but also understand whom to blame.

This process is not as easy for librarians as it is for police and teachers. Both groups make it very clear what a degradation in the quality of what they do would mean, and ultimately the threat or the reality of a work stoppage enforces that point. Librarians do not have such obvious options, in part because we have never succeeded or even really tried to define what represents an adequate or inadequate library, and even in greater part because we understand that work stoppages by librarians do not, at present, constitute a community disaster. Unlike teachers who, whether or not their work is valued are at least considered essential as babysitters to allow parents to go to work, we have no such easy justification. We therefore have to work to develop and market our own.

Fortunately, the fact that education and information are still important (even if vaguely defined) and that ignorance is not considered an acceptable alternative presents us with the raw material from which we should be able to shape our tools and develop our strategies. The opportunities are still there, but they are not as easy to realize as they would have been five years ago. And they will not be there forever.

Notes

1.   Drucker, Peter F. *Innovation and Entrepreneurship*. New York: Harper & Row, 1985.

2.   Drucker, Peter F. "Managing the Public Service Institution." *College and Research Libraries* 37 (January 1976): 4–14.

3.   Hedberg, Bo, et al. "Camping on Seesaws. Prescriptions for a Self-Designing Organization." *Administrative Sciences Quarterly* 21, 1 (1976): 41–65.

4.   Drucker, Peter F. "How to Manage the Boss." *Wall Street Journal*, August 1, 1986.

5. White, Herbert S. "Our Retreat to Moscow, and Beyond." *Library Journal* 119, 3 (August 1994): 54–55.

6. "The Growth of the Meatware Industry." *The Economist*, July 1993.

7. *Merwine vs. Mississippi State University*. A legal case in which Ms. Merwine argued that her failure to have an accredited library degree should not disqualify her from a position for which such a degree was specified. Judgment was made in favor of the university, despite the American Library Association's refusal to file a brief in support of its own accreditation process.

8. Harris, Roma M. *Librarianship; The Erosion of a Woman's Profession*. Norwood, NJ: Ablex, 1992.

9. Carmichael, James. "The Male Librarian and the Feminine Image: A Survey of Stereotype, Status, and Gender Perceptions." *Library and Information Science Research* 14, 4 (October-December 1992): 411–446.

10. Childers, Thomas. "California's Reference Crisis." *Library Journal* 119, 7 (April 15, 1994): 32–35.

11. "Parents Filling Gaps in Money-Strapped Schools." *Los Angeles Times*, June 6, 1992.

12. White, Herbert S. "Trouble at the OK Corral University Library." *Library Journal* 112, 4 (September 1, 1987): 154–155.

13. White, Herbert S. "Librarians, Journal Publishers and Scholarly Information: Whose Leaky Boat Is Sinking?" *LOGOS* 14 (1990): 18–23.

14. Drucker, Peter F. *Post-Capitalist Society*. New York: Harper Business, 1993.

15. Personal conversation by the author with Howard Jarvis, co-developer of the Jarvis-Gann initiative that became California's Proposition 13 in 1978. Spring 1980.

16. During World War II, Vidkun Quisling, a Norwegian, assisted the Germans in taking over his own country. The word *quisling* has been generically applied to anyone who assists the enemy in the overthrow and destruction of his own community.

17. White, Herbert S. "The GRATEFUL MED Program and the Medical Library Profession." *Bulletin of the Medical Library Association* 81, 1 (January 1993): 73–75.

18. Drucker, Peter F. *The New Realities: In Government and Politics, in Economics and Business, in Society and World View*. New York: Harper and Row, 1989.

19. Mason, Marilyn Gell. "Politics and the Public Library: A Management Guide." *Library Journal* 114, 5 (March 15, 1989): 27–32. (Extracted from the Lazerow Memorial Lecture Delivered at Indiana University's School of Library and Information Science in 1988.)

20. Paris, Marion. *Library School Closings: Four Case Studies*. Metuchen, NJ: Scarecrow Press, 1988.

Doing More with Less? If We Can Do It Now, Why Were We Goofing Off Before?

The title points out what we should see as the obvious danger in such easy compliance with the request that we work harder to compensate for the budget cut. However, you can be sure that the request, or rather the demand, will be made. Management often deals in word games. In all of my years in the corporate sector, I don't recall a single year, during good times and bad, that we weren't operating under an economy drive. Subordinate managers can't openly challenge this, but good ones learn to ignore the rhetoric and to concentrate on their own plans and programs. Faculty certainly know how to ignore academic librarians when they are told there isn't enough money to renew their favorite journals. They don't see this as their problem. And perhaps it isn't. We should either get more money, fight price escalation, or cut the subscription, and stop making a morality play out of a simple management decision.

Why is this refusal to accept the blame for what somebody else has done not obvious to us? Police chiefs make it clear that the quality of police protection comes from budgets and staffing levels, and any decline in public safety is the fault of the budget cutters, and never that of the already overworked cop on the beat. I have commented in earlier writings on the observation by Peter Drucker that some service professionals, and particularly social service professionals, are prone to the acceptance of the "moral imperative," that somehow with or without management support, they are responsible for accomplishing everything they feel needs to be accomplished.

This article was written with the intent to publish it as a "White Paper" in *Library Journal* in 1996. It was never submitted for publication because of space limitations.

Drucker notes that this is a foolish strategy, because it virtually guarantees a lack of support and interest. In the absence of other reasons that suggest the contrary, cutting budgets is always an attractive temptation. However, acceptance of the moral imperative also completely ignores the very basis of management structure. Responsibility can be delegated but never abdicated, and our managers share in both the credit and blame for an operation well or badly done. Indeed, since their responsibility and rewards are greater, they get more credit or blame than we do, or at least they should. Otis Bowen, the former governor of Indiana, noted this failing in our own strategy when he told us that it was his observation that librarians neither rewarded their friends nor punished their enemies— that ultimate concept of the political process.

Drucker, in a short article in the August 1, 1986 *Wall Street Journal* tellingly titled "How to Manage the Boss," noted that not only does your boss work for you, but is also your most important subordinate. In the corporate and academic sectors, our managers are paid to make us more effective and should presumably earn their salaries. Public library board members may not get paid, but nobody forced them to accept appointment and the responsibilities that go with it.

How does one deal with bosses in this environment of delegated decisions but retained responsibility? Obviously, very carefully. We don't present them with surprises, and we certainly don't offer ultimatums, because they will react to the style rather than to the substance. We present them with alternatives, which we have analyzed and for which we certainly have recommendations. However, they must decide and take responsibility. In a declining budget environment, those alternatives may well be painful for them, and the preference for avoiding decisions is understandable. However, the suggestion that we do more, try harder, or just do the best we can really has no substance. Ultimately, bosses must decide and take responsibility for their decisions.

What happens when budgets are cut? First of all, at least in some settings, there is the option for upper-level management to cut some other budget instead and shift the funds to you, and you can be sure that the reverse suggestion has already been made. They may also have the authority to increase revenues through higher taxes, unattractive as they may well find that option. Indeed, they may decide that they are better off politically in weakening libraries. That perception may be correct, and if so, it raises the question of what we might have done to persuade both our bosses and the taxpayers to a contrary view. However, in any case, the presumption that we can decrease library funding without negatively impacting the quality of service cannot be allowed to stand, because it makes the decision absurdly simple. We reward or we punish, and not only police chiefs but also schoolteachers understand this simple political principle.

It is important that we remember that while it may be easy to understand a budget cut during bad times, there is no consistent history of library budget increases during the good times. Certainly there are never any automatic increases. We must understand that the non-librarians to whom we all ultimately report have no real idea of what they should spend in support of the library. That is even true, except for collection size, in the academic sector. It is therefore important that we concentrate on our real responsibility. It isn't to save our parent organization money, although we can't say that out loud. Financial gurus are paid a great deal more to make sure we don't spend too much, and we don't have to take on their jobs. Our job, as professionals with unique knowledge, is to run an effective library, because, although our bosses may have forgotten, that is what they hired us to do.

The courageous and innovative corporate librarians whom I invite to speak to my special library students know that it is acceptable to have overspent your budget, as long as you can demonstrate that not spending the money would have been worse for the parent organization. It is easier to ask for forgiveness than permission if you did the right thing. We all know about government programs that spend all of their money until it is gone, and then argue the absolute necessity of getting more to avoid dire consequences. I don't recommend this strategy, but sometimes it works. In local communities these individuals may be in charge of poverty programs and spend according to levels of need and not funding. When they demand more after it is all spent, they usually get it, because no politician wants to be held responsible for TV coverage of hungry children. That costs votes.

With this as a background, we must understand that if our budgets are cut, something negative *must* happen, if only to protect against the next cut. Doing more with less, or promising to work harder, are both disastrous political strategies. Usually a cut in budgets means a cut in programs, but what programs? Those that matter most, or those that matter least? Choosing the first is potentially effective but also risky, and you might want to check how good you are at bluffing when you play poker. However, a budget cut even provides an opportunity, as many management writers have noted. It allows us to get rid of the tasks and responsibilities we never wanted in the first place. Perhaps it is a thankless task that nobody else wanted, and it was given to the library as part of someone else's budget cut. That happens a lot to corporate librarians. Getting rid of this unimportant task as your contribution to "economy" requires assertiveness, because quite simply if others control not only your level of resources but also your internal priorities, then you are not really being allowed to manage at all, no matter what your title says your authority is supposed to be.

Important as this is for library managers, it is even more important for their subordinates. Much of the management literature explains that what subordinates are expected to do, and with what resources they are expected to do it, is part of an informal contract. Part of what is expected used to be spelled out in job descriptions, but some administrators have found it convenient to turn specific job descriptions into meaningless gibberish. When this happens, and when administrators unilaterally modify the "contract," trouble can not only be expected, but it is deserved.

What budget cuts do suggest is that we work smarter, because there is no reason whatsoever to work harder simply to validate someone's capricious decision. Working smarter requires reassessment, and we end up eliminating some programs, cutting others, and even strengthening a few. The overall result may be positive up to a point, but only if the initiatives for change come from us and not those unqualified to make the assessment. Some administrators may simply opt for keeping the library doors open, and of course, that can be done without any embarrassing reference to what happens inside those open doors. Such sloganeering is always potentially attractive for politicians, but it can only happen if the professionals who know better remain silent.

If there is any positive news in a world full of declining budgets, it is that it allows good managers to show how good they really are, while it exposes the apple-polishing charlatans for what they have always been. Good management requires a realistic assessment of what options there are, and the development of strategies. And, of course, it requires that we make those who are responsible take responsibility, so that our non-librarian bosses receive either the credit or the blame they deserve. Former general medical practitioner turned Indiana governor Otis Bowen understood this instinctively, and I learned early in 40 years of management that to negotiate, there had to be something to offer—or to threaten to withhold.

Obviously we should try to build partnerships with our bosses, and in a partnership, their reward is that they will look good. Making our bosses look good is always much more pleasant than making them look bad. However, as Drucker has noted, this is not a process of making them look good first, in the hope that they will *then* show their appreciation. It is a process of negotiation based on the consideration of alternatives. If there are no alternative decisions, there are no negotiations and no real "partnership," except perhaps the kind which exists between those who wear boots and those who lick them. And of course, as all managers learn, blind obedience does not earn respect, but only contempt, and never more support. Management negotiation requires courage, and there are casualties in any such skirmish. However, what choice do any professionals have other than honestly and, at least initially, discreetly point out what only they know? Isn't that the presumed reason for their having been hired in the first place? If not for that, then why do they think they were hired? To be uncritically loyal and obedient? Any mayor or other official can always find toadies, but toadyism doesn't require any particular education or preparation. In fact, it only gets in the way.

Marketing As a Tool for Destabilization

Despite numerous library conferences that include the word marketing in their titles, it should be fairly clear that librarians do not market and that they never have marketed. Marketing—at least from the perspective of management practice—is a destabilizing process of creating in the client an awareness for a need of which that client may be totally ignorant. Indeed, that need may be served only after that hunger for a product or a service has been awakened.

The most obvious example of marketing has been the activity of the telephone system, which, after succeeding in getting just about all of us to purchase one black rotary telephone for our home or office, continued to make us aware of other "needs." These include push-button phones, multiple phones, color-coordinated phones, cute phones for the kids, cellular phones, car phones, call waiting, call forwarding, etc. We may or may not have use for all these things, but the point is that we never clamored for these features; the marketers told us we needed them.

Reprinted, with changes, by permission of the author and *Library Journal* 122, no. 3 (February 15, 1997): 116–117. Copyright © 1997 by Cahners Business Information.

Libraries Now Anti-Advertise

Another classic example is the development of the multi-billion-dollar pet food industry, limited to the United States and just a few other countries. In the rest of the world pet cats and dogs eat leftovers, or they must scavenge for themselves. Here we are urged to buy the more expensive brand to prove to ourselves (and perhaps to our neighbors) that we really love our pets. Marketers need not feel guilty because we buy only those things we are ready to buy. Lots of marketing campaigns fail.

Libraries do not market; occasionally they advertise what they already provide. However, increasingly we now anti-advertise, when budget cuts have made it difficult to maintain levels of service. Thus, budget cuts that cause a reduction in reference staff lead to a decision to curtail services, or instructions that reference librarians spend less time on each question to prevent backlogs. It is a classic example of the tail wagging the dog: allowing the budget to define the program rather than have the program define the budget, as management theorists have long urged us to do.

In the face of a reference service budget cut, might it not be better to stress to the remaining reference librarians that the quality of service won't be diluted? Obviously, when that happens we expect that long lines will form in front of the reference desk, perhaps snaking out the door and into the rain. This then becomes a great opportunity to summon the media to take pictures and interview those who have been in line since yesterday. Would such hoopla embarrass municipal administrators? Well, shouldn't it? Would it make them angry enough to fire us? Perhaps, but it might also make them take us seriously. There are risks in any management environment, and law enforcement administrators learned long ago to predict dire consequences at the first hint of a budget cut. And so the Democratic President and the Republican Congress, who can agree on virtually nothing else, agree that we must find the money to put "more police on the streets."

Paper-Training Our Officials

Public librarians caught in this vise seem to have no clue as to how the process works. The Urban Libraries Council (ULC) reports that the emphasis for public library boards and mayors has shifted to a simple strategy of keeping the doors open, and that money for continuing education and training (the very activities that clearly define a profession—just ask the lawyers and doctors on your own boards) is disappearing. While the ULC has noted this, there has been nothing on proposed strategies for dealing with this problem. We would certainly have to retrain our boards and civic officials, or perhaps train them for the first time—but that shouldn't be too difficult. There is a great deal of literature on how to train a puppy to use paper; it requires a combination of reward and punishment.

Mayors should be easier to train, but only if they are offered the choice between the opportunity to look good or to face blame for inevitable problems.

However, we now find the role of the public library redefined and re-redefined, almost always as a rationale for dilution of its "traditional" service provided without charge to patrons. Traditional as of when? The late 1990s, or 1970, or 1860? The role of any library, particularly the public library, has already been dramatically upgraded by other marketing efforts.

Hammering at Public Perception

The developers and distributors of computer hardware and databases have hammered away at the public perception of information adequacy, and this marketing campaign has been at least as relentless as that of the telephone companies. This means that all bets are off, that all attempts to define public library activities on the basis of what happened in the past are irrelevant, and that all this might make us incredibly important.

However, it also has the potential to make us trivial, if we accept simply keeping doors open as a priority, as well as adapting information services to whatever budgets we are handed. We will still be left with the responsibility for serving the information impoverished (children, the elderly, illiterates) whom information entrepreneurs in the private sector see little economic incentive to serve, except for teaching children how to play computer games. Are we willing to settle for what the computer industry and mayors leave us, or should we seek out and serve everyone who needs information, whether they yet recognize that need or not?

We were a lot more proactive at the turn of the century when John Cotton Dana at the Newark Public Library, NJ, undertook initiatives to serve the business community without charge. In the recent dispute between writer Nicholson Baker and [just resigned] San Francisco City Librarian Ken Dowlin, the latter seems at least simplistic if he argues that his Taj Mahal is "only" a public and not a research library. It is of course both and many more things, depending on the needs of each client, because the definitions are not mutually exclusive.

Money from the Municipality

If this library can do complex reference for a fee, it can do it without a fee for the individual and corporate citizens of San Francisco. The money must come from municipal officials, and in the overall context the amount is trivial. The library will get the money when giving it is politically safer than not doing so, and as experienced a politician as Mayor Willie Brown does not need to have that basic principle explained to him.

This all comes to mind because of the firing of Fred Glazer as West Virginia State Librarian, for reasons that are not at all clear ("Justice for Fred Glazer," Editorial, *LJ*, November 1, 1996, p. 6). I do not know Glazer personally, but I have long been impressed by his insistence that West Virginia, which can legitimately claim that it is poor, nevertheless undertake important library initiatives. I also noticed that while in other states governors sent messages to library conferences that they were always too "busy" to attend, in West Virginia they showed up in person. Where did that support for libraries in a state without money arise? Perhaps from Peter Drucker's observation that in the provision of services that people really want, cost is irrelevant. Obviously, any electorate prefers lower taxes to making detailed decisions, but how do you avoid that yawning death trap without the destabilizing process called marketing?

Don't Even Think About It

In a recent *LJ* interview ("Gave 'em What They Wanted," September 15, 1996, pp. 136–138), retiring Baltimore County Public Library (BCPL) Director Charlie Robinson suggested that library users might have to pay 15 percent of the cost of the public library directly. That doesn't sound so terrible, but what makes anyone think that this process, once started, would stop at 15 percent? Why not 25 percent, or 50 percent, or 75 percent? Hasn't anyone noticed the way in which the cost of higher education has been gradually shifted from the state legislature to the student?

Shifting costs is unthinkable. We might have to cut services, loudly proclaim those cuts, and blame the mayor. However, it might be better to argue in advance that services must increase because demand will increase; that the cost must be met by municipal administrators because that is their job; but that in any case benefits and rewards for decisionmakers will make it all worthwhile. Not all public librarians (or academic ones) understand the opportunity in destabilization. It was BCPL that proffered "Give 'em What They Want," a slogan not yet adopted by hospitals and medical centers, which makes us more aware of medical options. Perhaps that is why doctors receive more respect than librarians do.

Information Is Crucial

What a wonderful time this might be for librarians! Information industry marketing campaigns have already done most of the work by persuading us all that information is crucial. All we must do is to redirect the spotlight that Microsoft and America Online shine into our eyes so incessantly. We need to point out that librarians offer the most cost-effective way to manage and control the flood of information. It is still okay to use cost-effective instead of cheap.

What this requires is the development of an entirely new mission statement for public libraries, one in which our programs are not based simply on percentage changes from historical precedents that never had any rationale. That usually leads to less money, anyway. The process begins, as any management textbook will tell us, not with the "availability" of funds but with the definition of need.

As I now teach a course in planning and evaluation, two things have become clear. The first is that the planning process begins not with funds but with needs, or it is doomed from the start. The second is that planning for the library is a process that involves the assessment of alternatives. The determination of what will and will not be done must involve management above the level of the library, simply because they control the money and bear the responsibility. And, of course, there is money. If there was money in West Virginia, there is money everywhere. What is needed is a mechanism to describe the rewards for spending it and the punishments for not spending it.

Stress What Isn't Happening

That is why the destabilizing process of marketing—of creating expectations, hopes, fears, and perhaps anger—is so crucial for us in the present political climate. Marketing is not a synonym for publicizing what higher-ups tell you it is okay to publicize. As Drucker has often noted, the essence of management communication is exception reporting—stressing not what good things are happening but what good things are *not* happening.

It is depressing to learn from the recent Benton Foundation report that after two decades of declining budgets, declining staffs, and declining services, the vast majority of citizens still think their public libraries are "wonderful" (see "Polarized Perceptions," *LJ*, February 1, pp. 46–48). It is even more depressing to realize that some librarians consider that a compliment, instead of the trivialization it represents. Police protection is not considered wonderful, which is why police departments get more money while we get less.

What we need to tell people is not how wonderful our public libraries *are* but rather how wonderful they *could be*. The awakening of these dreams is the purpose of marketing, but it requires that we make people dissatisfied with what they now have. The telephone companies have no problem in deciding to do that. How about us?

Keynote Address: Fourth International Conference on Fee-Based Information Services in Libraries

SUMMARY. Despite the debate over free vs. fee libraries and services, libraries need to accept the responsibility of providing information to our users. Libraries, and fee-based services in libraries, need to lead the way in recognizing the need for libraries, developing the role of librarians as managers of knowledge, and creating our own future. The author makes the argument that knowledge work will be done by somebody, and if not us, then the end user. Providers of fee-based services have already staked out our jurisdiction and are on the right track. *[Article copies available for a fee from The Haworth Document Delivery Service: 1-800-342-9678. E-mail address:* getinfo@haworthpressinc.com *<Website*: http://www.haworth pressinc.com>]*

KEYWORDS. Fee-based information services, future of librarianship, knowledge management, free vs. Fee

This is your fourth Conference on Fee-Based Services, but only the first I have attended. I am interested to note that the conference program is primarily devoted to *how* you do what you do, and I will not intrude into a process in which my comments would really be uninformed. I would rather talk about *why* you do what you do, and why it is important that you do it. In addressing this topic, I am

Reprinted, with changes, by permission of the author and *Information Delivery in the 21st Century*, edited by Suzanne Ward, Yem Fong, and Tammie Dearie. Haworth Information Press, Binghampton, NY, 1999. pp. 5–11.

aware of some arguments that have been raised as to whether you should be offering fee-based services from libraries at all. It can be contended that fee-based services somehow attack and undermine the provision of free services. The argument is made that once services are provided for a fee, there will be a temptation to withdraw funding. The individuals who make this emotional statement offer no proof of any decision to withdraw already offered free services in order to offer these for a fee. Instead, there is plenty of evidence of reductions in funding without any alternative "temptation" of the kind being charged. Rather, library activities are curtailed because those who fund us would rather not spend the money, and we have offered neither any inducement to change their minds nor the threat of what would happen to them unless they did. The argument that services for a fee replace free services is, in my observation, totally without merit. Service for a fee replaces, for libraries, the absence of services.

However, those who might feel a legitimate concern about this issue must then accept the responsibility for seeing to it that funding for totally free services in all kinds of libraries is increased dramatically, and as you will see from my later remarks there is no real political or economic reason why funding for such *free* library services should not be tripled or quadrupled. There is certainly logic and validity in such a demand: first because it is worth it for the good of the community being served, and second, because the alternative is ignorance, which occurs when services are offered neither for free nor for a fee, is unacceptable if articulated. If your critics then took the challenge of free instead of fee as a crusade theme to demand and also obtain substantial increases in funding and staffing in both academic and public libraries, there would be no problem.

Indeed, Eugene Garfield's[1] argument that the need for information for the mind is as important as the need for food for the body is worth considering. Garfield has argued for the issuance of information stamps as a government subsidy to be used in libraries, to allow us to keep honest books as grocery stores are allowed to keep honest books when they deliver food in return for food stamps. However, this has not happened, and it is not likely to happen, since we don't even try.

Instead, the slogan "free and not fee" has become "free or not at all." However, "not at all" only means "not by us." We offer no objection when others offer services for a fee, even though this clearly still disqualifies those who cannot pay. The outrage at inequity extends only to our own participation. By providing services for a fee openly and honestly you are at least protecting our professional territory and our birthright. You are attacked because you are honest.

The real betrayers of our profession and of our clients are found in libraries such as the ones that:

1. Agree to the building of more and larger public libraries without demanding additional staffing before the first brick is laid.

2. Agree with the premise that academic libraries must do more with less without even examining what really happens when that nonsensical idea is exposed. What happens is that even greater

costs accrue to the institution, but they are hidden and not noticed in various academic budgets. Forcing the president to face the reality that the most cost-effective information access will require a substantial increase in the library budget is the most honest approach. It channels the money to those most competent to manage it. The alternative is simply a free-for-all.

3. Accept new responsibilities in public libraries for additional services, such as literacy programs or student services, simply because the public school or the charter school would rather dump this problem on the public library without additional funding.

4. Allow unqualified people to do professional work in reference or in online searching, particularly while we then do clerical work. Would surgeons, or any other professionals, allow such a scenario?

It is time to state some of the concepts articulated by Peter Drucker, for whose management wisdom I have unbounded admiration, and whose arguments certainly apply to librarians:

1. In the claimed absence of money, there is always money.

2. It is easier to get a lot of money than a little bit of money.

3. In the provision of a service or a product that important people consider essential, its cost is irrelevant, and

4. Your boss is responsible for everything you do and everything you do not do, and once your boss understands the importance of making you more effective, he or she becomes your most important *subordinate.*

It is not in what information for a fee workers do, but in our failure to apply Drucker's principles that we are betrayed. Drucker understands the importance of knowledge as we approach the next millennium, in both real and political terms. The search for knowledge or information has no avowed enemies. There is no pro-stupidity lobby. On the other hand, who actively supports librarians in presenting this argument? Stating that we would support libraries *if* we had money provides only dishonesty, because we will never have enough money to do everything. Peter Drucker has noted that in the political process there are no neutrals. If individuals do not support you as a primary or urgent priority they are enemies, because they are supporting some other priority. How many of our "friends" place the library first, ahead of whatever else they would like to do? Drucker is confident enough in his argument to posit that knowledge workers will be the most important profession of the next century.[2] However, he does not mention librarians, and he does not state who these knowledge workers will be. It is clear that other professions in such areas as business administration and computer systems engineering understand the importance of claiming to be knowledge workers, even if we do not.

By contrast the national newspaper *USA Today* mentions us quite specifically. In an article that identifies fields without a future for new recruits, the newspaper singles out bank tellers, telephone operators, and librarians.[3] The connection, at least in the eyes of the writers, is that these are fields that perform routine and clerical work that will be taken over by computers. We can and should certainly argue that such a characterization is inaccurate and unfair, but then where did *USA Today* get its perception of what librarians do? Probably from watching librarians, and we must all understand the danger that comes from the fact that this newspaper is read by policy- and decisionmakers.

There is beginning to be some recognition of a potential role for librarians as knowledge managers, but to a large extent in publications such as *Library Journal* this description is limited to special librarians in the corporate world. To a considerable extent, the role of academic and public librarians in the information process is seen as passive, as collecting and arranging material so that others can locate the information. For many librarians, their abdication suggests not a preference for free over fee, but rather a preference for not at all over either of these alternatives.

Knowledge work will certainly be done by *somebody*, as Peter Drucker predicts. The alternative of ignorance, particularly in a competitive society, is simply not acceptable. However, by whom might this work be done?

1. By us. Your group, in providing this service for a fee, is at least doing what needs to be done. Those who complain that you ought not do this while themselves doing nothing are only stressing their irrelevance.

2. By the end user. Here we encounter issues involving their qualifications and the cost effectiveness of "delegating" to individuals who, at least in academia and industry, are paid more. However, of even greater concern is their willingness to do this work. When the University of Alberta Libraries set up end user training workshops for faculty members, only a tiny number registered themselves. A larger number sent their secretaries and other clerical assistants. The greatest number ignored the opportunity.

3. By nobody at all. That option is indeed suggested by the University of Alberta reaction. After all, it is still possible to avoid the search for knowledge because ignorance is rarely admitted and rarely challenged by others. It is still comfortable and safe to pretend to know "everything" that is needed. In my corporate experience, I never encountered a presentation that began with an admission of ignorance.

4. Most probably, by somebody other than either librarians or the end user. This process may or may not turn out to be cost effective, depending on the qualifications of the provider. However, the fact that an "information for a fee" industry is growing around us is certainly obvious to all of you. The reason is quite simple. Part comes from the laws of physics. Nature abhors a vacuum. The other part comes from Drucker, as noted earlier. For important people to get what they want (or even just what they think they want), the cost is irrelevant. The British business journal *The Economist* points to the development of what is rather charmingly called the Meatware Industry (people as differentiated from hardware and software), and notes that meatware companies are likely to be profitable investments.[4] As noted earlier, in the absence of money there is money. Let's not confuse that truth with the observation that people don't want to give us money.

What then do we accomplish if we refuse to do this work for a fee, while also failing to achieve the funds necessary to allow us to do it for free? We then reduce ourselves to the clerical extinction which *USA Today* predicts. It is also the extinction that some library schools perceive as they seek desperately to jump out of what they see as a leaky and sinking boat into something dryer and safer. Does an insistence on not charging, if it results in not doing the work at all as a matter of principle, help our clients? No. The poor ones won't get served at all, and the others who can afford to pay can certainly find a vast range of other options, including the meatware industry. Such an approach serves nobody—certainly not the poor, certainly not us, and not even affluent clients. We could provide information more cost effectively, as indeed your group does.

For me, the solution for our clients, and of course for ourselves, comes from the acceptance of the work of Andrew Abbott and his book, *The System of Professions.*[5] Abbott makes three points that for him, and indeed for me, define any profession and that define ours if indeed we claim to be a profession:

1. The task of professionals is to address human problems amenable to expert service. This is the self-definition of self-styled professionals, from doctors and lawyers to plumbers and garage mechanics. What definition of expert service do we seek to carve out for ourselves?

2. Professionals compete vigorously for existing and newly emerging problem jurisdictions. Can we see the "information-based society" as such a problem jurisdiction?

3. Professionals seek to expand their jurisdictions by preempting the activities of other professions. Do these "others" include the

MIS people, information systems analysts? Do they include our encouragement of end user searching without having the vaguest idea how well they do it?

I believe that Abbott defines our future, if we are to have a future. Your own group has seen the need to stake out and defend your problem jurisdictions, and for this I salute you. I don't see many other librarians, particularly in the public and academic sectors, doing this. They are still promising that they, or at least their unlucky subordinates, will do more with less. However, even if this were possible it would be more clerical work at the expense of our professional jurisdiction. You are on the right track. I congratulate you, and I wish you well.

Notes

1. Garfield, Eugene. *Essays of an Information Scientist*. Philadelphia, PA: ISI Press, 1977.

2. Drucker, Peter F. *The Post-Capitalist Society*. New York: Harper Business Books, 1993.

3. "Future Jobs to Bank On: Therapists, not Tellers," *USA Today*, 11 April 1996, p. 1D.

4. "Tel-Tech Tales." *The Economist*, 327, no. 7817, p. 90–91. June 26, 1993.

5. Abbott, Andrew D. *The System of Professions. An Essay on the Division of Expert Labor*. Chicago: University of Chicago Press, 1988.

Our Conflicting Responsibilities: To Our Bosses, Our Staff, and Our Profession

In my column "The Conflict Between Professional and Organization Loyalty" (*LJ*, May 15, 1991, pp. 59–60), I referred to Joseph Raelin's categorization of professionals as either cosmopolitans or locals. Cosmopolitans make their professional responsibilities and image their first priority; locals are loyal to the home crisis.

I suggested at that time that librarians, while they perhaps aspired to the lofty perch of cosmopolitans, were at heart locals, doing whatever had to be done to "protect" the services ravaged by others. It is easy to get the American Library Association (ALA) Council to enact a sweeping condemnation of some national political leader, but just try to get it to blackball a city whose mayor cut the library budget, or a university whose president gave librarians a smaller raise than faculty—actions that would be substantive rather than cosmetic.

I have also referred to Bo Hedberg, who in 1976 warned against the danger posed by a management suggestion that we work harder and accomplish more to validate the decision to cut budgets and staff. Hedberg reassured us that this could never happen, because subordinates were not so stupid as to agree to simply work harder. Such an agreement would indict them for not having worked hard enough in the past. If budgets and staff are cut, then programs are changed, and the management that cut the budget must take the heat for its decisions. Hedberg was basically correct; however, it is safe to say that he hadn't met many librarians, who may place the "moral imperativism" of local service above their own professional status and careers.

Reprinted, with changes, by permission of the author and *Library Journal* 122, no. 7 (April 15, 1997): 50–52. Copyright © 1997 by Cahners Business Information.

Special librarians suggest that it is becoming harder to find corporate librarians willing to accept chapter and national assignments and other responsibilities. Downsizing, coupled with the perceived need to do everything just as before, is now swamping them to the point that they no longer have time for anything else, even during what used to be their free time. How did they decide to forgo all of their cosmopolitan responsibilities for local ones? Don't they understand that by validating one arbitrary staff cut they simply set the stage for the next one?

Things may have changed for the worse, but in my 25 years of corporate life I knew that if I showed management that I worked hard and effectively but also had other priorities, they would not only listen to but respect me.

Local Visions, Devil's Bargain

I am less concerned about how this stampede toward localism affects the individuals who make that choice than about the impact on innocent and hapless subordinates. Last September I attended an international conference in which some of the top U.S. academic library administrators expressed their vision of the role and importance of the university library in the next 10 years. The description was truly inspiring, but I was struck by their casual assumption that all this would happen while library budgets and staff declined. When management literature stresses that budgets result from negotiation after tasks are defined, how could the conclusion precede the justification and analysis? When library administrators have already made the devil's bargain that they will do a lot more with a lot less, to what sort of fate have they sentenced the subordinates they never consulted?

It was explained to me privately that library directors understood the financial pressure under which the university operated, and their allegiance as members of the executive team drove their actions. Perhaps accepting such a narrow role as "local" rewards them well with high salaries and plush offices. But do lower-level librarians share in this membership on the executive "team?" Will they now get larger raises than "mere" faculty? I hardly think so. What is the trade-off in responsibility for the library director as a local reporting to the president against his or her responsibility as a cosmopolitan, representing a staff and a profession in hard negotiations with the president?

I was told budget cuts affect faculty as well. True, but faculty respond as cosmopolitans. When budgets are cut, faculty do not increase their teaching loads or the size of their classes. Nor do they give up their sabbaticals. Budget cuts result in a dilution of the academic program and that, unfortunately, impacts students. However, if faculty can carefully point out where the fault lies, they are perhaps reacting most effectively. Absorption of more work leads to the demand for even more, because no one but us really knows what librarians do, why it is important, and how much of it we can accomplish.

Library Students As Locals

As a teacher, I'm disturbed to learn how much students who work in public libraries have already been poisoned by moral imperativism and localism. I have been asked by some how they can respond to patrons who justify their rudeness by saying they pay the librarian's salary. Supervisors sometimes counsel patience and forbearance, because such treatment "comes with the territory." It doesn't come with any territory I have ever inhabited, and I can only recall Eleanor Roosevelt's statement that nobody can ever put you down without your permission. I tell students that patrons do not pay your salary, they pay taxes, and from those taxes a great many services are provided. I urge them to suggest that those patrons try the "I pay your salary" argument the next time they are stopped for a traffic violation.

In one of my management courses I ask an exam question in which the director of an academic library has just received a letter from a professor stating that a librarian has been rude to him and demanding an apology from the library. What to do? The point of the question is that there's not enough information to decide. The librarian indeed may have been rude. Alternatively, it may have been a simple misunderstanding, easy to negotiate. The professor may be at fault. It might even be a case of sexual harassment, which must be referred to the highest levels of the administration.

However, perhaps 20 percent of the students simply write the apology letter, without even knowing for what they are apologizing. My nightmare is that these students will become academic or public library directors. What sort of protection does this promise for accused librarians?

What Bosses Owe Us

What managers owe their subordinates, in a library or in any other setting, is fairly simple. Bosses owe respect and protection, a fair salary, and job assignments that can be completed successfully with hard effort. This should then be followed by full and documented praise publicized broadly, perhaps even via library announcements and bulletin boards. That is every manager's cosmopolitan responsibility, whether or not that individual personally wants to participate in professional organizations or perform research. That minimum responsibility may throw managers into conflict with their locally oriented bosses. If managers can't do at least that much, then they owe it to their staff to resign and let someone else try.

My 1991 column took its cue from the *Challenger* shuttle disaster. Engineers had argued vigorously that a launch in cold weather posed dangers, but they were ignored. NASA management decided that the risks were minimal, that engineers always worry too much, and that the timing of the launch was essential, planned as it was to coincide with the President's State of the Union address. Mention of a successful launch would help the NASA budget. There are no good or evil people in this story—NASA management did not believe that the explosion would take place. The engineers were acting as cosmopolitans, the administrators as locals.

So far, fair enough. However, after the disaster, there was a rush to suppress all of this evidence and to classify the explosion as an act of God. It was no such thing; it was a bad management decision. Engineers were pressured to abandon their responsibilities as cosmopolitans and to join the ranks of the locals, for the "good" of the program.

Suffering Victims?

Do you see the connection to our own profession? If we are asked to accept budget cuts for the "good" of the city or of the university, do we tamely accept, as loyal locals, or do we at least point out what everyone already knows (except perhaps at libraries) that in the absence of enough money and staff bad things usually happen.

There has been a great deal of national publicity about the San Francisco Public Library's new $134 million building and the increase in public use it has created. Consequently, the staff is now swamped, and one TV story mentions a reference librarian so harried that she runs rather than walks to consult sources. Who would make such a devil's bargain to obtain a great deal of money for a building and not nearly enough money for the staff needed to operate it? Only a confirmed local, with less responsibility to the profession than to perceived city political pressures! However, perhaps the more interesting question is why the reference librarian runs instead of walks. She also must be a local, or she would clearly understand that she should continue to work at her normal pace and spot-light the danger of putting buildings ahead of staff. She should also leave time and energy for the rest of her life.

In San Francisco, the library staff ultimately helped to focus attention on some of the management problems. However, in too many places, librarians assume that being a suffering victim of someone else's irresponsibility "comes with the territory."

The Passion to Be in Fashion

There is an old joke about the mob rushing through the streets of Paris to storm the Bastille. Trailing the crowd by a full block is one heavyset fellow, panting and clutching his chest. When a caring bystander notes that he is risking a heart attack, and there are enough others to get the job done, he gasps in response, "You don't understand. I'm one of the leaders."

We always assume that we are supposed to be among the leaders in planning educational policy, although no one else seems to notice. When strategies were formulated in response to "A Nation at Risk," we were never mentioned or consulted. Our response was and remains the passing of angry resolutions to remind those in authority that we should have been included.

I see this problem recurring in our approach to newly developing information policy, the so-called information superhighway—a rather silly name. I am not a Luddite. I managed in the computerized information environment for more than 20 years, and I am one of the very large number of IBM alumni whom one can find in retirement communities.

Reprinted, with changes, by permission of the author and *Library Journal* 122, no. 11 (June 15, 1997): 48–49. Copyright © 1997 by Cahners Business Information.

Information Is a Means to an End

After my experience in the corporate and government information world, and my years as a board member of the American Federation of Information Processing Societies, I believe that the capable people in the hardware, software, and database development industries nevertheless do not understand what we presumably do understand: information access is a means to an end, not simply an end in itself. I use "presumably" as a qualification because when I see librarians employing circulation as the validation of their worth, I am not so sure. Circulation volume is a virtue only in a recreational setting; in an informational one it becomes a dilution of quality. Informational clients are looking for the exact answer, not six books, one of which might contain that answer.

More Information Isn't Better

It is reassuring to realize that not everyone accepts the "more information is good and most information is best" mantra. Tom Peters noted several years ago that a flood of information was the enemy of intelligence. However, we are still urged by the hardware and software people to discover the joys of surfing the Internet. Don't we already have too many couch potatoes? Are we so bored that we are supposed to enjoy the search for trivia? Will net surfing replace soap operas?

Whether some end users enjoy sitting at terminals is not really the issue, although those whose business is selling equipment certainly care and that is why they stress the fun features. A recent Hewlett-Packard TV ad shows an executive sitting at his terminal; the voice-over narration comments on how hard he is working. It turns out he is playing a simulated round of golf and has just sliced his tee shot into the lake. All of this may help sell computers, and obviously Hewlett-Packard thinks it does.

However, it will not take long for managers to suspect that their subordinates, who are spending a great deal of time sitting in front of terminals, might be playing games. Special librarians have long understood that it is not a good idea to stock recreational magazines because the management suspicion that any time spent in the library might be goof-off time always lurks just below the surface. How long before that suspicion dawns about "hardworking" terminal workers, or has it begun to dawn already?

Even when intent and usage are totally honest, the very ease of accessing tremendous quantities of information on terminals can work to the disadvantage of anyone looking for answers. Any industrial efficiency expert can explain why it is easier to find information in a smaller file than a larger one. Professors know this instinctively when they drag library materials they think they might need again to the smallest of relevant storage areas: their own offices. Even if librarians were fascinated by such quantitative measurements to define their value as holdings and circulation rather than qualitative ones, there were always constraints to keep them from running amok. Books had to be bought and that took money. Catalog cards had to be reproduced and filed and that also put a damper on our eagerness.

The New Information Flood

The present environment allows garbage to reach anyone without constraint, and garbage is defined very personally as something that must be looked at, although—especially in the case of unsolicited e-mail—it was never wanted in the first place. The creation and dissemination of information currently operates without any constraint except for the judgment of the originator and, like the rest of us, other originators believe that anything they might want to say is bound to be fascinating to the recipient. However, recipients have always had to balance the inconvenience of receiving too little information against the inconvenience of receiving too much.

Librarians—mostly special librarians—who have dealt with individually crafted computer profiles for selective dissemination of information have long understood this. Some users prefer broad sweeping profiles in which they endure garbage to protect themselves against missing anything. Others, who feel their time is already too constrained, would rather risk missing something than endure wasting their time reading what they don't want to read.

Those preferences change, as I can certainly attest as I move from academia to an active retirement as a writer and teacher without any managerial responsibilities. I have now removed myself from all e-mail contact, and some of my colleagues don't understand how I could do that. The reason is very simple. I realized that the great majority of what I was receiving no longer interested me, and wading through it cost too great a price. I can, of course, still be reached by telephone, "snail" mail, and fax. My protection is that all these require more effort.

It is reassuring that cartoonists now recognize this growing absurdity. Greg Howard, who draws "Sally Forth," has one character congratulated for having found an effective way to filter e-mail. This person only acknowledges messages from those who earn more than he does, although he admits that his mother is becoming upset. I don't doubt that the hysteria about *total* information access is starting to subside, as the recognition sets in that it can become a curse rather than a cure.

I don't really expect the hardware, software, and database marketing people to understand this because they still tend to believe that more is *always* better. However, as we enter the age of greater accountability, a period we have already seen through downsizing, the elimination of middle managers, and the summary dismissal of the in-house consultants, advisors, and facilitators (which some special and academic librarians seem so anxious to become), top management is starting to recognize that having unnecessary information can become both expensive and counterproductive.

Are We Knowledge Workers?

Just as Peter Drucker in the late 1980s accurately predicted the current wave of downsizing, he also predicted a bright future for knowledge workers. It is therefore disturbing to see a prediction published last year in *USA Today*. Those professions with a bright future are primarily those that harness and use technology, such as computer animation. The fields seen as having a dim future include telephone operators, bank tellers, and librarians. It is easy to see the common thread. These are the fields for which the work is presumably so routine and predictable that people can be replaced by computers.

We need to clarify our role, and I would suggest that we stress that it is not to enhance the work of the information highway paving trucks. Public libraries are now competing to receive free terminals from Microsoft. I can certainly understand why this makes sense for Bill Gates, who is smart enough to be a multibillionaire. What he donates is a full tax write-off and great public relations; moreover, librarians will now train future Microsoft customers.

We tend to repeat our strategic mistakes. As we decimated our salary and continuing education budgets to buy books when that was really our management's responsibility, we are now ready to decimate them to buy computer hardware. Not for the library staff. I would understand that tactic, because it would give us unique leverage and prestige. We buy them to train Gates's future customers. Perhaps he should donate computers to all of every library's end users, and perhaps he would if we pointed out the advantages to him. Or perhaps he already knows the advantages and is only surprised we have never asked.

Needed: Information Lifeguards

We have all noticed that as organizations swear eternal fealty to information access, they shrink and close their libraries. There is no future for us in chasing the mob on the way to storm the Bastille. However, if we can establish our credibility in protecting clients from the information deluge that threatens to drown them, then our niche in corporate, academic, and public environments would be secure. There are already enough information "get wet" instructors, particularly since those who want to sell us pools called terminals are understandably anxious that we learn to put our heads underwater. What is needed is a cadre of information lifeguards—not guides but protectors—because people who are drowning don't produce very much work.

After a recent talk I was asked by a law firm librarian who was spending a great deal of her time teaching lawyers how to search the Internet what I thought she should be stressing or doing instead. What I think she ought to do is point out to law firm administrators that access to the Internet presents both opportunities for information access and dangers for playing games and wasting time and money. Management needs to be aware of these issues and to promulgate ground rules for how the Internet should and should not be used on the employer's time.

Librarians: Logical Selectors

Some Internet blocking software programs also allow businesses to restrict Internet access by category. But librarians are the logical candidates to draft these ground rules, because they understand the alternatives better than anyone else. Moreover, and besides just teaching users how to access the Internet, librarians should also alert them to the opportunities for finding useful information and the risks of being buried in garbage and should stress that this risk can be minimized if librarians do the complex work for them.

That is what I believe the knowledge workers do ("Do We Want to Be Knowledge Workers?," White Papers, *LJ*, September 15, 1996, pp. 41–42), to benefit their employers and to save their own jobs. The issue concerns substance and not style—information access rather than teaching our clients to play net games.

In a recent issue of *LJ*, there is an exciting description of United Technologies Corporation's (UTC) plans to revamp its traditional library system into groups of information managers, research analysts, and knowledge facilitators ("Corporate Makeover," March 1, pp. 38–41). The article suggests that this should be the future direction for corporate special libraries, and I certainly agree.

However, I wonder if readers realize that this is also the only possible successful direction for academic and public librarians to take if they want to achieve prestige, respect, and funding, and if they want to end up on the right side of the *USA Today* prediction list.

Who Will Lead
the Unsuspecting
Lemmings Over
the Cliff?

The study and report by the Benton Foundation relies heavily on information supplied by the general public, which has already shown in previous contacts its total inability to select among alternatives, to rank order, and to relate desires to funding options. This information is then compared to recommendations made by representatives of organizations identified as library "leaders." However, the report confuses leadership with management authority and ignores the fact that managers and leaders have different and frequently contradictory priorities. Finally, this article argues that any meaningful strategy must come directly from the analysis and professional judgment of librarians unfettered by what outsiders might consider desirable or reasonable, and suggests ways in which such a strategy might be developed.

A study examining the prospects for our profession's future as we prepare for the next millennium is certainly welcome and very much needed, particularly when it is undertaken by the prestigious Benton Foundation and funded by the W. K. Kellogg Foundation, both groups

Reprinted, with changes, by permission of the author and the Trustees of the University of Illinois, from *Library Trends* 46, no. 1 (Summer 1997): pp. 83–91.

which have shown their interest in, and support for, the concerns of this profession. That the profession of librarianship faces an uncertain and perhaps even frightening future can hardly be doubted. Declines in support for public library and academic library activities, reductions in both staffing (particularly professional staffing) and funding, a decline in an insistence on the professional degree in hiring, and lack of support for continuing education—these are just a few examples. Other indicators of decline include the closing of many of the most prestigious institutions which prepared our future professionals (and without future professionals we become a dying breed), and the continuing trivialization of what we are and what we do by all branches of the media (e.g., the annual return of "It's a Wonderful Life" in which, in the absence of faith, something horrible like becoming a spinster librarian could happen). In the last few years, this trend has been aggravated by slick television ads for computer hardware and systems manufacturers which inform us that going to the library is no longer necessary since all information is "easily" and "rapidly" accessible on the system we are about to purchase. Finally, one needs only ride on airplanes a few times to discover the discomfort and puzzlement brought on by learning that one's companion for the next few hours actually teaches and researches in the profession of librarianship. These are simply random examples of problems in public perception and public support of which we are all aware. A study leading to a new and assertive strategy would be very welcome.

The first suggestion that this report is going to be disappointing comes from its very title, because *Buildings, Books, and Bytes*, while certainly a catchy title, is as much an example of trivialization as those cited above. Buildings, printed material, and computer access to information in other than printed form are merely tools for the carrying out of our mission and responsibility, if indeed we can ever decide what that is, rather than wait for others to tell us. Buildings, for example, are a necessary means to an end but never an end in themselves. Inadequate physical facilities make it difficult or impossible for librarians to do their jobs; adequate buildings at least increase the potential. In speaking at the dedication of a new public library in Findlay, Ohio, this writer congratulated the assembled civic officials and Chamber of Commerce representatives on making such a good start, but then asked them if they had considered how they now wanted to use this new opportunity to enhance public library service for the citizens, and what additional funding they were considering for access and staff. They were surprised at my comments, because they assumed that in building a new structure they had completed their task. Perhaps the most garish recent example comes from the city of San Francisco, where a new $134 million library has been completed without any thought to additional professional staffing. This is more than a waste; it is a danger, because the citizens of San Francisco now think they have supported their public library, when in reality they have perhaps only improved their skyline.

Books and bytes, as the report calls them rather simplistically, are also not the issue, but rather only among the options which allow librarians to bring more and better needed information and knowledge to the citizens of the community. Those options have always been subject to change and will continue to change. None of us recall what concern and anguish might have arisen when printed books began to appear next to manuscripts in libraries, but there was undoubtedly fear that libraries would now be spoiled forever. We do know that the introduction of typewriters and their use in preparing previously handwritten catalog cards caused much alarm.

If people think that changing the mix between printed books and computer access somehow "changes" what libraries are supposed to do, then that conception is both wrong and simplistic. When it appears in the opinions of the general public, this is not surprising because the public has always been initially suspicious of significant change as an attack on tradition and comfort. There was a similar outcry at the introduction of automobiles and the fact that they would frighten horses. Public negative reaction is temporary, provided that there is professional leadership from those qualified, through education and study, to know. What is significant in the introduction of computers in libraries is the fact that, when added to more traditional (which only means earlier) formats, they allow for far greater access to information than had previously been possible. In other words, all libraries, including small and geographically isolated ones, now become windows to the world's knowledge. That is the good news, but there are three pieces of potentially bad news, although the bad news is trivial by comparison. The first piece of bad news is that all of this will produce access to tremendous quantities of information, and that this will require filters. As syndicated management guru Tom Peters has noted, "a flood of information can be the enemy of intelligence." Expanded information access will require gatekeepers and evaluators. The second piece of news, which stems from the first, is that all of this will require a great many more professional librarians, because this is the most cost effective alternative. The third, of course, is that funding for libraries will have to increase dramatically. However, there is no acceptable alternative, because the alternative is stupidity and particularly stupidity while others are getting smart.

The issue of concern is not buildings, books, or computers; it is professionals to shape and manage the institutions we now call libraries. But what we call them does not really matter. What happens there is what does matter. The key issue of professionals is certainly never addressed by the general public in this survey, which never mentions librarians but only libraries. Indeed, there is evidence that they confuse librarians not only with the clerks who do important work in our institutions but even with the people who work in bookstores. That is not surprising and therefore not really disappointing, although the medical profession would never allow such confusion in responsibility to remain. What is disappointing is that the importance of professional librarians as the crucial element in addressing this problem is never addressed in the study title and content or by the presumed "leaders" whose only reference is to the fact that somehow librarians will "have to change."

It is perhaps time to review the definition of a profession and the roles of professionals to see whether we qualify or even want to qualify. The issue is certainly not assured within, let alone outside, the field. Also, as will be noted later, a number of library educators at prestigious universities have suggested that educational programs must distance themselves from the "field" of librarianship to avoid being swamped in the undertow. However, it is the premise of this article that we are and should be a profession, and that indeed the problems we face in the next century can only be addressed by the leadership of a profession which informs the general and political public of what it has no reason to know. That, of course, is what doctors and lawyers do but also what plumbers and garage mechanics do. It is, for this writer, the crucial issue in all of our consideration, and it is totally ignored in the report.

Merriam Webster's Collegiate Dictionary, 10th ed. (1994) tells us, in part, that a profession is "a calling requiring specialized knowledge and often long and intensive academic preparation." A slightly different but similar definition is provided by Andrew Abbott (1988), who argues that the tasks of professions are human problems amenable to expert service. Professions compete for existing and newly emerging problem jurisdictions; they work to retain jurisdiction over their problems, to change or extend their jurisdiction, or to preempt the jurisdiction of other professionals. It is easy to see how Abbott's point relates to our own field. Increasingly, our jurisdiction has been taken over by the computer and business fields which understand, even if we do not, the value of the territories called information and knowledge. It is hard to see how any study, and this study in particular, could hope to produce useful information for librarians without dealing with issues of professionalism and issues of territorial jurisdictions. But then the study hardly discusses librarians at all, and the general public being surveyed never talks about them. The emphasis is on libraries, but libraries are places which contain things. They have no innate value of their own, they are only what their professionals make of them.

The survey of the general public continues to tell us nothing more than what such attempts to quiz our users have always told us. This is not their fault because we continue to empower them without explaining the options and choices. We have seen in two White House Conferences that the general public wants everything, that it is not willing to prioritize, and that it does not want to talk about higher taxes. The first White House Conference in 1979 ended with over 100 unranked and uncosted recommendations, and such a wish list is politically unmanageable even if some in power might want to implement some of it. Of course, both this and the succeeding White House Conference assured their irrelevancy by insisting that the individuals being asked to decide first prove that they understood neither library issues nor library problems.

Thus these respondents indicate that they really want everything, and what they personally may not use is still also an acceptable addition. Thus, they want nice buildings, they want books (presumably the ones mentioned by Oprah Winfrey and also the classics), and they want computer access. Those with children, not surprisingly, want computer services, and there is general support for having the library play a role as a safe haven for latchkey children and adults who are functionally illiterate. We are told that senior citizens have a high regard for public libraries, but they were not asked why either they or their fellow senior citizens, as a group, consistently vote against all public funding initiatives, including those for libraries. Respondents had no objection to the role of librarians as pathfinders and guides, although some were surprised at such a role. That may be explained by the realization that some respondents don't even know who librarians are, as compared not only to the clerks in our own libraries but also the employees in book stores.

What can we make of such a range of responses, which espouse the value of everything and the cost of nothing? Very little if anything. The report suggests that there is optimism in the finding that a great majority of the public is "willing" to spend more in support of libraries, but that response cannot be believed. Support in the abstract is worth nothing, and the elected and appointed politicians understand quite clearly that there is greater safety in lower taxes than in better libraries. Even this last statement can be understood from the response that is, for this writer, the most depressing of all. Despite cuts in budget, in staffing, in services, and in hours of opening, the public is not distressed. It thinks libraries are "wonderful." Politicians know what that means. It means it is safe to cut the budget of libraries again. Police protection, on the other hand, is not "wonderful," and that budget must be enhanced. Nor are garbage collection and pothole repair considered wonderful. Money goes not to where people are happy but where they are unhappy. We have done a singularly incompetent job in making our users unhappy and angry, but this is never mentioned.

If library patrons can have their answers easily explained away, what of the responses of those individuals whom the report calls "leaders"? They are never identified as individuals, but they represent the institutions named by the Kellogg Foundation as Information Systems Management Grantees. This list of 18 organizations includes professional societies, major universities, large public libraries, and major library education programs. The spokespersons who represented these institutions are not identified by name, but it can be assumed that they are in high positions of administrative responsibility. That makes them managers, but does it make them leaders?

Perhaps as individuals they are leaders, but certainly not as a group, and it can be argued that successful managers, who have already achieved posts of high prestige and high salary, are particularly unlikely to expose themselves to the risks that leadership entails. The political process provides the most obvious example. Historians are now reaching the conclusion that the last United States president who was a leader was Harry Truman. Truman, we will recall, fired General Douglas MacArthur for usurping powers that belonged to the Chief Executive, although he knew that this would expose him to a storm of protest. He could, at worst, have assigned this task to an unlucky cabinet official and let that individual take the blame, but Truman fired MacArthur personally. We have seen examples of the other approach often since that time, most directly embodied in the decision by loyal staffers to "protect the President," presumably even from his own improper act. Most recently we have begun to confuse the style of individuals who tell us eloquent things with leadership. However, before they take any public stand they receive polls that tell them what the public wants to be told. That is not leadership.

The point of this digression is to explain why major officials, in professional society, elective office, and in the executive corner offices of major public and academic libraries, can hardly be expected to be leaders and risk takers. They have already achieved what they sought to achieve; why would they now want to antagonize those who elected them, or the university president, or the mayor? None of this then is their fault. The fault is with the study methodology which confuses leaders with important people. Important people tend to become more conservative because they have more to lose. In selecting the Kellogg Foundation grantees, the Benton Foundation researchers may have made what was for them a safe and perhaps politically expedient choice, but they have destroyed the ability to compare responses from the two disparate groups because, to a large extent, this second group says exactly what it knows the first group expects it to say.

Even with all of this explanation, there is one piece of unforgivable mischief. After stating in their public responses what they were expected to say—that libraries would continue to do everything and more even in the face of declining staffs and budgets—some of the participants then respond privately that what they had said publicly might in fact not be possible. It is unfair to brand such a double standard as hypocritical, but is this what any field (the report does not describe a profession, only "libraries") has the right to expect from its "leaders?" Management writers have understood for a long time that the characters of managers, who tend to be bureaucratic, and leaders, who tend to be impatient of organizational structure, are not only different but in large part contradictory. Cosgrove's 1988 analysis in *Campus Activities Programming* was then related to our field in an article (White, 1990), but it may be that the officials in the Kellogg and Benton Foundations do not read our literature. They can, however, identify top level managers. That part is easy.

The Kellogg and Benton Foundations are certainly correct in their sense of timing, because it is essential that librarians make some decisions about their future directions. Two possible roads beckon to us. The first is outlined by Peter Drucker, who in 1993 postulated that the most exciting future profession would be that of knowledge workers. This is because knowledge workers will do what is essential, and yet what the general public (and even corporate management and academia) will be unwilling and unable to do for themselves—unwilling because information is a means to an end and not an end in itself. This is particularly true in the working environment where individuals are judged by what they accomplish and not by how much time they spend looking for things. That realization will dawn even on the present population of 18 to 24 year olds who, quite typically for their age, are incapable of admitting any weaknesses. As these individuals enter the "real" world of the workplace, they will quickly learn that their managers are not impressed with how much time they spend online, particularly in chat rooms.

Drucker (1993) is undoubtedly correct in his prediction, but what is not known is whether the future knowledge workers will be librarians or others who can see the power base and the economic opportunity. Certainly a new commercial sector identified by the British journal *The Economist* (1993) as the meatware industry (meatware being the human beings who use the hardware and software on our behalf) falls into that category, and it has been identified as one of the hottest future growth industries. The question is not whether or not there will be meatware or knowledge workers, but whether librarians will be a part of this process. There are two things against us. The first is the public assumption that we are neither interested nor capable (although we certainly are better prepared for this work than any other field); the second is our own reluctance or perhaps lack of confidence, as indicated in this study through the reactions of our "leaders."

The second possible road is described in the daily national newspaper *USA Today*, which lists ten occupations (Kelly, 1996) for which the paper sees no future. These include telephone operator, bank teller, and librarians. The connection is obvious. These are three groups of people who, in the opinion of the newspaper, do clerical and routine work that computers can do more effectively. To some extent we still have choices but, as noted by John Barlow (1994), we will most certainly be relegated to *USA Today*'s perceived future for us if we insist that our business is containers of information rather than the content of those containers. Computers can manipulate containers far better than we can.

What then do the designated "leaders" see as our future? According to the report, they perceive the library's role (not even the librarian's role) as trusted guides, coaches, and path finders. If this does not send a shiver of excited anticipation down the spines of the reader, it is not surprising. A self-selected role in these areas, particularly at a time of downsizing and a fierce competition for funds, appears totally suicidal. This writer cannot imagine a U.S. president, governor, mayor, academic administrator, or corporate executive calling a news conference to announce that one of the higher priorities for his or her administration is the selection and nurturing of guides, coaches, and path finders. If we want to chart a unique professional role for the profession of librarianship, it must be by creating the unique jurisdiction about which Abbott writes so forcefully, without mentioning librarians (nor, of course, does Drucker). Only *USA Today* finds us worthy of specific identification. Our argument must be that what we do either uniquely or at least better and more cost effectively than anyone else is crucial, and that therefore we must be empowered to do it. Most directly, we must attack the absurd notion (certainly in management terms) that what librarians do has a cost, while what end users do is free.

Another way of describing these options might be in terms of the animal kingdom. Archilochus observed that "the fox knows many things, but the hedgehog knows one great thing" (7th century BC). Do we want to be the equivalent of hedgehogs, or rather, instead of foxes, guides, coaches, and path finders to the knowledge of foxes? Another alternative is posed, even if starkly, by library educators Nancy Van House and Stuart Sutton (1996). They suggest, although they are writing about library education and not librarianship, that we are likely to go the way of the panda: cute, well loved, coddled, and nearing extinction. It is these deans and other educators who also suggest that library education programs must distance themselves from libraries in order to survive. The intent of the Kellogg and Benton Foundations is commendable, but if they really want to come up with a document that this profession can use as a plan, they need to start over. First, they need to stop asking library users what they think. We already know what they think, and that unranked and uncosted wish list cannot be fashioned into any sort of strategy. Besides, why should we keep asking people who obviously don't know? Have we no confidence in our own expertise and our own judgment?

Second, they need to convene a conference of real leaders and potential leaders and not just of high level managers. Potential leaders in our field do exist but, unless we encourage and support them, we may stone them to death, because leaders are not always comforting or popular. The foundations might begin with some students in our library education programs who chose this career not because they wanted to emulate present librarians, but because they were certain that there must be a better way. Such students have to be identified early, before the bureaucracy of the library workplace, particularly in the demand that they be pleasant members of the mediocracy-driven "team," drives them to silence or to leaving the field. The foundations might also seek individuals who, as public, academic, and state library directors, have been censured, and perhaps even fired, for daring to suggest that librarians know more about planning and managing libraries than non-librarians. In both cases we have lost sight of the general management principle that good subordinates make far more trouble than bad ones, but they are worth it. In all fairness, it may not occur to professors of business administration that this applies to librarians.

For a third group of potential leaders, the foundations might look to working professional librarians, particularly reference librarians, who are frustrated by administrative policies that keep them from providing proper and adequate reference service, because administrators insist on pretending that the now decimated staff is still "adequate." These librarians may also be frustrated by the fact that much of what little time they have is spent in answering the routine and directional questions that clerks could easily answer, except that: (1) there are not enough clerks so the professionals become clerks; or (2) the patrons cannot tell who is a professional librarian, who is a clerk, who is a student, and who is a volunteer.

There are no guarantees, but a group of these free-spirited thinkers, unfettered by the realizations of their management bosses of what is or is not "reasonable" or "possible," might even come up with something we can use as a battle plan. And a battle plan is exactly what it must be.

References

Abbott, A. D. (1988). *The system of professions: An essay on the division of expert labor.* Chicago: University of Chicago Press.

Barlow, J. P. (1994). A taxonomy of information. *Bulletin of the American Society for Information Science, 20*(5), 13–17.

Drucker, P. F. (1993). *The post-capitalist society.* New York: Harper Business Books.

Kelly, K. (1996). Future jobs to bank on: Therapists not tellers. *USA Today*, April 11, p. 1-D.

London. (1993). *The Economist, 328*(7821).

Merriam-Webster, Inc. (1994). *Merriam Webster's collegiate dictionary* (10th ed.). Springfield, MA: Merriam-Webster, Inc.

Van House, N., and Sutton, S. (1996). The panda syndrome: An ecology of LIS education. *Journal of Education for Library and Information Science, 37*(2), 131–147.

White, H. S. (1990). Managers and leaders: Are there more differences than similarities? *Library Journal, 115*(11), 51–53.

Should Leaders Want to Be Managers and Give Up All That Freedom?

In an earlier column ("Managers and Leaders: Are There More Differences Than Similarities?" *LJ*, June 15, 1990, p. 51–53) I sought to distinguish between what managers and leaders do. We still may think that anything can be accomplished with good will and effort. The process of creating managers and leaders is much more complex.

In *The Peter Principle* (1969), Laurence Peter warned against creating managers not because of any particular talent but as a reward for performance in a lower post. The results can be disastrous: the very characteristics that may make for a fine worker (dogged determination, tunnel vision in the pursuit of an objective, abnormally high productivity) can make for intolerant and narrow-minded supervisors. We ought to be able to properly reward excellent workers without making them managers, but we rarely do this in libraries. How many reference librarians, no matter how excellent, can earn more than the head of the reference department? Yet there are situations in which reference librarians contribute more than their schedule-making bosses.

Irresponsible as it may be to promote someone to a management post who lacks an aptitude for or interest in management, that problem—despite Peter's concerns—can be controlled. Managers operate under rules and regulations, and run-of-the-mill managers can be taught to follow the rules and to apply them consistently. Excellent managers also know when the rules should be challenged or ignored, because rules are generalizations and can never replace common sense. However, we can and do live with managers who may lack imagination or common sense but who are fair and decent and at least apologize for implementing a general policy even when they know it's stupid.

Leadership Is Different

The issue of leadership is far more complex. John P. Kotter, in his book, *A Force for Change: How Leadership Differs from Management* (Free Press, 1990), is only one of many writers who has tried to persuade us of the difference between managers and leaders. We are often unwilling to hear this; we "train" managers so we think we can train leaders, perhaps by sending them to a two-day summer camp. Kotter acknowledges that while management as we now define it only goes back about 100 years, leadership is ageless. Management, which evolved from the development of complex organizations, was invented to fill a need. We can define managerial "success" pretty well, and in the corporate sector we do it through the bottom line.

Kotter describes differences between managers and leaders that appear almost contradictory. Managers, he notes, plan and budget, while leaders abhor such detail and instead establish directions. Managers organize and staff their operations, while leaders align people to their new directions. Managers control and solve problems. Leaders motivate, inspire, and energize. Managers aim at outcomes that fit both predictability and order, while leaders produce change.

There is little doubt now that management is in ill repute; we insist that we really want leaders. Kotter reports studies in which corporate officials complain they have too many strong managers who are weak leaders and they have too many people who are both bad managers and bad leaders. Perhaps surprisingly, while they wish for more strong leaders who are also strong managers, they say they would settle for strong leaders even if they are bad managers.

But do they really mean it? Kotter doesn't speculate, but my own experience in the bureaucracy of organizations (and there is hardly anything more bureaucratic than a library) suggests that we tend to find leaders who question dubious policies and procedures to be a great deal of trouble. As my students troop back to the campus after their job interviews, I perceive a preference by interviewers for individuals who "fit into group dynamics," who "work well in teams," but who in reality are willing to subsume themselves in a group consensus process. Leaders do not do this. Are we still sure we want them? Is it worth the effort of differentiating between a leader who asks valid, even embarrassing questions and a jerk who automatically questions everything? There are many supervisors who would rather not bother. In Paul Vincent Carroll's play *The Wayward Saint*, an elderly Irish parish priest suddenly and inexplicably starts performing miracles. The bishop is of course furious, as any manager might be. He notes that "saints cause nothing but trouble."

Leadership Isn't Easy

We try so hard to create leaders that we not only forget to remind them of all the opposition they will face but also forget to recognize that many people, particularly in a feminized profession such as ours, are groomed from childhood not to be leaders for fear of losing their popularity. I assure students, particularly female ones, that it's all right to be obnoxious some of the time; just try not to let it show during the job interview.

In one of his syndicated columns, Tom Peters stresses that the fit between successful management and leadership is not as automatic as we assume. He observes that managers, by the very nature of their jobs, are enmeshed in the need for detailed negotiations and decisions, something leaders try to avoid. Managers do what they do not because it is necessarily fun but because it is necessary. Leaders without management responsibility have far more freedom.

The Constraints of Management

There are many possible reasons why leaders might seek to become managers, but management's conferring of legal authority and higher salaries must lead the list. There is nothing wrong in having a leader become a manager. However, that individual must realize that authority brings with it *less* freedom and not the greater liberty that situation comedies suggest. Management is hard work: you don't control your agenda, and you frequently end up doing not what you want to do but rather what you must do. Not all natural leaders drawn to management may understand this.

An old proverb cautions us to be careful about what we wish for, because we might get it. When leaders seek the recognition that appointment or election confers, they also must recognize the limitations that a management post brings with it. For example, all presidential candidates promise greater efficiency, new services, and lower costs. The lucky ones lose the election. A wise observer of the French political scene stated that it didn't matter who won the election, because civil servants would continue to do what they always had done.

In "Library Leaders—Who and Why?" (*LJ*, July 1990, pp. 45–51), Alice Gertzog reported research that identifies me as a leader, and I accept that as a compliment. However, for most of my career I have been primarily a manager—in industry and government, as president of two professional societies, and as dean of a major library school. The limitations in any office are always there. The president of a society speaks for the entire membership, and therefore cannot call a senator a jerk, no matter how great the temptation. If wise, an American Library Association president will invite an equal number of liberals and conservatives and, of course, never just buddies, to speak from a platform. A dean cannot fight a university president without risk, because deans are responsible for the well-being of faculty and students, and angry presidents can punish the school and not just the administrator. Indeed, if the dean has tenure, punishment may fall indirectly on junior faculty and students.

As one of my former bosses once advised me, "The higher you get in management, the less personal freedom you will have." I accepted the trade-off between authority and constraint on my freedom willingly for many years, but in 1990 I let go of all management responsibility for the first time in 37 years. I am now simply a professor, lecturer, and author. I say and write whatever I want without fear that innocent victims might be punished in my stead. It is a heady freedom, making me far more at liberty to try to be a leader.

Turning Leaders Into Managers

It is still desirable, when possible, to make leaders into managers. You can't create leaders without major brain surgery, so the supply is limited. However, I think it is critical that people about to be named managers—particularly those used to the liberty of leadership without the constraints of discipline—be sternly counseled so they understand the limitations of promotion in a hierarchical structure or elected office in a democratic one. Managers are birds that choose to live in a cage, even if the cage includes a sauna. Leaders prefer freedom, and they constantly seek to "win." They do not, as the otherwise excellent 1996 Competencies Report of the Special Libraries Association suggests, willingly "take turns to let others lead." Having more than one competing leader may be trouble, but it is better than having none.

It is necessary to stress all of this because we still tend to confuse managers with leaders. In the recent Benton Foundation study ("Polarized Perceptions," *LJ*, February 1, p. 46–48), an impressive group of managers in societal offices and major libraries were rather casually introduced to us as our leaders, without any proof of their qualifications. Perhaps some of them indeed are leaders, but the probability is not very great. Successful managers usually have much too much to risk to allow themselves the luxury of trying to lead. Such managers are often not consensus-builders but rather searchers for safety and popularity. Or does anyone think that national politicians who check the polls before they express an opinion are leaders?

Planning and Evaluation: The Endless Carousel

During my 25 years as a manager in industry and government I knew that if I did not get to my boss first with my own proposals, I would have to implement whatever he or she decided to do without my input. I considered evaluation largely a nuisance, never realizing it was a valuable tool for demonstrating to the boss what was still wrong and what needed to be fixed. I have taught management during my 20 years in academia, but I never focused on planning or evaluation.

Only after my retirement, when I started teaching as an adjunct professor in the School of Library Science at the University of Arizona, did an opportunity arise. Arizona had separate courses in planning and evaluation taught by two professors, with no apparent coordination. When both of these courses became available, I was asked to consider teaching a combination: "Planning and Evaluation." It is now my favorite course. And, within a few days of examining the literature and reflecting on my experiences, two observations leapt at me:

Libraries Don't Plan

First, libraries rarely plan. Instead they react to what others have already decided in such areas as budgets and staffing and then "plan" to make the best of the situation. Proper planning, by contrast, is a proactive process: considering dangers and opportunities, then presenting these to our bosses as a series of alternatives

Reprinted, with changes, by permission of the author and *Library Journal* 122, no. 19 (November 15, 1997): 38–39. Copyright © 1997 by Cahners Business Information.

for which they will get either credit or blame. This represents partnership building with our own supervisors. Anyone who knows even a bit about management understands that, for our bosses, "looking good" results from specific decisionmaking alternatives. One obvious one is whether or not to spend money on the library. If they can "look good" in spite of—or perhaps because of—cutting our budgets, they will hardly consider changing a successful strategy of nonsupport. In a partnership, both parties have responsibilities. Ours include giving management the opportunity to look good and urging against decisions that will make it look bad.

Evaluation Needed

Second, libraries rarely use the opportunities for evaluation to find out what really happened. Instead, many of them rig the process to make sure that nice things are said by asking only those who are likely to be favorably inclined: the self-selected supporters who are found and contacted in the library. People who find us irrelevant or inadequate stay away. This then leads to such absurdities as the Benton Foundation finding that, after years of declining staffs and budgets, the citizens we carefully choose to poll still think the library is wonderful. Of course, that simply validates the most recent budget cuts. In other words, "surveys" that ask rigged questions of a carefully selected group of supporters will indeed make our bosses look good, whether they deserve to or not. As Anne M. Turner recently wrote ("Opinion Polls: A Savvy Tool to Raise Library Value," *LJ*, October 15, p. 40–41), the best library polls concern likely voters, not library supporters.

What is wrong with these strategies is most obviously seen in our failure to secure funding in comparison with such groups as law enforcement officers. Even when *LJ* happily reports "victories," we are usually talking about recovering something that had been taken away before—and sometimes even only part of it. We have all noticed that referenda for buildings are more attractive to politicians than referenda to increase operating funds. However, gaining bigger buildings and more branches without more staff is a pyrrhic victory.

Subordinates Worth the Trouble

Management analysts have long observed that better subordinates make the most amount of trouble. What makes them acceptable is the realization that they are worth all that trouble. In Marion Paris's dissertation "Why Library Schools Fail" (*LJ*, October 1, 1990, p. 38–42), administrators who had closed their library schools were asked what had prompted their actions. It was never lack of money, which should hardly surprise us, because library schools cost so little. Poverty, as a rationale for any decision affecting libraries, is a handy excuse but never the real reason. The real reason for closing library schools was the administrators' puzzlement as to what the school tried to accomplish and how this helped to support the parent institutions' objectives. As Paris heard repeatedly in her face-to-face interviews, "I never understood what they were doing in that school. They never seemed to want or need anything."

I had the same perception confirmed when a corporate administrator began our preliminary discussion about my assessment of his special library with the gratuitous observation that undoubtedly the company was spending too much money on the library. When I asked why, he commented, "Nobody ever complains about the library."

Planning is the natural process of determining what is needed to implement objectives. Mission statements and goals—not only plentiful but also highly altruistic—do not suffice because they are neither quantifiable nor measurable. However, management concurrence with our mission and goals, which is usually easy to obtain because it involves only "in principle" support, must then lead to the development of objectives. These are what you plan to accomplish within a finite period, certainly no more than a year (or budget cycle) for specific objectives. Those objectives must be measurable, so that we can determine whether or not we did what we planned.

Objectives should be presented to our bosses, in an early (before they have made decisions) and private (we don't want to embarrass them) meeting, for their concurrence, modification, and perhaps even enhancement. It is extremely important to encourage the boss to participate in developing objectives, both because pride of ownership matters and because their fingerprints can be traced.

It is only after objectives are agreed upon that we then develop, for our management, their implementation plans, which inevitably involve resources in staff, equipment, space, and dollars. You obviously cannot make your boss give you this money, but you can insist that there is a firm relationship between resources and objectives. If management insists that the funds are not there, then objectives must be modified. However, the resulting final objectives, which are agreed upon as being doable under the circumstances of available resources, become a public document, with the clear understanding that this is a shared decision between the library and its management. That is at least a sensible definition of a partnership.

How to Evaluate

What then is the role of evaluation and who should participate? Evaluation determines whether or not we have accomplished our objectives and whether those objectives should be modified, i.e., some are not as important as originally thought, or new and even greater priorities have arisen that require reranking. The general public, particularly if we include only our "friends" by forcing people to come to the library to participate, could only answer the first question if it knew specifically what those objectives were, what they were not, and, more importantly, why they were not.

On the modification of priorities, the general public's input might be useful for further directions but only if a reranking were really involved. "Would you support strong children's services?" and "Would you like more access to computer technology?" are not particularly helpful; cumulatively they add to an infinite total, and our funding is not infinite. Asking which of the two they think is more important would be more useful but certainly would lead to fragmentation and disagreements. However, "instead of what" is the real issue in evaluation for end users and to some extent even for librarians.

Librarians hate to rank order, and we have seen a new example in the urging that we embrace the overriding importance of literacy programs. I might or might not agree, but that is not the point. Rather, we should worry about adding resources, not trading off within our already meager budgets, and without even publicizing those tradeoffs. Alternatively, we might collect petitions of those who would like their own taxes, and not someone else's, raised. The Benton Foundation report found that the greatest level of support for higher taxes comes from those who pay the least, or perhaps none at all. That is not very helpful.

Making Decisions

The role of managers at all levels is to make decisions among alternatives. That process may be pleasant, but usually it is painful. The role of professionals in subordinate positions is to assist those above them who may understand the political generalities but not the specific options. Professionals are the experts here, and pointing out options is their task. That is the partnership between professional library specialists and our more generalist non-librarian bosses.

In 1980 I was offered the deanship of the Graduate Library School at Indiana University. Since I was already a faculty member and had asked to be considered, I was pleased, but I told the chancellor I could not respond to the offer without first asking a question: What kind of library school did he want this to be? One of the best in the nation, an average school, or the cheapest school that could still secure reaccreditation?

Those were *his* choices, not mine. If he chose the second or third alternative, I would decline his offer. If he chose the first I would happily accept, noting that this option would require much work from both of us. Certainly more from me but from him at least a willing ear to proposals that would probably cost more money. It would be worth it for both of us. However, if he chose alternative one, he could expect to be reminded from time to time of that decision. And he was.

It is acceptable for us to present alternatives in a way to encourage approval of our recommendations, but in every case administrators must understand the implications of their decisions in terms of credit or blame. We would prefer to dispense credit. However, if we are supposed to make our bosses "look good" no matter what they decide, they have no incentive for any decision but the cheapest one. And they don't respect us for such subservience. We already know that good subordinates are supposed to make trouble—in a good cause and for persuasive reasons. We also know that higher-level managers are puzzled by subordinates who never want anything.

Proper planning then leads to implementation of what we all agree can be accomplished with the resources provided. Evaluation is the assessment of whether or not the plans were successfully achieved. However, it also includes whether or not the plans need to be modified. Some of this comes from us, some from our users. The process is endless.

———■———

Embarking on the Information Superhighway While Downsizing and Outsourcing Libraries

In a recent column I questioned the premise that librarians should be asked to do more with less simply because somebody felt like giving us less. Such a demand should alert us not to indict ourselves for past incompetence, which is what happens when we meekly go along. If we are asked to work more effectively by eliminating pointless procedures mandated by others, we will be happy to oblige. If we are asked to suggest a reranking of priorities, we can certainly do this as well, although that will force our non-librarian bosses to make some very public and perhaps very painful decisions. However, the suggestion that we work harder because somebody would like us to is unthinkable, precisely because everybody really knows it is nonsense. Given our status and salaries, we probably already work much harder than anyone has the right to expect.

In June 1994 my colleagues in the Special Libraries Association (SLA) were gracious in inducting me into their Hall of Fame. Time conflicts did not permit me to attend the technical program, but one major session theme caught my eye, and it worried me. The speakers were leading corporate librarians, who addressed the question of how a library could continue to offer the same or even higher quality of service despite a decrease in funding and staffing. This, as we all know, is the present practice of *downsizing*, or as it is even called, *rightsizing*. It represents management jargon for cutting staff not because we know we can and should, but because we simply assume it. The absurdity in *rightsizing* should be obvious. Have any executives been fired because they previously condoned *wrongsizing*?

This article was written with the intent to publish it as a "White Paper" in *Library Journal* in 1997. It was never submitted for publication because of space limitations.

There are real issues which could but rarely emerge from this gibberish sloganeering. It may be perfectly valid to reduce the staffing of any organization, for a variety of reasons. However, this must follow an analysis of what procedures and tasks can be eliminated, or which might more effectively be performed by specialized contractors. A statement that staff will be cut but that nothing should change sounds like nonsense precisely because it is.

Corporate officials really do know better, at least when they must confront alternative impacts for their decisions. Assembly plants are not closed without a careful determination of how this affects the ability to produce products, and sales forces are not decimated without at least some prediction models of how new customers will be attracted and old ones retained. If libraries do not fit into that model—if the decision to downsize is made first and the impact thought about later, if at all—it is because many librarians have failed to demonstrate that impact when it really matters, *before* the decision is reached.

The SLA program topic is obviously important, but I see little point in a discussion which involves only the victims and none of the decision makers. What should have happened, in each of these corporate settings, is a meeting in which librarians spelled out the implications of any budget changes, positive or negative, just in case such possibilities are being contemplated. Budget cut considerations send out warning signals to anyone astute enough to watch for them, and downsizing is rarely a surprise. What librarians must explain is that, even in a climate of downsizing, keeping and even strengthening libraries might be the most cost-effective strategy. It will not occur to management unless we suggest it.

Any experienced manager understands that it is far easier to head off a decision before it is announced than to get it reversed after it has been publicized. Decision reversal is seen as a loss of face, a sign of weakness, and a bending to pressure. Protecting the library from cuts must emerge as higher management's own brilliant idea. If we want to change our manager's mind, we must do it prior to a publicly stated position, and seek that decision in the privacy of his or her own office.

All of this should explain why an SLA program on how to rescue quality service after the fact of a management decision which never considered that question is not only counterproductive, it is dangerous. The concerns about which these special librarians are torturing themselves in a public forum should instead have been posed to their own managers long ago, because facing those concerns and making appropriate decisions is what their own jobs require of them.

All subordinates understand that it is not wise to give the boss ultimatums, because the reaction will most often be to the style rather than to the substance. For this reason all bosses must be offered alternatives among which to choose, with a clear understanding of the implications of their decisions. That doesn't mean that clever subordinates can't rig the question so that managers will decide as we would prefer them to decide. However, the question of whether or not they would like to spend more or less money is, without implications, not a very useful question. And yet, it is precisely the question that most managers think they face.

What alternatives? Since situations vary, let me pose just three. First, do you believe that information for this corporation (or for this university, this hospital, this municipal government, this federal agency) is important, or that it represents an unnecessary frill we can do without, because ignorance suits us just fine? I think I can safely predict the answer to this question, but if somehow your management thinks information is unimportant, you need at least to know that.

The second question is whether the concern is about real economy, or a cosmetic appearance of pseudo-economy. Here, too, the answer is probably predictable, at least from the financial executives you should include, because political survivors with interest in nothing except how they look are not as certain to come out in favor of real rather than pseudo-economy. However, they will always insist that their hearts are pure. In any case, the issue must be raised, because otherwise it is somehow assumed that what librarians do has a cost while what end users do is free. That is only true if end users have nothing else to do, so they might as well do the work of librarians. Of course, given the fact that end users are paid a great deal more than librarians, if we have too many end users, then there are some *real* cutting opportunities. Since that discussion has not come up, we can assume that end user staffing is already, or is about to be, very tight. If so, then presumably end users should not do what others can do both more effectively and more cheaply, especially since our salaries are smaller. Should we pose such "theatre of the absurd" questions to our managers? I certainly would, particularly if your bosses have a sense of humor. In fact, this is exactly how I "managed" my own bosses for many years.

The third question, which considers the alternative of contracting, or in its fancier name (business professors are drawn to complex names as moths to a flame), *outsourcing*, raises issues that are not as simple. There may be validity in contracting, particularly if a contractor can supply individuals with particular skills our staff cannot reasonably be expected to have. Alternatively, the need may be only for part-time or temporary employees. At the same time, we should insist that the reasons for outsourcing not be purely cosmetic, and often that turns out to be the primary reason. The reduction of internal staffing (at whatever the ultimate cost) may give the *appearance* of economy, and sometimes appearance is considered politically preferable to reality. The federal government, as we might suspect, is particularly adept at this manipulative process. We are told that federal government employment has decreased, but we might be right to suspect that the total number of people being paid, even if indirectly, has increased. If you doubt me, just drive around the Washington suburbs to see all the contractor buildings that such "economy" has purchased with our money. We might begin our tour at Crystal City near National Airport, and I can't think of a more appropriate name for Wizard of Ox fans. The wizard, we must remember, was really a fraud who only pretended to have power. Economy can also be pretended.

If politically motivated and otherwise unjustified outsourcing will occur in any environment in which style is considered more important than substance, then why does it also occur in corporations and foundations which spend their own money, and which presumably have a commitment to knowing the truth? More importantly, why are libraries considered such handy candidates for outsourcing in any and all management environments? It is at least in part because the librarians are not known personally to the individuals who make these overall decisions. It is much easier to fire and replace with a faceless contract staffer an individual who is also faceless. Many librarians, in all settings but particularly the corporate one, have been so busy struggling to serve their normal users (who generally are not the people who make policy decisions) that they have ignored the people who control their own job future. It is usually not the person who voluntarily comes to the library, and academic, public, and school librarians might also consider how they fit into this structure.

Once we understand the problems and options, we should be able to develop a strategy. Subordinates whom managers know and like, and who help them directly with their information problems, are not as likely to be fired, particularly since all the financial structure requires is that we fire "somebody." I can illustrate with a very simple example. One of my former students took a job running a small special library, and nothing was really expected of her except that she respond to specific requests and keep material orderly. However, when she was married in her home town on a Saturday afternoon two-and-a-half years later, both the president and executive vice president cared enough to fly down in the company jet to attend the ceremony. Were they likely to replace her with a faceless contractor after that? I hardly think so. They might bring in contract personnel to assist her, but these will work under her supervision. She will continue to be in charge, because she has seen to it that she is known and important.

SLA has recently developed a statement of "Competencies for Special Librarians of the 21st Century." It is an impressive and potentially useful document, particularly if it is primarily intended not for us but for our bosses. If librarians were to use this list of needed competencies simply to punish themselves, much of the point will have been lost. Two of the stated competencies are particularly significant to the subject of this column. Number 2.3 states that librarians can only do their jobs if they can see the "big" picture of what happens and is planned within the organization. Number 1.11 argues that the librarian must be an effective member of the senior management team. Both of these concerns are crucial, but they are forfeited when management replaces its library managers with hired outsiders whose primary virtue is that they are cheap. I think SLA should have made this point, but unfortunately, it did not.

If senior executives are embarking on a cruise on the information superhighway without giving a thought as to what pilots or navigator skills are necessary, perhaps they need a road map from AAA. However, it would be even better if they got these road maps from our professional library associations.

Dangerous Misconceptions About Organizational Development of Virtual Libraries

Academic library leaders have generally taken the term *virtual library* to mean a concept in which as much information as possible is transferred directly to the offices of faculty members, usually through their computer terminals. Some of this information may come through the library, some may bypass the library entirely, but, in any case, it is suggested that this will reduce the need for faculty members to depend on the library for specific answers or general help. The conventional wisdom is that this new concept is considered attractive by faculty members, that it is favored by university administrators because they perceive it as a reduction in cost, and that it will also benefit academic librarians by increasing our status to the role of information advisors or consultants— but, in any case, by transferring costs from the library to the budget of the faculty member's department. This chapter suggests that all of these assumptions—of the virtual library's benefits for faculty members, benefits for university admin- istrators, and benefits for academic librarians—are totally erroneous.

Reprinted, with changes, by permission of the author and the American Library Asso- ciation, from *Restructuring Academic Libraries. Organizational Development in the Wake of Technological Change*, pp. 54–66, edited by Charles A. Schwartz. Copy- right © 1997 by The American Library Association, Chicago.

The phrase *virtual library* is sufficiently vague to allow anyone to apply his or her own definition, much as we can make almost anything we like of the "information superhighway," including a growing repertoire of bad jokes about traffic jams, speed traps, potholes, road repairs, and traffic police. The dictionary definition of *virtual* leads us to an approximation of the almost ideal library. However, what is that library, and what makes us think we are approaching it? Furthermore, whose ideal are we talking about? Ours, those of academic administrators, or those of our users? Finally, which users—undergraduate students; graduate students; teaching faculty, who care very little about research; research faculty, who care very little about teaching; tenured faculty who may care very little about either teaching or research; or university administrators, who no longer resemble faculty at all (even though they came from the academic disciplines) but whose information needs are now a cross between those of public officials and corporate executives? Or, do we think that all of these communities have the same information needs, something we can subsume under the term *reference*, which, if it is designed to serve anyone, is designed to serve the directional information needs of undergraduates (or at least anything else that can be answered in two minutes or less)? Perhaps we believe, even hope, that the virtual library will absolve us of the responsibility—and the cost—of providing reference service at all, as an expensive nuisance.

If there is anything we certainly do understand, it is that technology has made significant changes in the way information can be announced bibliographically and in the way it can be delivered physically. We also seem to understand that technology has broadened the definition of what we mean by "information," at least in the setting of the library. We used to define information in the context of what we, and perhaps others, considered worthy of indexing and announcing. In general, libraries limited such indexing and announcing to books and were usually willing to make the end user wait until we were ready to state that an item was completed. Journal articles were included in the worthy category if some group, usually a professional society, took the trouble to analyze them. But if this did happen, it was done in separate retrieval systems with various indexing systems that allowed for both gaps (the things nobody wanted to analyze) and duplications (the things everyone analyzed but differently). Other nonbook materials, defined not by value but by format (simplistically what could not stand up on the shelf unaided), were largely ignored.

Technology, which looks at information far more impersonally than we do, has some of the same faulty biases of announcement validity but, with its great speed of sorting and the storage capacity of machines, announces far more things than we were ever willing or able to consider. Moreover, the databases that sprang up more prolifically than weeds (because for weeds there are weed killers to get rid of the noxious ones and here there are none) "announced" things to end users whether libraries had analyzed them or not. This has created certain problems for us, insofar as requests for service can be described as problems. People now want more and more documents from us, and these are more likely to be materials we are not prepared for them to request (at least unprepared in that we have not yet rung the symbolic bell to indicate that people could come and get it).

There is, at the same time, an "out" for us. The organizations that are happy to announce documents directly to end users are also often willing to supply them directly, and more rapidly, than the workings of our own creaking interlibrary loan systems (which are based on the tenuous premise that the owner is just dying to drop everything to supply a copy to the nonowner). Document delivery services and interlibrary loan systems both cost a good deal of money, but cost is irrelevant to the provision of a service or a product that is considered essential. We should understand this (though we frequently do not) because management writers such as Peter Drucker have told us often enough that there is no safety in appearing to be inexpensive. There is only safety in being essential.

What, then, do we know about the options of new technology, the so-called virtual library? We know that there is more information and that it can be delivered directly to the terminals of our end users, particularly faculty members. Is this a good idea? The organizations responsible for developing databases, for selling hardware and software, and for pushing end user searching obviously think so; certainly it is a good business for them. Is it, therefore, a good idea for everybody else? We also know that even as this process of increased information access might be crucial for survival in a competitive world (and academia is a fiercely competitive world) and that it might be cost-effective (with more return on investment), it will be more expensive. Strangely, though we certainly know all this, to a large extent university administrators do not—some even think that the virtual library will save money for the overall university budget. Much as they might wish this to happen, we certainly know that it will not save money in aggregate terms.

Why, then, have we not told them the truth, and what is our professional responsibility for telling them even what they might prefer not to hear? I know of library administrators who will acknowledge privately that the virtual library will cost a great deal of money but that the cost will "fortunately" be charged to the budgets of the academic departments, not to the budgets of the library, and that, therefore, this transfer of costs—even if it involves an overall increase over the alternatives—is a "good thing" for us. How does that rank as a political strategy and, quite separately, as an ethical strategy?

It is time to assess the implications of the virtual library as they apply to (1) professional librarians, (2) university management, and (3) our end users, who range from uncaring freshmen to know-it-all professors, with administrators also figured in there somewhere. The order I have used is intentional, because the first and most important question is how all of this affects us. Librarians (but probably only librarians) might be shocked at such selfishness, but we need not worry. It is always possible, and indeed essential, to be able to rationalize that what is best for us also happens to be best for everyone else. This is a process that engineers call *retrofitting*—making facts fit conclusions—and, of course, our own researchers working under the time line of grants and dissertation schedules do this all the time. Elected political officials and university presidents do it instinctively or they do not survive. It is what Charles Wilson, president of General Motors, meant when he stated that, "What was good for General Motors was also what was good for the country." His statement shocked some, but on what other basis can anyone be president of General Motors? Therefore, if academic librarians are not willing to postulate that what is best for them is also what is best for the university and its faculty and students, they might as well cover themselves with ashes and live in a cave. However, reassuringly and comfortingly, the statement is true.

The Impact of the Virtual Library on Us

In the most direct and simplistic scenario, all information moves either directly from the data creator or, through us, to the terminal of the end user, who now functions quite comfortably without ever setting foot in the library or even contacting it. Where does that leave us? Obviously, without a role in information intermediation but perhaps still with a role in document supply for those items that the database providers are unable to supply. However, document supply, whether done well or poorly, is a clerical function, as is the operation of any stockroom or warehouse. What this role, then, presumably does is "rid" us of contacts with faculty members entirely. It frees our budgets of reference costs so that we can devote them more directly to meeting ever-increasing periodical costs. It frees the public areas for students who, at least in my observation, tend to use them for social contacts, except perhaps for the 48 hours just before a final exam. When I teach management, I stress that in the area of unionization the only ultimate power of workers is the threat, real or implied, that they will withhold their services. If the virtual library is on "automatic pilot," will anyone even notice that we are not there?

Some individuals, particularly in special libraries but also in academic libraries, suggest a new and higher-level role for librarians—that of virtual-information advisor or consultant or guru. It is an attractive concept but one that cannot succeed because of two major fallacies. First, one's acceptance of some individuals as being information experts or consultants is based on a confidence that those individuals really are experts who know what they are talking about. For example, I accept on faith that the service manager in an automotive repair shop used to be a master mechanic. If we are going to get individuals to allow us to teach them how to do their own information work, our credibility must be based on their confidence that we are truly experts who can do such searching better than they could. The fallacy in that argument from the typical view of the typical faculty member should be immediately apparent. Apart from one or two exceptional librarians on a given campus (who are usually explained away by the faculty as aberrations from the librarian norm), librarians have established no real credibility as being experts, more knowledgeable in the handling of their literature than the faculty. I am not saying that we could not do this, or even that there are not librarians who would like to do it. I only note that we have trivialized reference service to common-denominator "quickies" of directional services aimed primarily at undergraduates who want to know how the journals are shelved, when the library will close, or where the rest rooms are. Is it any wonder that our best reference librarians, capable of doing more than this, hate the time they must spend at the reference desk? For proof that all of this makes sense we need look only at the prestige and success of the occasional bibliographic specialist, who is embraced as a colleague by faculty in such diverse fields as history, French literature, and music. Their prestige stems not from their being librarians but, rather, from being seen as acting differently from the way librarians are somehow expected to act. I have on occasion been paid the dubious compliment of being told that I do not act like a "typical" librarian, and I still do not know how to deal with that. Such extensive reference service is probably worth our time and consideration, but do we foresee it in the virtual library—and would our budgets allow it? (I can anticipate the observation that the levels of information service I have suggested are undemocratic, in that they are geared to the importance of the client. That is obviously true, but who ever suggested that a university was a democratic institution?)

The greater reason that a strategy based on librarians as virtual-information consultants cannot work is the contemporary environment of downsizing—the elimination of jobs considered to be unrelated to the main mission of the parent institution. Corporations have few techniques for downsizing. They occasionally lay off perfectly satisfactory people (usually librarians) and they eliminate middle management slots, but generally they wait for attrition or early retirement and sometimes they force early retirement. They certainly do not add master's-level individuals to the payroll with job titles such as information consultant or advisor. Although they might contract such skills for a short time, they will not add them to the head count.

Academia, trapped in the tenure system that makes any new action difficult, is even more likely to count on attrition and retirement to trim the payroll (though it will take years to realize any savings from such techniques). It is easiest to eliminate the adjunct and part-time teachers, regardless of the impact on the classroom, and to leave vacated positions unfilled. I know of one university in which half the deanships are now vacant and no search committees have been appointed. A system such as this (in an environment ranging as far as we can see) is not going to invest in virtual-information counselors.

Still, it might invest in librarians who, as information *doers*, could make other employees, particularly faculty, more productive as teachers or researchers. That kind of reliance on librarians might make it possible to save money, probably the only justification in which academic administrators are now really interested. However, how are we even going to introduce this subject if we are not willing to tell them that: (1) Adapting to new information technology is a growing requirement for higher education; (2) it will entail a great deal of additional money from the university; and (3) if they agree to put the entire process under the control of librarians, the increased cost outlay could be lessened or at least controlled.

The Impact of the Virtual Library on University Administrators and Budgets

I did not realize until after I had joined academia in an administrative role how well my 25 years in corporate and government management had prepared me for what happens in universities, for I came to understand that the management process is substantially the same. However, academic administrators have far less flexibility in decision options than their counterparts in the corporate environment. Part of that difficulty is related to the tenure system, part of it comes from the faculty's stubborn refusal to concern themselves with whether something can be afforded (if they need it, they can make it an issue of academic freedom), and part of it reflects the faculty's similar refusal of a hierarchical relationship to administrators. In other words, faculty have a great antipathy toward authority and very little financial responsibility. Academic librarians understand the budget process quite well (because they, like administrators, have a good deal of responsibility with relatively little authority). Students, we understand, occasionally make noise but have virtually no power in academia simply because they are considered transients who will, in a few years, take their unpleasantness off campus. Librarians have no power either, in large part because their authority is recognized by neither administrators nor faculty (but, unlike students, we do not even make noise).

Long before I joined academia in 1975, I was given valuable information by my own boss, an IBM official who had spent several decades as a faculty member and administrator of an Ivy League university. When I complained about the negative impact of corporate politics, he told me that corporate politics were nothing when compared to academic politics. I have learned since that Robert Maynard Hutchins, former president of the University of Chicago, understood this even better when he noted that political battles in academia are waged so ferociously precisely because the stakes are so small! The issue in academia is one of intellectual turf—controlling a unique area of expertise that nobody else dares challenge. Professors with exalted titles or obscure specializations earn control over their turf automatically and, as I saw on many academic committees, everyone readily yields to the expertise of others that they do not understand.

Academic librarians control no turf as such. Our job is seen as purchasing material for the collection, the "heart of the university," but faculty retain a right to say what should be acquired. The job of librarians is to find the money with which to do it. It should be obvious that the faculty, by and large, are in no position to make decisions about priorities for the library because, at best, their knowledge is a balkanized one about the discipline or subdiscipline. Who but librarians can make a decision about the relative merits of spending additional money on the collection in English literature versus organic chemistry? Certainly not the professors in either discipline, and the faculty members in other disciplines are simply not interested.

At any rate, the "turf" that represents library collection development decisions has been abdicated to faculty, whereas budget responsibility remains with librarians. This tends to annoy administrators because pressures to spend more money on library materials follow relentlessly in the wake of both publication proliferation and price inflation—two growth patterns bolstered by publishers' realization long ago that librarians are often merely purchasing agents for the faculty. The strategy of library administrators in the face of this dilemma remains as predictable as it has proved disastrous. We beg for more money with which to meet rising prices, from both the administration and potential donors. We place all of our other priorities—including resource sharing, technology, adequate reference service, proper salaries, continuing education, and library operational research—on the back burner because the faculty do not see these as their own priority and because the administration is too preoccupied to consider planning much more than faculty pacification.

It is little wonder, then, that in such an environment librarians seem all too willing to cede the process of information intermediation—to abdicate their expertise in analyzing the content and the value of information to the desks and terminals of the faculty through the virtual library—because in such an organization, though costs may indeed be much higher, they will no longer be our responsibility. In that framework, the virtual library may be understandable, but it remains unworkable. Academic libraries will simply underlie what Robert Munn called "bottomless pits" and continue to be a constant source of annoyance to university administrators because there is always pressure to spend more money on research materials without any tangible credit accruing to administrators for authorizing such "necessary" expenditures. Actually, although academic administrators grouse that they are spending a great deal of money—perhaps too much money—on the library, the reality is quite different. They are spending an ever-declining percentage of the university budget on the library, and they are spending it precisely on the materials budget because they and the faculty have been unwilling to control price inflation by presenting a united front to threaten boycott—not as customers but as authors, a far more credible threat.

Librarians have not only transferred funds from all other budgets to the materials budget (at a time when they know that ownership is not nearly as important now as access), but they have abdicated what remained of their turf by allowing administrators and faculty to decide that the funding priority for the library is (in the view of these individuals, not librarians) the purchase of materials. Foisting off electronic materials costs on the end user in the virtual library is the next step in this pattern of planned invisibility.

It is a disastrous strategy for librarians but, perhaps more important, it is a disastrous strategy for university administrators. The growth of electronic access will most certainly increase university costs and, painful as this prospect is, university administrators must face it. However, that rate of growth might at least be alleviated if costs were centralized under the control of librarians, rather than decentralized and scattered among faculty cost centers (ultimately still funded from the same university budget). If university administrators are concerned about costs, they should consider a different approach—improving the productivity of faculty in the spheres of teaching and research. The purpose of information, after all, is to enable the recipient to do something better. Information is not an end in itself, it is a means to an end. Academic librarians should make a case that less money would be spent if librarians, suitably empowered, were given control over the university's information-access budget. To reiterate, successful management in any environment does not call for planned invisibility or appearing inexpensive or even frugal. Rather, successful management is to control the process and resources. (Perhaps I understood this instinctively when, as a 25-year-old corporate librarian, I argued that if there were not enough money to allow my library to buy a certain periodical, I wanted assurance that nobody else would be able to buy the same journal with corporate funds.) We should not assume that faculty will object to our becoming the managers of the information-access channels. As the following section will demonstrate, many might even be pleased or relieved, provided that they have confidence in our ability to manage the process in a way that would enable them to know what they need to know in order to accomplish their own research and curricular objectives, for which information is a means and not an end.

The Impact of the Virtual Library on Our Faculty Colleagues

The manner in which faculty members' work has long been romanticized is understandably their doing, not ours. When the general public thinks of what researchers do, film versions of Marie Curie and Louis Pasteur, Schliemann's digs at Troy, and the decoding of the Dead Sea Scrolls immediately come to mind. Undoubtedly, there are such people now, and some may even reside in the faculty of research universities. However, they are a small minority; and in institutions oriented toward teaching they may not exist at all. As Herbert Brinberg noted at an International Federation of Documentation conference, whereas basic researchers seek facts, applied researchers, technologists, and practitioners want specific answers to specific questions (rather than tools that "might" contain an answer), and managers need to know the range of their options. All three types exist among the clientele of a university library but, as notable a humanist and librarian scholar as Charles Osburn has observed, we treat all faculty as though they were researchers, even though basic research disappears rapidly under the siege of funded grants and contracts that demand not just an answer but the promised answer within a promised time frame.

As senior vice president for operations for the Institute for Scientific Information during the 1970s, I presided over the preparation of *Who Is Publishing in Science*, an annual author-address directory drawn from that year's *Science Citation Index* and various editions of *Current Contents*. I once worried about overlap and redundancy in the annual indexes until it was demonstrated to me that half of the authors appear in this collection of scientific and scholarly articles only once, never again. That single article, which may have sprung from their dissertation, is their life's contribution. And yet we presume in our treatment of faculty that all are basic scholars who must have access to scholarly raw materials.

Producers of databases and online services extend the same presumption to end users as a whole, who are supposed to be fascinated with access to more and more information tools. I can certainly understand why it is to the producers' advantage to do so. End users search more sloppily and, thus, more expensively than do librarians, and that means greater profits. But does that benefit the university? Is it helpful to the librarians? Is it even to the advantage of the mythical end user?

For many faculty members, the presumed fascination for information self-service in the virtual library does not hold. University libraries that offered end user training to their faculty have found that the level of interest is small, perhaps as small as five percent. Moreover, many of the faculty who do sign up send surrogates, such as graduate assistants and even secretaries. The business press informs us of the development of a new industry, rather delightfully dubbed the "meatware" profession, because the meatware people are the ones who use the hardware and software on behalf of the reluctant end user. I can only conclude that the market niche for the meatware industry was created by the failure of librarians to fill the gap because of either a reluctance to do so or a failure to persuade a management besieged by budget pressure to allocate the money which will now be spent in even greater quantities. Of course, there are end users who want to do their own searches all of the time, and perhaps more who want to do them some of the time. However, there are many who would be happy to delegate and even abdicate this process, *if* they could find someone willing to do it—and *if* he or she were someone they could trust.

Summary and Conclusions

The future leads to the possibility of some disasters, as well as some glorious opportunities. In what is bound to be an environment of increasing options, confusions, and costs, there may be several plausible reasons for academic librarians to decline from the process of acquiring and analyzing information, but all of them lead to disaster. One reason might be despair of getting adequate funds with which to do our jobs, particularly with ever-darkening clouds of publisher invoices hanging over our heads. Another reason might be our belief that end users *ought* to do such access and analysis themselves (just as we entertain that sort of morality plan in our insistence that students learn how to do their own searching). It may be that we really think that end users are better able to fend for themselves than we are. However, there is something fundamentally wrong with any academic library budget that puts a higher premium on buying things than on investing in staff.

We have a problematic future in the current conception of the virtual library because there will not be money to engage us as consultants and advisors, and because many faculty have seen no evidence of our willingness or capability to do the work that we now want to teach them to do. Our future, nevertheless, remains in the process of information intermediation. Furthermore, it is the only alternative that makes economic sense for the institution. Certainly, the waves of information that will be dumped on the terminals of people who are really being paid to do something else creates an economic disaster for the university. If administrators have been slow to figure this out, it is because the software and hardware people are not equipped to tell them and we have not been willing to say so. Our message is very simple: One cannot fritter away money into the budgets of countless and traditionally irresponsible user groups! You need to give us the funding. Unfortunately, the virtual library will entail a great deal of additional money. But if you let us manage and control these funds, the result will be a great deal more palatable for the institution.

What Is a Professional in Our Field?

Whether an individual is a professional has nothing to do with competence, only the potential for competence. There are more or less competent doctors and lawyers, and the same should hold true for librarians. One would hope that there are ways to weed out the incompetent and unethical, but that process works imperfectly in any field and particularly in a field like ours in which we have little say over who gets hired to run our major institutions.

Almost any organization with even the slightest degree of complexity—and that includes hospitals, law firms, and libraries—requires a mix of individuals with varied skills and specializations. Sometimes these people come from different professions; in a large library this might include accountants, personnel administrators, systems analysts, and computer systems managers. However, it also inevitably includes people who perform what we used to call—and what I still prefer to call—clerical duties, because a competent and proud clerk can be as valuable as an able librarian.

I realize it is now fashionable to play games with nomenclature. We no longer have janitors and garbage collectors, only individuals who do the same things. We also no longer have clerks and secretaries, only people who perform those duties. This would be a harmless game except that it can yield unrealistic expectations. I recall my discussions with the Indiana University personnel (pardon me, human resources) department when I told them I wanted a secretary who thought that was a proud and important post. I was not looking for an administrative wannabe. I suspect I would build better communications bridges with a competent circulation clerk than with a book distribution facilitator.

Reprinted, with changes, by permission of the author and *Library Journal* 123, no. 3 (February 15, 1998): 117–118. Copyright © 1998 by Cahners Business Information.

Getting the Right Staff Mix

The right mix of the right people may seem equally important in a hospital or a library, but the issues become more confusing in the library context. First, hospital job descriptions are specific and precise. Nondoctors may not perform surgery, and while doctors might be allowed to mop the floors, I have yet to find one willing to do it. Thus, we are always aware of what skills are available and what skills are missing or in short supply.

In libraries the delineations are not as clear, and, more importantly, patron expectations are not as clear. They get whatever they get, and we know from many of our own disastrous user surveys that they are invariably delighted with whatever that is. All libraries, no matter how bad, are considered "wonderful."

The second reason is that libraries are clerical traps. Clerical activities are both more visible and seen as more urgent. Without an appropriate mix of staff either of two problems can occur. One is that in the absence of professionals, clerks do what professionals should do. They answer reference questions because *someone* has to answer them. Try that rationale in an operating theater!

Why aren't there enough professional librarians? Perhaps because not enough were hired, perhaps because none were hired. However, we don't allow that to bother the politicians or the public who still expect that their "library" will answer reference questions. We know from both observations and surveys that the public cannot distinguish the qualified from the unqualified, and in our own desire to appear "democratic," we make sure they can't do so. Or, as clerks sometimes observe not inaccurately, it may be that they provide all patron service while the professionals attend meetings.

On the other side, in the absence of enough clerks, professionals will do clerical work simply because it must be done. That, of course, plays right into the observations of our patrons, who not only cannot differentiate a professional from a clerk (and let me stress again that clerk is not a derogatory term) but who also presume that all library work is clerical. The proper staff mix between professionals and clerks will vary, but in my observation it demands at least one clerk for every professional to assure a proper distribution of job duties.

It's unfair to our users for clerks to do professional work, just as it would be if nonprofessionals did hospital work. If some might want to argue that their clerks do better reference work than their professionals, that is irrelevant to the issue, because qualifications only allow for the greater probability of competence. It also suggests that these managers should consider replacing all of their professionals because they can certainly get better ones.

Librarians As Clerks

When librarians do clerical work, they are overpaid, implausible as that may sound. A proper mix of professionals and clerks should be easiest to achieve in an academic library where the clerks are usually students who are paid very little. Professionals are more likely to do clerical work in a small corporate library, where they may constitute the entire staff.

In the Special Libraries Association (SLA), these are the "solo" librarians, a large and rapidly growing group. However, if the library only has one staff member and that person is professionally qualified, then at least half of the time that person will work as a clerk. This is bad for our professional image as well as wasteful for the employer. How extravagant would it be to have a balanced staff of two to insure cost effectiveness?

The definition of a professional was basically answered for us all 60 years ago when Congress passed the Fair Labor Standards Act, designed to protect hapless 1930s employees from unsavory bosses who insisted that, while being paid for 40 hours per week, they had better work longer hours for free or be fired. The act protected clerical, production, and "nonexempt" (from the provisions of the act) workers. They could not be held responsible for how much they accomplished, only for the hours they spent doing what they were instructed to do. If they were asked to work longer, they had to be paid.

Individuals considered "exempt" from the provisions of the act were professionals who were held accountable not for how many hours they worked but rather for what they accomplished. While it was considered potentially possible for such people to work extra hours without pay on special and unique occasions, it was assumed that they would also have greater flexibility in taking compensatory time off, in receiving other considerations, and in being paid more. These people did not need protection because they could and would protect themselves. They were too important a resource to be alienated.

In the changing history of the workplace, we have found examples of employers who, as a result of ruthless and even senseless downsizing, expected employees to work longer and harder hours simply to validate their supervisor's incompetent decisions. At the same time, we also now find articles in which executives worry about how to persuade their employees to stay at a time of desperate labor shortages, when they are being wooed away by competitors. It is my observation that librarians always seem to get the worst of these pendulum swings, and that it is primarily our own fault.

Will Credentials Help?

Issues of who qualifies as "exempt" have been debated, but, in general, professional librarians have emerged unscathed, if for no other reason than that being a librarian requires an accredited master's degree and therefore carries, at least in principle, the same credentials as an MBA. Our graduates should have no qualms about the importance of their degree, as business school graduates never seem to lack confidence.

If we insist on the master's degree as an entry qualification we are probably safe in maintaining our exempt status. I am aware of institutions that would like to require the professional degree and yet make new hires nonexempt. Such suggestions are easily countered in today's political and litigious environment with the threat of a gender discrimination suit. Are we still singling out "female" professions, or are we also planning to hire engineers and MBAs as nonexempt? No city or county attorney would want to take that case to trial. The more interesting question for me is why some of these threatened librarians want to remain exempt. Is it because a few feel they deserve the prestige and recognition, or only so that they can continue working without pay after 5 P.M.?

One common way some organizations bypass the entire issue is to hire clerks (or at least individuals whose academic qualifications do not include the library degree) to run libraries, a practice quite common in smaller communities or branches that claim that they can't "afford" librarians. Is it possible to have libraries without librarians, or at least without an asterisk? Surely the American Library Association Council, always ready to act when censorship of pornography is raised as an issue, would leap to confront such a question that outranks and predates all the others about which it agonizes. Don't bet on it!

People, Not Technology

If the required staffing mix for libraries has been changed by technology, it is because technology allows us to replace some of our clerks with computers but makes the jobs of those who do what machines cannot do even more important. Technology allows even the smallest public library to access a huge information world for its users. However, that can only happen if every library—particularly the very small public library—has on its staff a properly educated professional librarian, because these capabilities become more crucial when there are no other librarians handy to consult. Is this affordable?

Because I lived in Indiana for 20 years, that state makes a handy and not atypical example. Indiana, like many other states, has a carefully graduated system that differentiates the smaller communities not required to have a professional librarian from the larger ones that presumably must have one, although that does not prevent pleas for exceptions. The process of professional self-abasement is administered by the State Library. Indiana also has a current budget surplus of more than $1 billion, but it has exhibited no enthusiasm for spending any of that to improve library staffing. What tiny fraction of this surplus would such a decision require?

However, even the library school participates in this process of self-trivialization by training quasilibrarians who can meet certification if not professional qualifications. What is certification in this context except a synonym for cheap? Real certification should begin with the master's degree and then require further acquisition of knowledge.

The danger is not limited to our field. I recall with admiration the ferocity with which the Indiana University Nursing School fought the argument that master's degreed nurses were not "affordable" and therefore the school should prepare cheaper degrees. The nurses have yet to win that fight, but at least they try.

Our own largest problem really begins with how we choose to define our profession. Andrew Abbott (in *The System of Professions*, University of Chicago, 1988) postulates that the task of professionals is to address human problems amenable to expert service. Professionals, he argues, compete vigorously for existing and newly emerging problem jurisdictions, and they strive to expand those jurisdictions by preempting the activities of other professions. Does any of this strike a responsive chord with librarians? Do we recognize that as we agree to do more with less, we really do less with less, and what we give up is our professional uniqueness?

Is There a Surplus of Librarians?

This question has been raised in our literature, particularly in letters to editors, for as long as I can remember. It is usually asked by angry and disillusioned individuals who discover that, after investing in their education, they can't find jobs. Their reaction should certainly be understandable to the luckier rest of us. I especially recall a rash of such letters in the mid-1970s when, partly as a result of Arab oil embargoes, we went through our last recession.

The argument that there might be too many librarians competing for available jobs, if raised today, might surprise economists. They fear that, with a national unemployment rate under five percent, our labor shortage may provoke inflation. It might surprise anyone who recognizes the importance of knowledge workers in the exploding universe of information. The advent of new technology to manage information has prompted a whole new business specialization called Management Information Systems—people who are only doing what librarians ought to be managing.

And yet there are unemployed librarians, perfectly capable unemployed librarians. For us to have missed out so much on both a booming economy and a booming interest in the work we have always done was certainly not easy to accomplish.

What Professionals Do

In my last column I mentioned the writings of Andrew Abbott, who in his book *The System of Professions* (University of Chicago, 1988) noted that professionals not only address human problems amenable to expert service, they also compete vigorously to protect their territories against outsiders and strive to extend those boundaries by taking away territory from "the enemy."

Who might the enemy for us be in such a scenario? The list is long, but at the top are the computer and business professionals who insist, based on no discernible qualifications, that they know what a proper information transaction represents. People who build and program computers or manage corporations don't necessarily understand anything about people's information needs. Moreover, there is ample evidence from *Wall Street Journal* coverage that the bottom line results as much from luck and timing as from wisdom acquired at the Wharton School. Why are we so passively willing to agree that such people know more about what we do than we do? Why do we insist on inviting them to and glorifying them at our conferences, where they prove through their platitudes that they are uninformed about what professional librarians do? They never invite us to speak at *their* conferences!

The list of self-styled experts also includes public library board members and university administrators who, aside from legitimately determining how much they want to spend, also conclude that they are qualified to decide results independently of staffs and budgets. We see an example of our abdication to this "first the verdict, then the trial" mentality when research library administrators involve their staffs in "planning."

That process begins with the conclusion that staffs and budgets will be cut but that we will somehow accomplish more because that is what the president has decreed. That is an easy decision for the president but an impossible task for librarians—*unless* they decide to narrow their territorial boundaries by inviting others to take over their turf. It is not what Abbott had in mind, but then what sort of turf do we want to claim for ourselves? That of second class educators? As techie adjuncts? Ordering and circulation clerks? Can we really expect the best students to invest in such a future?

I think I understood Abbott's thesis long before I read his book. In the late 1970s, when I was a professor but not yet dean at the Indiana University Graduate Library School, the university conducted a search for someone to head the university library. Some of the faculty, dissatisfied with the relationship with the former head, suggested that perhaps the post should go to a distinguished faculty colleague who would better "understand" them. After all, there were already plenty of "trained" (think circus animals) librarians who handle the daily details.

Protecting Our Turf

Does the scenario appear familiar? It should; it has occurred in major universities like Harvard and Cornell and of course at the Library of Congress and the National Library of Medicine. With very little leverage but the protection of tenure, and certainly with no authority, I decided to make an issue of this. Why? Because Indiana, unlike Harvard and Cornell, hosted a library education program and took tuition money from students who believed that the degree would prepare them for important professional jobs.

If Indiana appointed a nonlibrarian, I said I would call a news conference to demand that the library school be closed, to at least protect the university from hypocrisy. There is no dramatic ending to this story; all the finalists were well-qualified librarians, and two years later the university even made me dean of its library school.

We see this scenario recur when librarians agonize about whether it takes a library degree or management talent to be executive director of the American Library Association. Is it so outrageous to insist on both for what is after all a highly visible post for this profession? Does anyone know of a Surgeon General who is not a doctor?

I have tried to reflect on the writings of Andrew Abbott because it seems clear that the main reason for our presumed surplus of librarians is that we refuse to defend, let alone expand, our territorial boundaries, even at this time of national prosperity and affluence. Readings of our library publications might lead to the conclusion that we are living in an impoverished Third World nation, rather than in a nation with a booming economy and a disturbingly small rate of unemployment, worrisome for the avoidance of inflation.

Let me first make the most obvious point. To what extent can the "surplus" of librarians be traced to the many "libraries" that have no librarian at all? Because they can't be afforded? Let's not get silly. It is because communities and states would rather not afford them. Also, we certainly don't insist on making an issue of what seems our most important national professional concern.

In the mid-1980s we experienced a genuine shortage of children's librarians. My own keen awareness of this stems from constantly being berated because library schools did not produce enough of them. A complex combination of misjudgments by many people, including employers, educators, and guidance counselors, contributed to this scenario. There never should be a reason for the lack of prospective librarians to work with children.

Redressing Shortfalls

However, why we endured this shortage is for me less instructive than how we dealt with it. Because of what economists call "market factors," the shortage should have started a fierce competition for qualified children's librarians and a rapid increase in starting salaries. This would then have triggered increases in enrollment.

That never happened. Faced with a shortage of qualified candidates, public library directors might have informed their boards that hiring qualified people would require much more money and that hiring unqualified people was unthinkable. A failure to deal with that reality of management would keep the children's department closed for yet another year. However, when faced with the impossibility of paying enough under present salary scales to hire the qualified, library directors simply hired whomever they could afford. Adam Smith is probably shuddering in his grave.

Better Service, Not Self-Service

If we examine the territorial strategies that Abbott considers essential, it seems that we must redraw the dividing line between ourselves and our clients when it comes to providing information. We should not encourage self-service; we should provide *better* service and show our crucial role in managing information.

Should we perhaps stress information self-service to relieve the "pressures" on the library staff? To free the staff for what—even greater professional glories? Or should we be teaching all of our clients, including faculty, students, and the general public, why they should demand more professional services from us, even though there are so few of us that we are already harried? Only with that demand might there be more of us, to ease the political pressure on our bosses.

A Librarian in Every Library

The answer lies not in what is easiest or safest for us politically, or perhaps more convenient for our bosses. It lies in what is most cost-effective for the university, the municipality, the corporation, and for society as a whole. We must insist that honest books be kept, because without that publicized insistence nothing will ever happen.

Is there a surplus of professional librarians? When I see every task that ought to be performed by a librarian so performed, and when every institution that claims to be a "library" is staffed by at least one real librarian, then—if a surplus remains—I will agree. However, I don't expect that to happen any time soon.

Until then, I would suggest to our professional societies that their primary priority is not lack of books or terminals, or even coping with pornography on the Internet. The first priority should be having enough of us and making sure that we are empowered to make the decisions that will then address the other secondary problems.

Does that seem selfish? Of course, but what is wrong with that if it advances the common good? Does it seem aggrandizing? Not to a professional guarding and expanding territorial boundaries.

Library Outsourcing and Contracting: Cost-Effectiveness or Shell Game?

Competent librarians have used outside talent where appropriate for a long time. There were, in general, two primary reasons. First, an outsider could work more economically than we could. Frequently, this involved economies of scale. It might make no sense to buy expensive equipment for microfilming when a contractor could do the work as part of a regular workload.

It was also prudent to use subscription agents, particularly for international periodical titles. It allowed consolidation of purchase orders and avoided the need to deal in foreign correspondences and in foreign currencies. Even with the agency's service charge, the process was cheaper than the alternative.

At other times, we might employ a contractor whose skills were lacking in our own organizations and which we would be foolish to stockpile for occasional needs. This category might include translations from esoteric languages, or contracting with a systems consultant for a narrow and specific purpose.

Finally, librarians might decide to hoard their precious manpower slots by contracting out routine work that would waste our scarce staff time, recognizing that headcount ceilings have always posed a greater problem than budget ceilings. It might well make sense to have a contractor physically acquire the books and process them for shelf use, just as subscription agents would follow our bidding in obtaining periodicals. Note: obtain, not select, because this was and remains our area of special expertise.

Reprinted, with changes, by permission of the author and *Library Journal* 123, no. 11 (June 15, 1998): 56–57. Copyright © 1998 by Cahners Business Information.

Librarians understood then, as they should understand today, that we may get rid of as much of the routine work as possible, but that we hang on to our professional activities. We don't farm them out to contractors, and we would be equally foolish if we insisted that end users learn to perform our professional tasks and leave us with clerical routines.

Rational Outsourcing

Valid reasons for contracting out entire libraries were rare but did exist. In the mid-1960s, I directed the contractor-operated NASA Scientific and Technical Information Facility. Melvin Day, who headed NASA's scientific information program, decided to use a contractor to manage what was really a national library not necessarily because he thought it would be cheaper, but because he thought it would be better. A contractor could hire the best people outside the constraints of federal job descriptions, could reward them as they deserved, and even could be instructed by NASA to remove what the agency considered a less competent worker.

From my own admittedly prejudiced perception, the idea was a good one. The NASA facility was then in the forefront of information technology precisely because the emphasis was first on quality and only second on cost. That reality is as true today as it was 35 years ago.

Getting Honest About Cost

If things have now changed, it is not because we have lost sight of the reality that quality costs money. To check out that fact—and that people will pay—just look at pricing patterns for automobiles, houses, rock concerts, and Super Bowl tickets. Of course, there is a market for these products. Peter Drucker has told us that in the acquisition of what we really want, price is at least secondary and perhaps irrelevant.

What we have lost, to a great extent, is political honesty in dealing with the realities of cost-effectiveness as contrasted with cheapness—and I believe corporate officials as well as governmental ones lack such candor.

The drive to eliminate "waste" has always been with us, but this becomes more difficult when what one person defines as waste another deems essential. Academic library directors trying to cancel journals just because no one reads them understand the ferocity with which some constituencies insist that lack of use should be an irrelevancy.

This approach in both the corporate and governmental sectors, political in the most pejorative sense—meaning simply survival with or without any accomplishments—has confused and muddied the issue. If they were to tell us that they are cutting costs and thus also quality I might believe them, but they know that this won't get them reelected or promoted. What we want to hear is that costs are being cut even as quality improves. This is rarely possible. Yet we insist on hearing this, so it's what they tell us.

The Advent of Downsizing

We can see this phenomenon at play if we watch the stock market. When a company announces that it will reduce costs by laying off thousands of employees, it is considered good news, and the stock goes up. It's assumed that nothing that these people did really mattered and that anything cut was obviously wasteful.

The phenomenon that assumes that all cost-cutting must be valid is not new. Almost 40 years ago, when I worked for IBM—which was in retrospect really a well-managed company—the joking reaction to all of the frenzied activity, much of it simply for the sake of activity, was, "We're going to have economy around here no matter what it costs."

The process has become more refined over time. Now we "downsize." What do we downsize—the activities that were overstaffed to start with, or those no longer necessary? Management isn't smart enough for that. And so it downsizes and outsources what it can get away with trashing. That is rarely the executive staff, but it just might be the library.

Don't look for logic here, because it's usually absent. We must achieve certain numerical goals. Frequently, the easiest way is simply to force anyone over 55 into early retirement. Because these individuals are no longer productive? Studies indicate the exact opposite. It is done because it fits into an easy-to-implement formula.

Elected officials at both the federal and local levels, regardless of party, have learned this lesson well. The appearance of economy is more important than real economy. In reality, costs continue to rise. Why should that surprise us? There are more of us, and we constantly want more and newer services—including, of course, at libraries. However, politicians perceive that we do not want them to tell us the truth and would never forgive them if they did.

Fooling Us

What then do they do to create the impression of economy, even when it isn't real? By playing shell games—and the process is easy because the public's attention span is so short. The federal government has long used contracting, or outsourcing, as a tactic to present the appearance of economy. This is usually done by pointing out that the federal payroll has just decreased by several hundred thousand employees. What we aren't told is that the payroll of contractors has increased by twice that number.

If anyone thinks this is far-fetched they need only drive around Washington, DC, for a few hours. A whole community of outsourced contractors works hard doing what federal employees aren't doing. Nor is this necessarily bad. In some cases, outsourcing makes perfect sense; however, it probably makes no sense if the purpose is only style and not substance.

It also makes little sense if the purpose is simply to save money, regardless of quality. If government officials were to state that the only reason for outsourcing was cost, then the argument might at least be honest. However, we will never see that kind of honesty.

Public library directors report that their patrons demand improved services even as they are unwilling to pay for them. We must start telling the truth, by pointing out that you get what you pay for.

It's Even Worse at Libraries

The process of outsourcing as it affects libraries is particularly dangerous because cheapness simply for its own sake is easily defensible when there is no criterion for quality. If there are no qualitative standards for what happens in libraries, only quantitative ones (number of books processed, number of books circulated, even number of questions answered without determining how well they were answered), then it becomes easy to justify cheapness for its own sake even if it is not cost-effective.

Libraries are particularly handy targets for outsourcing precisely because everyone knows what they cost and no one understands what they need to do. How could anyone understand, when our profession stubbornly refuses to define quality and shine a glaring spotlight on its absence? So politicians actually accept no standards for public libraries except open hours.

If outsourced libraries report to a contracting officer who understands dollars but not libraries, and no professional librarians are involved in the selection, evaluation, and perhaps termination of the contractor, we should not be surprised if cheaper libraries are also automatically worse ones.

NASA used a contractor because that contractor could pay higher salaries if necessary. On what basis should we assume that a contractor that pays even lower salaries with little or no benefits can attract better applicants than a normal municipal hiring process, which offers salaries, benefits, and job security? We get what we pay for.

This is not cost-effectiveness by any definition, and it is not, as Ronald Dubberly suggests in the January 1998 issue of *American Libraries*, an example of "lean and mean" in municipal government. Rather, it is an example of incompetence and deceptiveness. We remain willing, as we were 40 years ago, to accept the appearance of economy no matter what it costs us.

Special librarians have now correctly postulated that, in order to be effective, corporate libraries must be involved in the corporate decision-making process at all stages. However, the Special Libraries Association has not stated the obvious corollary: none of this is possible if you have outsourced your library. You are dealing with cheap hired help who have no reason to care whether you succeed or fail.

When the Public Is Fed Up

The public will not tolerate outsourcing, no matter how cheap, if the results are unacceptable. In the summer of 1997, I spoke at the annual conference of Air Force librarians, which attracted a smaller group than in the past. Their number was seriously depleted by outsourcing and because few contract employees can attend national meetings unless their contracts specify it—an unlikely prospect.

Because there were uniformed Air Force officers there, I suggested that the government agency so interested in cost-cutting through outsourcing might consider replacing its own pilots from the plentiful and certainly much cheaper supply of Russian pilots who now had no planes to fly. No, I wasn't serious. However, why is it outrageous to hire contractors to fly our planes but not to select individuals who process and analyze the information that helps determine why they fly?

When I was involved in the NASA program, I saw a cartoon about two astronauts strapped in for liftoff. One asks the other whether they should be worried by the realization that every component was made by the lowest bidder. No, NASA never did always select the lowest bidder. However, if that is the only criterion for outsourcing libraries, shouldn't the public worry? And shouldn't we at least tell them that they will end up paying dearly for the deception being perpetrated upon them?

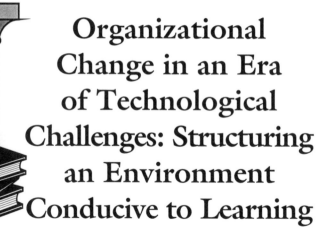

Organizational Change in an Era of Technological Challenges: Structuring an Environment Conducive to Learning

In the past year I have spoken several times, to diverse groups ranging from technical services librarians to reference librarians specializing in online reference, to library administrators, and to special and medical librarians. In each of these talks I have been asked to address, in varying forms, one very fundamental question. What changes, what opportunities, what dangers will technology pose for librarians as we prepare for the new millennium. Let me stress first of all that I never talk about what dangers this will pose for libraries. Libraries are far too attractive a concept politically for anyone to let go of them. We will always have libraries—in universities, in communities, even in our schools. However, what those libraries will be—whether they will have any useful role to play in the knowledge-based world in which we will live, or whether they will simply be storehouses of documents and rows of self-service computers—is very much open to question. Even more uncertain is what sort of librarians there will be: Will they be

Talk presented at the 1998 Conference of the Library Administration and Management Association, American Library Association, Washington, DC. July 1998.

299

important knowledge facilitators? Will they be irrelevant clerks? Will there be anything called a librarian at all? These questions are far more difficult to answer, and it is my purpose here to help you to shape that answer, rather than simply let the forces that shape our future wash over us. It is understandable that the new millennium looks like a watershed for us, and yet it is amusing that librarians are among the few people who know that the millennium begins on January 1, 2001, and not 2000. The rest of the world will celebrate early, with or without us. We might as well go along with the crowd.

In any case, all of this provides us an opportunity to take note of where we are and where we are going. What I consider my most significant management lesson was taught to me, quite inadvertently, by my varsity tennis coach way back in my undergraduate days. Never change a winning game, he told us. Always change a losing game. You might still lose, but changing your approach gives you the only chance of winning. My coach assumed that we would know what the score was. Do we know the score in the match we are playing? Is librarianship winning or losing? Is the score close?

We have been talking and worrying about the impact of technology on our profession, but really because some of us think it uncouth and selfish to talk about our profession, or our *institutions* for quite some time. Some of these issues seem amusing in the light of history. I recall one survey respondent who proudly checked yes to the question of whether or not the library was automated, and went on to explain that the library possessed an electric typewriter. Those questions, along with the passionate ones posed by Ellsworth Mason thirty years ago and longer—Should we use technology at all? Was it cost effective? Was it right?—are no longer relevant. Technology is certainly with us. As I now speak to the new level of concerns and issues, I somehow think of the old Japanese movies we can watch late at night if we have trouble falling asleep. Will Godzilla (the old and not the new Godzilla) revert to being the evil monster he once was and threaten to destroy Tokyo, or is he now a good monster who will help protect us from other, even worse monsters? I find the comparison apt, because quite aside from our own Godzilla—technology—we face other monsters. It was a challenging time to live in Tokyo, and it is a challenging time to be a librarian.

If I have somehow been less caught up in the emotion it is because I have managed in an environment of technology for most of my professional life. I have always understood, perhaps instinctively, that technology can be a wonderful servant but both a cruel and sometimes stupid master. From my early days at IBM, I have understood that computers large and small were very good at performing routine clerical operations—doing them accurately, doing them rapidly, doing them cheaply. One of the first IBM library automation manuals concerns the circulation control system for the Lake County Indiana Public Library, and that was in the 1950s. As a librarian I rejoiced at the potential. What libraries have always needed was fast, cheap, and accurate clerks, particularly if they didn't affect the head-count ceiling. With more such machines we could stock up on librarians rather than clerks, in the realization that libraries are clerical traps in which our bosses and users perceive clerical work as more important than professional work. In the absence of enough staff, we all become clerks. Technology could have helped us alleviate that danger, and to some extent it has. However, to a large extent, professional librarians are still allowing themselves to be sidetracked from their professional duties by clerical requirements. Often this happens because there are not enough clerks, and that may even make some sense in corporate and public libraries where clerks can be as expensive as librarians. However, it makes no sense in academic libraries where clerks are the cheapest and most plentiful resource imaginable—students. Furthermore, we have now added to the old clerical duties of checking in the circulation, shelving the books, and sending out the overdue notices, the new clerical duties of helping users to log on to computers so that they can do their own reference work. Are these clerical duties in a technological age? Are they perhaps paraprofessional tasks? And if they are professional tasks, are they ours, or should they be done by people paid by Bill Gates in training his future customers?

Obviously now the far greater use of technology is to put us in direct contact with lots more information more rapidly. Is this good? Well, that depends on what you want to use the technology for. Is it to play solitaire, to surf the Net to see what interesting things there might be, to find some tidbit of gossip in chat rooms or something titillating or pornographic? For all of these reasons, and for wasting time, they are wonderful—and that may be why kids love them. It still beats doing homework, and parents think it is more valuable than watching cartoons on TV. Somehow, using computers for any reason is considered a virtue. What is our role here, if any?

The far more important opportunity, perhaps for librarians but at least for someone, is in helping those who need access to information in order to do something else. This is the role of information intermediaries, and their role is easy to understand by anyone who has ever worked under pressures of time. These are the people who tell us what to look at and what not to look at, because technology also gives us garbage (and garbage is for us what we don't want) just as readily as it gives us gold nuggets. For me a valued information intermediary would have been someone who, after I returned from a week at ALA to Indiana University, informed me that in my absence I had received 240 e-mail messages, but that he or she had deleted 210 of them. Of the 30 remaining, the intermediary considered 10 to be quite important, and 20 perhaps of interest. Now that I am retired I have no access to an office information intermediary, and so I have done what you cannot do. I have removed myself from all e-mail, because the junk for me far outweighs the useful, and because I am now retired and my time is my own and therefore more valuable. Now, if you want to reach me, you have to write, phone, or fax. In other words, make an individual effort to reach me as a person, and not as a group of several hundred. Yes, I will miss some things, but that is my tradeoff, and it is a tradeoff decision which must be made by anyone who must make decisions in which time matters. That includes not only business executives and public administrators, but also professors. It includes anyone except for the low-level common denominator for which librarians appear to be designing their services—those who use libraries to have fun and waste time, perhaps even to avoid doing what they ought to be doing.

There is a more serious factor, of course. If we are awash in information, we might not find the correct information, or we might make decisions on the basis of what we think is all of the information, but it is not. When we encourage end user searching for the serious as well as the trivial, we are co-conspirators in this process. Have we tried saying to students and perhaps even to professors that they're not qualified to find this on their own? Professionals in fields like medicine say it all the time. The point I am raising is in asking whether or not the tremendous quantities of information, basically unfiltered in terms of the user's needs, provide an opportunity for us.

Peter Drucker, who is right far more often than he is wrong, certainly thinks it provides an opportunity for *somebody*. Drucker, whose wisdom about technology can be seen from his very early observation that automation was not about machines, but about how people worked and wanted to work, postulated over 10 years ago that the most important profession after the turn of the century would be the profession of knowledge workers. These would be the people who protected us from being engulfed in tidal waves of knowledge, and who told us what was important for us to read and what was not. I call these people information lifeguards, and I think it would be a job to which we are well suited. We have been swimming in knowledge-infested waters for a long time. Drucker does not mention librarians in his prediction about knowledge workers, he only predicts it will be a field for *somebody*. That other people are beginning to define knowledge worker to suit themselves should be obvious. We have a growing industry which provides information for a fee—some well, some badly. The point is that they are filling a vacuum we have left, and you all remember from your physics classes that nature abhors a vacuum. The most visible are the MIS people, who see this field as a subset of business administration rather than computer science, although it obviously combines both. So, of course, does everything we do, if we do it competently. Is Drucker correct in his prediction that this nation will be employing, and presumably paying well, a large number of knowledge workers? If he is correct, should we be at least a part if not even the dominant part of this field? Or are we too busy doing other things? What, exactly?

If Drucker does not identify us by name, the national newspaper *USA Today* does. In an article published two years ago for which I would not claim scientific validity but only a public perception and an important decision making readership, the newspaper identifies a number of fields for which it sees no future, precisely because of technology. Among these fields are bank teller, telephone operator, and librarian. Why this grouping? It may come from the simple observation that all of these are fields for which the advent of technology has reduced the number of people newly hired or replaced, and if so, there may be validity in both the observation and the lumping. Certainly, fields that are declining in staff at a time of booming economy stand out. For bank tellers their decline can be attributed, at least in part, to the growth of ATM machines. Banks like ATM machines because they usually make money on each transaction and eliminate labor costs. The initial rationale for customers was as a convenience when the bank was closed. However, I now notice people pulling into the bank parking lot and marching straight up to the ATM machine even when the bank entrance is open and only 10 yards away. Why would individuals willingly pay a service fee when they could avoid it? Certainly this developing habit does not bode well for bank tellers, whom I still prefer because one can interact with a live human being. The reason for this may well be that we have come to believe, because we have been sufficiently brainwashed, that *any* electronic transaction is somehow more worthy than a manual one. Does this same scenario apply to libraries? I suspect so, because we now have reports from both public and academic libraries of users, particularly students who represent our future users, who will only deal with terminal access, and who refuse to consult either a published source or a reference librarian. We have evidence, so far only anecdotal in sum, although it may be quantifiable for specific librarians (and there is a dissertation topic here for someone), that as libraries install terminals for end user searching, the number of reference questions declines. Should that trend keep library administrators awake at night? I certainly hope so, for at least two reasons. The first, of course, is that we don't know whether end user access to terminals without any monitoring, which amounts in medical terms to self-medication, may lead to incorrect or incomplete answers, of which the searcher will be totally oblivious. The second reason, of direct professional concern, is that having fewer reference questions leads to fewer reference librarians. On the other hand, if some library administrators somehow consider the decline in reference questions to be good news, because it took pressure off their already overworked staffs, then they should understand that all they have done is to validate the last staffing cut (no matter how illogically determined) and set the stage for the next staffing cut. If that is their value system—looking to create *less* professional work for ourselves—then it is probably I who will be spending the sleepless nights. Managers should understand that the only way to ever achieve staffing increases is by creating disparities between needed and offered service, a disparity which we will publicize with the explanation that the staff is not to blame. Furthermore, as Drucker has already noted, in the provision of a service that people insist on having, its cost is at best secondary and perhaps even irrelevant. I will have more to say about this in a few moments.

Perhaps the best example of how "with it" technology has fascinated us and overwhelmed our judgment of what constitutes quality is the elimination of hapless telephone operators. They are being replaced by voice mail and automated recorded options which take longer for the customer and may not even address the client's needs. However, this increased cost has been passed along to the client, and that makes the process appear cheaper, at least for the supplier. Are we sure that we librarians don't do some of this as well, by passing along costs, particularly in online searching, to clients who will end up spending more and doing it worse, with the only "virtue" in the fact that the cost won't be in our budgets? I am surely not the only one who has suffered from the difficulty of reaching a human telephone operator, with the substitution of a recorded menu of lengthy options which, despite their length, don't necessarily address my concern, particularly if my concern is complex.

Why do we accept such treatment, in telephone service, in bank transactions, and in libraries? Perhaps it is because we have been brainwashed into believing that *all* computer transactions are automatically preferable to what had preceded them. My most obvious example comes from the value system of our own vice president, Al Gore (although I am sure a Republican would have done the same thing) that the key to improving our school system lies primarily, and perhaps exclusively, in producing more computer access for the students. Not a word about libraries, let alone librarians. Can you understand why *USA Today* has us on its death list?

I am not a Luddite. The proper use of technology, in a library as anywhere else, can produce huge benefits. At the same time we are constantly bombarded by at least three arguments that are at best simplistic: (1) that using computers is easy, (2) that using computers is fun, and (3) that using computers reduces costs.

For an example of the first, I recall an America Online television ad which you may have seen. An individual urged by his friend to come with him to a basketball game demurs. He can't go, because he has to make travel reservations, because he has to send his mother a birthday present, and because his child has to go to the library to gather information for a report on dinosaurs. His friend assures him that all of this is *easy* with America Online, and as we watch in fascination, the tickets are purchased, flowers are ordered for dispatch to the mother, and the printer disgorges pages of information about dinosaurs. As the commercial ends, the two friends are on their way to the basketball game, although it is never made clear what the child has presumably learned from this. It is assumed, probably correctly, that we won't notice. This commercial, I should remind you, was also watched by mayors and university presidents, in addition to the general public. Perhaps it was watched by Vice President Gore. Can we begin to understand the assumption that using libraries and librarians is no longer necessary? All we presumably need is access to a terminal, and the tactic is almost certain to succeed as long as both public and academic librarians appear to have adopted the strategy (although *strategy* is hardly an appropriate word, suicidal comes more readily to mind). We seem to believe that the best way to serve our clients is to give them more access to more information—access to the good, the bad, and the irrelevant. We install terminals and shout "come and get it." Quality establishments which take pride in their professionalism, including five-star restaurants, don't shout "come and get it."

The selling of fun as a characteristic requires a little more subtlety. In a Hewlett-Packard ad, we are ushered into the sumptuous office of a busy executive, and we know he is busy because it is night time and yet he is still hard at work on his Hewlett-Packard computer. He gruffly rejects an attempt by the off-camera voice to ask a question by noting that he is very busy. Finally, he cries out in dismay. When asked solicitously what has gone wrong, he laments that he has hooked his tee shot into the lake. I consider this a very effective ad, because this company understands that computers can be and are being used for games as well as for real work. Bosses are slowly beginning to learn that a computer-engrossed employee is not necessarily a hard-working employee. I recall my own term as a university dean and passing a faculty office in which a game of solitaire was displayed on the terminal screen. Fortunately for them, faculty members don't have to account for their time. They need only to meet their classes, hold office hours, and produce an acceptable amount of publications and research. Most people are not as lucky.

The argument that computers result in cheapness should be surprising, because even IBM, before I left in 1964, had dropped the argument that using its computers made operations cheaper. Most cost effective, certainly, because it allowed us to do what could not have been done before at all. However, a simple cost comparison between a computerized and a manual operation is a comparison between apples and oranges. We can now do so much more, and while costs will most certainly increase, it will all be worth it. We probably will be able to replace some library clerks by machines, but we will have to hire other people who are more knowledgeable and more highly paid to use the computers to accomplish many new things heretofore not possible. It is one of the clearly understood characteristics of human behavior that when people learn that something is *possible*, they usually decide that it is *indispensable*. Properly used computers are certainly cost effective, but they are not cheaper.

I am certain that mayors and university presidents really understand this, as they understand that they have no choice but to upgrade their technology, to avoid unfavorable comparisons to their rivals—and universities as well as communities have rivals. However, understanding the reality that technology increases costs does not necessarily prevent an attempt to cut corners when there are those willing to be convinced that there "isn't any money." Astute observers recognize this as an old management chestnut which nobody except perhaps a few librarians tend to believe. Faculty certainly don't believe it, or at least they don't care. Municipal police departments don't accept the suggestion that somehow they should do more with less. An attempt to distribute operational costs to end users, which becomes the tactic when both universities and municipal governments advocate end user searching as an absolute rather than as one of the alternatives, is a shabby tactic at best. However, when universities distribute the cost to the faculty members whom they also pay, and pay a great deal more than librarians, it is also senseless from the standpoint of institutional cost effectiveness.

Technology provides opportunities for its proper use and for its misuse. For librarians to take advantage of the opportunity presented to them, two things are necessary. First they must understand and remember what they and their institutions are supposed to do. No real profession, as I will note later, allows outsiders to proscribe its agenda. Second they must understand what opportunities for greater professional activity technology now allows them, at least in part as a trade-off against having to do so many clerical tasks, but particularly because technology offers us the opportunity to redefine the limits of our own activities and to broaden and professionalize them. I will present to you two rather generic examples of this opportunity, one from technical services and one from public services. I will then close by suggesting what we must do as a profession to ensure that technology works for us, and not we for it. There certainly is no future in this second option, as bank tellers and telephone operators certainly understand by now. However, at least these people have not been prepared by undergoing graduate degree programs.

Back in 1964 Mortimer Taube, the president of Documentation, Incorporated, and one of my heroes and mentors, noted that even the rudimentary technology then available allowed us to reexamine the premises of our technical services operations. He made these comments as the Library of Congress was designing its MARC system, and noted that many of the ground rules of the cataloging system were constrained by economic pressures. He noted specifically the constraints of filing 3" x 5" catalog cards, and the damper which this placed on our ability to analyze, particularly subject analysis. He recognized, as early as 1964, that these constraints need no longer apply in a computerized environment. He also saw that knowledge and information were being produced and distributed both in increasing quantities and in a growing variety of formats. This led him to conclude that the double curse of (1) analyzing only books to the exclusion of more ephemeral material, and (2) performing only perfunctory subject analysis, was no longer a constraint, even with the technology then in existence. That, I need to remind you, was in 1964, and of course Taube becomes far more prophetic as we approach the end of the century. In 1964 I managed the entire NASA national technical information system on one IBM 1410 computer, and that machine had less storage capacity and less processing potential than is now found in any run-of-the-mill desktop computer. Addressing the options in the design of the MARC system, Taube argued that while it was certainly possible to design a MARC system which would simply take the manual Anglo-American cataloging rules and put them on a computer, this would be a wasted opportunity. And, as you all know, that is exactly what we did.

When I became a faculty member at Indiana University in 1975, I confidently predicted to anyone who would listen that academic library cataloging backlogs would be impossible to justify from this point forward, because our users no longer needed our catalog cards to inform them of what existed. They had other options for this, and would insist that we keep our materials processing operations current. Of course, at the time I had come from managing the NASA Scientific and Technical Information Facility, and then Institute for Scientific Information operations, where backlogs were not allowed to exceed one week. Backlogs are really not that difficult to manage once they have been analyzed. If backlogs are constant and not growing, permanent staffing is adequate but a special effort using temporary employees is needed to remove the one-time backlog. If backlogs continue to increase, then something is obviously very wrong. We are either processing too much material (a possibility which is most unlikely), or we are processing material in a cumbersome or ineffective manner. As a third possibility, perhaps the needed staff size was never determined in relation to what needed to be done.

In any case, I was completely wrong in my prediction. Processing backlogs may have decreased in some institutions, but in general they have remained unacceptably long. What is most disturbing is that university presidents seem to consider this as not germane to the assessment of their own administrative competence. Material lodging in a processing backlog has been paid for but is unusable. However, what is saddest about all of this is that we have lost, as Taube feared, the opportunity to improve both the quality and depth of information analysis. Given the growth in information volume, we have two options in separating the chaff from the wheat, and even a combination of the two. We can improve the depth of initial analysis, or we can improve the depth of assessment in the public service search process. Technology allows us to do either, or both.

When it comes to the implementation of public service, we really need only to implement the point Peter Drucker has already made. When Drucker stresses the need, in this highly technological age, for more information, for more rapid information delivery, for more complex inquiries, and he suggests the need for a new cadre of knowledge workers to differentiate the valuable from the useless for each individual client, he is, at least in my interpretation, talking about reference librarians. That any group, whether a corporation, municipality, or university, committed as it must be to maximizing its utilization of technology in the most cost-effective manner, therefore needs more reference librarians appears to me to be easily demonstrated. And yet, we have fewer reference librarians, coupled with the development of the perverse and absurd notion that the increase of technology decreases the need for intermediaries. Drucker certainly knows better, but those who have sought to persuade us that technology provides solutions and not just tools, to individuals as highly placed as the Vice President of the United States, have planted their seeds well and watered them carefully. What seems most absurd is that they seem to have convinced *us* that there is now less of a need for reference librarians. There really has never been in our profession a shortage of people who become librarians so that they can perform reference work, any more than there has every been a shortage of would-be librarians who want to work with children. The reality has become the fact that we don't allow reference librarians to do substantive reference work. We limit the time they can spend on a question, we encourage self-service without ever knowing how well it works, and we bury what few reference librarians we have under a mound of trivial directional questions. It should be obvious that we should divide, at least in larger institutions, directional work from ready reference from in-depth reference. This last could take hours for a question, or even days. Does that make it less worthwhile? For whom? There are still pockets of "real" reference librarians. In academia we sometimes call them subject specialists, but we also give them other duties, and hide them from the general public in upstairs offices. In corporate libraries, there are also still a few, but here as well end users are often urged to fend for themselves. In public libraries I know of no reference librarians who can devote however long it takes to answer complex questions. As a professor/administrator and library user at Indiana University, I could only identify a small number of reference librarians who were eager to accept a complex reference question from me. Most preferred that I do the work myself.

When this aversion by reference librarians to doing what they are supposed to do, either through personal choice or management edict, is combined with the arrogance of a new young user population which really thinks it can find everything for itself, where will the new knowledge workers come from? In some form the field will grow and prosper, because the need by decision makers for help they can trust is simply too great. However, will we have a role? Will we be able to use the opportunities of technology to expand our own responsibilities? Will technology serve reference librarians, or will they become the servants of definitions imposed by technologists? There is certainly no future for us in this second option, but even more importantly for those who have purchased the technology and also employ us, it is irresponsibility and waste of the worst kind.

To indicate how we might, on our own initiative, help shape the relationship between ourselves and technology, I want to refer you to the work of two authors who have written about professional roles, professional responsibilities, and professional options. Andrew Abbott, in *The System of Professions* (University of Chicago Press, 1988) postulates that the task of professionals is to address human problems amenable to expert service, and that definition is certainly broad enough to include developing technology which, after all, affects humans and their problems. Abbott continues by noting that professionals compete vigorously for existing and newly emerging problem jurisdictions, and that they strive to expand those jurisdictions by preempting the activities of other professions. Do we see how this affects us? Certainly those of you who are in academia are witnesses to the ferocity with which territorial battles are fought there. Indeed, it was Robert Hutchins, the president of the University of Chicago, who noted that territorial battles were fought ferociously in academia precisely because the stakes were so small. What territorial battles are we fighting or are we prepared to fight? Or do we happily give away our territorial jurisdictions, not because it will save the institution any money, but although it will cost more, it will make us look cheaper?

My second example comes from the writings of Joseph Raelin, who in an article entitled "Professional and Business Ethics—Bridging the Gap" published in the November 1989 issue of *Management Review*, sought to differentiate, among professionals, between what he called *cosmopolitans* and what he called *locals*. Cosmopolitans place their responsibility to their discipline and their professional colleagues ahead of the duties of the workplace; locals placed the pressures of the job ahead of professional standards. This was brought into focus for me by the explosion of the NASA space vehicle, with the death of seven astronauts including teacher Christa McAuliffe. The tragic explosion can be attributed quite simply to a conflict of value systems between cosmopolitans and locals. Engineers at the Thiokol Corporation warned against a launch in cold weather, because the O-rings might stick at temperatures below freezing. These were the cosmopolitans, and they concentrated on scientific principles. NASA administrators and even Thiokol administrators, on the other hand, were the locals. They noted that the NASA budget review process, to be started by the President's address to the new Congress, demanded a successful launch, and demanded it now. The professional worriers, the cosmopolitans, dealt with hypothetical and potential issues lacking in reality. The locals here were tragically wrong. They didn't intend to be wrong and kill people, obviously. It is just that their value system, as locals, led them to ignore concepts and principles for what they considered practical realities.

Those of you who work in academia know that the vast majority of your faculty colleagues are cosmopolitans. A professor of early European history teaches and researches in that field, quite secure in his tenure from whether or not the president likes the course or the research. If things get bad enough, and he or she is prestigious enough, the professor will simply take that specialization to another institution. Loyalty is to the profession, and the arrangement with the employer is one of mutual convenience. These are classic cosmopolitans, and they are respected for it. From my own experience in academia I certainly know, and so do you, that faculty do not adapt what they teach to the formal curriculum. They adapt the curriculum to what they want to teach, and curriculum revision in many library schools today is prompted by the recognition that we no longer have many faculty who want to teach cataloging, let alone be able to teach it. They want to teach what they know and what they enjoy teaching. It can even be argued that major academic institutions can only succeed if the emphasis is on cosmopolitanism.

Practicing librarians, by contrast, are classically professional locals. Loyalty to the institution exceeds all other criteria, and in the attempt to make an underfunded and understaffed institution still somehow appear to be good, professionals do clerical work and clerks do professional work, so that ultimately the clients can't tell the difference. Certainly *USA Today* can't. One might expect professional societies to fight for cosmopolitan professional approaches, and to oppose the emphasis on localism, but you all know they don't do it well, if at all. We concentrate on and try to salvage institutions. In the NASA context, we launch in any weather because the boss has told us to launch.

This is then what worries me as we approach the large question of whether we will adapt technology to serve our professional agendas, or whether we will adapt to the decisions made by others, and operate with smaller staffs because management made the budgetary decision without ever consulting us on the professional issues. Because I realize it may sound strange to you, let me close my comments by defining reference service as performed by intermediary cosmopolitans. We know what constitutes a proper reference transaction, and it varies from question to question. In other words, as cosmopolitans who know their professional responsibilities, we will take as long for each question as that question warrants. Whether or not that suffices to serve all of our clients is an issue that our non-librarian bosses must face.

I don't advocate an uncaring approach, but I do know that if we insisted more on being cosmopolitan rather than giving our own professional society awards to those who accomplished the most with the least, we might do better, and so might our clients. I now sponsor a professional development award at the Indiana University Libraries. The only limitation is that the activity being proposed cannot be directly job-related. That is the responsibility of the employer, and I am not going to make charitable contributions to forgive the employer's stinginess. I will only pay for the cosmopolitan emphasis. Where did New York Mayor Giuliani get the idea that, if he cut public library budgets, we librarians would find the money to take him off the hook for declines in library service, except from us? In fact, there is a program at this conference on how to raise money to offset the loss of money our bosses don't feel like giving us. Why on earth should they if they don't have to?

If the organizations in which we work are going to make proper cost-effective use of technology, it is going to mean a greater role for more of us, and it is going to cost our parent organizations money. So what? If they have to find it, they will. And if they don't like it, they can blame Bill Gates for having opened this Pandora's box. Gates's wealth and power is really now totally incomprehensible to all except perhaps editorial cartoonists. In one recent cartoon a White House staffer tells the President: "More bad news. Bill Gates has atomic weapons." I can only speculate on how much money he has earned since I began this talk.

I began with a comparison, for our field, to the movie scenario in which Tokyo residents worry about whether or not Godzilla will be friendly. I would prefer a different scenario. We know that the mongol hordes under Genghis Khan became a feared army when they learned to employ horses in their warfare tactics. Those horses had been around for a long time. What the mongols learned was the value of training the horses, of feeding them, of looking after their well being, and of making sure the horses understood who was boss. Do mayors, university presidents, and the Vice President of the United States understand whether computers serve people or people serve computers? I would like to feel confident. However, that becomes difficult when I see librarians scrape together what little money they can find in their own budgets and from grants to buy terminals, even if it is just so that end users can play. I have just been reviewing federal grant applications for the Institute of Museums and Libraries, and I am disturbed that librarians, at least in all of the applications I reviewed, requested search terminals for their end users, but never sophisticated hardware and software for themselves, something which would have given them prestige and power. The point I have been trying to make is that technology allows us to reexamine, redefine, and expand what libraries can and should do.

Mortimer Taube made that point in 1964, and if it was true then, it is substantially more true today. Up to now we have stubbornly refused to reexamine, let alone expand, what librarians can do to serve their clients, because we still stubbornly insist on dealing with quantity, with circulation and holdings, instead of quality. We insist on following our clients, and refuse to lead them. Our use of technology has been simply a process of adding more of it, either on our own initiative or under pressure from others, rather than begin with the process of deciding what we should do, what we can do now, and how to get from the second to the first. In the mongol warfare analogy I gave you, we may have improved the length of our spears and the aerodynamic quality of our arrows. But that is all. Those are still our weapons.

If that is all we do, libraries will survive. They will survive because having one is politically attractive, and because, unlike the medical profession, we have never established any minimum criteria for what constitutes a library. While libraries in that scenario will survive, they won't be very exciting, and I certainly would not recommend to anyone the obtaining of a degree to work in such an institution. Even in the school environment envisaged by Al Gore, which begins and ends with linking kids to terminals, there will still be the need for something called the library. Parents and grandparents still have a romantic attachment to us, and teachers will still need a place to send children for punishment. I realize that these are extreme scenarios, but I wanted to make you think, and I wanted to make you angry.

However, even as libraries will undoubtedly survive in some form, librarians, at least as professionals, might not. *USA Today* predicts this, and some library school administrators expect it, and so they find it prudent to abandon what they see as a sinking ship in both nomenclature and course content. I believe there is still time to change this, and that is why I continue to teach, to write, and to speak, even in retirement. However, this requires that we get our priorities in order, and not squander our energies at our meetings on non-library issues. It is for me paradoxical that as our elected professional leaders act as locals when they deal with our own issues, by always stressing the institution and never the staff, they often assume the role of combative cosmopolitans in dealing with the concerns of social activists, on issues in which anyone can and should participate but that are not part of this profession. If we expend our passions and energies in dealing with the Middle East and the Boy Scouts of America, how much energy will remain for us to address, using Abbott's terminology, expanding our professional problem jurisdictions?

The opportunity for this profession to redefine itself for the next millennium, and to redefine and expand our territorial boundaries as we deal with our clients, our bosses, technology gurus, and all other professions, probably still exists. However, the dangers also exist, particularly if we think that nothing fundamental has really changed. It has changed for bank tellers, it has changed for telephone operators, and it has changed for us. Luckily for us, the changes being implemented also give us even more important opportunities. The bank tellers and telephone operators are not as fortunate.

It is time to change our losing game. We can construct an environment conducive to learning, the prime subject of this conference session, only when we have first defined our role in helping to shape that process, and when we have addressed the option of learning by doing things yourself, as well as learning by knowing whom to ask, and insisting on a proper and complete answer. Both are part of the learning process. When I was an academic administrator, I knew that my power base was far less in what I could personally find the time to do, than in what I could persuade others to do on my behalf. Reference librarians have always been a large part of my power base, and I don't want that power base eroded by glittering and simplistic promises of what I can do for myself. I'm now officially retired, and that means that I am much too busy with what I enjoy doing to forgo the opportunity to delegate what I can delegate to others.

———————■———————

Library Managers Must Really Lead

I have devoted my last five columns to examining possible reasons for the failure of this profession to grow and prosper. But there must be reasons for this puzzling phenomenon beyond our own political ineptitude. Peter Drucker predicted a decade ago that knowledge workers had the brightest future, and Drucker is usually correct.

Certainly, those who have exploited the almost unlimited opportunity to provide more information have taken advantage of this development. Still, Drucker assumed that this deluge of knowledge would drown us and force us to seek people to manage that knowledge. Knowledge workers would assess knowledge on behalf of those who had neither the time nor the inclination to do so. In poker terms, it might be said that our profession was dealt a royal flush.

However, *USA Today* has listed librarians, along with bank tellers and telephone operators, as having jobs without a future, because these fields require clerical, repetitive tasks that computers can do at less cost. If both Drucker and the newspaper are correct, then what has gone wrong? How have we traded in that royal flush for a pair of threes?

Abdicating Responsibility

Partly, it seems that, in contradiction to Drucker's prediction, we react to information overload via the Internet and other online services by providing still more access and without making any attempt to separate the useful from the useless for each client. Has our professional battle cry become "Come and get it"?

At least some shadow of suspicion must fall on library managers, particularly high-level ones. These are not automatically our leaders, as the Benton Foundation assumes (in the 1996 *Buildings, Books, and Bytes* report), but the foundation can be forgiven for thinking so. Directors of major academic libraries certainly understand that full employment of new information options will require assessment and filtering and will cost universities a great deal of money.

University presidents understand this as well, much as they may hate to be reminded of it. However, they have no choice, because they must maintain such access if they want to compete for grants, faculty, and graduate students. Competition in academia is surely as ferocious as in industry. Since the money must be spent, it must first be found, and administrators understand that money that must be found will be found.

What is the most effective way to spend this money? Is it best to hire and enable enough of Drucker's knowledge workers, and are these really librarians? Or is the most cost-effective alternative one of pouring countless dollars into innumerable ratholes called "virtual access," with the assurance of a lack of accountability as well as duplication and overlap?

Have academic library directors discussed these alternatives in their monthly private meetings with their university presidents to chart the library's role in the changing university? I see no evidence of such planning meetings. Instead, I see financial edicts to cut library budgets and staffing, followed by dumping the problem of doing more on subordinate staff. But more of what? More housekeeping, more routine, more shifting of professional information work to faculty members who also claim to be swamped and who are usually paid a good deal more than we are? I fail to understand how this is cost-effective.

Public library directors face similar challenges and opportunities in the one-to-one monthly meetings they should have with the mayor to discuss the library's most effective strategies to support the urban mission. But if there are no such meetings, what does this suggest about their presumed "partnership"?

Public librarians certainly understand the danger of a "partnership" based on cheap libraries that keep branches open as long as possible. Such a definition says nothing about range of collection, professional staffing at the reference desk, or rapidity of access services. Public library directors know this is simplistic, but have they told the mayor?

Looking Dumbly at Ourselves

We see frequent examples of a silent acceptance of simplistic value systems in our own literature. We see the celebration of voter approval for new branches or a new central library. However, if that decision is not accompanied by a commitment to pay for new staff—particularly professional staff—what have we won?

There is a fundamental truth of municipal politics: bond funds to pay for construction are easier to justify than operating funds that pay for staffing that construction; the tax impact shifts from vague to immediate.

There has been much discussion about what really happened at the San Francisco Public Library, yet for me the scenario is absurdly simple. Plans were approved, amid much excitement, for a new, state-of-the-art central public library, incorporating both imaginative architectural design and advanced technology. It was predicted quite correctly that this magnet would substantially increase library use.

However, no one seemed to recognize the obvious corollary that building the magnificent new edifice would also require a substantial increase in operating funds, for access services, for materials, and most of all for staff. If the city was not prepared for that commitment, then perhaps it shouldn't have built the library at all. The citizens were misled into believing that innovation did not have an ongoing cost, and the staff was betrayed by making employees bear the brunt of misinformed public reaction. If the staff then reacted by assassinating its betrayer, why should anyone be surprised?

If we are to prove *USA Today* wrong, every librarian must take responsibility, but most importantly our managers must determine their priorities and strategies.

Making Myself Heard

As a semiretired manager and educator, I continue to teach, to write, and to speak at every opportunity. For 20 years, my management students learned that, in order to get credit on the final exam, they had to understand my belief that the single most important characteristic of any manager is courage. They also know of my standing offer to pay a reward, yet unclaimed, for the receipt of any public library annual report that states that "this has been a disastrous year." Surely, some years have been so, and it is not the librarians' fault.

In addition, for the last three years my wife and I have funded at the Indiana University Libraries a competitive award to support professional development. The only stipulation is that this development cannot be directly job-related, because supporting that is the employer's responsibility.

Library school alumni who received my fundraising letters as dean for ten years will recall my promise to never use their donation for anything that the state and university should provide. Why would I want to let those responsible off the hook? Why would I want to teach them that if they abdicate their responsibilities, I will bail them out? It was Drucker who noted that there is always money for activities that are important enough.

Lastly, we now fund an American Library Association award for promoting this profession, not just libraries as institutions. Initiative is crucial because, as Drucker has noted, the best way to predict the future is to create it.

Gadflies Need Apply

In a review of my most recent book (*At the Crossroads: Librarians on the Information Superhighway*, Libraries Unlimited, 1995), Michael Buckland, professor at the School of Information Management and Systems at the University of California, Berkeley, noted that while much of what I wrote might seem unpleasant, librarians should nevertheless read and discuss it. Fair enough.

I have been termed a gadfly, and I accept this to mean a person who stimulates thought and activity. However, I see little indication of discussion and debate about issues important to this profession. As someone originally educated as a chemist who then spent 25 years working with the literature of that field, I am struck by the contrast between scientists—who debate and disagree ferociously at their meetings and in their journals—and librarians—who insist most of all on pleasant congeniality.

At our professional meetings what could be rousing debate over such provocative topics as the use and desirability of filtering software to prevent pornography from reaching children is defused by inviting speakers who all agree with the same premise. It's no answer to claim that dissent is allowed via audience questions. This "feel-good" insistence that everyone at our meetings say what the program planners want to hear prepares us badly for the realities we face when we have to go home—that in truth there are at least two sides to complex questions.

Take Note of Alternatives

I now teach a course at the University of Arizona School of Information Resources and Library Science in case study analysis precisely because I recognize that we rarely analyze alternatives. Instead, we carve out a nonnegotiable principle, or we come up with fixes in order to survive. The most intellectually stimulating exercise is still the attempt to write your opponent's presentation, because it helps to understand that your opponent is just as committed and passionate as you are. All of this also would help us to understand *why* university presidents and mayors speak to us as they do.

In a recent talk at the Fourth International Conference on Fee-Based Services in San Diego—a conference our journals totally ignored, perhaps because they saw it as unpleasant—I said I would prefer that we offer all services without a fee. However, that would require our demanding and obtaining substantial increases in our staffing and budgets to let us do what we are supposed to do. Seeing little likelihood of this happening, I would far prefer that librarians charge rather than not provide these services at all or let someone else provide them.

Clearly, the responsibility for these decisions extends above us to our nonlibrarian bosses. I know that these comments contrast both with the view that it is better not to do anything at all rather than charge and the conclusion of some

Benton survey respondents that libraries must find more donations and volunteers in order to be both better and cheaper. What sort of "leaders" would devise such a disastrous strategy for our profession? Unless, of course, "leader" can be defined as the first lemming into the sea.

To groups that might be interested, let me state that I would happily accept an invitation to debate the most cost-effective future role for the professionally managed library. However, I would prefer not to debate another librarian. I would prefer my opponent be a mayor or university president.

Library Computers: Tools or Toys?

Once no VIP tour of any corporate or government headquarters could be considered complete without a visit to the computer center. Cool, immaculately clean, and impressive in IBM blue and gray, the center projected confidence. Those days are long gone. We all have seen enough computers to no longer be impressed by them, and today's more powerful computers are smaller and less imposing.

The exception: library schools, where a computer center tour may still be the first order of business for all prospective students. While Thomas Carlyle noted that the library was the heart of the university, he said nothing about the need for qualified librarians. Now our unacknowledged slogan may be that the computer laboratory is the heart of the library school, perhaps more important than the faculty.

I have been involved with technology for virtually my entire career, and I have recently found the text of a talk I presented to special librarians 35 years ago. I argued that it was less important that we used technology than it was to understand why we used it and why we didn't.

I haven't changed my mind, though my analysis is now more complex. The computer was then an important tool that could help us. Now, it's a crucial tool. However, it never was, or will be, something to use simply because it is there. Human beings must dictate what they want machines to do, never the other way around.

Reprinted, with changes, by permission of the author and *Library Journal* 123, no. 19 (November 15, 1998): 40–41. Copyright © 1998 by Cahners Business Information.

Technology and Its Limits

Some issues still debated in the 1960s have now been put to rest. Technology can be effective in performing repetitive clerical operations. As libraries are full of such operations and usually desperately short-staffed, that use of technology—once so heatedly argued in our literature—is no longer an issue. For us, strangled by low staffing levels, there is no reason not to use computers to do routine work. This then allows us to use staffing slots for professionals who do what computers cannot do.

At the same time, the issue of what computers cannot do—and more importantly what outsiders may incorrectly think they can do—raises significant issues of political turf. We must remember that, in spite of the simplistic approaches of some political bosses, librarians play not one but at least three distinct roles: providers of recreation, educators, and information intermediaries. These can collide depending on how funds, staff, and priorities are allocated.

We face a real emotional conflict between our roles as teachers (to which so many librarians aspire) and as information intermediaries who focus not on teaching others what we do but on ensuring they ask us to do what we alone can do. This conflict affects how we view technology. In one scenario, we stress teaching clients to become independent searchers, even as this makes them independent of us. In the other, we keep them aware of their need for our unique expertise. This protects our political turf, as it does for any profession.

Worrying About Our Education

As I look at the ways we integrate technology into the library school curriculum, two things worry me. The first is our emphasis on computers as tools to enhance only our educational role. This becomes most evident as we teach students to use enhanced database access to dump more raw material onto the terminals of the already swamped user.

More and more companies instead of libraries are serving as information intermediaries, evaluating information to shield clients from getting data dumped into their laps. With this, quality clearly prevails over quantity. Librarians who continue to brag about circulation statistics stubbornly refuse to understand how little that means. If we are simply competing for numbers, computers can beat us hands down.

My second concern stems from the observation that, in many library and information science programs, using computers has become the end in itself in curriculum design. I certainly agree that technology must be integrated into the curriculum but not as some sort of exotic hothouse bloom. This requires teaching about computers as a part of cataloging and of reference; in turn, this means that ideally teachers must be both librarians and technologists.

Fitting Faculty to Curriculum

Technology does not really change the purpose of either cataloging or reference; it only allows us to do both better. I can speculate as to why most library schools now teach about computers in separate courses without a library context. Perhaps we think we will look more attractive to university administrators as a technology school. It may also be that, as we rush to recruit faculty members who know only technology and have never worked in a library, we inevitably adapt the curriculum to those faculty. University faculty have always taught what they know and ignored as unimportant what they do not know.

We no longer select faculty because they fit the curriculum, we select curriculum because it fits the faculty. Law schools deal with this far more responsibly. When they hire nonlawyer academic specialists, they make it clear that these individuals must relate their teaching and research to the profession of law. Sociology, economics, and computer applications are taught as a subset of law. Our criteria should be no different.

Library education programs must of course expose students to hands-on experience with new technologies. At the same time, educators must recognize that if programs stress only the *how* of technological applications, then no matter how current the course, the student's learning will be obsolete in two years. It is far more important that we stress the *why* of technology in the context of our own responsibilities. We have the opportunity to develop and expand our singular ability to do what end users, systems analysts, and the computer itself cannot do. While we may study user behavior, we also can affect and enhance that behavior for the user's own benefit. Librarians who only give people what they request will always be recognized as clerks.

Our Role Is Unequaled

This should make it obvious why I don't believe that our academic programs can fit comfortably into disciplines of either technology or of social services. We exceed those narrow definitions. Needed interdisciplinary programs can be accommodated in dual degree programs. In the 1980s, at the Indiana University School of Library and Information Science, we had 14 of them, ranging from partnerships with history and comparative literature through journalism and chemistry to law and public administration.

The size of our programs should not be allowed to become the issue here. We must stress our uniqueness even as we interact with other fields. My standard response for ten years to observations that we were the smallest independent degree program at Indiana was that one school would always be the smallest. Why not let it be us and put the question to rest?

In any case, if we are going to eliminate the word "Library" from the names of schools that educate our professionals, we also must change the names of the organizations in which they work. Do "Municipal Knowledge Management Facility" or "University Information Access and Assessment Center" appeal to you? They don't to me, but the important thing is not what the titles are but that they match.

Peter Drucker, as usual, placed the issue into proper perspective years ago. Automation, he noted, is not about machines; it is about people and how they work. Library technology is about how machines can help us improve and expand what we are supposed to do. The problem we face is not with the word *library*. Rather, it is with how we have allowed others to narrow the definition so the public thinks of the library as a manually and computer-supplied warehouse and librarians as inventory clerks.

Claiming Our Territory

I have in several columns referred to the work of Andrew Abbott, who stresses that professions constantly strive to protect and to expand their territories. It's been true for some time that technology allows us at least the potential to expand our boundaries, as it is equally true that we have failed to see and take advantage of those opportunities.

Back in 1965, when the MARC system was being designed, the late Mortimer Taube noted that even the technology then in existence allowed us to rethink all of the premises of the cataloging process, up to then constrained, particularly in subject analysis, by the cost implications of filing 3" x 5" catalog cards. The most wasteful thing we could do, although it would certainly work, would be to simply take the *Anglo-American Cataloging Rules* manual and put it on a machine. And that, of course, is exactly what we did do. It can be argued that we did it well, but it was the wrong task.

Similarly, it is now possible for librarians to provide reference services of higher quality than ever before. If reference librarians claim this territory for themselves, they run no risk of competition from end user searching. It isn't even necessary to explain, in a knowledge-conscious society, that this is needed.

If reference librarians are beset by staffing cuts, they should—if they must—limit the number of searches they do but never dilute the quality. In that context, if huge waiting lines develop, necessitating appointments three months in advance, our nonlibrarian bosses would notice. If they realized we weren't bluffing, they would increase the staff. What else could they do, when confronted by our unserved patrons?

As our educators teach about the potential impact of technology on our profession, I hope they stress these growth opportunities. Unless they do this, the danger is not so much that computers will be toys in the playroom but rather that librarians will be toys in the attic.

Book Review

Gateways to Knowledge. The Role of Academic Libraries in Teaching, Learning and Research. Edited by Lawrence Dowler. MIT Press. 1997. xxii, 240 pp. Index. Hardcover ISBN 0-262-04159-6 $35.00.

This book contains the papers presented by 15 invited speakers at a conference at Harvard University with support from the Council on Library Resources, and was edited by Lawrence Dowler, Associate Librarian for Public Services at Harvard College. The book argues that this conference and these papers are about change: about suspending and adapting old ideas and rethinking and redefining the missions of the university and of the library. The book goes on to argue that in struggling to define the library of the future, librarians have too often bolted new technology programs and services onto existing library functions. It also argues that the purpose of the conference, and of the essays, is to think about the nature and qualities of electronic information. It is disappointing for this reviewer to note that none of this really happens, and that it is not the fault of the librarians. Rather, it is the faculty members among the invited presenters who make it clear that they have no intention at all of adapting the way they utilize information. They simply want all of it, and by general agreement, lots more. Because technology, presented to them without assessment, without intervention, and without evaluation ought to provide it. That they might either drown in the volume, or that, as a minimum, they will now spend their employer's salary money far less effectively by insisting on doing what they have always done, simply does not occur to them. They will not adapt at all, everyone must adapt to them. Clark Kerr has often noted this stubborn intransigence.

Reprinted by permission of the author and *Publishing Research Quarterly*, Winter 1998/1999.

In his introductory comments, Billy Frye, the provost at Emory University and a long time advocate of national approaches to library issues, shows an awareness of this danger. He notes that the *status quo* is certainly the most comfortable, but that the choices presented by emerging information technologies must be faced by all of us, and by this he means both librarians and professors. He points out that change is the order of the day from both the vantage point of economic exigency and educational philosophy. At the same time, he notes the danger of resistance to change from traditional faculty autonomy and independence. The papers which follow, not all by Harvard faculty members, but certainly all from faculty members selected by the Harvard planners for their continued insistence on total freedom to do what they like, sadly prove him to be correct. Certainly these individuals want, perhaps from the library if this becomes necessary, direct unfettered access to everything which they find of value or of interest. Moreover, they want all of the raw data, and they don't want it analyzed or filtered by anyone.

One of the speakers notes proudly that he now gets just about all of his information directly in his office and finds no need to visit the library. Richard Rockwell, executive director of the Inter-university Consortium for Political and Social Research at the University of Michigan, notes that in his view the information system of the future may resemble a mall of upscale boutiques and department stores. Librarians (and Rockwell is just about the only one who mentions librarians and not just libraries) will develop the mall and provide maintenance services, including opening the doors and sweeping the floors.

It is difficult for this reviewer to understand why librarians, either at Harvard or at the Council on Library Resources, would endorse a conference that so trivializes their own professional role. More importantly, the conference totally ignores a possibility that faculty might want to consider, or be forced to consider by those who pay their salaries: the reality that the great growth in information brought to us by technology, including the great growth of garbage, suggests that they need help funneling all of this stuff to their desks and terminals, and more importantly, in shielding them from what they should not be bothering to see at all. Peter Drucker, more than 10 years ago, predicted that the most important profession of the future would be knowledge workers, people who would do exactly that. Paul Horn, senior vice president for research at IBM, noted at a conference at the New York Public Library the growing role of librarians as mediators who find specific information in the proliferating deluge of data and create context for information as they connect users to it. However, neither Drucker nor Horn were invited to this pageant of self-congratulations in which faculty assure themselves that they are always right, need never change, and that everyone must adapt to what makes them comfortable. It is amazing that so many librarians buy into an arrangement which turns them into warehouse clerks, although, in the case of Harvard, a very large warehouse.

It is possible that real change in the way in which we assess opportunities and dangers, both the real cost efficiencies and the real endless cost overruns, will come from an alliance of convenience between desperate university administrators and savvy librarians. This spells out to faculty that they cannot simply continue to do what they feel like doing just because they have always done it. If and when this occurs, the leadership of this process will not come from Harvard University. At Harvard, the role of librarians in the operation of the library is so marginalized that it is a given that the director of the university library can never be a librarian, but must rather be a distinguished faculty member—the discipline does not really matter. However, faculty here do let librarians build gateways—or sweep the floor.

The Changes in Off-Campus Education

Twenty years ago, the Indiana University Graduate Library School was at the cutting edge in off-campus library education. We were teaching at eight locations in the state of Indiana and in one just across the state line in Cincinnati. This so worried the Committee on Accreditation (COA) of the American Library Association (ALA) that it dispatched an additional member for its accreditation visit to our regional campuses. The site visitors gave us a clean bill of health, and indeed I was later told by the COA chair that he hoped our approach might serve as a model for other expanded programs.

Nevertheless, the COA had every right to worry if we could assure an adequate standard of education for all of our students, whether in Bloomington or elsewhere. As I was largely responsible for the expansion of the program, I was concerned as well.

Can Off-Campus Teaching Work?

What sort of mix between traveling regular faculty and adjuncts could we tolerate and still maintain program integrity, and how often could we expect a faculty member who also had research obligations to make a weekly overnight trip, even if it were fully reimbursed? Could some courses be taught equally well, or perhaps even better, by adjuncts, while others had to be taught by

Reprinted, with changes, by permission of the author and *Library Journal* 124, no. 3 (February 15, 1999): 128–130. Copyright © 1999 by Cahners Business Information.

regular faculty? When an adjunct taught a course also taught by a regular faculty member, we knew we had to insist on consistency of coverage—but should we also insist on consistency of approach? To what extent should we assure each student time for consultation?

I never doubted the rightness of our approach, because we were a state university and the only one in the state offering an accredited library degree. We owed it to the students to provide them with an opportunity, but we quickly recognized that only certain courses could be offered: partly because of the availability of qualified instructors and partly because some courses required research library resources. Students in Gary could use libraries in nearby Chicago, and those in South Bend were graciously welcomed at Notre Dame.

However, some courses simply were not feasible in certain locations because we could not support them, no matter how much the students pleaded. Our approach to education might differ among locations, but quality had to be maintained. Students could not be penalized because they chose to split coursework between a regional campus and Bloomington. We knew better than to measure "success" by grade; we measured it by content.

When we began using interactive television a few years later, I found, in large part from personal teaching experience, that some courses—particularly lectures—could be easily adapted to a television format. Others, requiring interactive exchange among students and between student and professor, were simply not appropriate. Much as students always clamor for convenience, our insistence on quality had to override their own willingness to forgo it.

Expansion Without Funding

I had not recognized how much off-campus education had spread until I was asked to speak at Central Michigan University's fifth annual conference on off-campus library services in 1991. Here the issue was not providing library education courses but rather library responsibility for supplying adequate support, frequently without additional funding, for courses offered in distant locations.

Academic budget administrators understood, as they do today, the unit cost principle of cost per credit hour. Off-campus courses are almost always cheaper, particularly when they involve adjunct faculty and when support costs such as library services don't enter into planning decisions.

The Central Michigan University conferences dealt in large part with a problem with which all library administrators grapple: How do we deal with increased user demand when it is encouraged without concern for the increased funding and staffing that might be required? Public library directors will recognize this scenario, having already faced hordes of school children because of inadequate school libraries and because private charter schools have opened without any libraries at all.

Distance Education Expands

However, my main thrust here is graduate library education, where the most dramatic development—in only about five years—has been distance learning, sometimes called independent study, but in either case based primarily on the availability of the Internet. It is obvious that such a concept has many attractions. For universities and their hard-pressed library schools, it provides a wonderful opportunity to substantially decrease unit cost of instruction. For students who are geographically constrained—as are many potential librarians—it provides a wonderful option.

For the practitioner community, particularly those public libraries that neither pay interview nor relocation expenses, it allows them to hire cheaply. Finally, for politicians who will always favor expanded educational opportunities as long as they need not pay for them, this is an extremely attractive alternative. It should not then surprise us that electronic distance learning via the Internet has grown so rapidly. It represents a seeming win-win scenario.

How well does it work? What quality of education does it provide? The answer: we don't know. The concerns about off-campus instruction using flesh and blood teachers are only magnified in this environment. What courses are easily adapted to individual study programs? For what courses requiring interactive discussion and dialog is such an approach out of the question? If the basic contact between student and instructor is over the Internet, how much one-on-one consultation and advice is offered? Or mandated?

Hard to Evaluate

I am not suggesting that some courses don't work well, or that some schools don't run better programs than others, only that the rest of us can't tell, because there's no incentive for the school to keep honest books. It will insist that these courses are all just fine, which worries me, because surely experience teaches that some courses should no longer be offered.

All that schools tend to offer is the "proof" that distance education students get grades just as high as those earned by campus students, but we all know at this point, unfortunately, how little an A means. Nor will students complain about courses that allow them to complete their education. If they feel rancor, they will wait to display it when they are approached for a contribution by the alumni association.

All of this was foreseen some 25 years ago, when the Council on Postsecondary Accreditation (COPA) decided that practitioners, not educators, should assess quality in graduate education. Thus, ALA was made responsible for accrediting library education programs.

I saw how well the process can work in other fields when a legal accreditation team of practitioners stated that the Indiana University Law Library had inadequate space and holdings and they would be back in a few years to evaluate improvements. By that time, an addition to the law school had been completed and a larger and better-equipped and -staffed library had been established. Why? Because the law school understood it had no choice.

Practitioners Looking In?

Accreditation by library practitioners depends on two related factors: how much the practitioners care and how much educators fear the loss of accreditation. It should be obvious that practitioners have lost all interest in library education, except for occasional pique when their alma mater changes its name. Instead, they worry primarily whether a trained local graduate pool is available—not educated but trained. Educated students still must be trained, at the employer's expense. It is little wonder that employers may prefer candidates already prepared to tackle the backlog. Independent thinking and ideas are not required and may in fact be discouraged if they interfere with productivity.

If all of this seems harsh, look at the COA membership rosters over the past 15 years and at the composition of site visit teams. You will see how—by default—educators have taken over the responsibilities abdicated by practitioners. If COA members and site visitors are kinder and gentler to their brothers and sisters, this should not be surprising. Indeed, it is exactly what COPA was hoping to guard against.

As new interdisciplinary faculty members adapt the curriculum to their teaching interests, required courses are rapidly disappearing. Still, the importance of required courses was shown in my research study in the July 1990 issue of *Library Quarterly*. It reported that half of the graduates of a far-ranging sample of 13 library education programs were, ten years after graduation, in jobs or in libraries other than those for which they had prepared themselves. From this my co-investigator, Sarah Mort (now Cron), and I concluded that it was more prudent to emphasize required courses common to all parts of the profession.

Employers Hold the Power

Our study was never challenged, but it was ignored. Educators who read it disregarded it because it did not fit their plans. Practitioners ignored it because they had never read it. How many of you who read *LJ* also regularly read *LQ*? We were not always this fragmented. When C. C. Williamson postulated in 1923 that librarianship required education rather than training, his report generated fervent discussion. If practitioners are now dissatisfied with library education, whom but themselves do they have to blame?

Would library schools care if they lost accreditation? It depends on how employers react, because the question has been raised by recent events. The University of California at Berkeley has decided not to seek ALA accreditation because "accreditation for professional programs has little discernible value." However, Berkeley has not decided to forgo accreditation for its equally professional School of Law.

There is risk here, because, despite the high-flown rhetoric, administrators understand that those who seek to work in libraries still represent what one called their "cash cows." How will library employers now respond? Will they inform prospective librarians that Berkeley grads won't get hired? Will Berkeley's own university library now have the courage to reject these graduates? Or will rationalization and the emphasis on cheap convenience take precedence? If it does, we can be sure that other universities will also decide they need not consult us on what they teach our new recruits. If that happens, whatever sense we may have had of calling ourselves a profession will be gone.

What to Evaluate and What to Reward

In a recent syndicated column, management writer Dale Dauten pointed out that most people—and the best and most competitive people—try harder at whatever game they play if someone keeps score. Note that this applies only to *most* people; in management, no policies work all the time for all subordinates. Wise managers develop policies that will encourage the highest level of performance not only from the majority but also from the most valuable subordinates. Regrettably, some library managers stubbornly refuse to concede that subordinates perform at differing levels.

Adults must be told when they have failed but always in the context of understanding how they could have succeeded. However, if we are always told we have done well, even if we haven't tried, we learn nothing except to "feel good." I never hesitated to assign graduate students grades of B or C if they were deserved. I knew that not assigning those grades made the A worthless.

Dauten cited an experiment in which individuals participating in a six-month exercise regimen were vastly more likely to succeed if there were a $40 wager riding on the outcome. They had an incentive, even though it was relatively trivial. We need incentives and rewards.

Reprinted, with changes, by permission of the author and *Library Journal* 124, no. 7 (April 15, 1999): 62–64. Copyright © 1999 by Cahners Business Information.

Competition Leads to Results

Years ago, while I directed the NASA Scientific and Technical Information Facility, I had the opportunity to test the premise that competition improves performance. As in all large organizations, we had a mix of employees. Some never used sick leave even when they should have stayed home; others used every "allowable" day of it, even if that meant feigning illness during the last week of eligibility. These individuals fell into what is commonly called the "Friday/Monday" absence patterns.

Such malingering is easy to spot but nearly impossible to prove. I decided to develop and display a rank ordering of unrelated Monday or Friday absences as a percentage of available work days, ranking results by unit. I published it without comment. I hoped that the "healthiest" units (and I was careful to exempt identifiable medical problems) would brag about their standings and that the "sickie" units would take a ribbing from the others.

In turn, these individuals, who knew perfectly well the identity of the malingerers, might apply pressure that I as the manager could not. My plan worked, at least partially. Co-workers know far better than bosses who is productive. Yet we rarely give people any reason to try harder and to insist that their co-workers try as well.

People Want Recognition

That incentive comes from another Dauten observation: people like to be recognized and rewarded when they deserve it. He noted that the preferred form of recognition is financial, but far less costly approaches are available. We have all seen that hotels frequently honor an employee of the month, whose name appears on the marquee and who gains a preferred parking space. Dauten suggested that even something as simple as the public bestowal of a free pizza has a positive impact.

Libraries, in my observations, do none of these things. Our staff work anonymously toward objectives that are never known by upper management or clients and that may not even exist. "Do as much as you can" can't inspire either hard work or the hope for celebration; it satisfies mainly those who have no desire to compete and who relish their anonymity. Is it far-fetched to suggest that such joyless drones are not the kind of staff we want to cultivate?

In large part libraries function without recognition and reward because we misapply two principles. The first concerns what is called participative management. Managers have always understood that they should avoid micromanaging. They should make only those decisions for which they are responsible and leave to staff those decisions that can be reached by consensus or majority vote, e.g., the site for the library picnic. Vacations are usually scheduled best by giving first choice to those with seniority.

Strangely, some library managers insist on making trivial decisions but refuse to make important ones. While advisory input might be sought on hiring, personnel decisions rest with the top manager. It's not credible for managers to tell their bosses that an unsatisfactory staff member was hired by committee.

Improving Teamwork

Also, we misapply the team concept. All organizations require sometimes permanent, but more often temporary, teams. However, as management writer Gifford Pinchot noted a long time ago, teams are not anonymous; they consist of individuals who expect recognition and reward and to be judged as individuals. They may like teams if they believe that membership will help them. Sports teams have names on each jersey, as they cooperate in the shared hope for victory.

The process of allowing library teams to select their own recruits can work only when members believe that this will increase their own chance for success. We want new members not because they are fuzzy and congenial but because their probing and nagging will improve the team's performance and thereby earn us personal recognition and rewards. With this motivation, employees select the best partners and expel the malingerers, if not from the workplace (that's the job of management) then at least from their own group.

How many library teams can expel members? Dauten has pointed out—and we have surely all noticed—that many teams look just like committees; they emphasize anonymity and ignore individual credit and especially individual blame. Such teams aim not for success but for safety.

I have never found a satisfactory way to assign group projects in the 24 years I have been in teaching. If I allow students to form their own groups, then the best students would seek such partnerships and do very well. However, this would unfairly force the remaining students into weaker groups. Moreover, the "elite" groups might reject worthy new individuals, as well as commuting students not members of an on-campus social clique. Having experienced and seen the cruelty with which children choose sides for sandlot baseball, I could never impose such an unfair process on my students. All students must be allowed to make their own effort to do well.

The other academic approach is one in which the team is selected randomly by the professor, which is at least more fair for the total composition of the team. However, in both the classroom and the workplace it introduces not the probability but the certainty that some people will work harder and contribute more—and of course they will share the same undifferentiated evaluation.

Planning for Reality

How then do library managers adapt to the reality that most subordinates—and certainly the best subordinates—want to compete on a level playing field and be individually recognized, evaluated, and rewarded? I refer back to my column

"Planning and Evaluation: The Endless Carousel" (*LJ* 11/15/97, p. 38–39). Management goals must be important, doable, and accompanied by appropriate resources. We cannot vaguely encourage staff to "do the best you can" simply because we aren't brave enough to point out that good will demands resources.

In presenting our plans to the university president or the mayor we must concentrate not only on what institutions do but also on what individual staff members do. Also, we must relate these planned accomplishments to the larger objectives of the university and the community. Individual librarians below administrative levels have rarely met either the university president or the mayor, because these people rarely come to the library, and they have never been invited to meet the staff.

If planning leads to objectives that are meaningful, achievable, and quantifiable, then this process can also be translated into targets for individuals: minimum targets for the most mediocre and incentives for those who can do better. Quality is certainly more difficult to define than quantity, but it can be done. Professors must do it all the time. Managers also must be prepared to explain that qualitative criteria may not be as obvious as quantitative ones, but this does not make them unfair.

Fairness, Not Egalitarianism

The best and the brightest individuals will respond most eagerly to an achievable challenge. They need to see some potential individual reward on the horizon, if not money then at least recognition. In speaking at the installation dinner for the University of Arizona chapter of the Beta Phi Mu library honorary society, I suggested that if these new members were indeed more capable than others, they should never allow themselves to be buried in a faceless and creditless team, because they deserved the individual recognition. While fairness is always crucial, it is not the same thing as egalitarianism, which is always unfair in the workplace as in the classroom.

How then should we celebrate individual achievement? When financial rewards are not easily available, I like the idea of designating an employee of the month or of the quarter. Pizza parties can provide a celebration. Let us close the library one hour early for the festivities, and let us explain to our patrons why we are having the party—and invite them, too. Let us also make sure that we alert the media, both print and electronic. If television cameras are there, the mayor or university president also will be there, perhaps to claim credit for the idea but in any case to make the presentation.

Motivational speakers at our libraries and our conferences never share the honoraria they receive, and they are therefore not members of any team. Nevertheless, they like to point out that there is no "I" in the word "team." True, but there are "I's" in "accomplishment" and "credit"—and two in "recognition."

Technology and the Pressures and Opportunities for Document Delivery

Although those who teach public speaking strongly recommend against this, I must begin this talk with a confession. I do not like the term *Interlibrary Loan*. I find it both demeaning and inaccurate. It is inaccurate because it suggests some sort of process of applying for help, having that application reviewed and considered, and perhaps having it granted, perhaps after appraisal as in a pawn shop. Finally what has been requested is supplied when the supplier is good and ready. The requester is, in turn, duly grateful—that is, if the requester is still alive. It is also inaccurate because, certainly for the materials which in my special library experience comprise the vast majority of interlibrary transactions—journal articles—we are talking about requests via e-mail and transmission via fax. At least I hope so. I do know from my years as Vice President for Operations at the Institute for Scientific Information and the preparation of the *Science Citation Index* that the average length of a journal article is 10 pages. It obviously varies widely, but it was 10 pages in 1970, it was 10 pages in 1975, and I suspect it is 10 pages today. That is just about an ideal length for a fax transmission. My first objection is that, perhaps except for books and illuminated manuscripts or Gutenberg Bibles, we do not

Keynote Address, presented at the 30th Annual Colorado Interlibrary Loan Conference, Denver, Colorado, May 13, 1999.

337

lend, we supply a copy. Fortunately, the material with which we deal is not consumed in its use. I once disconcerted an earnest copy machine salesman who bragged that his machine could copy anything by asking him to make me a second sandwich from the one I had brought. Basically, we transmit printed pages, and they can be copied. Whether or not they may be copied involves a number of issues including the Copyright Law, and I'll talk about that later, and so of course, certainly more knowledgeably, will your next speaker. I will only say at this point that copyright is a cost but not an obstacle. Copyright owners want to get paid, they usually don't mind your copying.

I find the term interlibrary loan demeaning because it trivializes an important management business decision—that of determining the most cost-effective way of obtaining information for our clients. And for our clients information delivery is still primarily document delivery. In one sense our job is much easier than that of people who have to drag specific answers out of obscure and esoteric materials. That is ostensibly the job of reference librarians and bibliographic specialists, but as I noted in a talk at Appleton, Wisconsin, last month, at least in my observation, there are fewer and fewer reference librarians willing to undertake complex reference work, despite the fact that there is now far more information, and finding specific answers is now far more complex.

For this talk it suffices to point out that there are now far more documents. As a sci-tech librarian and teacher of the Literature of Science and Technology, I enjoyed pointing out that every day enough scientific information was produced to fill 25 complete sets of the *Encyclopaedia Britannica*, and that more than half of the chemists the world has ever known went to work that morning, even allowing for vacations and sick leave. The data I used was from the 1970s, and I am sure the deluge of information has gotten greater.

Not only has this society become very good at producing lots of information—not necessarily always valuable information but sometimes you can't tell until you see it—it has also become very good, through the improvements in technology which are also a large part of your conference, at telling everyone what is out there. This is called bibliographic access. Almost all libraries, no matter how small or how geographically isolated, now have widespread access to bibliographic information, to what is out there. It is rapid, it is at least relatively cheap, and it is at least as accurate and complete as the originator made it.

What follows bibliographic access is document access for the things that somebody, perhaps a librarian and perhaps a user, now wants to see based on having learned about it. Whether or not the material will prove to be as valuable as we thought it might be is something we can't tell. We look at lots of material which, after looking at it, we decide was not as useful as we thought it might have been. Think of your daily newspaper and your own rapid turning of pages in sections in which you have no interest. We have gotten used to this, nobody calls the paper to demand that the paper remove the bridge column from their home-delivered copy. If bridge is not your game, you skip it. Closer to our own field, I know from many years of experience with SDI (selective dissemination of information) systems that any "hit" rate about 50 percent or 60 percent is really quite good, particularly since users sometimes act annoyed when we inform them of something which they already know. What greater proof of relevance is there than that?

My point is that bibliographic access leads to document access, and if you are not prepared to support document access, perhaps you'd better limit or eliminate bibliographic access; shut down the terminals and tell your clients they may only know what is in your acquisitions list. I know that is absurd, but it is equally absurd to tell people, "Yes, that really looks like a very useful document for you, but you can't have it because it is too much trouble for us to bother to obtain it." Those options are, of course, not very meaningful, but they would not be available to you in any case. Our clients are no longer dependent on us for bibliographic access, but then they often come to us for the documents. What are we going to do then? Yell at them for having found things without our permission?

Document access comes in two forms. The material you acquire in the belief that somebody will probably ask you for it, and the material you wait to acquire when and if somebody asks you for it. The two categories are not mutually exclusive, but they are in any case part of a perfectly natural management process—it is what the business schools call the "make or buy" decisions. What we acquire in advance of request is the "make," what we wait to see if anyone asks for it is the "buy." That does not mean that one value system is better than the other. The material in your collection is not automatically more valuable to the requester's need than what you do not have. If you think it is, try telling a requester, "We don't have any of the things you have asked for and we aren't going to acquire them as long as there are still other things on the shelves. Read one of those and don't be so picky." I don't recommend it.

The decisions about what to make and what to buy are not infallible, with us or in the commercial sector, but librarians who know their collection and know their users can almost always make better selections than a process which is totally reliant on user demand, and that is particularly true in academia where the demand that something be bought may for the requester be as much of an expression of ego as one of need, and please bear in mind that you are hearing this from somebody who spent 20 years in academia, as a full professor, as a dean, and ultimately, as a distinguished professor. Studies by Allen Kent at the Hillman Library of the University of Pittsburgh showed that half of the material in the humanities and social sciences had never been charged out even once. I think even the worst public librarian selects better than that. I also know that any corporate special librarian who selects so badly that half of the material is never used even once has no future in that organization.

I stated earlier that the decision to purchase and the decision to acquire later are not mutually exclusive. Many librarians, at least some of the ones I have encountered in major research universities, express a value system which I, as an innocent faculty member user, find strange. They tell me that what I want is in the library collection but that it is charged out, *as though that were an answer.* The attitude seems to be, for these librarians and I hope none of them are my former students—we have done our job, you are just out of luck. Richard Trueswell— the same Trueswell who told us the 80/20 rule (80 percent of requests are met from 20 percent of the material) and that is crucial to remember because it means not only that you can't buy everything but also that you shouldn't buy everything— Trueswell also told us that your chances of getting from the library today what the library already owns is at best 50 percent.

You will begin to appreciate why at least some librarians at Indiana University, although certainly not what I would consider the good ones, considered me troublesome, when I tell you my response to being told that the material I had requested, to be used in the preparation of my next lecture by the end of Friday, was charged out. I answered: "We seem to be having a communication problem. I asked you for a copy of this book and you are giving me an inventory report on your collection. I never insisted on seeing a particular copy. I'll take any copy, and if you like we can find out from the publisher how many copies were printed. I'll take any copy, and if yours is charged out, would you please get me another one. By Friday."

I know that many libraries refuse to borrow what they already own. This means, particularly if there is already a waiting list ahead of me, that I would have been better off if you hadn't bought the book. I suspect I know why libraries are reluctant to borrow what they already own. They somehow think that the process you call interlibrary loan is unnatural and designed to be minimized. I would suggest that the very opposite is true. If you are borrowing a lot, it means that you have been frugal and conservative in your initial purchase decisions. However, that also means that you must treat the acquisition after request and without purchase as a normal economic transaction, to be budgeted and paid for just as you pay for what you buy. Above all, get rid of the idea that interlibrary loan is a favor. Favors are performed slowly and reluctantly if at all, and that is absolutely correct. You owe more to your own clients than you do to strangers, and if that is true today, it will be even more true tomorrow, because of the concept of accountability. How dare you spend time helping somebody else when you complain that you don't have enough staff to help your own clients? Margaret Otto, when she was library director at Dartmouth College, once posed a problem to me when I consulted with the New Hampshire Library Network. As an excellent library collection in the state of New Hampshire and yet a private Ivy League University, Dartmouth was being asked to supply a great deal of interlibrary loan as part of so-called cooperative agreements, when in fact those agreements were really one way. She lent a great deal within the state, the rest of the state might be willing to lend to her, but they had nothing she needed. The University of New Hampshire might have a public responsibility to lend, but what was hers in a private institution? She felt guilty at the realization that interlibrary loan deprived her own faculty and students of service. I told Margaret to raise the question with the university president. He could either give her additional staff and money with which to be good neighbors, or take full responsibility if Dartmouth was perceived as uncooperative and selfish. It was not the library director's responsibility, it was the president's as a public relations issue.

  Many of the problems which now plague interlibrary loan—and I have contrasted bibliographic access versus document delivery to a six-lane divided highway versus a rutted one-lane road—come from two myths which, for a long time, we have perpetuated. The first is that interlibrary loan is a wash—we lend and we receive and the two balance out somehow. It is not a wash—the relationship between the University of Arizona and the Sierra Vista Public Library is not an egalitarian relationship of borrowing and lending. Nor need it be, if we keep honest books. We refuse to acknowledge what the process called interlibrary loan really costs. The most recent figure I trusted came from the 1970s and a study by Westat Research. That study, with fully amortized costs, was then $31/transaction, and it was attacked for being much too high. I suspect it is now probably closer to $50. I don't know about your state, but some states supply as "much as" (and I say this sarcastically) $10 to help defray the costs of the supplier. Where did $10 come from? It has no scientific validity, it is a political figure. The problem is that the suppliers know what it costs them, and if they don't know, they should know. If they don't compete anxiously for the privilege of supplying documents, it is probably because they suspect that they will never break even on $10 per transaction, and they are not really anxious for more business at that rate. And, yet, I would suspect that, as in any normal business transactions, the quality of service will not really improve until organizations compete, ferociously if you like, for the privilege of filling your next request. Sending the request through a state library for clearance simply adds a middle man and delays the process, and ultimately only helps to decide whom to stick with this burden without being most unfair.

  As I stated, the process of acquiring what you haven't already bought is a perfectly natural business decision which librarians, as managers, need to make. However, I have also suggested that sometimes you acquire what you already own, simply because you cannot provide it. A study of interlibrary loan by a consortium of midwestern liberal arts colleges (schools like Coe and St. Olafs) reported that the majority of what they borrowed from each other, they already owned—it is just that they couldn't locate the document or book or journal to meet the demand. I will only give you one more example of what I suspect you already accept instinctively to be true. In 1965 the National Library of Medicine set up the Medical Library Assistance Act, designed to subsidize at that time the process of allowing small medical libraries to acquire material from larger medical libraries. The obvious assumption was that what would be borrowed were rare and esoteric titles. The most frequently borrowed title in the initial survey was the *Journal of the American Medical Association* (*JAMA*). *Lancet* was second.

What I have been stressing and will continue to stress is that we begin to consider interlibrary loan, or simply the process of acquiring what we never acquired in advance of request, or what we did acquire but now can't deliver, as a normal part of the operation of our library, including its cost. Indeed, it will be an increasing part of the operational cost, and that is good because it is preferable to either alternative—buying everything in anticipation of need, or telling clients that this is not a good library and they are out of luck. However, in addition to the issue of cost, there is yet another issue to be considered. Who is going to do this work, quite aside from the money?

Interlibrary loan, as you all know, is a labor-intensive process, and for some libraries acquiring labor is even more difficult than acquiring money, because of headcount ceilings and hiring freezes. That is certainly true for public libraries, it is particularly true for special libraries such as corporate libraries. It is not necessarily true, or at least it should not be true, for academic libraries, who have easy access to a plentiful and cheap resource, if they can pay them. Samuel Sass, a prominent special librarian working for General Electric, argued in the literature more than 30 years ago that special librarians tended to be moochers of the resources of other libraries, and that they should make greater efforts to become lenders. I disagreed then, and I disagree now. Special, or for that matter, all small libraries cannot afford to get into a labor swap effort. What special libraries should supply, in response to receiving interlibrary loan, and of course they are net borrowers, is money. Money is still for all libraries, except for student labor in academic libraries, easier to get than people.

Twenty years ago I consulted over a period of several years for the Weyerhauser Company, a forest products business in the state of Washington, on the operation of its Research Center library. That library, because of limited holdings and expanding research interests even before the widespread availability of database access, was requesting between 100 and 150 interlibrary loans per week, virtually all journal articles, from the University of Washington in Seattle. Service was slow, and relations were not too pleasant. I made many recommendations during the course of my consulting assignment, but the one of which I am most proud was also the simplest. I suggested that, rather than submit interlibrary loans in huge quantities to the University of Washington, they contract for the hourly services of a University of Washington library science student, who would be provided with a large bag of nickels (the then-rate for photocopying). The student would call each morning to receive the list of needed articles (perhaps 30 or more), would proceed to make the photocopies from the bound journals, return these to the shelves, and have a package of copies ready by 4 P.M. that afternoon. The company mail vehicle, which always traveled to the Seattle Main Post Office, would be instructed to stop daily at the Suzzalo Library to pick up the material. One day delivery! However, I made one further recommendation. The corporation should make an annual tax-deductible contribution of $15,000 to the University of Washington Library in return for this courtesy. Corporate officials argued that they already contributed large sums to the University of Washington, but I stressed that this didn't count, because none of that money ever goes to the University Library. And that is what they did.

If obtaining later what you did not initially purchase or what you did purchase but can't supply becomes a natural management transaction and not a huge surprise (absurd as that might sound), then what you need is not a purchase budget but an access budget, some of which obviously goes for purchase, but much of it probably will not. The reason for allowing librarians this flexibility is that this is the most cost-effective approach. It makes such perfectly good sense that I am puzzled that the process of access versus purchase budgeting is used by virtually no academic libraries, and no public libraries of which I am aware at all. It is used to some extent in special libraries, but some of these libraries also attempt to pass along this cost to the requester or the organization in which he works. I consider this a particularly nasty and unethical process, and I will explain in a moment.

Right now let me address the implication of copyright, and to stress that, to a great extent, copyright compliance affects the cost of access but not access itself. I first became aware of this issue when I hosted at Indiana University in 1977, a conference at which librarians, authors, publishers, and government officials were all asked to comment on what was then the new copyright law. I intended to call the conference proceedings, which ALA published, "The Copyright Dilemma: A Rational Outcome," but I dropped the second part of the title when I realized that there was absolutely no agreement on the part of the speakers as to what the law specifically meant in specific situations. Some of that has been clarified, but some confusion still remains, and I must point out that at least some of this comes from the definition of "fair use," which was added to the bill largely at our insistence. Copyright owners did not particularly want a concept called fair use, they would have preferred to be paid for every copy made. It was Richard de Gennaro, then library director at the University of Pennsylvania and later at the New York Public Library and Harvard University, who pointed out that if fair use was interpreted as seven separate individual transactions from the same title, it should pose no problem for libraries at all. He argued that anything needed seven times should have been purchased, because there are plenty of titles purchased that are not used seven times. He suggested that libraries use interlibrary borrowing records to guide their purchase decisions.

Further modifications in copyright legislation might impact costs, but you already have my view that it does not necessarily impact access, only its cost. That is a problem, but is it our problem? It is if we assume, as Peter Drucker has suggested, the role of moral imperativists, those who insist that with or without money, they still have to do everything or it will be their fault. I would rather not carry that burden. In an ALA session in Washington last year, I shared a platform with a number of speakers, including Pat Ward, director of the library at American University in Washington, D.C. Pat expressed the concern that changes then being considered in copyright legislation would increase operational costs for libraries. I told her that if she believed this, she should inform the president of American University at once, in case he wanted to fight against this legislation, because if it passed, he would have a problem. He would either have to give the university library additional money, or he would have to explain to faculty and students why library service would get worse. Somehow, it rarely occurs to us, in any library setting, whose responsibility this really is. All we can do is run as good a library as we are allowed to run.

The management issues for librarians in considering their access alternatives are therefore, I believe, three in number: 1. What do we acquire in advance of need because we believe it will be requested? 2. What do we wait to acquire when it is requested, making the decision then as to whether we want to purchase or simply to acquire for that one user? The economics here is simply the purchase cost divided over the expected use versus the one-time temporary acquisitions cost. 3. What do we acquire as part of option 2, although we also acquired it as option 1, because we cannot now supply it within the time frame needed or at least reasonable. There are individuals fascinated by ownership as opposed to access. Many of these, I am afraid, are librarians. Libraries do not generally keep that most significant of Trueswell statistics—what percent of the things we own were we unable to supply?

There are, of course, also library users who are more fascinated by ownership than by access, but they are relatively small in number and restricted to academic research libraries. Public library and special library users don't really care where you get the material from, as long as you get it. Ah, yes, browsing. It is a public library phenomenon, but it is an overrated phenomenon even there, except for fiction. Academic and special library users rarely browse. They don't have the time, and the material is too widely dispersed in large libraries.

As a professor at Indiana University, I conducted a small and totally unscientific survey among my academic professorial colleagues. I asked them: "If I promise you that 90 percent of what you request will be furnished to you within 96 hours, and half of that within 48 hours, do you really care, and for that matter is it any of your business, where that material came from?" Their unanimous response was that they had absolutely no reason to care. The level of service I was suggesting sounded a lot better than what they were getting now.

It is a sad truth that we have allowed this activity to become trivialized, with an emphasis on process rather than on quality of results. Allen Veaner, at one time the director of the library at the University of California at Santa Barbara, noted rather bitingly in a paper published in *College and Research Libraries* that despite the tremendous improvements in technology, we had not made a great deal of progress in improving the delivery of documents to our patrons. Rather, he suggested, we had made a great deal of improvement in the sophistication of explaining why they ought to wait.

All right then, if the mechanisms exist and the issue is basically one of money for a basic library service, who pays? You already know that, in my view, the prime candidate is the requesting library, since it presumably made the make or buy decision as a normal business process explained to its own bosses. If, on the other hand, those bosses prefer a cheap to a good library, then you have to make sure that everyone understands what they decided. You already know that I am a great believer in the work of Peter Drucker. It was he who noted that in the absence of money, there is always money for whatever is important enough to do. Where else does the money for flood relief, for earthquake repair, or for troop deployments in Bosnia come from? None of it was anticipated.

The second area of responsibility falls to government agencies at all levels, local, state, and federal, particularly if the transaction involves two libraries both in a particular political jurisdiction. Encouraging resource sharing through one-time acquisition rather than full purchase is obviously more cost effective for them, and you can make that point. However, you must also make the point that having them opt for the cheapest option—not supplying desired information at all—has a political price for them when it is publicized.

The third and final group which needs to be mentioned is the requester, and I have already noted that some libraries seek to make the requester responsible for what is obtained on his or her behalf. I have considerable ethical problems with this approach, and when you hear me state them as indeed I have stated them, you may be glad that you don't have me as a library user. What is the rationale for seeking to charge me? I did not make the decision on what you would buy, and by not buying this, you have already penalized me once. Do you now seek to penalize me a second time because you are the one guilty of failing to anticipate what I would ask you for? It is obviously a rigged response, but I consider it fair based on what these libraries try to do. I can honestly state that in 20 years as a faculty member at Indiana University, I never paid for getting something on interlibrary loan, I simply refused to. Whether my approach was typical, or whether I got away with this because I was a full professor, then a dean, and then a distinguished professor, I do not know. However, I believe firmly that I was right.

Perhaps we should base our charges to our customers on the historical and traditional Chinese way of paying for medical services. According to that tradition, doctors are paid regularly while people are well. Payment stops when the patient becomes ill and is resumed only when the patient recovers. I like the approach as it applies to medicine, because it gives the doctor an incentive for curing you. Under the present system, his only incentive is in keeping you ill.

We might develop a similar charging system in libraries. If we provide what you have requested within 24 or 48 hours, you pay us a fee for our competence. If it takes between 48 and 96 hours, the transaction is a wash. If it takes more than 96 hours, we start owing you money, and, as with overdue material, the longer it takes, the more we owe you. In fact, I consider this overdue material. It is material you are late in delivering to the client. As overdues are designed to provide some incentive, so might this.

The one group which cannot be asked to subsidize the process of providing material not initially purchased or not now available in the requesting library is the document supplier. That should not surprise you, because we have been asking suppliers to assume at least some, and perhaps most or all, of this burden for a long time, and we have certainly noticed that it doesn't work. If the supplier now has no incentive for rapidity and efficiency, because that only causes more requests, that process will get worse, for at least two reasons. The first is the sheer growth in the process as bibliographic access continues to improve and the volume of material continues to increase. The second reason is that library managers are increasingly being asked to do exactly that, to manage, and that means taking responsibility for decisions which serve their own organizations.

If what we now call net lenders are going to be asked to continue and even increase their activities, it must be demonstrated to them and their own management quite clearly that they will not lose money every time this happens. This requires first of all that we determine the costs of this process as accurately and as believably as possible, and that we reimburse every cent of incurred cost. I have already noted that academic libraries, which fortunately also have the best collections, are best organized to be able to use the money to hire cheap and available student labor.

However, I have an even better idea for improving the quality of this service, and that is in providing a financial incentive above the actual cost. I hope that does not shock you, but you might agree that the best way to improve quality of service is to get providers to compete for the privilege of being allowed to supply these documents. Isn't that the kind of competition on which most quality of service provisions in this country have been based? I can even visualize the scenario. The director of an academic library summons the Head of Interlibrary Loan to her office. That individual, who knows what is coming, is visibly nervous. "I've been looking over the statistics of our own document supply to other libraries over the last three months. Can you explain this continuous decrease?" "Well, we've been losing customers to Trans-State University, which claims to be faster than we are." "Well, that just means that you will have to improve your responsiveness to match and surpass theirs. Don't you understand, we need this money?"

That's how improvements in document supply, to a maximum of 48 hours after receipt, and, of course, receipt is almost instantaneous using e-mail or fax, could be achieved. The technology exists. What is lacking is the recognition that this is important and worth paying for. And that is an awareness we librarians must create.

Never trivialize what you do in the attempt to be cheaper, because you will never be cheap enough. Concentrate on being good at what is obviously important. And it really is obvious, because no administrator or political leader is likely to come out in favor of ignorance or stupidity. Nobody I know in the real world I have inhabited for some time in the field of librarianship ever asks for things just for the fun of it. If people ask for something, that's enough of a reason for providing it. And, of course, technology not only makes it possible, but also makes what we can accomplish so much more important.

I have not talked at all about the new forms of access which are developing rapidly and which do not deal with printed copies at all. We deal here with information which is available only electronically, and not in printed form at all. Do our clients have the right to access this material? Of course. Do they have the right to expect even this to be a normal request to the library? Of course, unless we want to be so suicidal as to suggest that the library's role in providing access to needed information is limited by format. I am afraid that at least some librarians have been guilty of that form of snobbism, preferring to deal in books rather than reports because books looked more attractive and were able to stand up on their own. As a special librarian going back to the 1950s, I am aware of those biases—indeed the rapid growth then of special libraries came precisely from the fact that a new kind of library had to be developed in many institutions which would understand that sometimes technical reports, or patents, or art slides, are more crucially important than books to some users. However, the problems in providing electronic information are usually not mechanical. They are economic, and, of course, it is the need to deal honestly with economic issues which we must address in moving material—whether from the shelves of library A to the user of library B, or for moving material from a database to a downloaded file. In my experience those who have or own information don't mind selling or sharing it. They just want to be properly reimbursed. And this is really where I began this talk, and where I will end it. Operating a vending machine is easy, but it costs money. So does interlibrary loan.

Public Library Reference Service— Expectations and Reality

At the 1992 conference of the New Jersey Library Association Reference Section, I was asked how public library reference librarians, beset both by increased user demand and declining support, could continue to provide adequate reference service. My short and simple answer was that this is not possible, and accepting this premise would save much guilt and anguish.

Declining resources provoke changes and, ultimately, declines in services. Everyone should understand that. It's an ugly and bankrupt strategy to absorb more work in the face of budget cuts, even as some managers encourage it and some employees naïvely believe it. It is bad for us if only because it emphasizes clerical quantity over professional quality. Cuts in resources require new plans, strategies, and priorities—and this will be painful.

The management literature stresses that this should uncover activities of lesser importance, that can then be proposed to be cut. This might even be said to be healthy, because during times of affluence—if librarians can remember such times—this never happens. No credible manager would suggest to the staff that we simply work harder to make up for the funding shortfall because that implies we are malingerers. Librarians must understand that if declining funds do not bring devaluation of service that politicians notice, they not only validate that last budget cut but ensure the next one.

Reprinted, with changes, by permission of the author and *Library Journal* 124, no. 11 (June 15, 1999): 56–58. Copyright © 1999 by Cahners Business Information.

Whose Expectations?

None of this was new in 1992, but the conference theme suggested to me an even larger and more important question. Whose expectations of public library reference service? If we consider public library users, then we should know that their expectations are already too low. Unfortunately, our customers adapt graciously to declines in service, even as they fight ferociously against cuts in garbage pickup and pothole repair. They adapt, or they simply stop coming. If our users accept reference service at any level provided, it is because they have no way to compare.

Those precious few who are truly disappointed and offended are sometimes labeled by us as unreasonable, and eventually they leave. Swamped as we are, we may even be relieved. Studies that simply ask how users like the library always produce a positive response. This may keep us from being fired, but it is not useful if we are trying to stress unmet needs. No, users cannot be trusted to define the expectations for reference service, because they will settle for far too little.

Ask Administrators? No

If not the customers, then who? Certainly not the municipal administrators. They focus on cost and the avoidance of trouble, not quality of library service. They measure a library by what it spends, and they think that services should all be maintained despite resource cuts. That must seem silly even to them, but if it works it will be repeated. Sometimes these people are even sleazy enough to suggest that since they have no money, we should get out our begging bowls and find it for ourselves.

I wish I could suggest that top library administrators should define adequate reference service—and in a few situations they do. In many others, however, administrators simply become extensions of and messengers for municipal officials, primarily concerned with avoiding trouble.

Paul Wasserman and Mary Lee Bundy of the University of Maryland noted in the 1960s that a surprisingly large number of library administrators were already in the jobs from which they expected to retire. Such individuals are less likely to fight their bosses on behalf of staff. They have achieved their goal and have little to gain and much to lose by assertiveness.

Let Reference Librarians Do It

Reference librarians themselves are in the best position to determine the expectation of public library reference service. They know that the amount of time spent on a reference question cannot be predetermined by administrative fiat. It is 30 seconds in some instances, several hours in others. Imposing arbitrary time constraints places the budget ahead of the need and in effect trashes the need. If reference librarians are prevented from dealing properly with the reference question, shouldn't they at least tell the customer what an unsatisfactory level of service they are providing and that they could do better if they were allowed to?

Yes, they should. Reams of literature tell us that marketing creates an awareness of an unmet need. Did any of us really know that we needed cellular phones, call forwarding, and call waiting until the phone companies promoted them? Once we probably thought that one rotary telephone per home was enough.

How much need for reference service exists in the public library? We will never know as long as we keep telling people that we are already too busy. And then two things will result: some patrons go away and never use a library again, and those with money will go elsewhere. Neither option is a solution for our clients, or for us.

Knowing Whom to Blame

It is of course essential, in creating the dynamic tension of a recognized but unfilled need, that we know whom to blame when that need is not satisfied. But libraries are very bad at shifting responsibility to the real decision-makers; note the bitter comments of reference librarians who endure abuse from those patrons willing to acknowledge their dissatisfaction.

Has it never occurred to us to tell these individuals that we are all on the same side and that they should blame those responsible? Librarians now find themselves experiencing burnout—and, unlike others in that situation, burnout at low pay. We don't know how to shift responsibility where it belongs. We keep it on our own sagging shoulders.

Our increasingly employed tactic of directing reference clients to terminals does not absolve us of professional responsibility, even when these clients, and particularly the younger ones, comply and even when they insist that with a terminal they can do their own reference work. They use the terminals and then leave. Having done what? Having found what answers to what questions? Correct answers, or complete ones? Shouldn't we know? Shouldn't we care? Does the definition of a professional lie in the answer to these questions?

Claiming Our Expertise

Librarians have one clear, publicly understood area of expertise: reference service, or "information intermediation." Information and the avoidance of ignorance are recognized priorities throughout the nation, in communities as in corporations. Many lengthy discussions with wage and salary analysts have persuaded me that such reference service, as well as the more extended activity of bibliographic compilation, is a professional activity that they understand and accept, particularly when we use computers to do it.

Explanations of the professionalism involved in cataloging puzzles them. Doesn't the Library of Congress already do all of this? We can certainly argue but it is hard to win. Reference service is our professional ticket into the 21st century if we choose to take that ticket to the cashier's window. It should not be hard to demonstrate that we can find more relevant information on a terminal than an 18-year-old who has gained facility in net surfing and playing computer games.

How then should public librarians deal with the gap between potential and reality in reference service? By defining that gap as honestly as they can and recognizing that it is far wider than the public suspects. What will happen then?

Two Possible Tactics

Reference librarians have at least two possible tactics for response, and instinctively and mischievously I am drawn to the first. Why don't we do what doctors do? Let's give our reference clients appointments and then keep them waiting for 30 minutes as a matter of principle, so that they will have an even greater appreciation of what we do.

OK, that won't work, thought it might be fun to claim to be back-logged at least as much as electricians and plumbers (or, in Arizona, people who do yard work). However, we could certainly follow the second approach. If we are forced by budgetary constraints or administrative edicts to provide lesser reference service than we know we can and should provide, then at least we should inform the customers.

We should tell them that of course we could do more but that we are not allowed to. And, of course, we should tell them who made that decision and how little money it would take to get it reconsidered and reversed. Making our customers dissatisfied and angry is the first step toward a solution.

We're Professionals, After All

Let me offer another caution. Peter Drucker has noted that the shortage of nurses has grown even as the number of nurses has increased more rapidly than the number of patients. This suggests that nurses might be bogged down by duties—usually clerical ones—that do not require their unique skills and preparation.

Do reference librarians, equally in short supply to perform real reference work, face the same danger? Of course they do, but confronting that issue requires that we differentiate between the responsibilities of cosmopolitans and locals. Eight years ago I introduced my readers to that differentiation, articulated by Joseph Raelin ("The Conflict Between Professional and Organizational Loyalty," *LJ* 5/15/91, pp. 59–60).

Of course, professionals sometimes must perform clerical work on an emergency basis. However, if they do clerical work regularly because not enough clerks were hired, they betray both our profession and our clients by taking on such assignments.

They even betray our employers, because doing so accepts the premise that libraries need not be cost-effective. Once this is accepted, it is only a short step to hiring contractors because they are cheap, not good. There is even a perverse logic in that final decision. If the work that is going to be done is clerical, we might as well hire cheap clerks to do it.

If this seems strange to you, it is only because you have accepted your role as a silent, loyal, and unquestioning local, even if doing so betrays your cosmopolitan professional responsibilities. Reference librarians certainly know better than anyone else what they could be doing and are not being allowed to do, and this is particularly true in an environment in which computer technology gives a tremendous edge to such professionals. However, if reference librarians don't make this point, even as municipal administrators and their own librarian bosses would rather they not make it, no one else will ever know.

Edmund Burke

All that is required for the triumph of evil is that good men do nothing.

$*$ $*$ $*$

Your representative owes you not his industry only, but his judgment; and he betrays instead of serving you if he sacrifices it to your opinion.

—Edmund Burke

These two quotes from Burke—the first clearly attributed to him in *Bartlett's* but never formally verified, the second from his 1774 speech to the electors of Bristol—have played a key role in shaping my philosophy of the professional responsibilities of a librarian. It is certainly crucial that we protect the right of library patrons to access the information they want and need, but we must do more than simply react to the expression. Whether we work in academic, public, government, special, or school libraries, it is our foremost responsibility to assure unfettered and complete access to ensure that the library—through its collections, its access services, and its professional staff—makes this a reality and not simply an empty gesture. Whether for recreation, for education, or for information, our patrons deserve quality and timely service. Burke reminds us not only that this is our responsibility, but also that without our assertiveness it probably will never happen. The development of technology, which increases potential access to both the important and the trivial, which, in turn, blocks the patron's ability to find the important, only increases our opportunities and responsibilities.

Reprinted, with permission, from p. 30–31 of *Speaking Out! Voices in Celebration of Intellectual Freedom*, edited by Ann K. Symons and Sally Gardner Reed. American Library Association, Chicago, 1999.

Librarians have fought courageously against those who, because of their narrow viewpoints or their selective definitions of what information is worthwhile, have sought to hamper our ability to serve our patrons responsibly and equitably. Those fights have included battles against the FBI's badly thought out suggestion that we report library users with "foreign sounding" names, and our consistent opposition to those who, in their own narrow interpretations of what constitutes legitimate information access, have attempted to censor the works of Kurt Vonnegut, Anne Frank, and Mark Twain, along with so many others.

However, Burke also reminds me that our war is not limited to providing access to what we already have. Our first and greater responsibility is to assure that we are in a position to determine the quality of our libraries, their budgets, and their appropriate staffing. Particularly in an era of technology in which it becomes easy to be drowned in trivia and junk while looking for the significant, it is crucial that librarians provide not only access to information but also professional guidance to help assess that information. Burke teaches me that these concrete actions are far more important than slogans. Quality is still more important than sheer quantity, and we owe our patrons our professional judgment.

Librarians and Information Technology: Which Is the Tail and Which Is the Dog?

This article will argue, perhaps in contradiction to the discussions which precede it, that providing end users with more information does not really address their problems and, in fact, does not even identify them. Users want information in order to do other things, and this means that they must not only have the best information, but also not have it buried in quantities of other information which may be wrong but are more likely to be irrelevant and thereby misleading. Most importantly, our users need some assurance that what they found is the best that could be found. Dealing with these concerns does not require access to more information, it requires a process to sift the chaff from the wheat. Computer programs used by the end user cannot do this, but computer use by qualified information intermediaries on behalf of, and to protect, the end user can. This growth of specialists has been consistent for any field in which both complexity and options have increased, and the suggestion that computers can be programmed to do their own self-filtering effectively is at best naïve. Peter Drucker has predicted that the most important profession in the next century will be knowledge workers, and knowledge workers are not the same as computer systems specialists. The most competent ones are likely to be reference librarians using sophisticated hardware and software, tools which the end user does not know how to use.

Reprinted from *Library Trends* 48(1): 264–277, Summer 1999. By permission of the Board of Trustees, University of Illinois.

This entire issue of *Library Trends* deals with knowledge discovery or data mining, a relatively sophisticated application of electronic databases. However, most database use is not sophisticated, particularly through CD-ROM and the Internet. This puts databases increasingly into the hands of people who are ill-equipped to search them, but who do not necessarily know how ill-equipped they are. Unfortunately, the impression has been created that *anyone* can find not only the right information but also the "best" information by simply sitting down at a computer terminal. Librarians have unfortunately promoted and encouraged these misconceptions by their own insistence that end users search for themselves and to stop bothering the "busy" librarians. In this exercise, end users may or may not find the "correct" information, but they may also find huge quantities of information which are, for them, irrelevant or misleading. End users will then use whatever they found without ever knowing because we refuse to use our expertise to help them. Based on my own experience over the past half century in dealing with a wide range of information problems and services, I will use this article to point out the problems inherent in such simplistic and abdicative approaches.

I made the decision to become a librarian during my junior undergraduate year as a chemistry major in 1948. Part of the reason was my growing awareness that I probably faced very little of a future as a chemist except by working in a laboratory, and I didn't really want to do that for the rest of my career. The other reason came from the growing realization that neither chemistry students nor chemistry professors really knew how to find information in a university library. They would find "something" and make do with that. Whether they had found the best information or all of the correct information they would never know, although they would never admit that they had not found everything they should have found. Students were occasionally caught in that deception, faculty never were. All research reported from the literature was claimed to be complete, and that claim was simply accepted as true. At the time, I knew virtually nothing about librarianship, except for the observation that most librarians were humanists and had not the vaguest idea what chemists were talking about, but that they discouraged such conversations in any case. Researchers "were supposed to" find their own information. If faculty, but particularly students, were helped in anything but the most simplistic directional assistance, we were simply encouraging sloth. While I did not really know what librarians did, because I don't ever recall using my high school library, I was blessedly unencumbered by that ignorance. I only knew what I felt librarians should do, at least for chemists, although I learned quickly that it also applies to other fields. Librarians could and should find the correct information to meet the specific needs of each patron, in part because these individuals were untrained and incapable of finding it for themselves, but primarily because they would rarely if ever admit that shortcoming. Students sometimes get caught in providing incomplete and erroneous information, particularly if the instructor only assigns what he or she already knows. Working professionals are rarely caught in that deception, and the higher their level of prestige and importance, the safer they became. Indeed, if what they claimed to have found from their "research" was totally unintelligible to others, their claim to brilliance was safest of all.

I had no way of knowing then how correct my totally unsupported hypotheses were but, in the almost half century since becoming a librarian, almost equally divided between operational management and administration in the area of scientific information and the academic pursuits of academic research, teaching, and administration, I have learned the truth of my assumptions many times over. What has surprised me, and continues to surprise me, is the passionate unwillingness of many, if not most, librarians to assist the foundering (even if unconfessed) client to find what is really needed to meet an information need. Thus librarians who could carve out, particularly in an age of computerization, that which geometrically magnifies the amount of information (both useful and useless for the individual need), the crucial role of what I call information lifeguards and Peter Drucker calls knowledge workers, stubbornly refuse to do so. They prefer to handle administrative and clerical details, to build "gateways" to knowledge, and in any case never to intrude into the researcher's right to founder, thereby leaving us with the "rights," as one researcher invited to speak at a sponsored library conference suggested, to build boutiques of information and, when necessary, sweep the floors (Rockwell, 1997). This is certainly not any sort of professional agenda which a real profession, as described by Andrew Abbott (1988), would select for itself. There will be more about Abbott's premise and our failure to seek a road other than an insistently clerical one later in this article. For the moment, it will suffice to note only that this strange reluctance to take professional responsibility for what we presumably know perhaps uniquely, but certainly better than our clients, serves neither them nor us. It is a philosophy wrapped in the professionally self-deprecating "give 'em what they want," and I have suggested to medical librarians that our practice of simply showing clients to terminals and explaining how to use them without any attempt to determine how well they did in meeting their own needs amounted in their field to an encouragement of self-medication. It was the equivalent of saying to patients "Here is the pharmacy. Help yourself to whatever you want."

I learned very quickly, as a sci-tech librarian at the Library of Congress, the Atomic Energy Commission, and the aerospace industry, and well before my introduction to information technology by coming to work for IBM and later NASA nine years into my professional experience, that the scientific literature grew even more rapidly than I had assumed. Statements that each day enough scientific articles were written to fill several complete sets of the *Encyclopaedia Britannica* may have been inaccurate or even apocryphal but, even if they were close, they confirmed the impossibility that any individual, but particularly individuals who sought necessary information for the purpose, not of its own virtue but to be able to do something else with it, a process which would also require time, was doomed to fail. On a more specific note, I recall that, during my own vice presidency at the Institute for Scientific Information in the early 1970s, this company annually announced and described 200,000 new organic compounds, and that wasn't even all of them, only the most important ones. The literature growth in other fields may not have been as dramatic but, in any case, the "ease" of accessing information on computer terminals with which all now live as re-magnified this problem. Technology, whether in databases, listservs, or e-mail, brags about the large quantities of information we now receive. Whether or not it is good information is our problem as end users and, of course a growing problem as technology becomes "more efficient" in quantifying our access. Could librarians help here? Has it occurred to them to offer? Drucker has noted that, in his view, the most important profession after the start of the new millennium will be knowledge workers. Who are these people going to be? Drucker does not specify, but might they perhaps be the information lifeguards I call reference librarians? Or do they all have to have MIS degrees?

I am indebted to my long term colleague Herbert Brinberg (1986) for a cogent and simple definition of why different groups of people need and want information, at least in a professional setting. Chat rooms, playing solitaire online, and browsing for pedophilic and pornographic literature does not count, at least within the context of this article. Brinberg argued that basic pure researchers wanted only raw materials which they would then sift for themselves. Applied researchers and operational workers wanted specific answers to detailed questions. Upper level managers needed to know what their decision options were, and the implications of these options. Brinberg noted, quite correctly, that these different users required approaches suited to the individual need and not some overall policy. Some clients want only minimal help, others would happily turn the entire problem over to a librarian, if it is a librarian they trust. Twenty years in corporate information work has taught me that.

Librarians tend to treat all clients as though they were basic researchers, who only want to be pointed at information sources, although this is particularly true in academic libraries. However, even in the most prestigious institutions, there is very little basic research going on. This has been noted by such diverse sources as the *Chronicle of Higher Education* and humanist scholar/librarian Charles Osburn. My own confirmation comes from the Institute for Scientific Information's publication of "Who is Publishing in Science" (WIPIS). During the years (1970–1974) when I was connected with this publication, fully half of the authors cited for publishing in the literature wrote only one publication and never again. Even when they wrote more than one, it might well be the well-known process of extending one particular piece of research (such as a dissertation) into as many satellite articles as possible.

However, even if we prefer to deny the premise, well supported as it is, that only a few faculty members do a great deal of research and publishing, a great many others, particularly after they achieve tenure, do very little or none at all. However, even this research tends to become applied research, in the social sciences and humanities as well as the physical sciences, particularly because of the increasing influence of government grants and contracts. Such work is applied precisely because it seeks to "prove" what the funding application postulated.

Disproving your own hypothesis might be honest, but it would endanger the chances for additional funding. Most research is then decidedly applied because it seeks to accomplish two things: (1) validate the hopes expressed in the funding application, and (2) demonstrate the need for additional funding. Most "research," including academic research, does not seek raw materials. It seeks "proof" for what we already "know" to be true. The finding of contrary information, whether by the researcher or a librarian, is not always accepted graciously. As noted earlier, we can not only pretend that we found all of the needed information, but also that the conflicting data we did find was not found at all. This is not intended to be cynical, only an accurate observation. In all of my years in the corporate and academic sectors, I know of no scheduled policy or decision making meeting which was ever postponed because the literature review was incomplete. We have what we have by the deadline, and whatever that is we claim to be enough.

If librarians fail to serve applied researchers within the framework in which they work, they tend not to serve the administrators who seek to know what their options are at all, and we must remember that not only in industry but also in universities there are powerful administrators who long ago stopped doing research, if indeed they ever did research, but who in any case make policy decisions which affect the status and operation of libraries and librarians. Why librarians adopt stances and policies which are so consistently counter-productive is outside the scope of expertise of this writer and perhaps belongs instead in the field of psychology.

One thing we have long observed about any information system users is that they want what they want, and they object to having this cluttered by what they do not want. Not all of them, of course, and it is observation that suggests that no library reference service policy is ever totally appropriate. Different people want to be served in different ways, and the good thing is that, if we ask them how they want to be served, they will tell us, although that only works if we don't edict policies which label those who really want to be helped as either selfish or lazy. If that occurs, they will perhaps do the work themselves or more likely abdicate it to an assistant or secretary, or most likely pretend they didn't really need to know. That option is still open to them, as indeed it was in 1948.

However, one thing we should understand, because it is confirmed by operations research studies, is that individuals find the ideal information file to be the one that contains everything they want and nothing else. Faculty members who remove library books they might want to use again to that most relevant of all small files, their own offices, understand this instinctively. Since it is not usually possible to create an ideal world in which we have everything we want and nothing else, individuals react differently to the dilemma. In the 1960s, when I managed one of the earliest selective dissemination of information (SDI) systems for 600 NASA scientists, engineers, and contractors, we found that some individuals happily tolerated lots of "garbage" to make sure they received everything they really needed. Others, who already felt they received too much, bridled at even one notification which they considered as outside their area of interest. We fine tuned profiles to meet these ranges of individual preferences. That phenomenon of individual difference in preference exists today, even as librarians, and to some extent information technologists, insist that one size fits all as we buy information off the rack.

If individuals who work for a living and need information in order to do something with it have not changed, then of course what has changed has been the growth of a technology which brings more information directly to people more easily and more rapidly. It can even be argued that the provision is also more economical. What is not more economical is the human process of sifting out the chaff from the wheat, no matter how many clever software programs are developed. If this sifting is to take place, who should do it? The more greatly stressed, untrained, and probably more highly paid end user? Or one of Drucker's specially prepared, and often more lowly paid (at least in the case of librarians), knowledge workers or information intermediaries?

We can see an increasing reliance on intermediary specialists in many fields, if not in this one. Many of us recall the days when individuals spent Saturday afternoons working on their cars, including carburetor adjustments. Improvements in automotive technology, obviously for our own benefit, now make this impossible, although it is argued that the inconvenience of having to take our cars in for diagnosis and service is far outweighed by the advantage of having better performing cars. We have also seen this increase in specialization in fields such as medicine and dentistry. My regular dentist recently sent me to an endodontist for needed root canal work because he did not specialize in endodontistry. That individual, finding he was unable to save the tooth, sent me to yet another specialist for the extraction. We can certainly recall when one dentist would have done all the needed procedures.

The examples of automotive mechanics and dentistry are only two of what is really a wide range of examples which could be cited to demonstrate the growth of service specialist professions throughout the economy to allow us to take advantage of the greater opportunities and options which more complex technology, in all areas, now affords us. As opportunities become greater and procedures more complex, we rely increasingly on specialists, and economists confirm that the service sector—the people who do for us what we are now either incapable of doing or unwilling to do is the most rapidly growing field not only in the United States but in the developed world. That the particularly emphatic changes, growth, and complexity in the information sector should have given rise to a swelling cadre of what Drucker calls knowledge workers, and what I prefer to call information intermediaries or simply reference librarians, seems completely obvious. Indeed, it was obvious to Drucker, and his prediction may yet turn out to be completely true. The growth of management information systems (MIS) as an academic discipline is just one example of this phenomenon. However, what is disturbing, at least to me, is that the emphasis here is not on adapting machines to people, it is rather adapting people to machines. The extent to which this has now become the operational mantra of what once were called our library education programs are in charge of our institutions. Certainly the emergence of a new class of educators in our fields, who not only have no idea of what libraries are and do, but who also see no need to learn, tends to confirm this fear.

Why has the development of highly paid specialists who help the general public deal with new options, opportunities, and complexities, completely bypassed this field? How is it possible that, as both the quantity and the importance of information grow at a rapid rate, the number of reference librarians in academia, government, and industry declines (Abbott, 1988). It occurs to me that there are at least three reasons. The first is the fact, first noted by me in 1948 and since repeatedly confirmed, that information ignorance does not need to be admitted and is usually not admitted. Whatever we have is "enough." How, indeed, could we admit that we don't know anything? As a consultant in the assessment of corporate libraries and information centers, I have found quite a few which were inadequate, some whose librarians realize they were inadequate, but none whose users felt their library service was bad. What complaints they utter concern collection access, but even these criticisms are muted. The reason is obvious. If I am doing a good job, and deserving of promotion, salary increases, and grant funding, I must first state confidently that I am doing well and that somehow I know everything I need to know. The process is not as simple in automotive repair and dentistry, because a car which still does not run, or a tooth which still hurts denies the premise that everything is fine. Since end users and upper management either genuinely do not know or at least refuse to acknowledge how inadequately information processes serve them, it is incumbent that the people who presumably do know, the professional librarians, make the point not of how wonderful libraries are but rather of how inadequate they are and how good they could be. That librarians suicidally never made this point is, however, a part of my third reason and will have to wait.

The second reason comes from the incessant propaganda with which the developers and sellers of computer systems, both hardware and software, constantly bombard us. These messages tend to fall into three categories: (1) using technology is easy, (2) using technology is fun, and (3) using technology saves both time and money. This article will only cite one example of each of the first two because, thus prompted, the reader can certainly find his or her own. The best example for me of the argument that the use of technology is easy comes from a frequently aired television commercial for America Online. In it a young man urges his friend to come with him to a basketball game. The friend declines. He cannot go because he has to order airline tickets, he must send a birthday present to his mother, and because his child needs to go to the library to locate information on dinosaurs. The friend reassures him that this is all "easy" with America Online and, as we watch in admiration and fascination, the tickets are ordered, flowers are dispatched to his mother, and the printer disgorges pages of encyclopedia information about dinosaurs. What the child is supposed to learn from all of this is not clear, but it is assumed the viewer will not notice.

The second example of the point that using computers is "fun" is best demonstrated for me in a commercial for Hewlett Packard, which demonstrates ingenuity which I consider very effective. We are ushered into the plush office of a very busy executive through the use of an unobtrusive camera. We know he is an executive because the office is so large and tastefully furnished; we know he is busy because it is late at night and he is still hard at work on his Hewlett Packard computer. He rejects our interruption by stating that he is very busy and has no time. Suddenly he moans in anguish. When asked solicitously what has gone wrong, he replies that he has hooked his tee shot into the lake. We all know, and managers have learned, that computer terminals behind a closed door are a potential for doing work and also for wasting time and playing games. Hewlett Packard would be foolish not to stress this second feature, because it probably sells at least as many computers. I am not criticizing either company here for doing what obviously is intended to sell computers. That is their primary responsibility to their stockholders. The problem is not only that these advertisers have a lot of money (I haven't even mentioned Microsoft), but primarily that there is no counter-strategy by those most negatively affected, librarians.

The third argument, that the use of computers saves money, is of course nonsense, and even IBM had stopped stressing this advantage way back when I worked there in the early 1960s. It is both foolish and unnecessary to claim that computer technology is cheaper, when it is far easier and far more important to demonstrate that the proper use of technology (and even some of the improper use) is cost effective. However, it is wrong to make straight cost comparisons, because this would be a comparison between apples and oranges. Indeed, the use of technology is clearly potentially cost effective in libraries, primarily because it allows that far more effective work be done. However, we must deal not only with the additional hardware and software costs, we must also deal with additional professional staffing costs to use the advanced technological opportunities more effectively. That is why I now have the "privilege" of paying three dentists instead of one. It is good for my dental health. I am certain that corporate, government, and academic administrators really understand this as well, but perhaps I am wrong. Certainly librarians have made no attempt to make a point which should be easy to make—access to more information by more highly paid people who don't really know what they are doing costs more. Obviously.

The mystique that somehow having computers is enough to assure success in information and in education is perhaps best exemplified by the present federal argument, expressed by Vice President Albert Gore, that the solution to our educational problems is making sure that all school children have computers. Presumably not librarians, because they are not necessary. Learning to use computers is both "easy" and "fun."

All of which brings me finally to the third reason. I have always understood, in many years working with information technology, that vendors prefer end user searching to librarian searching. End users have more money, there are more of them, and because they search more sloppily they will spend more. I do

not resent this strategy because it makes sense—for them. However, silent acquiescence makes no sense for us.

The great problem for this profession is the lack of any sort of professional philosophy about what libraries are and what librarians do. The issues are
no longer discussed in our professional literature, and our library education programs
have moved away from any consideration of institutional management. Instead,
we have become survivors trying to cope under a barrage of budget cuts which
never consider the implications of those budget cuts simply because nobody
makes upper management face them. As an adjunct professor at the University of
Arizona School of Information Resources and Library Science, I now teach a
course in planning and evaluation precisely because I am painfully aware that, to
an overwhelming extent, librarians do not plan. Instead, they react to what others
have already decided about the future of the library. Planning, by contrast, is an
early process of pointing out to upper management the alternative implications of
various decision options before those decisions are made. Librarians have largely
abdicated any confidence that they understand what they ought to be doing far better
than anyone else, the essence of any professional discipline. Thus, the Baltimore
County Public Library motto of "give 'em what they want" rather pathetically
sums up the vision of many librarians. It is not "give 'em what they need" or even
"make 'em aware of what they could have and should have."

Nor do libraries really evaluate. Instead, they rig questionnaires
which only ask people already in the library, and therefore an obviously biased
constituency, how they "like" their library. As compared to what? The responses
may be predictable, but they are also not only useless but dangerous when we recall
Drucker's injunction that the essence of management communication is exception reporting—what ought to be happening but is not happening.

There are three distinct roles that libraries can play, and the later
named ones are far more important and offer far more potential than the earlier
ones. The first is the library's role in recreation. It is the easiest to explain and to
justify, and it is indeed the role, particularly for public libraries, that our clients
most easily identify. It is also, of course, the most trivial and becomes the most
dangerous during the budget review procedures which have become standard in all
management operations. These reviews force the ranking of priorities, and recreational activities (parks, libraries) can never compete against the priorities of police
protection, road repair, and public health. When libraries are judged in this environment, the evaluation usually comes out as "of course we favor good libraries,
but. . . ." In the context of the information world, this sometimes comes out as "of
course information is important, but what has this to do with libraries?"

The second role, in education, is the one which probably the majority
of librarians embrace. In this context, we don't so much answer questions as teach
students to answer their own questions. It is certainly a different approach from
that practiced by plumbers and mechanics who are not likely to teach us how to
fix our own leaks and transmission. However admirable one might consider this

role as an objective, it cannot succeed as long as the "other" educators, be they teachers or professors, fail to acknowledge us as partners of equal importance.

This trivialization of our educational role can be easily seen, on the one hand, in the willingness of teacher unions to sacrifice librarians to retain teaching slots. On the other hand, we must recognize the failure to grant (as at institutions like Harvard) faculty status to librarians, and the constant pressure to take both faculty status and tenure away from librarians. That pressure sometimes comes from administrators, but I have failed to see it ferociously opposed by the American Association of University Professors (AAUP). Finally, the failure of our "fellow" educators to accept us as full brothers and sisters can be observed in the traditional low, almost invisible, status of library programs and particularly library research within the federal Department of Education and the research-oriented Institute for Education. Educators have now neatly finessed this problem by transferring library programs to the Institute of Museums and Libraries, again with us in the junior positional listing and under the directorship of museum experts. And yet nobody in this profession, in its leadership, and in its professional publications finds this objectionable, let alone intolerable.

The third role, that of information intermediaries, is clearly the one which, in this age of growing information output, growing information access, and therefore growing information confusion, poses the greatest potential for this field, as Drucker recognized in his stressing of the importance of knowledge workers. However, acceptance of role number three causes a potential direct conflict with role number two, that of educators. In role number three we do not teach end users to solve complex problems without us, even as that educational exercise is at best problematical because we do not know whether such users whom we have turned loose in the information ocean ever find what they need—no I did not say want. WANT is, particularly for the unprepared, as irrelevant here as it is in medicine. In accepting our roles as information intermediaries, we seek rather to make our clients dependent on our unique expertise. To place this into the context of a profession's responsibility and sense of expertise, I will now return to the writings of Andrew Abbott (1988), briefly mentioned at the beginning of this article, and his definition of a profession. Professions, Abbott argues, have the unique responsibility of addressing human problems amenable to expert service, and I interject only to note the words *problems* and *expert*. Abbott continues that professionals compete vigorously for existing and newly emerging problem jurisdictions, and that they strive to expand those jurisdictions by preempting the activities of other professions.

The reader can certainly understand what sort of expanding jurisdiction, as well as amenable problem areas, computerized access to information represents, and it should be equally obvious what the other fields are at whose expense we should be expanding our jurisdictions. That the growth of computer-based information access not only provides opportunities but also changes the ground rules is certainly clear today. Indeed, it has been clear for thirty-five years.

In 1964, in what can be argued to have been the very beginning of the technological information age, my friend and mentor, Mortimer Taube (1964), the president of Documentation Incorporated, noted that the development of the MARC system by the Library of Congress, and its reliance on what is now seen as rudimentary but was still exciting technology, allowed librarians to rethink and completely restructure their cataloging rules, particularly with regard to subject analysis. That analysis, Taube noted, was constrained by the economic problems of having to file 3" x 5" catalog cards, and this limited subject analysis to the perfunctory level of perhaps one or two broad subject headings. Even the computer technology available in 1964 removed that limitation and allowed for analysis in far greater detail. Taube expressed the concern that the library profession would fail to see this opportunity and simply devise techniques for computerizing the Anglo-American Cataloging Rules. And that, of course, is exactly what we did do.

However, by far the greatest opportunities thirty-five years later lie in the expanded role for reference librarians to claim for themselves Abbott's territorial role in doing what others should not do and, more importantly, could not do. That we have failed to seize this opportunity is most evident in the decline in the number of reference librarians, even as we are deluged by reports of growing information files, growing information needs, and growing information complexity. Justifying additional reference librarians as the most cost-effective strategy for dealing with this issue should be relatively simple. However, we continue to see the strategy of National Library of Medicine administrators of teaching medical practitioners to search for their own information online, even as we are also told that the development of Health Maintenance Organizations (HMOs) increasingly turns the doctor into an overworked production employee with neither time nor energy for undertaking information searches at the end of a fourteen hour working day. Since medical librarians are both much cheaper and better trained for information searches, the solution should be obvious, yet no one sees and no one clamors for it.

In the absence of management courses in our library education programs, in the lack of professional discussion concerning our management strategies, and in the absence of research literature on this topic, it is difficult to understand why librarians insist on following a suicidal policy of shifting professional duties from their own desks to terminals to those of the end user, while they retain the routine activities which make them look like clerks. And yet they do. In reviewing grant funding proposals for the Institute of Museums and Libraries, I found numerous requests for additional money with which to purchase hardware and software for our end users. There were no proposals for funds to purchase tools to be used exclusively by librarians, to give them skills end users could never possess, and to make them more important. These are not disciples of Andrew Abbott.

Just as Peter Drucker predicts, the growth in the role of information intermediaries or knowledge workers is certain, even as the part which librarians will play is not nearly as certain. Once we get past our fascination with teaching children to play computer games on the premise that playing on computers is somehow more virtuous than playing soccer or basketball, and once we understand that having adults waste time on computers playing solitaire, surfing the Net aimlessly, or downloading anything for any reason or for no reason is more educational than watching soap operas on television, we will be left with the information needs of people who work for a living, and who need information in order to do this work. Herbert Brinberg (1986) has given us a clear indication of who these people are.

In addressing information needs of end users, there are two things we need to keep in mind. The first is that here, as in any other segment of society, we delegate what we can delegate, and save for ourselves only what we must do ourselves. The development of terminals in executive offices has not reduced the number of administrative assistants, precisely because having more assistants at our beck and call makes us more powerful. The second is that ignorance does not need to be admitted. Complete knowledge will be claimed whenever an admission to the contrary gets in the way of the primary objective.

For end users to delegate to information intermediaries, there are still two additional requirements. The first is that the user must trust the intermediary. Trust cannot be simply claimed, it must be earned. However, once it is earned, it is freely and openly given. Good reference librarians, whom clients insist on using even if they have to wait until they come on duty, understand this and appreciate this, and their bosses should also understand that clients usually know who the good librarians are. The second requirement is one of convenience. Clients want to be helped on their schedule and not the institution's. However, technology can be very helpful here. American Express learned long ago the virtue of establishing an 800 number telephone staff twenty-four hours per day. Whoever answers the phone has complete access to your file and can help you. The Social Security Administration has learned the same thing. Its 800 number is staffed 8 A.M. on the East Coast until 6 P.M. in Hawaii. You never get the same person twice, but it doesn't matter. The person who answers the phone is well trained, has complete access to your file and organizational policies, and can either put you on hold or call you back while he or she seeks either clarification or approval from a higher level of management. Is this possible for an online reference service? Of course it is!

Given acceptable options, clients will treat the increasing opportunities and options in information access exactly the same way they treat increased complexity in automotive repair and financial investment decisions. We delegate to a specialist whom we trust, and who will work within our time frame. A high level executive made the point quite clearly. He was delighted at the improvements in air transportations, which now allowed him to fly far more rapidly without the delay of refueling in a luxuriously appointed corporate jet. However, that did not prompt him to learn how to fly—not as long as he could hire a qualified pilot.

References

Abbott, A. (1988). *The system of professions*. Chicago: University of Chicago Press.

Brinberg, H. (1986). Unpublished talk presented at the Conference of the International Federation for Documentation (FID). Copenhagen, Denmark. September.

Rockwell, R. C. (1997). Using electronic social science data in the age of the Internet. In L. Dowler (Ed.), *Gateway to knowledge: The role of academic libraries in teaching, learning, and research* (pp. 59–80). Cambridge, MA: The MIT Press.

Taube, M. (1964). Unpublished talk presented at a meeting of the Washington, D.C. Chapter of the Special Libraries Association. May.

———————■———————

Why Outsourcing Happens, and What to Do About It

In the past 40 years, contractor organizations—known in some circles as the Beltway Bandits—have completely engulfed Washington, D.C. Of course, some of these organizations do very good and useful work, but there is no way for the public to tell. In official double-speak, the replacement of 600,000 federal employees by 1 million contract employees is always presented as a reduction of 600,000 and may even necessitate the expansion of certain activities. However, no public official will ever admit it.

Blame us citizens if you like. We insist on more services but don't want to be told they cost anything. And so we are told that they cost nothing. "Look at all the outsourcing we are doing." If it is said rapidly enough, people begin to think that contractors are free.

Let me make one thing very clear. The outsourcing of libraries has nothing to do with real fiscal economies. It has everything to do with the cosmetic *appearance* of fiscal economies. Funding authorities, public and private alike, usually outsource libraries because they think that it isn't important to employ knowledgeable librarians who are committed to the mission of the organization.

But whose fault is that, in the final analysis? The keepers of the purse strings (who are usually not firsthand library users) can't make an informed decision about the cost-effectiveness of replacing you, their in-house library professional, with a cadre of unknown contract information workers if they don't even know who you are or what you can do for them.

Reprinted, with changes, by permission of the author and *American Libraries* 31, no. 1 (January 2000): 66–71.

A case in point: One of my former Indiana University/Bloomington library school students took a job in the corporate library of a firm whose managers had not the vaguest idea of what the library could do for them. Indeed, she was informed on being hired that her most important job would be bundling up old newspapers for the Boy Scout paper drive, because the company president was active in the Boy Scouts of America.

Naturally, she made sure that all those papers were properly bundled up. But she also did a great deal more, and not only for her regular users. Instead of operating the library on a purely reactive basis—giving people only what they asked for—she trusted her own clear understanding of the firm's overall mission and provided both direct users and higher-level management with information she knew they needed, even though they never requested it.

Some two-and-one-half years later, both the president and executive vice-president flew several hundred miles on the corporate jet to attend her Saturday afternoon wedding. How likely were they to outsource her job after having established such a personal connection?

The people who make outsourcing decisions about libraries are not evil. Facing a political problem, they deal with it as best they can. They accept bids from often unknown and only perfunctorily evaluated contractors because they don't really know what difference a professionally run in-house library makes to their operations.

In a talk I gave to Air Force librarians in 1997, I suggested facetiously that if the Air Force really wanted to reduce staffing it should contract out the flying of its fighter planes to presently unemployed Russian pilots, many of them quite qualified, and certainly all of them cheap. Although the librarians understood I was joking, a handful of uniformed flight officers in the audience registered shock.

Obviously, the military doesn't contract out the operation of its aircraft or missiles because those functions are too important and too sensitive. But then why contract out military libraries, when qualified senior librarians help determine why we fly the planes and aim the missiles?

When Outsourcing Pays

Of course, it's possible to achieve better service quality, although usually at a higher cost, by contracting out an entire library. This is what the NASA Scientific and Technical Information Administration did in the early 1960s—a contract project for which I served as executive director from 1964 until 1968. Division director Melvin Day and his staff decided that using a contractor would afford them greater flexibility in securing quality. They could instruct the contractor to hire high-quality people regardless of seniority or government pay scales, and just as simply order the contractor to remove or reassign a particular unsatisfactory contract worker, something the government cannot do with its own hires. To ensure success, however, NASA retained a staff of professionals whose only job was writing, modifying, and monitoring contractor requirements.

The plan worked because Day's primary concern was not cheapness but cost-effectiveness; it often comes at a higher price, but is worth it, and is a perfectly valid reason for outsourcing.

There are several other valid reasons for outsourcing library operations:

- It is often more cost-effective to hire an organization that already has the skills and the equipment to perform such specialized tasks as translation, systems design, and large-scale microfilming. Just make sure that the contractor understands what you want done, and that he or she reports to a librarian rather than to a contracting officer who may not have a clue what is needed. I was once strongly urged, in the contracted management of the ERIC information system, to cancel a contract with Dialog because it is based in California. I was told to deal instead with a Washington, D.C., vendor because of the public relations value of awarding a government contract locally. It never occurred to the contracting officer that Dialog was providing proprietary services and databases.

- The use of a contractor is a great way to eradicate backlogs and reassign repetitive and routine operations that involve little if any intellectual contribution, such as processing book orders selected by the professional in-house library staff. Just about all organizations operate under headcount ceilings, and it makes sense to save those slots for the highly skilled people you want to interest in a career appointment.

Of course none of us want to squander money, and if those were the only reasons for outsourcing library operations (usually at the recommendation of the librarian in charge), there would be no problem. But the dollar savings aren't worth it if we lose something we really need in the process.

Management guru Peter Drucker saw all this when he stated that people don't care about cost when a product or service is something they really want. I have never heard of a military commander who decided to cut the size of a landing force in half because the rest of it wasn't in the budget. Kosovo wasn't in the budget, either.

That's true in any endeavor where the stakes are perceived as high. One of the cartoons I recall from my NASA days depicts two astronauts strapped in for lift-off. One asks the other if it gives him confidence to know that every component in the spacecraft was produced by the lowest bidder. The cartoon is funny because we presume that the statement is a wild exaggeration, and that NASA writes very careful specifications for what it buys. How carefully written are the specifications for the provision of your library's service?

Your senior management can always outsource another activity, and probably will once they realize that no contractor could possibly match the quality of understanding, caring, interest, and proactivity you contribute to the organization's mission. Why not stop by one of their offices and personally hand over a relevant informational item you've never been asked for? Perhaps they'll offer you a cup of coffee—and remember your name.

Does your senior management know what you do? Do they know what service cutbacks will result if they deny your requests for staff increases or cut your budget? Or do your reports pretend that everything is just fine?

The presumed savings of outsourcing libraries, even if real, just don't add up to the cost of one sophisticated fighting vehicle that can be lost by accident. Unfortunately, what libraries are supposed to do is rarely, if ever, discussed except in the aggregate—the number of books purchased, items circulated. The G & C Merriam Company, which has specialized in publishing high-quality dictionaries for many years, once successfully challenged an army RFP for pocket dictionaries. The specifications dealt with the number of words to be defined, but as Merriam noted this was nonsense without criteria for how well those words were to be defined.

It would be just as nonsensical if the specifications for military libraries, or any other type of library for that matter, detailed only the numbers of books to be purchased, periodical subscriptions to be placed, and the number of reference questions answered. How *well* are patrons' questions answered? What of the questions that the patron never asked but a qualified librarian should have anticipated? And who will judge the library's performance? A contracting officer certainly isn't capable of it; probably the end user isn't either.

Information retrieval has become far more complex and crucial as we enter the technological age. We won World War II largely because our technology continued to improve while our enemies could not keep up. What was true then is even more true today. I once visited the CIA library in suburban Washington and expressed surprise that so much of the collection resembled that of any other library. It is not the collection that matters, I was told. It is the questions that need to be answered.

Beat Them by Joining Them

No librarian can sit back and simply deliver documents as they are requested. Any contractor can do that, and in that case the cheaper the better. In its recently developed mission statements the Special Libraries Association stresses that to be effective special librarians must be privy to planning and decisions at the highest levels, so that the library can support those activities. In other words, there are limits to what can be outsourced.

A library's management must be comprised of people who can be trusted to sit in on policy decisions. As executive director of the contracted NASA Scientific and Technical Information Facility, I was never privy to everything.

However, several high-level NASA staff members, one of them in the office next to mine, did have that knowledge, and made sure that I knew what I needed to know—not just to react to directives, but to work proactively. That, at a minimum, is what needs to happen in a contract operation.

Of course I also dealt with contracting officers. However, those contacts were not substantive in the information context because the contracting officer didn't know enough. In the dictionary RFP context, he could determine how many words we were to define, but never how we defined them. It takes other lexicographers to do that, just as it takes senior librarians to monitor the contractor.

The key is communicating up the chain of command, not only what you have done (you'll brag about what went well in any case) but what you can accomplish on their behalf with adequate resources. As management guru Peter Drucker noted long ago, the essence of effective management communication is exception reporting—what went badly, what didn't happen at all, and why it's bad for the organization.

Does upper-level management know what you do, and what you're capable of? How many of your superiors would come to your wedding?

Authority, Responsibility, and Delegation in Public Libraries

When my management students—particularly those who already work in public libraries—deal with case studies, I can expect a specific reaction to one problem. At the suggestion that a particularly volatile issue should be brought to the board for policy resolution, some students say that the board doesn't like to be bothered by such potentially embarrassing problems. I respond that, while this is probably true, board members also don't want to learn from the local newspaper that the library is being sued. Their strategy is authority without responsibility.

The relationship between library boards and directors is clear—at least in principle. Boards make policy; directors run the library. Problems occur when those simple lines are crossed, because boards refuse to make policy, preferring to second-guess our policies, or when they insist on making daily decisions about library operations.

Learning How to Delegate

The relationship between any administrator and his or her governing body must be negotiated, then spelled out in carefully written language that leaves no room for misunderstanding. In lower-level relationships, that is called a job description, and it must be specific enough to anticipate most circumstances. However, when "other duties as may be assigned" cover 80 percent of the tasks, what may be comfortable for the supervisor is useless for both the subordinate and the organization.

Reprinted, with changes, by permission of the author and *Library Journal* 124, no. 15 (September 15, 1999): 59–60. Copyright © 1999 by Cahners Business Information.

The latitude to make certain decisions in your job falls under the heading of delegation, that much-praised but little understood (and even less practiced) management principle. Delegation encompasses not only the freedom to make decisions but also the freedom to make some wrong decisions. You should discuss and negotiate how many wrong decisions are acceptable, but it seems clear that the worst situation is one in which there is fear of making any decision because it might be wrong. When that happens, we have paralysis, the worst of all management situations.

My students know that for many of my Monday class discussions, I draw from Sunday sports television, because management issues are so clearly spelled out by intrusive cameras that record every facial expression. Most professional football teams have the coach send in or signal the next play for the quarterback. However, that decision is based on assumptions about the defense, and defensive coaches on the other team are also sending in signals. For that reason, quarterbacks may change the play at the line of scrimmage. This latitude is part of delegation.

Most of the time such changes avert a disaster, but sometimes they cause one. When that happens, the coach must practice immediate self-discipline—his management duty—and suppress his frustration. On Monday he can decide whether this quarterback makes too many mistakes and must be replaced, but even a new quarterback must be allowed some leeway. Still, during the game he must avoid destroying team and player moral.

Any coach (or any public library board) who suggests that quarterbacks, or directors, are free to make decisions only if they're correct assures the development of robots who will choose safe decisions over smart ones. Managers, be they library board members or football coaches, must avoid the easy temptation to scream at subordinates in public for making honest mistakes. It immediately destroys all initiative.

We Need Contracts

Because all managers make some mistakes, and because good managers make more mistakes than poor managers simply because they are more willing to make decisions, higher level managers need contractual protection against arbitrary punishment. Football coaches and even star quarterbacks can of course be fired, but contractual protection specifies how long they must be paid.

Any individual responsible for highly visible and controversial decisions would be a fool to take a job without contractual protection. That includes superintendents of schools, university presidents, and tenured faculty members; even untenured faculty must usually be given a year of notice. But this most obvious protection almost never extends to directors of public libraries, who serve at the "pleasure" of the board. Library directors have a very uncertain relationship with the body that appoints them, because board composition often changes with no input from them.

Legislative Protection

Why is there no protection for public library directors? Unlike police and fire chiefs, they are not covered in protective legislation. The absence of such legislation usually points to the absence of a noisy lobby behind it. Why can police chiefs make more political noise than public library directors? Is their public image more positive? Sometimes, but invariably they are more visible.

However, the absence of legislative protection does not rule out the negotiation of contractual protection. Any agreement between two parties that does not adversely affect the rights of third parties tends to be legal. Public library directors should be able to negotiate contract terms the way coaches and school superintendents do, including settlement pay for termination.

Then why don't they? And, more importantly, why don't state library associations apply pressures and suasions to urge library boards to include such contractual language? Tactics could range from blacklisting noncomplying libraries from participation in interlibrary loan to a public exhortation that no one take a job under such terms.

There are many explanations for such failure, but at least one can be attributed to the mixed nature of such associations, including both librarians and their employers. It would be far-fetched to call this "sleeping with the enemy," but it's too simple to explain that this affords an economy of scale in association headquarters staffing. There are many issues for which librarians and their employer boards can make common cause, especially if those board members are committed enough to join a state association. However, they will differ on other issues, and employment protection for directors is probably one of them. The Chamber of Commerce and AFL/CIO may agree in condemning international competitors, but they have not yet discussed a merger.

When Users Don't Pay

For a classic example of authority without responsibility, consider the situation of individuals who live in one library taxing district but use libraries elsewhere, perhaps near where they work. That imbalance will continue to grow as residents of bedroom communities filter into the main city for their jobs, then go home for dinner.

Librarians have known this, but we have pretended not to notice. It is more pleasant to simply serve everyone. However, it is politically unjust and perhaps legally shady. We condone what is really mooching by trying strenuously to avoid knowing the real costs of service. Fortunately, net lenders increasingly understand the impropriety of stealing from their own clients to support strangers. In stores, you can be prosecuted for shoplifting or paying whatever you feel like. Is it so different to borrow something from a library you do not support?

Much as we worry about the unfairness of such inequities, they are not our professional or even ethical problems. The problem belongs to the state legislature under whose jurisdiction all of these users reside. Unfortunately, state legislatures would rather not deal with it. The problem will grow, because an increasingly mobile commuting population will want to use the most convenient library, particularly if it is also the better library, as larger and older urban libraries may be.

Certainly the citizens who built a better library deserve protection against having it plundered, but who will pay for this use? It could be the individual borrower, under either an annual or transaction fee designed to recover costs. It could be the borrower's own taxing district, if officials recognize that this is cheaper than raising the standard of the local library. However, most logically it should be the state legislature's job.

Punting the Problem

A legislature in one Midwestern state has neatly abdicated its own responsibility with a "solution" as bizarre as it is Machiavellian. These solons decided that cross-district borrowers should indeed pay some sort of annual fee. The determination of that fee could easily have been made through studies carried out by library and public administration schools.

However, the legislators preferred not to be confused by facts. They mandated a fee small enough so that individuals would pay it without protest to the legislature itself. If lawmakers calculated correctly, they have every reason to feel smug. They have spent no money and have not alienated voters.

Who then is left holding the bag? The public libraries that lend to commuters who pay no taxes and the local residents who support those libraries, mistakenly assuming that what they have paid for belongs to them. Public librarians in this state will acknowledge privately that the mandated fee is much too low but hope that someday it can be increased. Is there a basis for that hope?

Why do we as managers agree to something that violates all rules of fairness, as well as those of authority and responsibility? When I hear these expediencies defended as "all we can get" and "better than nothing," I understand the primary reason for so many of our political dilemmas. We are such passive and amiable victims.

Is Our Mission One of Providing Only Information or Providing Knowledge?

It has been many years since Peter Drucker noted that automation was not really about machines, but about how machines could help individuals work more effectively as they desired to work. Technology, in other words, is a tool toward achieving an end, and not an end in itself. As technology is then applied to our work, it allows us to access a great deal of information—rapidly and cost effectively. However, information is not an end in itself, it is rather a tool for allowing us to achieve something for which information can be useful only once it has been turned to knowledge, and that knowledge has then been utilized to do something else. In an article in *The Atlantic* several months ago, Drucker updated his earlier observation by noting that what individuals wanted as an end result has not been changed by technology, although they may now approach those ends differently.

It was Drucker's recognition more than a decade ago that, while there would now be a great deal more information available and easily accessible, this really compounded the problem for those seeking knowledge in order to be able to do something with it. He therefore postulated that the most important profession after the start of the new millennium would be the profession of knowledge workers, experts who would sift and filter huge volumes of information to provide the information needed to address a problem—the knowledge as differentiated from the trivia

---

Talk presented to Tucson Health Sciences Librarians, November 3, 1999.

and garbage (and, of course, one person's jewels of knowledge are another's trivia). In making this prediction, Drucker was probably only extending his observation, and also your and my observation, that as technology and other advancements made life more complex, there would be a greater need for expert services to protect, filter, and interpret. To see examples of this, you need only think of what is now under the hood of your automobile. The machinery is now far more effective, but the price you have paid is that it needs to be tended by experts. Much of it can no longer be tended to by the owner in the driveway on a Saturday afternoon, because the owner has neither the expertise nor the tools, many of them expensive and electronic. Serious maintenance can no longer be done by the corner service station mechanic, because he also lacks many of the tools. We accept our reliance on help from the "service professions," probably willingly and gladly. However, in any case we have no choice. The price of improvement has been complexity.

To relate this experience to a field health sciences librarians can certainly understand, you certainly recognize that the field of medicine is now full of referrals, from generalists to specialists. The entire premise of Health Maintenance Organizations (HMOs) is that you must first see your primary care physician, who will solve the simple problems, but then refer you as needed to specialists who can help you. You call that process triage, and in some HMO waiting rooms, it is performed by nurses. To cite one simple personal example, last year I was unfortunate enough to require dental work which included fillings, a root canal, and an extraction. No one dentist will now do all of these. I needed three separate appointments, with three specialists.

When Peter Drucker predicted the importance of an emerging profession of knowledge workers, he was undoubtedly drawing his conclusion from his observation that more information might or might not include better information, but that in any case, the best information would be harder to find in a large information file which also included "garbage." Operations researchers have known this for a long time, in their observation that the "perfect" information system contains that which is of interest and little if anything else. University professors have always sensed this instinctively when they remove library materials of interest to their own offices, not necessarily because they need it now, but because it will be easier to find when and if they do need it.

Peter Drucker's prediction of the importance of knowledge workers did not extend to a forecast of who these people would be. However, the fact that others can see an opportunity even if it is vaguely defined, and perhaps particularly because it is vaguely defined, can be seen from the growth of academic programs in "information management," whatever that might be. As I learned in my physics classes long ago, nature abhors a vacuum, and this vacuum will most certainly be filled. There will certainly be knowledge professionals to filter for the hapless end user what is not only useful but also the most useful. The process of identifying and empowering knowledge workers is being delayed to some extent by the insistent clamor by hardware and software manufacturers that finding what you need is both "easy" and "fun." Why they stress these characteristics is not difficult to understand. Selling their services to individuals who inevitably search longer because they search more inefficiently improves profitability. However, managers in industry, government, and even academia are beginning to understand that the use of technology as an information finding tool so that it can be turned to knowledge is a process which can take place more or less cost effectively, and so they must continually search for cost effectiveness. The premise that "everything" can be found "easily" and "rapidly," so that if it wasn't found in the first five minutes, it obviously does not exist will linger only with our enthusiastic if also naïve child clients. Or perhaps it will linger also with librarians, who believe that once we have "trained" the users on how to log on and off, our work is finished. Is such naïvely suicidal behavior possible? Stay with me.

In the days before the ease and fun of technology was incessantly preached to us, at least some librarians understood that their professional future lay not in quantity but in quality. In the 1920s the Special Libraries Association (SLA) adopted a motto which is still applicable today. That motto is "Putting Knowledge to Work." That is more specific than a motto of putting knowledge in a large pile of information onto the desks or the terminal of the client. In the mid-1960s, when I managed over 600 Selective Dissemination of Information (SDI) profiles as Executive Director of the NASA Scientific and Technical Information Facility, I understood that while a few users wanted everything which might be of interest and would endure wading through what might not be, the great majority considered themselves far too busy to do this. They willingly took the risk of missing something useful as the price for not getting material which is not useful. A number of them even chose the very non-scientific option of specifying that they did not want to be informed about things for which there was not at least a complete English-language abstract. The trade-off between quality and quantity as a part of cost effectiveness and time management continues to this day, even as perhaps some of you might regret it. It most certainly applies in the field of medicine. As you well know, the rise of HMOs has turned physicians into production workers. The nuggets of knowledge may well exist on *Medline*, well mixed with what is for them the trivial, but they now have little time and less energy to spend on information research. If you don't tell them what at least you have selected as potentially important for them (and please, no more than 10 items per week), they will never know. Do you begin to see your critical role as knowledge professionals, in partnership with the medical professionals?

At a conference of the International Federation for Documentation (FID), Herbert Brinberg, then president of Aspen Systems Corporation, noted to his Copenhagen audience in 1985 that the information needs and preferences of our professional clients could be divided into three categories: 1. Basic researchers were looking only for raw materials, and would gladly assume the responsibility for sifting through this to find what they needed. 2. Applied researchers and operational managers were looking for specific answers to specific questions. They had already determined what they thought they needed to know, and in many cases were only looking for confirmation or proof for what they hoped and assumed was the case. 3. Higher-level administrators needed to know what their options were, as well as the implications of implementing these options.

Brinberg noted, and indeed I have also observed, that librarians tend to treat all of their customers as though they were basic researchers. In universities this might be considered to make some sense, except for the studies by Ladd & Lipseth reported regularly in the *Chronicle of Higher Education* that there are very few basic researchers left in our universities. At least part of this is because of the importance of research grants, which to a large extent pose a hypothesis as a basis for funding support, and then seek for the proof of the validity of that hypothesis. It might be acceptable one time to tell your funding body that your valuable findings are just the opposite of what you had assumed, but don't make a habit of it. To a great extent, our academic clients are seeking only to fill in the gaps in the garment they have already woven. The fact that academic librarians don't deal with what Brinberg describes as the needs of high-level administrators at all may help to explain why there is often so little interest in the administration building in what the library does, only in what it spends.

Why we would treat clients in the public library as though they were academic researchers searching only for raw material is even more puzzling. As we have all seen, users of all sorts of qualifications and preparation march into a public as into an academic library, are shown to a terminal and perhaps taught how to operate the terminal, and then are left to their own resources. Eventually, they leave, usually without ever talking to us again. Certainly we make no attempt to intercept them. They leave, having found what? Correct answers, incorrect answers, incomplete answers, obsolete answers? They will now act on the basis of what they now *think* they know. What is our role here, when we have made no effort to ascertain the question, or to determine how well that question was answered? How does this "professional" role compare, for example, with that of doctors? Would they suggest that, because they are so busy, we simply step into the pharmacy warehouse and help ourselves?

It should not really surprise us that there is a large body of popular opinion that thinks we perform no professional role at all. They see us as amiable record keepers, and they fail to understand why somebody needs a graduate degree to do what they think we presumably do. In an article about three years ago, the national newspaper *USA Today* identified three fields for which it saw no future, precisely because of technology. Those jobs were those of telephone operator, bank teller, and librarian, because they all involved tasks which would be done by computer, and without the need for human interaction for such repetitive and routine tasks.

Before we become angry, we should probably ask ourselves if we don't really believe it ourselves, at least a little. As we stress the virtues of the "virtual library," are we now suggesting that end users can undertake all (and not just routine look-up) information transactions? I realize that this is what hardware and software companies tell them, and I can certainly understand both why they do it (they stand to make a lot of money) and why people tend to believe this (they have a lot of money to spend on convincing us). We know that political leaders, and not just the editors of *USA Today*, have come to believe it. Vice President Gore, the technological/educational spokesperson for the present administration, has argued for the need to provide every school child with computer terminal access. This is perhaps admirable as far as it goes, but the Vice President never mentions the need for libraries or librarians. Apparently self-service computers are enough to find whatever one wants. Can we be certain that a Republican Vice President would not have said the same thing? We all watch the incessant television ads.

Apparently librarians at Harvard University have watched those ads, and believe them. The Harvard libraries, with assistance from the Council on Library Resources, sponsored a conference presumably dedicated to building "gateways to knowledge," but primarily dedicated to trivializing our professional responsibilities. Perhaps not surprisingly at Harvard, where no mere librarian can aspire to become director of the university library, speaker after speaker extolled the library's "role" in channeling raw information to the desks and terminals of the scholars as really all we needed to do, and even more tragically, all they needed to have done for them. Speakers noted proudly that, with the new technology, they never had to come to the library at all any longer, and I can only surmise that this would free them of the need to interact with librarians. Only one "scholar" speaker mentioned librarians as people, and he saw their role as managers of a boutique, opening the doors for customer access, and sweeping the floors as necessary.

What then do we see as our own future role? Is it simply to serve as a facilitator allowing people to do their own work? What other field, let alone profession, would set aside such a role for itself? Do we see ourselves simply as educators who step graciously aside once students have learned? If that is our perceived role, what success have we had in persuading the "other" educators, be they classroom teachers or university professors, not only that we are their total equal but that we are exactly like them? It isn't much fun to claim membership in a club which won't even admit you. Or should we be carving out the role of knowledge professionals which Peter Drucker predicts as a fantastic future—for somebody?

Before we can even decide, we must have some understanding of what a profession is and what professionals do. Andrew Abbott, in *The System of Professions* (University of Chicago Press, 1988), spells out the characteristics. Abbott argues that professionals accept the task of addressing human problems amenable to expert service, and it should be clear that *human* (not machine) problems, and *expert* are all key words here. He notes secondly that professionals vigorously fight to protect their jurisdictions from inroads from other professions, and third, that professionals strive to expand their jurisdictions by preempting the activities of other professions. You may want to give some thought to how well we protect and expand our jurisdictions, in our dealings with technologists, MBA and MIS specialists, and with our end user clients.

During my term as Dean of the Indiana University School of Library and Information Science, I had one experience which, in hindsight, is really quite amusing. I was called by the Dean of the Faculties (in many institutions the Vice

President for Academic Affairs) to pass along the complaint from one professor. Apparently one of my masters students, using her own computer and charging for the service, had compiled a literature search which an undergraduate had then used as part of his assignment. What was I going to do about this? I countered with a question. Had my student done a good or a bad literature search? I was told that the search was obviously very good, because its high quality had alerted the professor to the likelihood of involvement by someone else. I responded that if the search had been excellent, I would seek out my student to congratulate her on the quality of her work. What she had done is exactly what I was teaching my students to do, to assist clients by the use of their own particular talents and expertise. Sadly, neither the dean nor the professor had any idea that this was what librarians did.

Since I have certainly conveyed to you at this point my own view that our profession's future lies not in the role of second-rate educators and technological enablers but as first-rate and unique knowledge evaluators, let me close with the observation that others are beginning to see the same opportunities. The Special Libraries Association, which for a decade had stepped away from the simple role spelled out in its motto and embraced a special librarian role as an information guide, trainer, and facilitator, has apparently realized that these are the first jobs eliminated during a downsizing exercise. Hopefully convinced by the closing of a number of special libraries, SLA is now holding workshops to persuade its members of the importance of claiming organizational roles as knowledge experts.

In the last two years, at least two prominent librarians, F. W. Lancaster (*Library Journal*, September 15, 1999), and Allen Veaner (Newsletter of the Willamette University Library, Fall 1998) have argued that the library profession must rethink its future role. Lancaster argues that we may have become besotted by the claims made on behalf of technology. He cites in particular a 1997 report published by the European Commission entitled "Public Libraries and the Information Society," which states flatly that the ultimate goal of libraries is to provide access to any type of information for anyone, at any time, anywhere. Technology can already provide the answers. Lancaster asks what justification could exist for such an assertion.

Veaner argues passionately that we combat the simplistic arguments presented by the media and the software publishers, and that we abandon our modesty. He states that librarians know how to produce, organize, and manage information, and that we are particularly well qualified to distinguish the valuable from the worthless, something that end users who believe that anything not found in a few seconds does not exist, cannot do.

Let me close by stating that if you, as Health Sciences Librarians, would like to follow the steps outlined by Andrew Abbott, you have every reason for success, precisely because the medical information field is so swamped in information, and because medical practitioners are so swamped in overwork. You have two groups to persuade. The first consists of hospital and health sciences center administrators, to whom you must demonstrate that work done more rapidly, more correctly, and more cheaply by health science knowledge professionals is more cost effective than having it done by the more highly rewarded but already overworked medical practitioners. You should not be afraid to invoke the assistance of financial analysts in this process, because financial analysts are neutrals without an ax to grind. Make sure your management understands that you will carry out this work according to the *qualitative* standards of your professional responsibilities, and that you would not think of cutting corners any more than any other professional working here. The *quantitative*, how many people you can serve, how large the backlogs might be, depends on them and the funding and staffing they provide. You will take responsibility for qualitative implications good or bad; they must take responsibility for the quantitative ones.

The second group you must persuade to cede you this territory of knowledge work are your clients, and I can assure you that the vast majority will happily allow you to do as much for them as you are willing, but only *if they trust you.* Trust cannot be demanded, it is voluntarily ceded, not to organizations but to individuals who are personally known and respected. The good news is that this trust, once given, will be renewed unless or until you betray it, and I have already stressed that you, like any professional, must never allow funding or staffing limitations to let you perform careless, shoddy, or incomplete work. This is of course true in any library setting in which librarians consider themselves professionals, but the dangers resulting from poor work are far greater for you. Make sure that your bosses know.

We know from a number of examples, particularly in academia, that learning how to access still more databases is not a particularly high priority for professors, and probably also not for doctors. Invited to participate in such training programs, many decide instead to send graduate assistants, student assistants, and even secretaries. No, your clients will not fight you for this territory, they have other territories to protect, but not from you. If you stake out your claims as knowledge professionals, you will have participated in what is clearly a win-win exercise. The results are good for you. They are also good for the organization that hired you to use your professional skills for its best advantage.

Where Is This Profession Heading?

I began my White Papers column on February 15, 1985, and this, column number 123, is my last one. The opportunity to comment on a wide range of professional issues has been wonderful, but I have decided it is time to stop.

I am now past my 72nd birthday and officially retired for more than five years. While I will probably continue to teach, speak, and write somewhat, I intend to enjoy more theater, classical music, and sports. I will remain for at least two years as vice president of the Coordinating Council of the unincorporated retirement community of 25,000 that is Green Valley, AZ (once an administrator always an administrator), but, basically, I hope to change gears and perhaps even slow down. I may even find more time to use our excellent public library.

While some columns have taken a lighter tone, my concerns have always been serious. I want to thank a whole range of *LJ* editors with whom I have worked. They have occasionally dabbled with my sentence structure to place periods where I usually prefer semicolons, but they have never suggested that I should avoid a particular subject or eliminate a thought.

My greatest appreciation goes to John Berry, who initially invited me to write this column and who devised a title I originally thought corny but have come to cherish. I have had little direct contact with John in the last few years, but we both know that we disagree on several professional issues. I am certain that he has disagreed with some of my columns, as indeed I have disagreed with some of his editorials, but he has never sought to dissuade me from a topic.

Reprinted, with changes, by permission of the author and *Library Journal* 124, no. 19 (November 15, 1999): 44–45. Copyright © 1999 by Cahners Business Information.

What Is Our Unique Role?

As I write this last column I continue to be puzzled by my failure to understand our professional objectives—as opposed to sociopolitical ones (we have lots of those). What is our unique role and our unique contribution? In the 50 years I have been a librarian I have at least known why I entered this field.

As an undergraduate studying chemistry, I recognized very early on that there was little successful communication between scientists and librarians in my institution. Science students and professors did not know how to find things in libraries and therefore often settled for incomplete information. Librarians, I observed, tended not to understand what the scientists were talking about because they had studied the humanities or social sciences.

I hypothesized that a library career could achieve that communication and save me from a lifetime in a smelly laboratory. I posed that hypothesis to every library school dean I could identify while I was in the military during 1946–47 and received unanimously encouraging responses. I returned to City College of New York to finish my undergraduate degree, then used my G.I. Bill benefits to obtain the library degree.

Where It All Began

I began my professional career as an intern at the Library of Congress without regular library work experience, and in that I consider myself fortunate. While generalizations are unfair, I have since found in 25 years as a library educator that at least some students with library work experience have had all initiative crushed, accepting the premise that their clients, particularly in academia, are superior to them. That is not modesty but self-denigration, and it is professionally suicidal. Sometimes the customer is wrong.

I am firmly convinced that my initial instincts were correct. Many library users, particularly academic library users with advanced degrees, don't know how to find what they seek and, more tragically, don't even know that. The advent of library technology, with a greater emphasis on cost-effectiveness in an expensive and important setting, has increased the need for specialists to serve as intermediaries between highly sophisticated information sources and the still largely uninformed and untrained end user population.

The number of specialists has grown in many fields, from automotive repair to medicine. As a youngster I found that my dentist did fillings, root canals, and extractions. Most recently, I needed three separate appointments with three different specialists. In the information field the need for specialists has been recognized by such astute observers as Daniel Bell, Alvin Toffler, and Peter Drucker. That gap has been addressed, not always honestly, by a whole cadre of newcomers who now deal with "information systems."

Libraries, Not Information

I always thought a proactive library was an information system, and when I directed the NASA Scientific and Technical Information Facility I understood that I was really running a library. Even in the 1960s, that library depended heavily on computer processing and a variety of output formats, but libraries always vary in content and methodology. They are not defined by format.

We may love printed books, but books may be our avocation, not our profession. The Chance Vought Aircraft library I managed contained 3,000 books, 800 periodicals, and 150,000 technical reports, but it was certainly a library. So is an art museum's library that collects slides. And, of course, if your main collection happens to be slides or reports, that is what you analyze most carefully.

For me, a library is what it does, and that depends on its clients and their needs. Who determines those needs? For any profession, there should be a great deal of consultation, but the ultimate decisions must rest with those who have been educated and prepared to make them. That is true in any professional field, but it is also true whenever we acknowledge specialist expertise. We usually listen respectfully to plumbers and garage mechanics. Then why not as often to librarians?

What Price Modesty?

I'm puzzled at our modesty in stating our claims. When we embrace the slogan of "give 'em what they want," isn't that more appropriate for a newsstand, that lowest common denominator of client interaction?

When academic institutions like Harvard decide that any prestigious faculty member is more qualified to officially lead its library than a librarian, do you see this as a gratuitous professional insult? Should it then surprise you when the President of the United States follows suit in appointing a "Librarian" of Congress (actually most recently the Historian of Congress)?

I registered my concern in a letter to then-Harvard President Derek Bok. He replied quite courteously that I was the first librarian from whom he had heard about this issue and that he had received no complaints from any Harvard library staff. Was this really a problem, he asked, or was my reaction personal? How was I supposed to respond to that?

ALA Ignores Librarians

As readers of this column know, I have commented regularly that our major professional organization, the American Library Association (ALA), constantly stresses support for libraries but never for librarians, even when their jobs are eliminated by outsourcing. Perhaps we can admire such altruism, except that ALA never bothers to define what differentiates a good library from a bad one, or, for that matter, what deserves to be called a library at all.

I think our priorities are reversed. We cannot have good libraries until we first have good librarians—properly educated, professionally recognized, and fairly rewarded. Some librarians state with pride that neither they nor anyone else they know chose their career to become rich. Perhaps not, but I have also never taken a vow of poverty nor promised to forswear all hopes of Caribbean cruises.

Do some of us think that being poorly paid and disrespected makes us better librarians? I don't see the connection. I have always wanted to be rewarded as I deserved to be and have insisted that my worth be compared to that of individuals who do work of similar complexity and importance. Isn't that what salary equity is about? Do we understand that low pay usually leads to low respect?

Where Are the Librarians?

Our insistence on stressing the institution over the people who work there leads to some unfortunate side effects. The 1996 Benton Foundation report, which sought to examine our future, was entitled *Building, Books, and Bytes*, as if those were the main characteristics of the future library. There was nothing about the people who would be needed.

We tend to celebrate in *LJ* whenever a community has decided to build a new main library building or add branches. However, construction usually comes from bond funds, which are easier to justify because the impact is not as visible for the taxpayer. However, it requires a very visible commitment to run new facilities, with funds for staff, materials, and technology. Do we understand how politically foolish it is to accept new buildings without a formal written commitment for the needed operating funds? Without that commitment, we dilute the quality of our library for the sake of allowing our bosses to brag about quantity. Sometimes we do it ourselves.

Letting Our Bosses Know

As I teach management and observe other managers, I recognize how little librarians tell their administrator bosses about options developed in our planning. What are the opportunities, the dangers, and the alternatives for executive decisions? Upper management decides on the basis of alternatives, then gets credit or blame based on how those decisions work. Ultimately, the library's quality depends far more on them than on us. Trying to make *us* feel guilty because of *their* failure to support needed services is absurd. However, to their delight, with librarians, it often works.

Regular readers of this column will recall that when I was offered the deanship of the Indiana library school, I first asked how good a school the university wanted. I had no interest in managing a bad, cheap school, but, if the chancellor wanted one of the best, it would take work from me and a commitment to resources from him. I offered a partnership based on mutual respect. Affection is not required, but respect often leads to affection.

I have just signed with Libraries Unlimited for a third and final collection of my writings and speeches, to be published next year. I have titled it *Librarianship—Quo Vadis?* (Where are you going?) because I remain dismayed at our failure to take stands on professional issues, even as we eagerly take stands on sociopolitical ones.

Concern, Not Consensus

Faced with such crucial concerns as outsourcing and the downplaying of libraries in professional education, ALA appoints large bodies including both victims and perpetrators in the hope that they will somehow reach "consensus." Can any of us recall the last time a truly courageous and imaginative breakthrough was achieved through consensus? Was it *AACR2*, or was that as bland as consensus usually is?

We continue to invite speakers to our conferences who know nothing and care less about our professional concerns and who prove that ignorance in their talks. More than 10 years ago at an ALA conference, we heard a self-appointed representative for the homeless speak passionately but irrelevantly, because he ignored librarians and libraries. That talk was published in an ALA journal and then selected as "one of the best" of our literature for a 1989 compilation. Is there a better example of self-trivialization?

C. Northcote Parkinson noted back in 1957 that the time and energy spent on a problem were inversely proportional to its importance. Change *importance* to *relevance*, and we have a potential ALA poster for display in all of our libraries.

Index

About the Author

Herbert S. White, retired Distinguished Professor at the School of Library and Information Science at Indiana University in Bloomington, is author of the popular column "The White Papers" in *Library Journal* and of the books *Librarians and the Awakening from Innocence* (G. K. Hall, 1989) and *At the Crossroads: Librarians on the Information Superhighway* (Libraries Unlimited, 1995). In all White has written more than 150 books and articles on topics of library administration, supervision, and library automation. He is also widely recognized for his work as a consultant, speaker, and reviewer.

White received his master's degree in library science from Syracuse University. During the fifty years of his involvement in the library and information science profession he has served on a variety of boards and committees, including as a member of the American Library Association (ALA) Council and its Committee on Accreditation, and as Chair of Government Relations Committee of the Association for Library and Information Science Education (ALISE). He has received numerous awards, including the American Library Association's prestigious Melvil Dewey Medal. He received the Book of the Year award from the American Society for Information Science and was given the first Lifetime Professional Award by Syracuse University School of Information Studies.